IN PURSUIT OF PROOF

IN PURSUIT OF PROOF

A History of Identification Documents in India

Tarangini Sriraman

OXFORD
UNIVERSITY PRESS

OXFORD
UNIVERSITY PRESS

Oxford University Press is a department of the University of Oxford.
It furthers the University's objective of excellence in research, scholarship,
and education by publishing worldwide. Oxford is a registered trademark of
Oxford University Press in the UK and in certain other countries.

Published in India by
Oxford University Press
22 Workspace, 2nd Floor, 1/22 Asaf Ali Road, New Delhi 110 002, India

© Oxford University Press 2018

The moral rights of the author have been asserted.

First Edition published in 2018

ISBN-13 (print edition): 978-0-19-946351-0
ISBN-10 (print edition): 0-19-946351-4

ISBN-13 (eBook): 978-0-19-909408-0
ISBN-10 (eBook): 0-19-909408-X

Typeset in Berling LT Std 9.5/13
by The Graphics Solution, New Delhi 110 092
Printed and bound in India at Repro India Ltd., Mumbai

For Amma and Appa

CONTENTS

TABLES AND FIGURES

Tables

Figures

ACKNOWLEDGEMENTS

Recently, a student who was just beginning to research the history of fin-gerprinting in India asked me with undisguised befuddlement whether I did not think it strange that Indians needed British colonial authori-ties to identify them. In a sense, he was wondering whether having a fingerprinting system for administering subjects was not the ultimate measure of India's enslavement under British rule. This conversation impelled me to go back to the bible of colonial inquiry into this tech-nology, William Herschel's *The Origin of Finger-Printing*. Sure enough, this colonial administrator did write, in no unmistakable terms, of how fingerprinting was needed to tide over 'the great difficulty of adminis-tration in India' and how 'the decisiveness of a finger-print is now one of the most powerful aids to justice' (Herschel 1916: 9). Herschel's narra-tive was so far removed from the violence of colonial rule in India that terms like 'justice' and 'the difficulty of administration' did not seem dissonant to him. While having governments and bureaucracies—that have sunk their teeth deep into democratic rule—identify the people of India may seem like a vast improvement, I know better than to argue the cogency of identification (ID) regimes in contemporary times. I write this book, however, with the keen conviction that while the com-pulsions and rationalities behind ID documents can never be properly justified, the immersion of 'the enumerated' and 'the documented' into these material processes is worthy of commemoration and critique. So, I would like to start by thanking this student, Aniruddh Sheth, as well as my history students at Azim Premji University, who constantly remind me that my writing should always reflect a piquant sense of wonder and never be detached.

My greatest thanks are due to Ravi Sundaram who unstintingly went over and beyond his mandate as co-supervisor overseeing the writing of my PhD thesis. My intellectual debts to him have snowballed to the extent that I am no longer able to separate my writing process from his interventions. He was and continues to be generous with that most-valued resource in pedagogy, namely, time. He has never grudged me a meeting even when weighed down by professional and personal commitments. I will always warmly remember his strictures to never renounce the conceptual premise and to remove all judgement from my already privileged authorial voice. I am also very grateful to Ujjwal Kumar Singh, my supervisor at the University of Delhi, who has been both gracious and democratic in guiding the thesis, as well as astute in his comments on the early drafts of this book. Had it not been for his timely intervention, I may not have been admitted after my interview at the University of Delhi owing to an ironic lapse of leaving the address column blank in my application form! Another person I would like to thank at the outset is one of the most gifted and prodigious scholars that I have met, Chitra Venkataramani, who needed no coaxing to design the cover for this book. I would like to extend a very profuse measure of gratitude to Awadhendra Sharan, aka Dipu, the many-time Oscar winner in the best comments by any scholar category. I have lost sight of the many voids of conceptualization that Dipu has helped fill in this book—without his help, this book would have lacked texture and density. Vipin Kumar, who was also a visiting colleague at Centre for the Study of Developing Societies (CSDS) during my stint there, has been equally sharp. He has both elevated my writing and rescued me from some of the innumerable errors in this book.

I am grateful to Sanjay Palshikar for helping me plot this project in its nascent days. Not barring her inimitable research advice, Radhika Singha has vastly contributed to improving my legal and epistemic understanding of this field. Nivedita Menon, who was examiner for both my MPhil and PhD theses, has helped shape my thinking on citizenship, affect, and materiality. I would also like to thank Veena Das whose comments on a peer-reviewed article in *Contributions to Indian Sociology* went a long way in forcing me to rethink the relation between ID documents and culturally moored emotions. Thanks are also due to my many former colleagues from CSDS, but especially to Priyadarshini Vijaisri, Aditya Nigam, Hilal Ahmad, Ravi Vasudevan, Ravikant, Sarada Balagopalan, Prathama Banerjee, and Rakesh Pandey. Other mentors I would like to acknowledge include Marie-Helene Zerah, Veronique Dupont, and Jules Naudet at the Centre de Sciences Humaines (CSH). I can hardly forget the time when Jules not so gently reminded me to not ignore the gauze-like narrative thread connecting paragraphs and chapters. Indivar Kamtekar's comments comparing ration cards in the 1940s and after 1990 have also helped a great deal in rethinking my chapter on wartime identification. Yamuna Shankar and Navin Menon at the Children's Book Trust graciously gave me the permission to use Shankar's cartoon published in *Hindustan Times*. Vandana Solanki came up with the maps for Govindpuri and has helped me understand the urban geography of the place. Sithal Chordia and Shampa Saha have been unstinting in their assistance with transliteration and transcription of interviews. Monisha Punith helped me put together an indispensable archive of Aadhaar-related news articles and official reports. Prasad Khanolkar put me in touch with Chitra and indirectly aided with the cover of this book. P.K. Datta encouraged me to undertake a comparative historical study of censuses.

I am overwhelmed by the close reading that Usha Ramanathan has favoured this book with. She has pointed out glaring inaccuracies, helped me soften my irrevocably academic narrative style, and asked me to be less subtle in places where power was at stake. Vqueeram Aditya Sahai has been an indispensable companion to this book, whose advice to pay heed to conceptual distinctions and ideologically charged terms I have particularly valued. Mahesh Rangarajan has been a great friend who needed only to run into me in the random eating joints of Delhi to then follow up, with great gusto, on my career and research pursuits. Aman Sethi has been an unlikely but exemplary friend whose rigours of investigative journalism have hopefully rubbed off on me.

It is easy to forget the creature comforts of institutional research life. In a bid to not elide the immense benefits of working in such establishments, I would like to name a few places that have provided not only the much-needed financial support but also elaborate office facilities. I would like to start with the university where I work at present, Azim Premji University. If it were not for Venu Narayan, the Director of the School of Liberal Studies I work in, as well as the university's generous financial assistance, the last leg of archival work for this book would not have been possible. Thanks are also due to S.V. Srinivas who has never ceased to push me to finish this book. Alex Thomas has been taskmaster extraordinaire, frowning away at every paragraph he read and turning each idea over its head. I would like to also warmly thank Varuni Bhatia for helping me stay warm during a research stay and Sharmadip Basu, aka Toy, for giving up his office desk without a second thought when he went on leave. The combination of teaching and research would have been deadly had it not been for my close friends and colleagues in Bangalore, Sunil, Sunandan, Asim Siddiqui, Proteep Mallik, Abhigna Arigala, Shantha Bhushan, Sriram, Usha Rajaram, Jayanti Mukherjee, Stefi Barna, Neeraja Sundaram, Rahul De, and Sonali Barua.

I would like to thank the present Director of CSDS, Sanjay Kumar, for his warm hospitality and the institution at large for its generous visiting fellowship at a critical time. While I have already identified several colleagues at CSDS, I would like to thank Praveen, Jaishree, and Sachin for helping me navigate the ins and outs of the already-made-easy research life there. I would like to also thank the former director of the CSH, Basudeb Chaudhuri, who is among the most large-hearted persons I have met. The CSH has been a wonderful place to work in and I am immensely grateful for the postdoctoral fellowship I received at this institution. I would also like to thank the present Director, Leila Choukroune, who urged me to keep publishing as much as I could. Priyanka, Guillaume, Dolma, Shailaja, Pushpa, Mahesh, and Amit have been extremely helpful in figuring out various logistics of applying for conference travel, fieldwork, and using library facilities and other amenities. I am also in awe of the efficiency and expansiveness of the many people who work at Teen Murti and extend scholars the most unselfish courtesy. I also recall with great warmth my very many forays into the National Archives of India (NIA), the Delhi State Archives (DSA), the Central Secretariat Library in Delhi, the Maharashtra State Archives (MSA) in Mumbai, the British Library and Wellcome Library in London, and the superlatively helpful staff in all these institutions. Thanks are due also to the very many kind people who helped me at the Kroch Asia and the Olin Library in Cornell University, the staff at Ratan Tata Library, the office staff in the Political Science Department, and the librarians at CSDS. The people at English and Foreign Languages University (EFLU)—formerly, Central Institute of English and Foreign Languages (CIEFL)—library in Hyderabad have also been very forthcoming in their assistance.

I have also received two generous international research grants and would like to thank Cornell University and the Charles Wallace India Trust, London, for enabling research mobility and access to precious resources. Thanks are due in no small part to Daniel Bass, Valerie Foster, and Anne Blackburn at Cornell University, and Richard Alford in London. Kelsey Utne was instrumental in helping me steady my wobbly feet in Cornell. I have also been able to present my work at several destinations, including Kolkata, Pune, Shimla, Singapore, Istanbul, and Zurich; and I am grateful to the discussants at all these places. I would like to thank Pratiksha Baxi for the many opportunities that Law and Social Sciences Research Network (LASSnet) has afforded me both in the short and long term. Thanks are particularly in order to Matthew Hull who generously gifted me a copy of his book, *The Government of Paper*, Tarini Bedi, Vasudha Chottray, and Fiona McConnell. Nayanika Mathur has been a lovely fellow traveller on the ethnographic road of documentation. William Stafford Jr has been a truly inspiring researcher who has helped me theorize richly through ethnography. It has been great to have Raghav Kishore to share urban history notes in the DSA. I have learned much from Ranjit Singh, a great fieldworker on the subject of Aadhaar. It has been a humbling experience to read Shrimoyee Nandini Ghosh's work and to have engaged in discussions with her on the lives of paper. Himanshu Upadhyay has shared, at a moment's notice, his notes on relevant Comptroller and Auditor General (CAG) reports. It was also pure joy to have overlapped with Ishita Tiwary, Shireen Mirza, Sunalini Kumar, Sandeep Mertia, Satakshi Sinha, Siddharth Narrain, Ritika Kaushik, and Sagar Tewari in CSDS. Soofia Siddique, Moggallan Bharti, and Abdul Rahman have been more friends, less colleagues, and wonderful to be around. I am also grateful to Aparna Balachandran for lending me her copy of Bhavani Raman's book, *Document Raj*. Santana Khanikar has blurred the lines between being a friend and a saviour during my days at the University of Delhi. Sohini Guha has encouraged me to balance my job hunt with research perseverance. I also cherish all the help extended by the editors at Oxford University Press who fixed a whole world of embarrassing mistakes. Any remaining errors are certainly my burden to bear.

I am reserving a full paragraph to simply begin expressing my thanks to the many people who made possible the fieldwork for this book. Just to name a few such people, I would like to thank Shailesh, Amarnath Kashyap, Udai Bhan, Saroj, Mukhija, R.T.L. D'Souza, Karnail Chand, L.D. Pahwa, Osman Ali, Jai Bhagwan Jatav, Sohanlal Sharma, Subhas Chopra, Khataria, R.L. Kain, V.P. Singh (the former food official!), Ramesh, Bagri, Haneesh, and Chhajuram for their affection, hospitality, and infinite generosity. I have pestered Sunil Kumar Aledia, again and again, with my countless queries about urban procedures and minutiae in matters of Delhi housing and he has never once grudged me a detailed response. I would also like to thank the people of the Department of Food and Supplies, Delhi, the Unique Identification Authority of India (UIDAI), the Delhi Urban Shelter Improvement Board, and the Aadhaar enrolment centres for talking to me and sharing precious resources with me. I am also grateful to Rama Matthew for helping me procure and navigate hostel accommodation at the University of Delhi and for being the quintessential local guardian.

I would like to thank Harmeet Kaur Rai who emerged out of nowhere and has continued to remain an endearing constant in my life. Physiotherapist par excellence and BFF material, Harmeet took a broken version of me and never ceased to build confidence in my own stamina. Could I ever finish writing this part of the book without thanking my best friends, Zarin Ahmad, Jayani Bonnerjee, Meera Gopakumar, Sushmita Pati, Saumya Premchander, Malavika Sasikumar, Anannya Baruah, Anuja Kelkar, Parvathy Ravindran, and Anumitra Ghosh Dastidar? They are the enablers of the *sakhi sammelan* that I have never stopped craving in my living memory. Also, I need to thank Poorva Rajaram for reminding me of the existence of this glorious term and the need to seek it out at every given instant! Let me not forget to add that her remarkable MPhil dissertation helped me rethink my own ideas on enumeration and ID in the final stages of this book.

I would like to thank Ina Sathe and Jay Sathe, who have extended material and moral support in my research journeys. They, in addition to Raju, Sunita Patnaik, Tulu Patnaik, and Arjun Patnaik, not only made research simple after I left the familiar pastures of Delhi to work in Bengaluru but also made me yearn my Delhi visits every time. I am so grateful to my darling, bold and beautiful sister, Ramya, for being a rock of support, Soma for being a great brother-in-law, and their devilish brats, Siddharth and Nishant. My mother, Kousalya, and my father, Sriraman, have given me every strength possible to write this book, plied me with humour, obliged me with heated debates, and instinctively understood my need for academic seclusion. It is to them that I lovingly dedicate this book. I must add that my father, who edited this book with a fine-toothed comb, managed to survive a potent combination of terrible punctuation and ever-winding sentences. I would like to finally thank Gopal, my manic friend and companion of 11 years, for his exhausting and rejuvenating effervescence, erudition, and love. I wish to remind him that he enjoys a status in my life that goes way beyond simply being a technological messiah and a sounding board for intellectual provocations!

ABBREVIATIONS

AAP	Aam Aadmi Party
AAY	Antyodaya Anna Yojana
AIR	All India Radio
APC	Agricultural Prices Commission
ARD	Authorized Retail Distributor
ASA	Ambedkar Students Association
ASHA	Accredited Social Health Activist
ATMs	Automated Teller Machines
BISP	Benazir Income Support Programme
BJP	Bharatiya Janata Party
BPL	Below Poverty Line
CAG	Comptroller and Auditor General
CCO	Chief Commissioner's Office
CEO	Chief Executive Officer
CGHS	Central Government Health Scheme
CIDR	Central Identities Data Repository
CIEFL	Central Institute of English and Foreign Languages
CP	Connaught Place
CPI	Communist Party of India
CPWD	Central Public Works Department
CSDS	Centre for the Study of Developing Societies
CSH	Centre de Sciences Humaines
DBTL	Direct Benefit Transfer of LPG
DDA	Delhi Development Authority
DIT	Delhi Improvement Trust
DLF	Delhi Land and Finance
DMV	Department of Motor Vehicles

DNA	Deoxyribonucleic Acid
DP	Displaced Person
DRO	Delhi Rationing Organization
DSA	Delhi State Archives
DTIDCL	Delhi Transport Infrastructure Development Corporation Limited
DUSIB	Delhi Urban Shelter Improvement Board
EC	Election Commission
ECA	Essential Commodities Act
ECHS	Ex-servicemen Contributory Health Scheme
EFLU	English and Foreign Languages University
EID	Enrolment ID (number)
eKYC	electronic Know Your Customer
EPDPA	East Pakistan Displaced Persons Association
EPIC	Electors Photo Identity Card
FCI	Food Corporation of India
FIRs	First Information Reports
FPS	Fair Price Shop
FPSC	Federal Public Service Commission
FSO	Food and Supply Officer
GIS	Geographic Information System
GNCTD	Government of National Capital Territory of Delhi
HCU	Hyderabad Central University
HRO	Housing and Rent Officer
HSS	Harijan Sewak Sangh
HT	*Hindustan Times*
ICDS	Integrated Child Development Services
ID	Identification
ID4D	Identification for Development
ISBT	Inter State Bus Terminal
IT	Information Technology
J&K	Jammu and Kashmir
JDY	Jan Dhan Yojana
JJ	Jhuggi Jhopdi
JNU	Jawaharlal Nehru University
JRC	Jhuggi Ration Card
KYC	Know Your Customer
LASSnet	Law and Social Sciences Research Network

LIC	Life Insurance Corporation
LPG	Liquefied Petroleum Gas
MBBS	Bachelor of Medicine, Bachelor of Surgery
MCD	Municipal Corporation of Delhi
MGNREGS	Mahatma Gandhi National Rural Employment Guarantee Scheme
MHA	Ministry of Home Affairs
MHRD	Ministry of Human Resource Development
MLA	Member of Legislative Assembly
MNIC	Multipurpose National Identity Card
MP	Member of Parliament
MSA	Maharashtra State Archives
MTNL	Mahanagar Telephone Nigam Limited
NADRA	National Database and Registration Authority
NAI	National Archives of India
NCT	National Capital Territory
NCTD	National Capital Territory of Delhi
NDMC	New Delhi Municipal Council
NFSA	National Food Security Act
NGO	Non-governmental Organization
NGS	Non-gazetted Section
NMML	Nehru Memorial Museum and Library
NPR	National Population Register
NR	National Registration
NRCs	National Resident Cards
NWFP	North West Frontier Province
OBC	Other Backward Class
OMCs	Oil and Marketing Companies
OTPs	One-time Passwords
PAHAL	Pratyaksh Hastantrit Labh Yojana
PAN	Permanent Account Number
PDS	Public Distribution System
PEPSU	Patiala and East Punjab States Union
PGMS	Public Grievance Monitoring System
PILs	Public Interest Litigations
PoA	Proof of Address
PoI	Proof of Identity
PoS	Point of Sale

PSUs	Public Sector Undertakings
PW	Price Waterhouse
RC	Refugee Registration Certificate
RCRC	Resettlement Colony Ration Card
RSS	Rashtriya Swayamsevak Sangh
RTI	Right to Information
SBI	State Bank of India
SC	Scheduled Caste
SDM	Sub-divisional Magistrate
ST	Scheduled Tribe
SWJN	*Selected Works of Jawaharlal Nehru*
TISS	Tata Institute of Social Sciences
UAE	United Arab Emirates
UID	Unique Identification
UIDAI	Unique Identification Authority of India
UNDP	United Nations Development Programme
UNHCR	United Nations High Commissioner for Refugees
UPA	United Progressive Alliance
UPI	Unified Payments Interface
UPSC	Union Public Service Commission
UT	Union Territory

INTRODUCTION

Yet the means have repeatedly outlived their original ends and gone on to shape new ones. It is through means that institutions bite into real people, not through their ends or objectives. Means require their own history, and their own kind of history.[1]

When a fire broke out in his slum, Rajendra, a resident of Govindpuri in south Delhi, waited for the embers to settle down and then gingerly stepped over the burnt remains of his house. His perilous search was not in vain. For, shining in all the sooty mess of mangled plastic, rubber, wire, fabric, and cement, was an unmistakable shred of laminated identity card. While half of the V.P. Singh Card—issued in 1990 to surveyed slum residents across Delhi by the central government headed by the then prime minister V.P. Singh—had vanished, leaving in its wake a trail of dark inky marks, the other half had survived. Rajendra decided that all was not lost. If the marks and what remained of the card were allowed to tell the tale of his loss of a precious document in a fire accident, he could still perhaps carve out a claim to a resettlement plot. In the years that followed this incident, Rajendra decided to take no chances. He pinned all the identification (ID) documents that he had slowly accumulated—his voter ID card, his son's and wife's voter ID cards, the surviving shred of the V.P. Singh Card, a survey slip, and his photograph—to a piece of cardboard which he carried on his person most of the time.

In some ways at least, Rajendra's tale led me on a thorny historical (mis)adventure where I searched for ID documents that were salvaged, fashioned, and willed into existence by all sorts of people—officials, slum residents, refugees, migrant workers, and assorted middlemen. As I went about inquiring into popular modes of identifying oneself, one's family, and community, not surprisingly, I hit upon a colourful panorama of the rich ways in which people, especially urban poor subjects, avoid falling into a bureaucratic and administrative abyss of proving who they were and where they lived. This was, of course, no epiphany taken by itself. What, on the other hand, was remarkable was the bold insertion of various subaltern subjects into the very processes that classified, quantified, and identified them.

This book plots an ethnographic history of the Indian state which governs its subjects through the ID documents that such people, considered in their myriad roles, have either helped produce or produced themselves. In other words, we will see how popular forms of knowledge are salient to the fashioning of infrastructures of ID. In this book, I argue that it is owing to the contributions, contestations, and collaborations of 'the enumerated' in the making of ID documents that the Indian state has been able to carve out niches of administering subjects in marginal spaces. The self-enabling iterations, narrations, and inscriptions of identities of the book's many protagonists have filled bureaucratic and administrative voids of evidence at different junctures in the welfare-based history of the Indian state. These moments include the Second World War, the Partition, the Licence Raj, an obscure yet momentous enumeration initiative in 1990, and the production of a biometric number identifier. In order to make sense of all this, we need to first properly name and demystify the ethnographic object of this book, namely, the 'ID document'.

ID Documents as a Unique Subset

ID documents are a unique subset of bureaucratic writing. However, to understand this, we need to briefly map the field of the recent remarkable literature on documents. It has been argued that documents are more than just 'cultural texts' and 'receptacles of meaningful knowledge' (Riles 2006: 12). Annelise Riles writes that documents are not just 'artifacts of modern knowledge practices', they are also 'knowledge practices that define ethnography itself' (Riles 2006: 7). So, instead of viewing ID documents simply in symbolic terms as designating or indexing the state, this book takes a cue from social anthropology (Appadurai 1986; Hull 2012a; Kopytoff 1986; Mathur 2016) to observe the movement of assorted documents within local economies, social, and cultural spheres, such as the bureaucracy, the refugee registration office, the ration office, the urban housing office, refugee squatter settlement, the slum, and the enrolment centre. However, rather than satisfy itself with plotting the popular life of ID documents, the book goes beyond to demonstrate the popular making of ID documents.

This book on ID documents draws parallels from the wider and recent literature on documents in a significant aspect, namely, its immersion in the genealogies of writing practices in order to record claims. In the work of these scholars who trace such genealogies, a narrative arc can be traced: standardized writing gained gradual ascendancy over orality; written records gained traction over mnemonic habits; written depositions and petitions came to be privileged over verbal declarations and scribal practices; and bookkeeping replaced more informal audit practices (Clanchy 2013; Goody 1986; Ogborn 2007; Poovey 2010; Raman 2012). A similar trajectory can be plotted for ID documents which were consolidated over time where earlier, processes of recognition did not rely on thorough practices of verification. Depending on their genre, states in medieval and early modern Europe used bills of health, bills of mortality, health passports, nomad passbooks, and beggars' passes in order to parcel off privilege, police suspicious sorts, and track mobility (Caplan and Torpey 2001; Groebner 2007; Salter 2003). However, the turn of the twentieth century saw the emergence of more systematic regimes of proof. This, of course, did not mean the disappearance of discretionary forms of privileging the unwritten word or older forms of mutual recognition; however, they would now have to be recast within newer regimes.

The various moves in this book of plotting ID documents across welfare sites are inspired by the historical and anthropological scholarship on documents, where too writing is explored as a material practice[2] (Hull 2012a; Mathur 2016; Raman 2012). In such scholarship, the power of writing proliferates and pervades life in everyday bureaucracy and society. This is true not only of Western societies but also their counterparts elsewhere. Brinkley Messick's (1993) work attempts to demonstrate the formation of a textual polity in the late nineteenth and early twentieth century Yemen where contracts, deeds, and the written Sharia idiom and discourse were central to the creation of Islamic states. One of the most powerful interventions within this field, Matthew Hull's *The Government of Paper* traces the movement of the file in the urban bureaucracy of Pakistan. Hull spends considerable time showing how documents matter in their form, materiality, and linguistic genre, as much as in their function within the 'political economy of paper' (Hull 2012a). As he shows in his book, files on land allotment, housing, and compensation obscure more than they reveal the truths about development and welfare dissemination.

This present book is inspired by Hull's work as well as that of many other enterprising ethnographers of 'documents' who critically invoke Max Weber. Weber senses the inevitable modernizing effects that bureaucracies have on society. Therefore, even though he sees bureaucracies as delivering legal-rational authority of the kind that modern states cannot do without, he is darkly pessimistic about its effects on people. He writes that the more perfectly the bureaucracy develops, the more it is 'dehumanized', the more completely it succeeds in eliminating from official business love, hatred, and all purely personal, irrational, and emotional elements which escape calculation' (Weber 2006: 216). Historians and anthropologists have noted, however, that documents spawned by the bureaucracy can enable intimate cultural encounters between the state and touts, the state and activists, activists and the poor, the state and its political subjects, considered in their many hues. These artifacts[3] produce rhetorical, aesthetic, and discursive effects of transparency and opacity, engender structural violence, and provoke emotions of panic, exhaustion, and pride within and outside the bureaucracy (Brenneis 2006; Cody 2013; Gupta 2012; Hull 2012a; Mathur 2016; Raman 2012; Riles 2006).

All this said, it is critical that we treat ID documents as a unique and somewhat more distinctive subset of documents. Through both their presence and their absence, they raise spectres of surveillance, welfare fraud, terrorism, illegal refugee crisis, and urban disorder. ID documents, unlike letters, petitions, lists, records, and reports, mark persons and their bodies in varied aspects of geographical location, occupation, and social background defined by parentage, especially of the father, racial descent, and caste. The categories they contain, like name, nationality, address, family, gender, caste, and fingerprints, far from being random,

have a lengthy history and a place in systems of classification, codification, and standardization of information (Breckenridge 2014; Caplan
and Torpey 2001; Higgs 2004; Singha 2000; Torpey 2000).[4]

While some early ID documents in India, like alien certificates,
plague passports, plague inoculation certificates, pilgrim passports, coolie agreements, and descriptive rolls for convicts (Singha 2000; Sriraman
2013c), were fleeting and contingent on their historical value, they
were remarkable in their weighty contribution to 'the enduring material infrastructure' (Hull 2012a) of counting, identifying, and classifying
people on paper. Such documents do not always correspond to people's
identities and affective selves. Even if their production, retrieval upon
loss, and circulation may be controlled by middlemen, ID documents
willy-nilly throw up conundrums of one's own recognizable self. The
story of ID documents everywhere is caught up tragi-comically with
the slippage between ID and identity. In other words, the provocation
for a good deal of scholarship on ID documents has been the incongruous efforts of administrations to calibrate a synchrony between people's
'handheld documents' and their bearers' 'heartfelt' (Bakewell 2007)
but shifting regionally, ethnically, and socially enmeshed identities.
Tibetan refugees, Turkish Cypriots, Brazilian slum residents, and indigenous subjects in the Argentinian Chaco region experience hauntings,
crippling anxieties, fears, and misapprehensions when they encounter
specific genres of ID documents and the citizenship claims that such
papers hold and withhold (Gordillo 2006; Koster 2013; McConnell
2013; Navaro-Yashin 2007).

The relationship between ID documents and welfare processes is
also far from being straightforward. Identification documents function simultaneously to reinforce the state as an arbiter of people's
welfare claims and render it liable to popular manipulations. If they
occasionally make people and their representations legible, they more
often obscure and render opaque the claim-making and the welfare-
allocating process (Das 2006; Tarlo 2003). Such documents, especially
when seen through a grid of technological innovations administratively
termed as e-governance and lately biometric governance, extend
certain illusions of transparency, incorruptibility, and social inclusion.
However, such new-age ID documents, such as the Aadhaar, owing to
their self-legitimizing markers of biometric authentication and, ironically, their inconsistencies and error-prone modalities, can yield 'new

opacities' (Mazzarella 2006: 486), an indifference to 'social cleavages in modern India' (Mazzarella 2006: 487) and politics itself (Ferguson 1994).[5] Barring a few exceptions, much of this scholarship tracks the movement of ID documents in general, but does not really touch on their popular production. Rather than interest ourselves purely with the effects of ID regimes, and alternatively why welfare processes fail, this book will preoccupy itself with the collaborative aspects of creating ID documents and claim-making in the domains of food and housing.

The Artifice of ID Documents

There is a disarming, self-certain, and self-authorizing allure to ID documents and electronic identifiers, if one were to bear in mind the relatively recent ascendance of the unique number identifier, Aadhaar. With newer additions to the ever-swelling inventory of forms of identity that Indians must possess and allied linkages that they must perform, there seems to be no end to the cathartic stories that apparently throw us all together in pursuit of proof and their entitlements. These stories only validate and rarely question the nature of the state's, and by extension subjects', deep immersion into ID documents. Very few people then wonder whether ID documents really make the tapestry of persons, commodity entitlements, and proof hold in an innocuous, seamless weave. For instance, even a single trip to an urban ration office where numerous poor subjects wait in line to apply for a new ration card is enough to know that welfare entitlements are not pre-existing entities which can be readily claimed. There can be a maddeningly exponential number of reasons why such a subject cannot get a new ration card: the photograph on the old ration card may correspond to a different person; the food inspector on duty may have reported that a family does not stay in the designated residence; the very genre and protocols of the ration card may have changed owing to the vagaries of changing food policy; and the card may not have been seeded to a biometric number identifier.

The tying of commodities, entitlements, persons, and state authorities has to be contrived at every given instance. Some of the welfare initiatives this book considers, such as the post-Partition refugee housing schemes, the resettlement of slum dwellers at the dawn of the neoliberal era, and the production of caste certificates in the age of digital inscription, attest to this. The non-negotiable emphasis on proof often stymies administrations as much as the people whose information is, at times selectively and at other times indiscriminately, placed under the microscope. In the rough and tumble of transacting welfare initiatives such as the provision of food rations, resettlement housing, educational scholarship, reservations, concessions of age relaxation, fee waivers, and waivers of job criteria, governments only too painfully realize the magnitude of the business that lies ahead of them. Their mandate is statistically, visually, and informationally befuddling. As they scour applications, look for incriminating inconsistencies, pounce on revealing untruths, chance upon subversions of the document, or the spectres that inhabit paper, the officials often find themselves cursing their job descriptions. Their roles fall in the interstices of a ritual-prone and writing-obsessed bureaucracy, error-filled and time-consuming technologies of information gathering, and a society brimming over with subject statuses that defy all characterization. As these anxieties threaten to spill over into the daily administrative routine, state functionaries seek to exorcise and mitigate these phantoms of imposture, fraud, and overlapping identities.

In the city spaces of a place like Delhi, the welfare of poor people, historically speaking, often impinged on the enumeration of families whose dwelling spaces could not be fixed. Such families impalpably crossed sovereign national boundaries, moved into urban quarters which were legally dubious, and resided in households which spilled into each other. Worse still, the temporalities of 'occupying', 'squatting', or 'passing through' certain spaces of refugee camp, slum, satellite township, village, or transit accommodation were to be borne out in standardized application forms and supporting documents. Welfare claimants were then required to mark their presences as much as their 'identities' as urban dwellers in application forms that were conditioned by officially defined kinship norms and the 'factum of residence'. Confronted with the impossible mandates of administering complexly self-identifying poor subjects, the everyday state could not afford to neglect or disqualify popular genres of evidence. What resulted was a popular insertion of paper-mediated narratives of residence and family into the very factories of welfare production.

In this book, ID documents are presented less as the artifacts of a sovereign state and more as the byproduct of engagement of subaltern subjects with the welfare establishment. The book is hinged on the premise that the question, 'how is a welfare claim pieced together', cannot be separated from the question, 'what resources do states have to identify people applying for benefits and entitlements'.

How States Administer Societies

The question of identifying subjects often translates into one of rendering subjects legible to the state gaze as it is often broadly believed that states can govern well only when they 'see' their subjects within a uniform administrative format. It is here that James Scott argues that the state wishes to make its subjects visible and legible through censuses, surveys, and naming and identification practices. He terms these practices 'simplifications' and 'abstractions' on account of the reductive and universalizing functions that 'cadastral surveys and population registers, the invention of freehold tenure, the standardization of language and legal discourse, the design of cities, and the organization of transportation' can perform (Scott 1998: 2). Through such practices, 'complex, illegible and local social practices' can be smoothed out into 'a standard grid' and 'centrally recorded and monitored' (Scott 1998: 2). Scott's interest here seems to lie in explaining the administrative erasure of social practices and their replacement with more convenient standards in the making of the high modernist state. In this, he omits to consider that perhaps these complex social practices, far from making the state gaze inconvenient, could enable the state to see subjects better.

In her critique of James Scott's *Seeing Like a State*, the historical ethnographer of Brazil, Mara Loveman, regards the state to have failed in building a modern infrastructure of governing subjects. She attributes this failure to the state's 'visual acuity' that was devoid of indigenous forms of knowledge (Loveman 2007: 10). She suggests that it was because the Brazilian state did not open its gaze to local metrics and conditions that it ended up diluting its own imperative to render subjects visible. Contra Scott and pace Loveman, this book then regards the possibility that states have governed marginal subjects through a rich repertoire of alternative inscriptions of identity. We will see how the subjects who feature in this book inscribed multiple legibilities and negotiated opacities of welfare entitlement in ways that substantially transformed the state gaze in urban poor spaces.

By considering how states administer through the popular production of ID documents, this book distances itself from an ethnocentric
(mainly Eurocentric) discourse of 'citizenship' in the sovereign welfare
state (Giddens 1982; Marshall 1994; Turner 1990). In order to explain
why, we will first need to examine histories of state identification and
citizenship in Europe and why the normative ideal of the 'citizen' is
universally tenable neither in all Western countries nor in urban poor
social locations in India. Critically, we will see how even within Europe,
the Enlightenment project encompassed not simply freedom and
equality but also domination as it came up against its own racialized
biases and category anxieties in the field of ID practice. Finally, this section will show how classical Foucauldian definitions of governmentality
that underlie administrative practices may occasionally not be tenable
in their intended Western cultural milieu and often not in other parts
of the non-Western world.

Let us start by noting the most formative moment of them all in the
historical narrative of Western citizenship. In the wake of the French
Revolution, municipalities became the consecrated sites of registering
births, deaths, and marriages, where earlier the churches had the power
to endow civil statuses. France expanded the realm of citizenship
rights to enable the civil registration of Jews and Protestants, where
such a right had been denied by the church. The new French Republic
effectively achieved this feat by delinking civil registration from the
authority of the church and parish records (Noiriel 2001). At a certain
point in time, France attempted to go beyond assigning civil statuses
that challenged aristocratic structures to wear down the bourgeois
trappings of republican authority. Working-class movements definitely
contributed to the enhancement of citizen rights and the appropriation
of identity cards from capitalist oppressors played no small role in the
making of the rights discourse in Europe. In his introduction to Karl
Marx's *Civil War in France*, Friedrich Engels gives us a detailed exposition of the French Commune and its many social experiments, such as
the move by the workers to remove registration cards from police jurisdiction and vest the powers to issue them instead in the mayors of the
arrondissements of Paris (Marx and Engels 1891). A historical process
that seemed to span an eternity involved the expansion of the franchise
and voter registration to include workers, non-propertied men, women,
and religious minorities in Europe and America. Many of these rights

were granted under the aegis of a gathering welfare state. The famous sociologist Anthony Giddens positions citizenship in the interstices of class struggle, ruling class ideologies, and surveillance technologies of the welfare state in England and Europe. He writes, '[t]he formation of welfare measures has from the outset been closely intertwined with the surveillance and control of the conduct of the underprivileged' (Giddens 1982: 178).

These universal narratives of class emancipation through citizenship practices of ID are bounded by a certain Enlightenment discourse of reason and equality. The global erasures of citizenship of immigrants, those thought to be racially inferior, refugees, and political undesirables have run headlong into the tide of this discourse. The commemorative processes of mass enfranchisement and citizen registration have been accompanied by pronounced state moves to stall the movement of some classes into emancipated zones of sovereign belonging, for, after all, classifications are central to making and unmaking citizens and sealing off others. Scholarship on ID documents has sought to uncover how classifications are necessary to sort the world into categories that constitute the state's knowledge of them across the world (Bowker and Star 1999; Robertson 2009; Torpey 2000). It has been argued that the state comes into being through acts of identifying, classifying, and enumerating its citizens and aliens. Timothy Mitchell (2006) has, for instance, proclaimed the state to be 'an effect' that constitutes itself through intricate practices like issuing passports, collecting taxes, instituting border checks, and passing immigration laws.

Nobody captures this better than John Torpey, who in his pioneering scholarly work, *The Invention of the Passport*, demonstrates how states slowly acquire a monopoly over the legitimate means of movement. With the evolution of the modern passport system, states come to displace private entities 'in their power to authorize and forbid movement' (Torpey 2000: 8). Various terms such as 'illegal migration', 'internal movement', and 'undocumented migration' have gained currency almost entirely as a consequence of this extension of the 'bureaucratic construction' of the modern state (Torpey 2000: 8–9). The twentieth century has been special in that the two world wars prompted not just a rash of surveillance practices but also some serious thinking on comprehensive databases. Edward Higgs undertakes a broad sweep of the documentary transformation in Europe while noting especially

Britain's scrutiny of its populations within and beyond its borders. When the Second World War crept up on the people of Britain, the government was able to perfect its national registration programme (introduced tentatively during the First World War) by linking registration with rationing, thus ensuring effective conscription and recruitment of labour. The arrival of war also meant that the relative flexibility that marked movement across state borders vanished. By the time of the Second World War, countries like Britain, Italy, and Germany began to issue passports systematically. Higgs captures the national administrative sentiment when he writes, '[i]n a world in which citizens were being mobilized for total warfare, all foreign nationals became a threat' (Higgs 2004: 140).

While noting the state's artifice in constructing itself as the sole arbiter in matters of ID, this book would, however, like to gently steer the reader away from a history of ID documents framed within a hegemonic Enlightenment modernity of equality and its antithesis, domination. It instead draws heavily on a discourse that illustrates 'the reciprocal relations between the power of the state and the power of the civil society' (Lau 2006: 2), though I would like to replace the term civil society with the term 'marginal groups'. Let us consider a couple of instances where such a relation has been operational. In the early twentieth century, America attempted to sort its subjects into those constituting an informal immigrant workforce who had to be regularly subjected to surveillance and those who could come and go freely as passport-holding sovereign citizens (Torpey 2000). In their pervasive search for undesirable immigrant populations, the US reserved special attention for the Chinese community whose movement alone impelled a crop of legislations. In the way that Estelle Lau tells her story in the eloquently titled book, *Paper Families*, what stands out is not the overbearing documentary state weighing down on a haplessly harassed community, but rather the reflexive practices of both the Chinese community and the US Immigration Services, who moulded their material lifeworlds in response to each other. Chinese immigrants created a web of interdependence that consisted of 'fictive kin and the needed family histories, landscapes and the use of stereotypes' (Lau 2006: 2). Lau writes that the Chinese learnt to memorize their family histories and they even sold crib sheets, family trees, and village and household maps. They also used the racist inability of American authorities to discern

differences between the Chinese to subvert immigration policy. The
Immigration Services did not remain inert either: they learnt to modify
their file and record-keeping practices to include evidence that opened
out into the information proffered by the immigrants themselves (Lau
2006: 8).

In South Korea, another scholar Kim writes, the state was again
entangled in an intimate relationship with its Korean Chinese immigrants who sought to press their case for ethnic citizenship by presenting document-borne genealogies of their families. These documents
forcefully demonstrated their blood-based ties to the country. Here too,
family histories were reconstructed and 'family genealogy books, letters
with South Korean kin, old photos, endorsement letters' were consolidated in rapidly increasing numbers (Kim 2011: 771). Through these
ID encounters with Korean Chinese immigrants, the South Korean
state learnt that it needed to upgrade its systems of ID. Where evidence
either had to be sourced from several records or arbitrarily gleaned
from interviews that tested the knowledge of the kin and resemblances,
such genres became untenable over time. This state settled for the use
of deoxyribonucleic acid (DNA) testing as an ID practice overwhelm-
ingly, as a reliable alternative to the bureaucratic nightmare of verifying
the authenticity of disparate shreds of evidence. Even though DNA
testing was an expensive and time-consuming process that offended
immigrant sensibilities, the South Korean state decided that this was
infinitely preferable to processes that relied on record-based testimony
(Kim 2011). This case also shows how ID practices were reconstituted
through mutually informative encounters between the state and
its subjects.

Family as a Category of Governmentality

In his famous excavations of governmentality that have helped carve
out tunnels of comprehension about modern states, Michel Foucault
has repeatedly drawn our attention to those elements of individual lives
whose development fosters the strength of the state. Foucault defines
the attributes of governmentality in a remarkably interdisciplinary
sense by conjuring a transformation in the historical economic, juridical, and political contexts of modern states. Where earlier, sovereignty
and the political capacities to end life were the primordial markers of

rule, they are now replaced by a science of government and the exercise of 'power over life' itself. This science is best fulfilled in the site of the body as well as through the production of population as a normalized collectivity (Foucault 1991). In this, he has been alert to a philosophical and political necessity to demonstrate how modern states produce 'docile bodies', create a political economy by controlling populations, and achieve an ordered course of the everyday world. However, it is states considered in their dispersed bureaucratic effects and not in their totalizing effects of juridical authority that secure this order (Foucault 1991).[6]

The modern (state's) conception of 'power over life' is rendered possible through two poles. The first pole of setting up power is centred on 'the body as a machine' and this is achieved through procedures of anatomo-politics which target the individual's body for 'integration into systems of efficient and economic control' (Foucault 1984a: 261). The other pole consists of 'regulatory controls' or a 'biopolitics of the population' and is targeted at the 'species body, the body imbued with the mechanics of life and serving as the basis of the biological processes' (Foucault 1984a: 262). It is the population that is the primary unit for intervention and discipline in the study of 'political economy' and 'the science of government'. Along with the population, individuals must be produced not as juridical subjects but as 'working, trading, living beings' of 'a political technology' that optimizes life itself (Foucault 1988: 146, 156). Such a technology is wielded by an all-encompassing police, which becomes a discipline over time and embraces all spheres of administration, people's relationships with property, and their social relations. Interestingly, the family falls somewhere between the individual and the species body and does not form a category of governmentality in Foucault's framework. The family can be an 'instrument' and 'a privileged segment' of biopolitics in that it is necessary for the regulation of 'sexual behaviour, demography and consumption' (Foucault 1991: 100). However, the family is of 'secondary importance' and it derives its significance only in its capacity as an element of the population (Foucault 1991: 100).

While this book acknowledges the capillary and generative capacities of power, and salutes Foucault's comprehensive field of inquiry replete with insights into local state forms, it wishes to enable a more situated reading. In this book, some of the mechanisms of how urban

administrations function will come across as classically Foucauldian—
housing surveys, food censuses, ration cards, refugee certificates, and
metallic tokens. Other regulatory controls such as permits and licences
are less evidently compelling, signifying a more repressive and universally resented state apparatus (Foucault 1984a: 262). Yet other practices like biometric number-based identifiers that feature towards the
end of this book have been described to be synoptic and hypermodern
in the technological surveillance they perfect. With the exception of
the Aadhaar, the many genres of ID in India have been shaped, to a
great extent, by the mandate for protagonists (officials and subjects,
for instance) to identify themselves in relation to each other, the social
worlds they inhabited, and the materially demanding administrations
they were a part of. This book at times alters and at other times critiques the Foucauldian conception of governmentality by arguing: (a)
the operation of the family as a category of governmental knowledge;
(b) the family's pale imitation and mutation in urban poor residential
spaces; and (c) the prevalence of popular practices and templates of ID
and modes of administration that could not otherwise exist. Let us, for
the moment, consider family as a category of governmentality.

One of the pioneering works on ID documents, *Documenting
Individual Identity* by Jane Caplan and John Torpey (2001), has presented untold genealogies of state ID and historically delineated the
individual as a documented subject. It does not, however, address the
deep cultural investment of state bureaucracies in the enumeration of
families. It must be said in the authors' defence that this is a deliberate
omission, as the title of the book suggests. The unusual ethnographies
of Chinese immigrants in America and Korean Chinese immigrants in
South Korea, featuring in the previous section, are revealing on the point
of how states administer through practices of familial identification. Lau's
(2006) book, *Paper Families* (2006), demonstrates this not simply in the
non-Western World but quite specifically in a country like America. The
Hukou household registration system of China and the *Koseki* system
of national registration of Japan gesture to an alternative conception of
governmentality that produced citizenship through a social order that
reinforced a heavily disciplined family norm rather than a minutely
managed individual identity. Such norms are at once patrilineal and
patriarchal as they have necessitated municipal registration of individuals as units of the household, facilitated the passage of male heads of

the household into samurai roles, privileged loyalty to the master of the family, and only recognized the rights of male sons to inherit property (Brown 2008; Ogasawara 2008; Winther 2008). Even in recent times, the *Koseki* system holds women back from securing legal status if they are outside the institution of marriage (Ogasawara 2008: 96).

While loyalty to the nation composed of conforming and self-disciplining families does not lace practices of governmentality, the bureaucratic imagination of the state in India has definitely perpetuated the household as a unit of enumeration. In India, governmentality was forged through ration card practices that subsumed individual identity within a family without requiring them to register within a nationally maintained household register. Though the voter identity card individuated identities by extending republican entitlement to all its citizens, its introduction to India was gloriously belated with the Electors Photo Identity Card (EPIC) being inaugurated only in the year 1993. Where ration cards were concerned, they were initially issued to individuals within a city like Delhi, and the transition to household-based ration cards in 1952 laid down the parameters for familial identification. The family-based food card, which over time came to be dubbed the household consumer card, supplied the rationale for welfare categories like ordinary rations and supplementary rations, head of the households and dependents, and terminology like bogus ration cards and ghost beneficiaries. An individual whose name figured in one family's ration card could not be present in another. The ration card became a cultural necessity for a family living through the Second World War—as several provinces and states issued family ration cards even during the war— and the era of the Licence Raj, where norms of commercial austerity were sought to be ubiquitously enforced. Much later, ration cards came to be used by families as a mortgage to ward off debt and to secure bail for friends and relatives (Sriraman 2013b). Today, the household consumer card carries all sorts of health advisories and moral precepts for families that span concerns of reproductive health, unwanted pregnancies, female infanticides, and malnourishment among newborns. If one were to flip through the leaves of ration cards issued after the year 2000, one would find, for instance, adverts such as the indispensable health functions that inoculation shots administered to mothers and newborns fulfil and information about where to get different types of contraceptives (see Figure I.1).

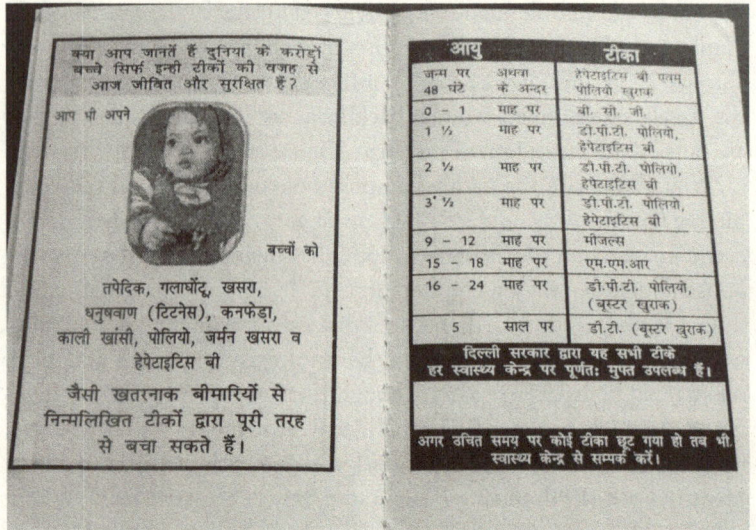

Figure I.1   A Leaf from the 2004 Ration Card Booklet Serves as an Advisory Circular for Families
Source: Department of Food and Supplies, Delhi.

While today we may accept that the Aadhaar has finally launched India into a biometric project that individuates identity through the unique number identifier, the ration card and the job card (tied to a legislation on rural employment called the National Rural Employment Guarantee Act) continue to be ID documents that provision families rather than individuals. As such, these ID documents, post Aadhaar, continue to spur individuals to identify themselves as members of families who seek out the paternalist role of the state. That said, we have been witnessing the transformation of the state into a neo-liberal actor that is withdrawing from providing universal food benefits under the public distribution system (PDS). With the passing of the Food Security Act, 2013, the PDS is conceived to have much more coverage than before; however, families continue to be targeted rather than universally provisioned. One other way in which the state is steadily withdrawing from providing welfare is in terms of its inclination towards making payments through machines rather than through intermediaries, in cash rather than in kind. Though a few chapters touch on these issues, the book does not seriously pursue the implications of such a neo-liberal transformation of the state, unlike a few other recent works like *Red Tape* (Gupta 2012) and *Paper Tiger* (Mathur 2016).

The other point to note is that it was not merely the ration card through which family as a category of governmentality imbued the Indian developmental state. An ID document like the RC too was designed to answer the question of who the head of the family was. The application form for this certificate required the refugees to be candid about present and missing family members and their relation to the head of the family. Though not an archaic colonial piece of legislation, the Delhi Refugees Registration Ordinance, 1947 inaugurated a governmental ethic of care that equated women with children and idiots, and drove female refugees into the protective paternal arms of the male head of household. Under this ordinance, it was only a male head of a household who could register any refugee members of the family present with him. He had to take charge of 'a female, a minor, a lunatic, an idiot or a person incapable by reason of some physical infirmity of attending at the registration centre'.[7] Chapter 3 argues that the RC was hardly an indispensable ID document for refugees seeking compensation. However, even when it was not demanded, and even when other forms of 'collateral evidence' or alternative forms of self-identification were accepted, housing authorities, who had to identify squatter beneficiaries for resettlement, were still interested in establishing the male head of the household. It is evident from this that even in their welfare-providing roles, states often administer by assuming that political subjects are male and that the only consent which matters is that of men.

In her book, *The Sexual Contract* (1988), Carole Pateman embarks on an impressive and necessary mission to contest the theories of social contract of male Western political philosophers. These theories subtly accomplish the consolidation of paternal right as political right, coercion as consent, and subordination as contract. Where the political deed of entering the social contract assumes universal consent preceding it and promises universal freedom succeeding it, the social contract smuggles coercion mainly of men against women into this transaction. The birth of modernity is forged through an unmistakably sexual contract between the state and men which results in freedom, fraternity, and political obligation for men, and domination and the appropriation of consent for women.

Men's domination over women, and the right of men to enjoy equal sexual access to women, is at issue in the making of the original pact. The social contract is a story of freedom; the sexual contract is a story of subjection. The original contract constitutes both freedom and domination. Men's freedom and women's subjection are created through the original contract—and the character of civil freedom cannot be understood without the missing half of the story that reveals how men's patriarchal right over women is established through contract. (Pateman 1988: 2)

The story of the Indian postcolonial state's contract to provide care and welfare for its citizens parallels Pateman's fable of the farcical constitution of universal right and consent in Western political philosophy. The application form for the Hindu and Sikh refugees—who embody in many ways the quintessential citizen—in that it requires men to account for and claim responsibility for the women travelling and living with them, positions the state as a provider that can care for women only through acts of paternalism and patriarchy.

In the momentous years following the Partition, there was, however, one prominent exception to the norm of the male head of the household and the subsuming of women's political consent in ID documents. As the first general elections of the country, extending to the people of the country the long-awaited promise of universal franchise untainted by colonial rule, dawned on India, the election commission (EC) and the first chief election commissioner, Sukumar Sen, found themselves in the unenviable spot of ensuring the inscription of every individual, unmediated by gender, family, lineage, religion, or caste, in the electoral rolls. One can then well imagine Sukumar Sen's dismay upon finding that around 28 lakh women had not given their names and had to be struck off the electoral rolls. These women, who constituted nearly 10 per cent of the total female electorate in five states, namely, Bihar, United Provinces, Madhya Bharat, Rajasthan, and Vindhya Pradesh, had, instead of giving their own names, described themselves as the wife or daughter of so and so. In his All India Radio (AIR) broadcast to the nation on 2 August 1951, Sukumar Sen deplored this callous failure on women's part to discern the enormity of the franchise for 'their complete social and economic emancipation'.[8] In alluding to this absurd practice of concealing their names and identities, Sen said:

Here, then, was a curious senseless relic of the past which would prevent a woman from having even an independent identity of her own, and she must be known as the wife of so-and-so or the daughter of so-and-so. Our women must realize that it is degrading to themselves not to be allowed to have their independent existence in their own right apart from their relationships to the male members of the family.[9]

While acknowledging in an abstract sense the role of 'social custom', Sen was curiously silent on the role of men in denying women this historically hard-earned right and rested his case entirely on the ignorance, illiteracy, and superstitious beliefs of women.

In his introduction to *Provincializing Europe*, Dipesh Chakrabarty writes of how the Indian state extended citizenship to its people in both the performative and the pedagogic registers. Rustic or not, literate or not, peasant or erstwhile prince, everybody enjoyed the right to vote in India and was enabled to vote owing to the EC's progressive practice of issuing ballot papers in which the symbols of parties were emblazoned. The illiterate voter could recognize the party through the symbol and exercise her or his vote. It was at such critical junctures that the performative aspects of citizenship were privileged in the understanding that a peasant too could be 'a full participant in the political life of the nation' (Chakrabarty 2008: 9). However, at other times, voters had to be educated on their rights and responsibilities through canvassing, campaigns, and rules and regulations about eligibility, disqualifications, and so on; and Sukumar Sen gestured at the use of novel modes of publicity such as folk dance, music, and drama to educate and socialize the masses. Republican authorities could not help expressing their frustration that women could not be incorporated into citizenship in either the performative or the pedagogic register. If electoral rolls were the only way to know and identify women voters and women did not consent to being recognized despite all educational campaigns, then how could they be regarded citizens? Among the means Sen hit upon to enable women to exercise their vote without fear of having their anonymity or social inhibitions compromised was separate polling stations for men and women. While lamenting the irrational part that social custom played in these matters, Sen said that perhaps having separate polling booths for men and women in states where purdah was strictly enforced would enable women to exercise their vote.[10]

This book, however, stops short of characterizing the tale of how the Indian state administers through ID documents as one of how it administers men primarily and women only by extension. While the

Indian state was definitely interested in identifying men and administering them primarily, women did not always submit themselves to
erasure and co-option. The book is interested in recovering moments
where women come up with their own modes of inscription and it
traces the matrix of patriarchal norms of bureaucracy, gendered welfare norms, and family within which they do so. Chapter 4 collects
the stories of women whose lives were altered by an ID initiative in
the slums of Delhi. This chapter delves into an intensive ethnography
of how ID cards which were termed V.P. Singh Cards, ration cards,
and metallic tokens were issued to families with a view to establishing
their eligibility for resettlement in a future where their houses may
be demolished. This initiative provoked affects among mothers who
feared for daughters that slipped away from them and wives who felt
wronged by the promiscuity of their husbands; in other words, such
anxieties caused them to insure themselves through ID documents,
both formally issued and counterfeited. Women also used ration cards
to secure bail for their relatives and though this book does not outline
some of these narratives, I describe elsewhere how women were able to
utilize the ration card and the performative idioms therein to navigate
the masculine spaces and the hegemonic male norms of the police station (Sriraman 2013b).

The Popular Making of ID Documents

The historical canvas of this book is spread over moments as dispersed
as ration card production in late colonial wartime India, refugee evidence arbitration in the aftermath of the Partition, the licensing era
and management of commodity fraud, the making of housing proof
in a slum, and the electronic transition to a number-based identification form. These moments, while they may appear random, have been
carefully chosen because they yielded ethnographic and epistemological narratives of an evolving urban welfare dispensation which had to
constantly improvise its genres of ID. The high point of such improvisa-
tion featured when the subcontinent was severed and a sea of refugees
poured into the two states on either side, carrying with them their
anguished citizen claims and their affectively marked shreds of paper.

Given that rehabilitation was a politically and culturally laden
project, when read especially against the postcolonial promise of an

expansive citizenship, denying housing, employment, and education to a class of potential national subjects on administrative grounds seemed unacceptable. So, though the nascent Indian nation-state issued RCs across the many constituent states, these ID documents were limited in number and the period that they pertained to. Given that few refugees could satisfy the exact stipulations of producing an RC or their registration number, several genres of documentation came to be accepted in its lieu. These alternative forms of 'collateral evidence'[11]—as they came to be called in rehabilitation discourse—had to be mobilized into the infrastructure of ID, if administrators were at all serious about catering to the legitimate figure of (the Hindu and Sikh) refugees in these parts of the country. This book considers, among its case studies, the housing applications of West Pakistan refugees who carried with them evidentiary pieces of their journeys lived in camps, transit accommodation, and places of 'squatting'. Though they were not exempted from an aesthetic and material mandate of 'truth', makeshift and tentative scraps of paper like letters of recognition, bills, affidavits, and private employers' certificates that possessed only a semblance of the authority of official writing were still admitted into evidence. Since these scraps of paper contained residues of time and space inhabited before, during, and after migration, their production amounted to a 'narrativization' of identity. A normatively defined project of imbuing postcolonial citizenship rendered it necessary for the state to enable moments of self-identification where infrastructures of evidence had to be fashioned out of the residues of one's journey strewn across lived time and space. Refugees had lost their enduring degrees and certificates, pension papers, and the like, owing to the circumstances of travel. A certain governmental latitude had to inform the processing of applications for education, employment, and housing owing to a deficit of genres that readily recognized a figure like the refugee. The absence of an infrastructure of ID to verify the identities of welfare claimants did not, however, result in the same latitude for East Pakistan refugees in West Bengal.

ID documents are made in more ways than one. It is not simply when people recognize themselves and create their own forms of ID, and send them to authorities for authentication through proper channel, that ID documents are 'made'. This was more or less the story of how people fashioned ID documents soon after the Partition, as described in this book. The book also records various other poignant moments and modes of making ID documents which allowed the Indian state to administer subjects. In the slums of Delhi after the year 1990, ID documents were counterfeited and presented to officials, who often had to accept them because the urban authorities had no means to cross-check if they were genuine. Having possibly lost the original record of cardholders who were counted in a housing survey and issued identity cards, these authorities could at best gauge the legitimacy of these documents depending on how old or new the cards looked. The slum residents of Govindpuri, a locality in south Delhi that forms the field site for Chapter 4 in this book, deemed these counterfeited V.P. Singh documents to be the result of a necessary *kalakari*. Such kalakari was devised to counter unfair housing classifications between those who arrived before and after a critical 1990 survey in the slum. In cases where one particular card termed the V.P. Singh Card (apart from the backdated ration card) was the most reliable temporal marker of the slum resident's urban presence, the authorities could not make do without it. While a lot of administrative discretion surrounded the acceptance or the rejection of these cards—I witnessed one official berate a woman for producing what he assumed was a counterfeit card—their utility could not be overlooked. Where the tangibility of the document (in terms of its newness or oldness) could not be determined, these ID documents circulated freely and pandered to familial desires surrounding resettlement. The book does not suggest a seamless continuity between the post-Partition moment of ID making and the counterfeiting of ID documents in 1990. It merely conjectures that the administration of subjects dwelling in 'in-between spaces' (the rural and the urban, one nation and another, illegal and legal) required the everyday state[12] to imbibe and allow evidence that was otherwise out of their reach.

A Material Critique of Citizenship

If the book has suggested so far that the documentary state has evolved in a dialectical relationship with the subjects it identifies, and if the very definition of governmentality has been complicated, then it is time to challenge governmentality as something that works similarly for everybody. While foregrounding popular and subaltern discourses of citizenship, the reader will note the deliberate use of the term 'subjects' rather than 'citizens' in this book's discussion of the urban poor. This is because marginal subjects dwelling between legalities and those dwelling in sovereign spaces have all had to endure different governmentalities. Partha Chatterjee who came up with an original thesis of governmentality in India, sees its operation mainly in political society, a space that is inhabited by population groups such as slum residents, migrants, refugees, and the labouring classes. The space of political society is marked by paralegal arrangements and an absence of the conception of law in general. The terms of association in political society starkly stand out in contrast to civil society. Groups in political society negotiate with authorities, mediate through local leaders and politicians, and manipulate rules. This sets them apart from civil society where a sublime discourse and rights framework of sovereignty is operational, enabling its middle-class, law-abiding, and law-savant citizens to claim their rights, demand their due, and engage in civil terms with authorities.

Partha Chatterjee talks about political society when he writes: 'The activities of governmentality required multiple, cross-cutting, shifting classifications of the population as the targets of multiple policy, producing a necessarily heterogeneous construct of the social' (Chatterjee 2004: 36). While Chatterjee writes of a dynamic governmentality at work in political society and though he defines the composition of political society itself in an expansive and heterogeneous manner, he does not see the relevance of governmentality in civil society. I find this dichotomy of civil society and political society somewhat troubling because it is produced through sharp distinctions between these population groups in terms of what is politically possible as well as in policymaking. However, more significantly, while the state can devise multiple classifications and policies to govern the people of political society, the subjects of political society can only draw on a limited repertoire of negotiations with authorities. In their claim-making, poor subjects living in slums, for instance, are regarded to draw only on the politics of patronage or the language of moral rights.

The stories in this book differ from this assessment as we will see how subjects have demonstrated a certain infrastructural and administrative ingenuity in rendering ID documents in their form and function appropriate to their specific needs. In so doing, they have shown an

astute knowledge of various modalities of making claims, such as citing law, performing law, invoking penal rights such as first information
reports (FIRs), drawing up public interest litigations (PILs), and sending petitions alongside drawing on 'paralegal' arrangements. So, even
though urban poor subjects are not labelled as 'citizens' in this book,
they arguably deploy different languages and strategies of citizenship;
in other words, they can drive policy and not simply be governed by
policy. Citizenship need not be the preserve of any one class of society,
nor need it be bound up with any single skill set of interactions (such as
negotiation) with state authorities. This book features manual labourers, 'refugee squatters', slum residents, and rural migrants in Delhi,
and their efforts in drawing up affidavits, declarations, identity cards;
demanding special or supplementary ration cards; creating 'collateral
evidence'; counterfeiting ID documents; and keeping personal or
community records and archives. We will consider how, inter alia, the
popular production of ID documents occurred in realms that straddle
the formal and the informal and shaped the very administration of the
poor in urban spaces.

In his novel, *The Circle of Reason*, which traces the operation of
reason and modernity outside Europe, Amitav Ghosh (1986) conjures
a surreal scene in which Karthamma, a pregnant woman aboard a ship
headed from India to Al-Ghazira in Egypt, refuses to bring forth her
child unless she is given the right forms to sign. As the people on the
ship marvel at how an ignorant village woman can possibly be in the
know of things as nuanced as birth certificates, one of the ship inmates,
Professor Samuel, interjects with a sharp rejoinder. He drily remarks
that the woman believed in the form because the man who brought
her on the boat casually mentioned that her child would become a
Ghaziri and enjoy cars, houses, and big buildings. All she needed to do
was to sign a few forms and so, Karthamma decided to take the man
at his literal word. The forms would be a passport for the child into
Ghaziri-ness and they would alone deliver the child from the negligent
hands of the Indian state. So, Professor Samuel, who was as lacking
in bureaucratic authority or medical pedigree as anybody else on that
ship, decides to indulge the woman in her craving for her son's Ghaziri
citizenship and enacts a ritual of state certification. He first dresses
himself in a suit, wears a tie, and swings a suitcase jauntily before he
approaches the cabin to see Karthamma. However, before he sees her,

he asks Alu, the protagonist of the novel, to tear out a page from his beloved book, *The Life of Pasteur*. Professor Samuel proceeds to scribble his own signature at the bottom of the page next to the English word 'Signed'. He then explains his actions to Alu by saying, 'she's in no state to tell the difference between a form given to her by a government babu and a sheet of paper held under her nose by a suited-booted stranger' (Ghosh 1986: 200–1). Sure enough, the woman accepts that her son will not be orphaned by Egypt's laws and goes into labour. Karthamma's insistence on seeing a form that assured her of her son's prospects is a powerful instantiation, in general, of marginal subjects' conviction in the material aspect of citizenship. Her anxious resolve to obtain a tangible assurance of her son's citizenship claims can be read as a rich signifier of how subjects who dwell in the margins struggle to gather whatever resources are available to protect themselves against administrative denials.

In work that has engaged with the urban poor, citizenship has been noted to be manifest in piecemeal, insurgent, and emergent spheres of marginal dwelling. James Holston witnesses an insurgent citizenship in Brazil's slums where alternative legalities were forged through adverse possession or the unauthorized possession of land over a long period of time. Such a citizenship, fought over land deeds, involving the circulation of documents valid only within localized contexts, and won through minute legal and administrative battles, can rise only from 'the sites of metropolitan degradation' (Holston 2009: 249). Veena Das (2011, 2012) records an 'emergent citizenship' in Delhi's slums where poor people's aspirations for an urban future that is filled with uncertain possibilities impels them to marshal material resources such as ration cards. She also writes that a certain moral obligation on the part of the state to preserve life and related to this, certain 'legal impulses' towards the poor in the 1980s allow the scripting of a citizenship that is framed in an evolving temporality. She demonstrates this through an ethnographically rich story where local authorities in a Noida slum issued an intriguing substitute for the ration card. Here, the residents were able to exchange their ration cards (both original and counterfeit) to get new cards which were labelled *pradhikaran patra*. While this substitute ration card was issued only for three months, the stamps issued on the document indicated that the residents used it beyond that period (Das 2012: 328). Veena Das's corpus of work regarding the urban poor, seen in its rich and composite entirety, supports a certain narrative of marginal dwelling in which terms like 'squatters', 'slum', 'occupation', and 'unauthorized colonies', as well as objects like the substitute ration card, allow for the consolidation of unnamed laws and liminal models of governance in marginal spaces. Ritajyoti Bandyopadhyay too suggests a citizenship through the hawkers' movement in Calcutta (present name Kolkata) which allowed for a 'state–union complex' that enabled the state to mobilize 'the pre-existing knowledge' of the hawkers into the ethnographic tools needed to govern them (Bandyopadhyay 2009: 119). Pace all these scholars, the chapters in this book will also show that it is not just law in marginal spaces but also ID documents that circulate in such spaces which themselves undergo change.

Citizenship, however, needs to primarily be defined in the broad sense of sharply contested and socially preluded claims to political equality. The caste system in India has supported a structural violence that has bled into the very contours of how people from the lower castes identify themselves. The slim volume of stories, essays, and poems of Dalit writing, called *The Exercise of Freedom*, alerts us to the dynamic and ever-transforming modern matrices of power through which caste operates. The many texts of this book alert us to the insidi- ous and clandestine ways in which bureaucracies and college adminis- trations preserve caste at the centre of privilege, education, jobs, and well-being (Joseph 2013; Tharu and Satyanarayana 2013). This volume underscores how school report cards, loan application forms, and col- lege identity cards viciously iterate and reinstitute caste leading to the heartbreaks and suicides of Dalit youth. This edited book must be read afresh against the backdrop of the recent suicides of Dalit students, which have inspired and strengthened the undaunted and powerful Dalit-led movements in Hyderabad Central University (HCU) and, to a lesser extent, in Jawaharlal Nehru University (JNU).

In January 2016, Rohith Vemula, a Dalit student from HCU, com- mitted suicide following the suspension of his scholarship and eviction from the hostel. As he hanged himself with a banner of the Ambedkar Students Association (ASA) that he was a member of, the Dalit stu- dents of HCU spearheaded a social movement which questioned the treatment of Dalit students on campus and protested the censorship of radical thought in universities. The tribunal that was appointed in the wake of Vemula's death found the Vice Chancellor of the university,

Appa Rao, to be guilty of exclusionary practices and supported the demand for a Rohith Vemula Act that would penalize authorities who were culpable of institutional discrimination against Dalits. Even as a case was being made out against Appa Rao under the Scheduled Castes and the Scheduled Tribes (Prevention of Atrocities) Act 1989, a thick cloud of scepticism was cast over Rohith Vemula's 'Dalitness' (Teltumbde 2016). A question hung uneasily in the air, 'how can these various authorities be held accountable when Vemula's caste was unknown?'[13] Almost as soon as the question was asked, several newspapers jumped into the fray to question the truth of 'the institutional murder' when Rohith's caste identity was itself trapped in ambiguity.[14]

Such strange journalistic stances notwithstanding, poignant stories emerged detailing the caste of Rohith's mother who was from the Mala (Scheduled Caste [SC]) community in Guntur and forced by her negligent foster mother into a marriage with a man from the *Veddera* community.[15] Rohith's mother, Radhika Vemula, repeatedly asserted that Rohith grew up as a Mala living in a Mala village and considering that her husband divorced her, there should be no doubts over his caste status. However, it was only when the Guntur collector, who initially expressed confusion, declared in his report which was submitted to the SC commission that Rohith was indeed Dalit, and also produced his caste certificate, that this question ceased to be asked, at least for a brief while.[16] More recently, the Guntur collector recanted his submission—suspiciously as a consequence of 'petitions against the claims of the scholar's family'—and sent a notice to Radhika Vemula asking her to prove her son's caste. She was warned that if she failed to prove her son's SC status, Rohith Vemula's SC certificate itself would have to be revoked.[17] Thus, caste and the very category of caste violence, even where it is ordained through bureaucratic rituals, can never suffice in enacting justice or even simply acknowledging a crime. The very tenability of proving the criminal neglect charge against Appa Rao and the enforceability of the Scheduled Caste and Scheduled Tribe (Prevention of Atrocities) Act hung uncomfortably on Rohith's, and by extension every putative Dalit student's, Dalitness and its material corroboration, the caste certificate. The social movement in the University of Hyderabad that unfolded in the wake of Rohith Vemula's death was and is forced to deal with the stalling of the penal inquiry until the caste certificate—the product of a garbled process of administrative fact-finding—was produced as a witness to the crime. As Teltumbde puts it, '[t]his seemed to suggest that if he had not been a Dalit, the crime would have been no crime and if he had been a Dalit, he would really get justice' (Teltumbde 2016: 11).

This book studies, among other things, the early framing of caste and caste-ness in the welfare discourse of the nascent Indian postcolonial state at a formative moment, namely, the dispensation of housing compensation for refugees in the aftermath of the Partition. The Harijan Sewak Sangh (HSS), an autonomous central agency that played a critical role in influencing the process of lower caste refugee selection and omission, tried assiduously to establish the caste-ness of Dalit refugees. A.V. Thakkar or Thakkar Bapa as he is fondly called, the General Secretary of the HSS, was emphatic on the point and said at a point that it was important to ensure that compensation goes only to *pakka rakka* Dalit refugees.[18] Intriguingly, this body, which was so keen on marking the Dalit refugee by asking for proof of identity in matters of monitoring the allocation of compensation, took the question of Dalit representation within its own committees very lightly. Thakkar Bapa treated caste as an 'exceptional norm' and as 'a liability' in matters of ensuring Dalit representation within the bodies of HSS (Deshpande 2014: 407), but he believed that caste was an insurmountable reality when it comes to welfare allocation. His insistence on seeing proof of the Dalit refugee showed that he wished to put a fine point on the caste-ness of Dalits on occasions where the state was liable to provide for lower caste groups, while underplaying it at other times when representation was due to them. The intractable insistence on proof of caste for housing compensation prompted self-declarations of identity by Dalit refugees, and Chapter 3 describes how, in the absence of dependable ID genres, authorities had to accept these forms provided they were not materially suspect.

In the postcolonial history of welfare governance, the mere production of the caste certificate did not always satisfy authorities who believed that impersonation and fraud outpaced conventional documentary processes of verifying identity. As the twenty-first century dawned on the Indian documentary state riddled with self-doubt, it was no longer deemed enough to verify age, caste, or economic status, for now the state required nothing less than the authentication of subjects as well as the ID documents that attested to the bureaucratic truths that they contained. This century brought with it a new form of identity for Indians, termed the Aadhaar, where their biometric details were captured, linked to a centralized database, following which 12-digit unique numbers were issued. It was only by carrying out biometric authentications of individuals and linking existing ID documents like the ration card, job card, and caste certificate to the new unique number identifier that the ultimate alibi against welfare fraud and manipulation of citizen benefits could now be secured. Where caste certificates were and continue to be mired in a regional politics of reservations, red tape, insurgent caste mobilizations, and power brokerage, the move to link them irrevocably to a centralized database may only deepen bureaucratic biases against people of the lower castes. What is worse, the turn to biometric verification threatens to compromise the post-colonial possibility of privileging popular forms of evidence. Earlier, lower-level officials, refugees, 'squatters', slum residents', and touts of all manner submitted ID documents that contained residues of their personal histories, social relations, and everyday life. Now, with the gathering hegemony of Aadhaar, the doors of such bold narrativization are shutting resolutely against them.

Delhi as a Research Site

The book is located in the shifting spaces of Delhi's administration and urban poor dwelling. My choice of Delhi as the setting to tell the story of how the Indian state administers poor subjects and how these subjects made such administration possible is informed by a host of considerations. This book does not consider Delhi as an ideal research location simply owing to its geopolitical importance, cultural hegemony, or its claims to being repeatedly 'the seat of empire' (Frykenberg 1986: 1). I take my cue from Delhi's prolific historian, Narayani Gupta, who regards the city 'as a museum' on account of its layers of social and political history interspersed with geography (Gupta 2002: xv). Just like other cities such as Bombay (present name Mumbai) and Calcutta, Delhi too has witnessed a profound number of 'critical events' (Das 2006; Tarlo 2003), such as the Second World War, the Partition, the Emergency, and the 1984 riots, and the aftermath of all these events has impinged on its urban ordering. Alternatively, Delhi has allowed for several moulds of casting and recasting citizenship on account of different historical waves of migrating urban poor (Nair 2005). In its capacity as the provincial capital city of colonial India and an independent India, Delhi has enabled civic and national authorities to engineer the lives of the poor and micro-manage their urban aspirations. The turn to urbanization, characterized by the acquisition of tracts of village land, the Second World War, and the Partition simultaneously, entailed a spurt in the number of Delhi's poor and a certain imperative to intimately govern them (Gupta 1986: 153). The involvement of scientists and experts in the planning of Delhi was to the effect of producing Delhi as the centre of infrastructural modernity and 'technocratic modernism' (Sundaram 2010: 17) and dispelling memories of congestion, squalor, and chaos. All this necessitated systematic interventions that targeted the mobile, heterogeneous, self-reflexive, and hybrid classes of the urban poor in Delhi.

Within the urban imaginary of this book, the city is shown to be the nerve centre of colonial wartime rationing, postcolonial refugee rehabilitation efforts, housing and large-scale spatial planning drives, and a laboratory for Emergency austerity measures. In the year 1990, Delhi was chosen for a massive enumeration and ID drive of the slum population and the city administration issued a plethora of ID documents in the wake of this survey. This survey and ID drive lay down the parameters for recasting housing policy and reordering the city, and in so doing, caused intense class tensions in the decades that followed. Delhi was also one of the first cities to warm up to the national unique identification (UID) number initiative termed the Aadhaar, with the government grandly announcing that it would achieve 95 per cent enrolment in the National Capital Territory (NCT) of Delhi. This project, imagined and presented as a technology that will set India free from corruption, leakages, and misappropriation of benefits, entailed issuing a unique number to each Indian resident. While declaring her intentions to integrate the number with a rash of centrally sponsored and locally implemented welfare schemes—some of which were inspired by the UID project's premise of electronic de-duplication— the then chief minister of Delhi, Sheila Dikshit, proclaimed that 'the unique identification is a revolutionary method to overcome bogus beneficiaries and duplication'.[19] Such was Dikshit's gusto that she urged the engineer of the UID initiative and one-time chief executive officer (CEO) of Infosys, Nandan Nilekani, not to drag his feet with enrolment in the city.[20] Its undeniable novelty as a genre of state ID and its claims of rendering administrations paperless notwithstanding, the UID initiative had to undertake breeder document authentications and measures to secure existing ID documents through biometric linkages. It would not be out of place to suggest that the Aadhaar did not depart in any significant sense from the hoary tradition of intensely scrutinizing ID documents and their urban poor bearers in Delhi or their bearers anywhere in India.

If the city was an actor that ordered the modalities of knowing, recognizing, and certifying subjects, it was simultaneously moulded through many modernities and many artifacts. As Awadhendra Sharan puts it, we need to approach the city by paying attention to 'the words through which these [urban] worlds were made up and seen' (2014: 2). In his book, *In the City, Out of Place*, which frames the environment as the historical site of Delhi's urban configuration, Sharan closely follows 'social surveys and scientific standards', 'the emotional registers of pain and prejudice', and 'the vocabulary of planning, governance and the measures of risk' to understand how the city was instituted (Sharan 2014: 2–3). Jyoti Hosagrahar, in her book, *Indigenous Modernities*, asks us similarly to consider how 'Delhi is a city of many cities: imagined, lived and controlled, the landscape has been re-created, rebuilt and made meaningful by the daily acts of inhabiting as well as planned interventions' (Hosagrahar 2005: 3). Following these authors, this book is interested in seeing how the city was administratively able to provide for its subjects during crises of food scarcity, political turmoil, impoverishment, and periods of austerity like the Second World War, the Partition, and its aftermath, Licence Raj. Considering that these urban crises shaped popular modes of dwelling in the city and simultaneously constituted significant moments of ID production, it is only apt that this book studies urban welfare governance and its related regimes of proof.

Methods and Reflections on Multi-sited Ethnography

Research around urban welfare governance put me on the path of exploring documentary practices of rationing families and controlling commodities, ID genres of certifying and knowing refugees, and paper forms identifying designated 'squatters' and 'slum dwellers' entitled to compensation. Considering that these paper forms allowed poor subjects to inhabit the city in layered, disparate, and liminal ways in between the legal and the illegal, in ways that sought to render the liminal into the formal, it was important to throw the net not just far and wide but low and deep. While a traditional immersion into the state archives seemed in order, my close reading of letters, private notes, memos and memoranda, news excerpts, reports, primers, bills, acts, and petitions was framed to pay minute attention to several things. These included the use of administrative legalese, the rhetoric of sovereignty and fraud, the penal language, and the linguistic imagining of 'deviants' built into the application form and the ID document. A discourse analysis of application forms, survey forms, certificates, licences, ration cards, affidavits, and statements of declaration entailed an alertness to the following: the definition of proof (what an ID proved and what it was not supposed to prove); the material aura of the ID (how old and used it looked, for instance); certain habits of self-representation by the official and the applicant; and the absence of certain genres of identity cards in Delhi as compared with their presence elsewhere. Other critical details of my close reading included: attending to protocols and preferences of addressing authorities; the selective relevance of certain types of application forms, licences, and permits to elite classes; the insertion of (gendered and bourgeois) authority into the application form; the significance of notes, notations, and overwriting; and official and popular construction of timelines within an affidavit, statement of declaration, or survey form. The archives that enabled these discursive pursuits included the National Archives, Delhi, the Delhi State Archives (DSA), the Maharashtra State Archives (MSA), the Central Secretariat Library, Nehru Memorial and Museum Library (NMML) Archives in Delhi, and the India Office Records, London. What I wished most was to scour these archives to discern suppressed voices of the subaltern figure in the firm conviction that marginalized 'historical subjects exist beyond the knowledge regime of the archive' (Ghosh 2006: 22).

But this book does not plot a historical ethnography simply within the state archives, nor does it content itself with reading colonial and national archives 'against the grain' (Stoler 2002: 100). It embodies a certain aspiration towards a multi-sited ethnography. Such a term does not simply entail diffusing research across an exemplary profusion of sites of ethnographic inquiry but rather across different social worlds and everyday spaces. A multi-sited ethnography, unlike traditional (Malinowskian) ethnography, does not occur in a 'bounded group in a single place', but unfolds in several sites as an empirical response to a theoretical question and as part of the research process (Nadai and Maeder 2005). An ethnography for a research subject like ID documents—in that it touches the deeply familiar, 'the already known', the mundane, and the trite—is an ideal case for a multi-sited ethnography (Marcus 2005; Riles 2006; Strathern 2006). Traditional ethnography would require an immersion into 'perspectives, categories, logics of subjects who are presumed to be other' (Marcus 2005). Such work can be undertaken in bounded cultural spaces such as a clan, a forest-dwelling community, or an aboriginal population. Multi-sited research would require us to dig into sites like the dispersed bureaucracy; locations where enumeration and ID take place (camps, enrolment centres, slums); places where the administration faces crises of legitimacy and legal jurisdiction; the spaces where the poor live and work; 'paper shrines' (Hull 2012a: 113) where applications are received and processed; and the furtive recesses of the archives. Multi-sited research, perforce, requires methodological agility and this book has therefore entailed the use of different methods like archival work, discourse analysis of laws, speeches, letters, policy texts, reports, judgements, newspapers, oral narratives, and interviews with subaltern governmental actors (like low-ranking food officials) and subjects dwelling in critical historical and cultural locations. The fieldwork has involved qualitative interviews conducted over the course of four years, that is, 2010, 2011, 2013, and 2014, with a range of officials in the Department of Food and Supplies, Delhi, the Delhi Development Authority (DDA), erstwhile fair price shop (FPS) holders, non-governmental organization (NGO) representatives, representatives of the Unique Identification Authority of India (UIDAI), and computer operators in enrolment camps. Chapter 5, which has involved additional fieldwork over a year, is situated in two prominent sites of Aadhaar enrolment, namely, the centres that were set up in north Delhi to issue Aadhaar and a bus terminal whose porters applied for the Aadhaar. Chapters 2 and 4 involve a heavy reliance on oral narratives, collected over three years, of subjects such as low- and middle-ranking food officials and the residents of a slum in south Delhi.

The oral narratives that yielded testimonies from food officials, NGO representatives, and slum residents were, to a limited extent, intended to reconstruct a certain empirical understanding of how an ID initiative unfolded in 1990. Given all the philosophical difficulties of engaging with the fuzziness and selective acts of omission and inclusion in memory, I have tried, in Chapter 4, to corroborate the popular and official versions of events with their sketchy appearances in newspaper reports and official documents. However, this book does not trust oral narratives to do what archival texts promise the researcher and it does not intend those narratives to merely fill the void of official documents. As Ranajit Guha points out, official documents such as the departmental dispatches found in the minutes and reports on counter-insurgency only deny the complex modes of existence of peasant subaltern consciousness. Where such insurgency is deeply rooted in cyclical and mythic notions of time, official documents broadly index these surges of rebellion to be linear and secular (Guha 1999: 3). Guha writes that certain kinds of archival knowledge, both in their narrative and analytic forms, achieve the submergence of peasant consciousness into official writing. Oral narratives are needed to counteract the hegemonic and subsuming tendencies of the official archive. The use of this terminology, that is, oral narratives, is deliberate as it entails a certain dense self-insertion into another time that one has lived and seen. Such narratives require grappling with 'the difference between the time of the events and the time of their telling, the time of history and the time of discourse, the distance between the narrated and narrating self, the time of history and the time of telling' (Portelli, cited in Narayan 2010: 113). In addition, they have to negotiate fragile distinctions between 'the factual and the artistic' narratives, 'events and feeling', memory and record (Portelli 1998: 66).

In this book, the use of oral narratives of slum residents recognizes the complex power of this historiographic device in rendering conflicting emotions and memories of the 1990 ID initiative. These emotions include nostalgia for the leader, V.P. Singh, a certain fear of losing the card, anxieties about timelines of entry and occupation, pride that they were original occupants, and jealousy where they were not treated on par with original occupants. In cases where residents inventoried their affective practices of mobilizing ID documents within the historical milieu of the initiative, I have used their narratives to plot the life of ID documents in marginal spaces. In a limited sense, this book also makes use of original and translated Hindi fiction, Hindi newspapers, and archival sources in the firm conviction that the popular should not be divorced from the vernacular even if it cannot be conflated with it. In other places, I have made use of Indian English fiction, especially where certain narratives have been invested with the power of recreating historical, existential, and surreal situations of the bureaucracy and the administration.

The field of ID documents is strewn across 'different but complexly connected sites' (Nadai and Maeder 2005) to which one can trace practices of circulation, mobilization, imitation, appropriation, and affective negotiation of paper. It may seem like a wild arrangement of field sites, but the homes of retired food officials who issued and withheld ration cards during the era of the Licence Raj in Chapter 2, squatter settlements whose refugee dwellers were minutely scrutinized in Chapter 3, a slum where an ID initiative was first announced in Chapter 4, and a bus terminal where mostly Dalit rural migrants sought to acquire and mobilize the Aadhaar were locations that were carefully chosen to empirically probe the historical production of welfare through practices of ID documents.

Structure of the Book

On first glance, the book's choice of themes for a historical ethnography or the very proposition of a historical ethnography spread across such a vast timescale, from the last decade of colonial rule to the present moment of biometric identity production, may seem absurd, or at the very least, foolhardy. However, this book is written as a response to a certain trend in literature on ID documents. Typically, scholarship in this field has been driven by the cultural epistemes of the nation whose presence haunts and preordains practices of ID. Predominantly, histories of passports and contemporary analyses of national ID cards have framed ID in national discourses of state formation, sovereignty, immigration, nationality, and citizenship. This book attends to the largely unheeded task of systematically plotting the history of documenting and identifying subjects within the dispersed urban milieus of welfare governance in late colonial and postcolonial India.

Chapter 1 attends to the 1940s and 1950s period in India, which together characterized a period straddling the colonial and the postcolonial and witnessed unprecedented documentation in terms of the scale and models of ID undertaken. This was owing to the concurrent developments of the Second World War, political dissidence, the Partition, and electoral preparation. Surprisingly, however, the wealth of identity documentation spawned in India during this period has received little and sometimes no scholarly discussion.[21] Drawing on primary official and popular sources, Chapter 1 essays the analysis of the significant war period across the Indian colony, in terms of initiatives to identify and classify, while focusing on Delhi in terms of the ID documents produced, the most prominent of which was the ration card. The wartime enumerative categories of 'head of the family' and 'dependent', the official norms of 'individual' and 'family', the commercial taxonomies of 'dealer', 'distributor', and 'consumer', the administrative criteria of residence, address, date, and the evidentiary attributes of serial number, signature, fingerprint, all prefigure as salient entry points into the postcolonial welfare economy. This chapter is committed to demonstrating the wartime crystallization of the ration card into an indispensable administrative marker of family and residence, as well as the material significance of ration cards in real and imagined encounters of corruption implicating cardholders and petty and high-ranking officials.

Bureaucracies are made out to embody ideal organizational norms and the self-definition of a bureaucrat is a person 'without anger and fondness' (Albrow, cited in Hoag 2011: 82). Chapter 2 asks: what happens when low-ranking officials encounter ID documents in a society saturated by emotion-laden practices of kinship and ritual? Documents of rationing summoned deep interpretive traditions of governance and enabled the fluid negotiation of administrative boundaries of rules. The chapter makes a case for the deep presence of lower-level officials and official intermediaries in the knowledge production of the welfare economy. The chapter deals with the period designated Licence Raj, which marked a new era of socio-economic control of various food, cloth, and other commodities. Certain urban affective dilemmas of issuing ration cards to middle-class subjects, regulating the food commerce of hospitality (wedding, funeral, and festival gatherings) through rationing documents, and raiding the godowns of hoarders and smugglers presented themselves to food officials during the Shastri and the Indira Gandhi years. The chapter advances an argument that ID documents can lure, tantalize, and animate officials located within a culturally ordered bureaucratic world. During this period, officials crafted, on the go, affidavits and declarations of the kind that had no precedent and no basis in existing administrative legislations. Such mobilizations were inspired by the extended social context of kinship obligation and the self-representation of the food inspector as a culturally ordained *annadata* and destroyer of evil practices of smuggling food.

Chapter 3 traces how the Indian state administers, through popular practices of ID documents, in the marginal spaces of refugee settlements in the city. The Partition, which brought in its wake a sea of displaced populations that deluged both countries, threw up conundrums of ID that straddled the philosophical and the feasible, the material and the intangible. With the exception of Calcutta (present name Kolkata), Delhi received a disproportionate number of refugees compared to other cities, and their rehabilitation called for a massive infrastructure of enumeration, classification, and ID of the refugees and their families. Given that there were no pre-existing genres of recognizing the refugee figure so alien to the memory of the colonial state, civic and rehabilitation authorities had no choice but to accept and privilege alternative or 'collateral evidence' that emerged from the makeshift documents and narrated itineraries of refugees and refugee associations. While an official ID document that was termed the RC did emerge, it was unrealistic for authorities to undertake rehabilitation on the strength of the scarce possession of this document. However, urban authorities did not exempt (Dalit, upper caste Hindu and Sikh) refugees from certain encumbrances of enacting their caste, nationality, displacement, markers of entry, occupation, and presence in marginal spaces of the planned city. In the face of this, the chapter shows how such authorities had to consider and selectively accept the productions of self-identifying communities and individuals.

Chapter 4 unfolds in a slum cluster which came to be historically noted for being the first of its kind to benefit from an initiative that involved the creation of hitherto unseen identity cards and metallic tokens. This initiative had at its helm the former prime minister, V.P. Singh, who sought to demolish historically sacrosanct administrative criterion of a stable home by issuing ID documents to those squatting on government land. Three genres of ID documents were issued to slum residents as part of this initiative: (a) a ration card; (b) an identity card also called the V.P. Singh Card; and (c) a metallic token. Had it not been for the popular contours of this initiative and the slum residents who enabled it, the creation of a regulatory housing discourse in Delhi would not have been possible. In the popular memory of slum residents, this exercise is remembered for its remarkable move of erasing residence and identity proof as prerequisites to acquiring these documents. Such a move, however, forced the enumerating official to make alternative inquiries of the performative kind into what constituted proof. The administrative factum of residence so sacred to ration card enumeration defied easy characterizations in the absence of reliable ID cards and officials relied on extra-documentary, aesthetic, material, and affective practices of counting and verifying families and their dwellings. This initiative paved the way for the crystallization of an urban legalism that was both precarious and kind. This chapter dwells at the same time on the micro-practices of enumeration during the initiative and the anguished political struggles of slum residents around ID documents after the initiative. Based on an intensive ethnography, this chapter argues that bureaucratic practices of issuing ID documents take on aspects of marginality in sync with the dwelling spaces of slum residents. These ID documents allowed residents to set up a diverse range of truth, that is, material and emotional claims on welfare (mostly housing) benefits, through practices such as counterfeiting, securing FIRs for lost cards, and filing right to information (RTI) petitions against counterfeiters. This chapter also demonstrates how these marginal practices of ID, unique to subaltern realms of dwelling, were mediated not by the individual but by the family, its perception, and its affects.

Chapter 5 starts by acknowledging the novelty of biometric systems in that they rely not merely on an identity card but more crucially on complex and comprehensive databases. Considered within the history of documenting welfare beneficiaries in India, the Aadhaar is also unprecedented in the sense that the number is presented as a digital, portable identity and is plotted as part of 'a larger administrative and technological regime' of cloud-based authentication (Bennett and Lyon 2008: 3). Aadhaar's novelty, however, is not confined to what its engineers pitch it to be but what it may very well uncork and bring forth, that is, that which is not yet present (Heidegger 1993), and its newness is to be imputed to its continuous making, remaking, and what it will help reveal in the unfolding and deferred fact of its creation. As newer and newer imaginations of this electronic number identifier are unleashed on Indians, especially poor Indians, the Aadhaar may foreclose the marginal subject's ability of moving within the welfare ecology, especially if s/he does not belong to this number-based community (Amoore 2008; Franke 2009). The chapter confines itself mainly to probing the processes of enrolment for the Aadhaar and secondarily to the implications of linking it to existing ID documents. Through fieldwork that was undertaken in three different sites, namely, the enrolment centres of the Aadhaar, the Department of Food and Supplies, Delhi, and a bus terminal in Delhi which was home to a community of rural migrants (the bus coolies), the chapter sets up two related arguments. The first is that the production of Aadhaar as a dematerialized form of identity was one that curiously entailed an immersion into intensely material acts of verifying applicants and authenticating their ID documents. However, once it was created, the Aadhaar was invested in its own universal acceptance as the only alibi against welfare fraud in an age of sophisticated identity card manipulation. This leads up to the second point: its strides towards a gathering universality meant that the Aadhaar was ill-suited to an urban welfare ecology that was deeply moored to intricate administrative definitions of shifting address. The rural migrants who are the subjects of this chapter were poorly served by Aadhaar which sought to congeal their documented selves, even as the welfare establishment was itself implicated in a rapidly shifting matrix of caste and regional politics. While the porters had their own forms of ID and others which the government partially sanctioned, the UIDAI, for a long time and until very recently, refused to recognize any of these alternative narrativizations of identity for purposes of enrolling these subjects.

The book concludes by considering how welfare regimes would perhaps benefit from recognizing that claims can neither be purely electronic nor documentary. More critically, the welfare establishment in India would do well to garner insights from its own history of drawing on popular constructions of identity.

Notes

1. This is an extract from Simon (1993: 10). I, however, came across this formulation first while reading the 'Introduction' of Estelle Lau's book, *Paper Families: Identity, Immigration Administration and Chinese Exclusion* (Lau 2006: 3).

2. By the material practice of writing, I mean the discursive and the linguistic relationship of official and popular forms of writing, such as letters, files, maps, permits, licences, petitions, and ID documents, with state bureaucracies and local administrations and by extension, with power.

3. While several anthropologists have used the term 'artifact' to mean different things, I use the term to signify specific things in the context of the book. I imply the deeply consequential and universally acknowledged discursive effects that certain ID genres enjoy among both those who enumerate, identify, and certify and those who will themselves be enumerated, documented, and verified. This would mean that while an artifact may have been introduced as an ID, it becomes artifact only after it secures a certain validity of 'proof' among urban authorities of occupation, residence, family, and refugee status (in this instance). Alternatively, an artifact need not resemble an ID in the strict sense of the term. Take, for instance, the number-bearing metallic token of the slum residence that features in this book. Insofar as it is treated as proof of a certain temporally marked occupation of the slum, it too serves as an artifact.

4. Such a definition of ID documents begs the question: are ID documents the result of enumeration or identification, or is there no difference between these two acts? I would say that they are related but not interchangeable and at times, one devolves into another and at other times, they remain distinct. In fact, I have tried, in different chapters, to locate the instances where they devolve into each other and the junctures at which they remain distinct. Also, not all moments of enumeration and identification are invested with the same densities of impinging on subjects. Each such act is also experienced differently depending on the communities and the minorities in question. It is argued that ID carries the mandate for processing 'stigmata' of persons, involves more precise modes of authentication, and is considered to enact the 'individualizing gaze' (Torpey 1997: 842). Identity cards and identity practices are also believed to be utilitarian enterprises, intended to exercise social control over specific individuals and groups such as labour, nomadic groups, and political undesirables (Higgs 2004: 139; Kaluszynski 2001: 132; Longman 2001; Singha 2013). Such practices do not—unlike enumeration—necessarily shore up the administrative power of the nation state through the use of statistics. Enumeration machineries are distinct in that they validate and inflate the power of bureaucracies and statistics bureaus (Black 2001; Zureik 2001). Hannah Arendt (1967) writes that the greater the extent of bureaucratization, the more is the state's propensity to violence; however, she fails to assign the place of enumeration in such a process. Enumeration is also meant to generate national and social consensus. In Japan, household registers

entrenched local power structures and male aristocratic authority as men alone, in their capacity as heads of household, could enter the samurai class (Winther 2008: 27). However, enumeration and identification as modes of knowledge production often do not operate parallel to each other, and the former devolves into the latter because enumeration often results in enrolment and documented forms of ID. For example, censuses were undertaken in Israel with the explicit intention of issuing identity cards selectively and discriminatingly to Jews, Arabs, and others (Zureik 2001).

5. While a later chapter will cover a wider range of critical scholarly and activist interventions around Aadhaar, here is a tiny sample arranged such that the reader gets a sense of the sweep of time over which this project has gathered steam and critique: Ramanathan (2010), 'A Unique Identity Bill'; Khera (2011), 'The UID Project and Welfare Schemes'; and Jean Drèze, 'A Unique Identity Dilemma', *The Indian Express*, 19 March 2015.

6. These bureaucracies and local-level administrations operate by tightening the screws of 'panopticism' in institutions like the hospital, the asylum, and the prison. This term is used to convey a universal technique of power which coaxed individuals into falling in line with disciplines that surveilled them with military efficiency (Foucault 1984d).

7. Section 4, Delhi Refugees Registration Ordinance, 1947, *The Gazette of India, Extraordinary*, as found in 117-P147, Office of the Regional Commissioner, Abu, Rajputana Agency, 1947, National Archives of India (NAI).

8. AIR Broadcast Talk by the Chief Election Commissioner on 2 August 1951, '28,000 Women off the Electoral Rolls', 8030/46 (3), Political Services, H Branch, 1951, Maharashtra State Archives (MSA).

9. AIR Broadcast Talk by the Chief Election Commissioner on 2 August 1951.

10. AIR Broadcast Talk by the Chief Election Commissioner on 2 August 1951.

11. See 53/31/50, Non-gazetted Section (NGS), Home, NGS Section, 1950, NAI and 60/209/49, Home, Establishments, 1949, NAI.

12. The many essays and books that invoke the everyday state describe it in terms of a blurring of the boundaries between the state and society, official state roles and social identities. Within the everyday state, the distinction between the formal and the informal economy is also fuzzy. The state, in this definition, is not a discrete, homogeneous, monolithic structure, aloof from society. Such a state in India mingles impersonal norms of a formal rational bureaucracy with sociocultural values, 'vernacular discourses', and ritualistic beliefs (Corbridge et al. 2005; Fuller and Harriss 2001; Harriss-White 2003).

13. The Dalit student movement has, in particular, insisted on the institutional roles played by the Bharatiya Janata Party (BJP) Union Minister for Labour, Bandaru Dattatreya, and the Ministry of Human Resource Development (MHRD) in abetting the suicide of Vemula. See 'Students Demand Action against Union Minister for Role in Scholar's Suicide', *The Wire*, 18 January 2016.

14. Nagaraja, Gali, 'Fresh Inquiry Ordered into Rohith Vemula's Caste', *The Times of India*, 22 June 2016; 'Controversy over Rohith Vemula's Caste Refuses to Die Down', *The Indian Express*, 27 February 2016.

15. See, in particular, Sudipto Mondol, available at http://www.hindustan-times.com/static/rohith-vemula-an-unfinished-portrait, accessed on 10 November 2016.

16. Saubhadra Chatterji, 'Official Certificate Scotches Doubt over Dalit Identity', *Hindustan Times*, 20 January 2016; Nikhila Henry, 'It's Official, Rohith Vemula was Dalit', *The Hindu*, 15 June 2016.

17. 'Guntur Collector says Rohith Vemula was not a Dalit, asks Mother for Proof', *The Economic Times*, 15 February 2017.

18. A.V. Thakkar to Sevakram Karamchand (Working Secretary, Displaced Harijans Rehabilitation Board), 14 February 1950, Subject File No. 1, Part 1, F. No. 1 (A) 1936-55, HSS correspondence, Rameshwari Nehru Private Papers, Nehru Memorial and Museum Library (NMML) Archives.

19. 'Dikshit Suggests Larger Role for Aadhaar Numbers', *Hindustan Times*, New Delhi, 11 January 2013.

20. 'Sheila Dikshit tells Nandan Nilekani to Speed up Project', *The Times of India*, 21 June 2012.

21. This is also owing to a general paucity in the historical scholarship of ID documents in late colonial and postcolonial India. Radhika Singha's work on ID practices in the colony and across sites of British imperial expansion has been a refreshing exception in this regard (Singha 2000, 2013). Radhika Mongia's article on the emergence of the passport across racialized sites of crossing imperial borders is also noteworthy (Mongia 1999). However, apart from the passport, ID documents have attracted little attention in Indian scholarship. Veena Das's work that touches on FIRs and more recently ration cards (Das 2006, 2012), Emma Tarlo's work that has dwelled on sterilization certificates (Tarlo 2003), Ravinder Kaur's discussions of the RC (Kaur 2009), and Sanjay Srivastava's article on fake ID documents in Delhi's slums (Srivastava 2012) are notable exceptions. However, there has been no full-length book that consistently delineates a history (straddling the colonial and the postcolonial) of ID documents in India.

I

WARTIME IDENTIFICATION
The Early Ration Card

Shortly before rationing was actually introduced, a film showing the procedure for getting a ration card and for drawing one's ration was, with the full cooperation of the local cinema managements, shown in the cinemas in Bombay and was very effective in explaining matters to the public in general. The Bombay artisan or labourer, even if he could not read, was often a keen cinema 'fan' especially after the wartime rise in wages had put spare cash in his pocket.[1]

In the years following the outbreak of the Second World War, colonial subjects became familiar with a new genre of ID documents that came to dominate their everyday social and economic life in an enduring sense. The ration card or, more imprecisely, the rationing document—imprecise because there was a deluge of documents within this category—was the first mass-scale ID introduced during colonial rule just a few years before the eclipse of the empire. In introducing this document, the colonial authorities were not responding to any one economic crisis or set of political considerations; and once introduced, this document did not remain moored to fulfilling a narrow mandate of extending a basic entitlement, controlling prices, or enforcing austerity. However, to comprehend the afterlife of the ration card, we must begin by dwelling on the critical historical moment when a multitude of these documents were introduced with no seeming uniformity to them and yet with careful forethought. While the rationing document was inspired by the very instrumental politics and economics of imperial sovereignty and necessity, it conjured up all manner of anxieties about how it could be (mis)used. Its very existence was seen as tempting offences and crimes of corruption and fraud. Rationing documents became rhetorically and discursively indispensable to a late colonial discourse of legality. At a time when authorities were desperately trying to enlist indigenous support for the war, rationing permits, cards, and certificates fulfilled a unique mandate of enacting norms of legal propriety and transgression.

This chapter will present a picture of the various wartime initiatives to identify, enumerate, and classify subjects in what constituted a historic and unprecedented moment of colonial documentation. What rendered this moment so unique? Though colonized subjects were no strangers to ID documents—pilgrim's passports, passports, epidemic-related detention and inoculation certificates, descriptive rolls of convicts, and alien's passes being examples (Singha 2000; 2013; Sriraman 2014)—the 1940s heralded a new genre and politics of ID documents where entitlements came to be linked to stable residences and enumerable households. The immediate relevance of these two categories of a verifiable address and a 'proper' family to miscellaneous undertakings of welfare, such as food distribution, housing, and employment guarantee, is treated today as common sense. In contemporary times, if these norms are responsible for all kinds of marginal subjects like slum residents, refugees, migrants, and homeless persons falling through the cracks of welfare provision, it is surely imperative to evaluate the historical processes that were responsible for normalizing these administrative criteria of eligibility. It is fitting that we begin by attributing to the ration card the historical responsibility for the very pragmatic approach to welfare schemes today where queries of 'head of the family', concrete house, and permanent address are part of routine administrative inquiry. So, the first question this chapter addresses is: How does the ration card get rendered into a mechanism for certifying residential address and household? Secondarily, we will see how the family cannot be treated as a cut-and-dried administrative category of ID—a theme that is reinforced in disparate ways throughout this book—where households can be counted with ease and without any great enumerative complexity. Even in this early phase of the document, the ration card came to be culturally imbued in terms of the Indian family. Finally, I demonstrate the different genres of rationing documents introduced at this time as vital to the fashioning of a discourse of legality where definitions of fraud and corruption came to be yoked to the proper use and misuse of ration cards, for instance.

I wish to trace the genealogies of the rationing document which was stubbornly capricious in its origins and the role that this document, taken in its various avatars—cards, permits, and coupons—played in shaping welfare governance. So, while the later chapters may see the focus shift to the role of other ID documents in ordering welfare discourse, the historical primacy of the ration card is critical to this phase. While other genres of ID documents like refugee certificates, electoral rolls, and miscellaneous licences and tokens will be introduced in this book, their continued centrality to the plot of welfare governance pales in comparison to the all-pervasive ration card in wartime and postcolonial India. This is because no other ID document was akin to the ration card in its ability to unify and consolidate both the norms of residential address and household. In so doing, the rationing document became disembodied from its preliminary colonial function of handling wartime scarcity, feeding priority sections, and managing political dissent. Over time, it came to mobilize demographic information about subjects for wide-ranging social and economic purposes, invest the Indian family with a singular documented identity, consolidate proof of residence, or alternatively cast a pall of doubt over the enumerable home, and thus animate welfare discourse.

If this fits the classic story of governmentality where information-gathering and enumeration are undertaken via the ID document for the efficient management of populations, the book will introduce complications along the way (Foucault 1991). Questions such as the liability of the written form to the possibilities of its imitation, repurposing, and appropriation and the document's role in making welfare processes opaque, muddy the story of power-knowledge (Caplan 2009; Das 2006; Groebner 2007; Hull 2012a; Raman 2012; Tarlo 2003). Above all, the ration card became an artifact that foregrounded the family and normalized gendered welfare roles, such as head and dependents, within the economy of food distribution and housing. The many variable genres of the rationing document, like the supplementary coupons and the heavy manual labourer's ration card, were, to a great extent, the byproducts of mobilizations by indignant religious communities, trade unions, and other collectives, who refused to be denied the means to travel, gather, observe festivals, and act in adherence to their belief systems. Cultural forces of community identity, emotions of kinship born out of religious affinities, and ritual practices of collective worship informed the enactment and relaxation of documentary norms of ration card-based commerce and welfare. All these factors should also give us pause in drawing inferences about the strictly disciplinary aspect of the wartime ration card.

The setting in which I will narrate this story is the colonial capital province and later the postcolonial national capital of India, namely, Delhi, as the various moves to enumerate persons and families and to calibrate parameters of identity and eligibility were orchestrated from this city. During the war, Delhi became a nerve centre of colonial activity, buzzing with the schemes and contrivances and the comings and goings of different colonial representatives, diplomats, and native gentlemen, all of whom had a stake in how they were fed and how their everyday privileges were regulated. For the purposes of this chapter, we will see how it was crucial to generate certain genres of rationing documents for specified urban groups, such as manual labourers, industrial workers, millhands, government employees, and policemen, across various cities. Once rationing commenced in Delhi, there was an imminent danger of riots by various communities deprived of supplies they perceived to be optimal and essential to their cultural existence (even if those supplies sufficed in a basic nutritional sense). For the purposes of ration card enumeration, government officials also worried about how to demarcate the boundaries of a city that was spilling into the ubiquitous countryside that eventually engulfed it. The food-based ration card and the cloth permit also spurred everyday anxieties about holding social gatherings such as weddings, funerals, and festival gatherings. Finally, the comprehensive nature of the rationing scheme also implied a zealous scrutiny of applications for non-essential commodities like petroleum, electricity, and tyres and tubes, which were of considerable value in a city that was the very hub of elite bustle. However, before tracing the intricate ways in which Delhi's urban residents and spaces came to be shaped by ration card practices, there is a need to first inquire into how this document was framed as a colossal necessity during the Second World War.

The Cross-cultural Basis of Rationing

The 1940s and 1950s—a period that straddled the colonial and the postcolonial—were a period of unprecedented documentation in terms of the scale and models of enumeration undertaken owing to the concurrent developments of war, political dissidence, the Partition, and electoral preparation. Even though this period stands out within the history of documentation, it has not, with just a few exceptions, been singled out for historical treatment. This is despite a very stark reality unique to the Indian postcolonial economy, namely, the decision to retain commodity controls and the ration card even though most other countries like the UK and the US believed the ration card to have outlived its use after the war.

Much like elsewhere, rationing in India was deemed significant for various classes of commodities, both essential and non-essential. Given the urgency of shoring up supplies for the imperial war effort, the consumption of every commodity, ranging from paper to electricity, flour to cement, sugar to tyres, was a subject that demanded attention at various levels of the colonial bureaucracy. Internationally, both America and the UK were available as models of wartime rationing, where controls over food and fuel were deemed vital both for regulating prices and for conserving commodities invaluable to the military industry. In America, it was not only staple consumer goods like gasoline, sugar, tyres, and meat that were made available only through ration books and tokens but also other items like farm equipment, typewriters, cars, and stoves ('Rationing of Consumer Goods' 1942). In overseeing the implementation of these disparate controls, the War Production Board and the Office of Price Administration believed that different rationales informed the rationing of the variable classes of rationed commodities. If a commodity like rubber was important to ration because its supply had been directly hit by the Japanese attack on the Dutch East Indies which was responsible for the erstwhile stream of raw rubber into America, then certain other goods like steel were important to conserve because of their critical role in generating other industrial goods.[2] In America, the system of rationing documents was complex, with a confusing array of rationing authorities, a profusion of genres of coupons and certificates, and a multitude of nomenclatures like uniform coupon rationing, point rationing, differential coupon rationing, and so on. British India presented a similar intricacy as the wealth of ration cards, permits, and certificates of both essential and non-essential commodities in the colony was undergirded by a nuanced regime consisting of separate rationing offices, distinct chains of command, and discrete rationing orders spelling out the rules and regulations of use of different rationed consumer goods.

In the UK, plans to ration certain essential commodities were in place even before the war began, as the food administration there was alert to the possibility of an attack on the food lines. In his insightful work on the war economy where he furnishes comparisons between the British and Indian models of rationing, Indivar Kamtekar writes that in the UK, rationing did not extend to staple commodities of consumption, like potatoes, bread, flour, and oatmeal, and in this sense, could be contrasted with India where foodgrains were amongst the first few commodities to be controlled (after motor spirit) (Kamtekar 2002: 196). The model of rationing in India indicated an imperial and geographical bias where only urban areas were meaningfully rationed, thus departing from the system followed in the UK where commodity rationing was more ubiquitous across regions. Finally, Kamtekar also speaks of how the import of rationing was unique to these different landscapes: In Britain, the ration merely determined what a person ate; in India, it might determine whether a person ate at all. British rationing carried, for the majority of people, connotations of equality; Indian rationing offered, to a minority of Indians, a promise of subsistence (Kamtekar 2002: 196).

If this paints a certain benign picture of British rationing, that was far from being the case. The rationing initiative in Britain bore insidious linkages with the infamous wartime national registration (NR) programme. This programme was designed to help 'sort' British men with a view to determining their indispensability to their district and axiomatically, their availability for the war. If compulsory enlistment for the war was enforced through this register, how could people be induced to enter the register in the first place? This was accomplished quite simply by centralizing the register in London and tying it to the food department's ration programme (Thompson 2008: 147). The production of special colour and number-coded identity cards, issued as part of the NR programme alone, entitled British men and women to lay claim to their ration cards. Ration books could be sent only to the addresses of individuals who were present on record in the NR's Central Index (Thompson 2008: 149). By making sure that their nutrition during the war was predicated on their military compliance, British men were neatly boxed into serving their nation. This British practice of linking a ration book per person with an ID through a number identifier was also one of the earliest precursors to the now eerily familiar contemporary technology of biometric de-duplication in different parts of the world. The demographic information was mounted on a centralized database and changes in addresses would have to be updated if people wished to continue receiving their rations (Thompson 2008: 149). However, such a stringent, disciplined, and intricate model could not be applied in a colony where one of the rudimentary reasons to implement rationing was to feed and assuage a hungry and dissenting population (Srimanjari 2009: 48, 60). The rationing programme in colonial India was not used as a bait to enforce compliance to an extraneous coercive scheme of enumeration.

Another point of comparison between Britain and India needs to be made about the actors behind the massive information-gathering enterprise that preceded rationing in both these countries. In Britain, unlike India, private initiative was relied upon to generate demographic information—crucial to at least one type of rationing—to compensate for undependable census data. In India, as we will see, authorities covered such a deficit by undertaking special food censuses purely as a government initiative. In the year 1940, Britain's Board of Trade requisitioned Price Waterhouse (PW) accountants to collect the information necessary for the administration of the system of clothes rationing. These PW experts were to produce a statistical database based on a numbering system that could identify those making rationing claims, and establish their veracity because it was also geared to generating specific information about the clothing habits of the population (Amoore 2008: 24–5).

Finally, we arrive at the question of propaganda. The rationing drives in all these countries were bolstered by aggressive propaganda campaigns that entrenched the relationship between everyday civilian life and the priority war efforts. In Britain, short propaganda and publicity films were made during the Second World War to demonstrate the wisdom of rationing and the best practical ways to use the ration card or clothing coupons. For example, one such film in the archive of the Imperial War Museum, *Rationing in Britain* (1944), describes a day in the life of an average middle-class English family, where the daughter consults a magazine in which a column named Your Coupon Problems offers tips on how to prudently spend the 24 clothing coupons issued to every family over a period of six months. Using nightclothes for 'patching, mending and making things over' is, for instance, suggested as a means to save the clothing coupons so that the woman can look good even during the war.[3] In India, Henry Knight (1954) tells us, short films were made to educate the unlettered labourer to use the ration card. Besides these films, advertisements were issued both by various government departments, such as the Department of Information and Broadcasting, the Department of Food, and the Railway Board, and by indigenous and foreign companies, such as Bata, Burma Shell Company, Diamond Charcoal Gas Producers, Kirloskar Gas Plant, and Goodyear Tyres, which exhorted people to buy less, waste less, and spend less (petroleum, coal, charcoal, rubber, tyres, electricity, food, and so on). A very curious form of economic nationalism was on display in these advertisements that sought to cash in on the colonial war-induced shortage of certain commodities to promote their own brands. These companies would paint themselves as being enterprising (by providing alternative fuels like charcoal gas in place of petroleum to complement the war effort) and helpful (by furnishing advice on the prudent and economical use of rationed commodities).

The Department of Information and Broadcasting, for instance, did not hesitate to appropriate nationalistic sentiments and figures to generate wartime colonial propaganda. It came up with advertisements that depicted the Japanese to be megalomaniacs who saw themselves as 'demi-gods' racially superior to Indians like Iqbal and Tagore, and who did not hesitate to steal swadeshi rationed cloth and pass it off as their own.[4] Such advertisements implicitly asked Indians to comply with rationing norms, for doing so would aid the morally righteous imperial effort. This colonial discourse also projected acts of hoarding, black marketing, and other violations of ration card norms as only aiding the Japanese and slowing down the very patriotic endeavour of saving more for the threatened colony. A splash of advertisements in *Hindustan Times* (*HT*), all advising caution against the hoarder who lurked amongst colonial subjects, stood testimony to this move. These advertisements mentioned 'the cultivator, the dealer and the customer' as the three men legitimately concerned with food, and then underlined the presence of the 'unwelcome fourth man' or the hoarder, an abhorrent figure who threatened the well-being of the people and the authorities through his illegal trade (Sriraman 2011: 53). In short, these films and advertisements mostly reinforced the normative expectation of patriotism implicit in the various demonstrations of the prudent use of the ration card (see Figure 1.1).

Figure 1.1   British Wartime Propaganda against the Hoarder
Source: *HT*, NMML archives.

The Historical Context of Rationing in India

If rationing was introduced in India during the war, it was also meant to address contingent crises of monsoon floods and crop failures in Madras Presidency, Bombay, and Bengal, the abrupt disruption in the flow of imports from a regular supplier of rice, Burma, which came under Japanese attack, and a famine of legendary proportions in Bengal in the year 1943 (Sriraman 2011: 53).[5] Something that just cannot be missed in the wartime period from 1939 to 1945 was the enforcement of military regulations to safeguard India's food supplies. At the helm of these extensive regulations was the formidable Defence of India Act, 1915, which was now repurposed into the Defence of India Act, 1939, and the various control orders issued under it which sought to monitor and regulate the sale, stocking, supply, movement, and transfer of foodstuffs across the country. That a piece of national legislation pertaining to security should accord so much penal space to the safeguarding of grain and sugar supplies is telling of the symbolic and material significance of food and other essential/non-essential supplies to the British colonial state at a time like that.

Nominally, food rationing was introduced in the year 1939, with Bombay being the first city to be rationed. However, for all practical purposes, we can assume the scheme to have materialized only in the year 1943. It was only after the official endorsement of rationing by the Foodgrains Policy Committee and consequent to price control conferences between 1939 and 1942 that the formal decision to ration commodities was taken in the year 1943. Japan's invasion of the three suppliers of rice in the Far East, namely, Burma, Siam, and Indo-China, distressed neighbouring countries and forced the British colony in India to look for alternative sources. On the one hand, in Bombay where rationing was first introduced, the damage done to growing crops by pest and floods was hard to undo, and, on the other, there was a sudden rise in food prices owing to the Japanese occupation of Burma (Knight 1954: 195). The Bengal famine produced the rationales for 'deficit' and 'surplus' zones, the creation of the Basic Plan which governed the movement of food between these zones, some government action in deficit areas, and adequate preparations in surplus areas (*Report of the Foodgrains Investigation Committee*, 1950: 2–3).[6] With the high risk of famine and famine conditions surfacing in other states and provinces, there was an onus on the administration to regulate the normal chan-nels of trade and supply of food. No foodgrains were permitted to be removed from one province or state to another except in accordance with a central plan or the Basic Plan.[7]

Historians and economists project rationing to have been a palliative measure for the discontented civilian population and a wartime neces-sity for the 'priority sections' (Bhattacharya 2001; Kamtekar 2002; Sen 1981; Srimanjari 2009). Srimanjari writes that hungry subjects hardly needed goading to participate in civil disobedience.[8] Sanjoy Bhattacharya regards feeding the swelling numbers of the Allied Forces and the impracticality of generating local food supplies around Burma given the difficulty of the terrain of the Japanese battlefront as forming impulses for the British to increase food production and make plans for rationing. The purchases of cereals by the army constituted a huge burden on the food establishment as it had to provision British and American troops and two million Indian soldiers (Joseph 1961: 23). Scores of men fighting for the British Army, soldiers in the Maratha regiments, policemen in the Bombay City Police, and labourers in the mills and other industries of Bombay and elsewhere, on whom the colonial national security of India depended, were in urgent need of food replenishments. Many ranks of civilian employees, those working in the provincial civil services, workers involved in the war industries, plantation and mine workers, and unskilled labour employed in military and civilian building projects were covered by rationing schemes (Bhattacharya 2001: 84–7). The military scare was sounded: official inquiries reported the imperative need for a separate ration scale for army soldiers whose food needs in the year 1943 were estimated to be 650,000 tonnes of foodgrains, of which wheat constituted 500,000 tonnes and rice 150,000 tonnes (*Report of the Foodgrains Policy Committee* 1943: 34).

Many factors, other than famines and the need to keep the labour and military force well-fed, were pressing on the administration to do something to regulate food supplies and to make it available to a greater cross-section. These were: the impossibly large queues forming outside food supply stores; the strikes by grain merchants; and the danger and the incidence of hoarding among householders and private traders. A lot of dissident activity in Bengal might have also nudged the British to act. Bengal Congress leaders reportedly incited people by telling them that extensive exports of foodstuffs from India to South Africa, Canada, Australia, and England were taking place even as Indians were deliberately being forced into famine conditions (Srimanjari 2009: 113). The Bengal *Congress Bulletin*, in its 1943 publication, alleged that Indians were being forced 'into the Army and the labour for war production' (Srimanjari 2009: 113). If much of the Quit India resistance was undercut by the widespread arrests of Congress leaders and the communist compromise with colonial leaders,[9] it did not prevent local leaders from fomenting food riots and hoarding (Bhattacharya 2001: 208). Colonial leaders were aided by the Communist Party of India (CPI) Central Committee in launching the Grow More Food campaign to address local disquiet and handle such riots. In Delhi, the Quit India Movement raised worries of attacks on vulnerable sites of food and cloth production, with patrols and pickets organized in anticipation around the Delhi cloth mills and grain dealers' shops (Legg 2007: 117). Basic supplies were scarce enough to conclude that such attacks and riots could unhinge the war effort seriously, thereby reinforcing the argument for rationing.

Amongst the various price control conferences that took place between 1939 and 1942, the one in 1942 suggested in all gravity the centralized purchase of foodgrains, with a view to address insufficient supplies in deficit areas (Mooij 1999: 66). The Food Advisory Council formally endorsed the plan for rationing on 3 March 1943, while the Foodgrains Policy Committee did so when it submitted its report in the year 1943 (Knight 1954: 202).[10] Within a year of the Committee arguing that rationing was indispensable in all large centres in India, 103 cities and towns came to be rationed in British Indian provinces and princely states; and by October 1946, the number of towns and rural areas rationed was approximately 771, covering a population of over 150 million (Knight 1954: 189). By 1947, both the urban and rural areas of Madras, Bombay, Travancore, Cochin, and Mysore were under rationing, though the rural areas were not statutorily rationed. Initially opposed to rationing, Punjab introduced it in the cities of Rawalpindi, Amritsar, and Lahore in 1944 and Shimla did so in 1945. Even surplus provinces like Assam, Orissa, Central Provinces, Sind, Bihar, and United Provinces introduced it in some of their towns in the beginning of the year 1947 (Knight 1954: 191) (see Figure 1.2). Food rationing was introduced in Delhi on 29 May 1944—interestingly, long after it was introduced in other places like Bombay and Calcutta—under the Delhi Rationing Order of the same year and much after other commodities like motor spirit and tyres and tubes were rationed in Delhi. The rationing department of Delhi came into existence at the same time in May 1944 and remained functional until March 1954.[11]

Sir Henry Knight, Advisor to the Governor of Bombay during the Second World War, was considered responsible for the introduction of a rationing system in the Bombay province, which was upheld by central food authorities as the best in India and became the basis for models used in other provinces and states. He recorded three prominent models of rationing, namely, statutory, non-statutory, and controlled

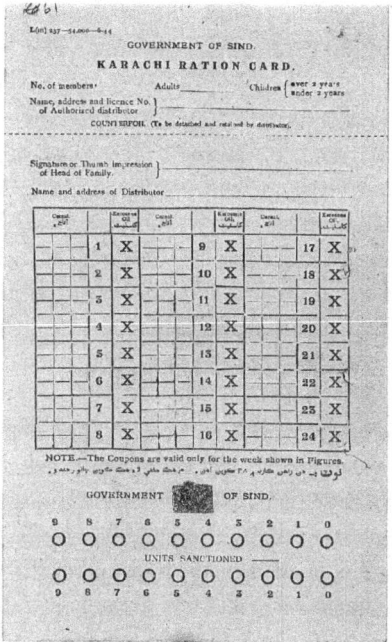

Figure 1.2   The Karachi Ration Card
Source: NAI.
Note: Issued by the Government of Sind, the ration card was unique in that it was
printed bilingually in both Urdu and English.

distribution. In areas where statutory rationing orders were given, the
provincial or state administration had to count the population and
regulate the acquisition and the movement of rationed foodstuffs. In
the absence of a ration card, the subject was not entitled to any food
supplies and subjects were forbidden from importing food into the
rationed area. The period till which the ration card was valid was subject to change, as were the quantities that the cardholder was entitled to
obtain. Statutory rationing was usually enforced in urban areas because
the food administration found it extremely impractical to regulate the
large numbers of the rural masses through rationing documents. Where
statutory rationing was imposed, private imports of rationing stuffs by
traders were banned and individual consumers were allowed to import
rationed foods only against the cancellation of appropriate coupons

on ration cards for specific periods. While consumers could not obtain rations without ration cards, establishments could not do so without ration permits.[12]

Non-statutory rationing was the model common to rural areas. Here, private imports were not prohibited; and ration cards were issued to non-producers and to those who produced much below their needs or insufficiently. Those possessing a ration card were entitled to a fixed scale of ration, but it was not legally punishable if they tried to procure supplies without a ration card and nor were the authorities obliged to supply the ration. The third model of rationing went by the name of 'controlled distribution' and was prevalent in some districts across India. This was also termed informal, partial, or unofficial rationing. Here, private traders were allowed to issue family ration cards and the supplies that they provided could vary from those strictly supplied in other places at the time (Knight 1954: 191). Even though traders were permitted to open ration shops, they could do so only after obtaining a licence. These traders opened retail shops under the control of district officers and were assisted by voluntary organizations. They were operational in rural or semi-urban areas.[13] The Famine Inquiry Commission made clear in its report that in matters of colonial food provisioning and regulation, the priority was the protection of cities and industrial areas (Famine Inquiry Commission Report, cited in Sen 1981: 441). Scholars writing on food entitlement and regulations during this period criticized the colonial administration for ignoring the needs of rural India. Amartya Sen describes the famine and post-famine conditions in rural Bengal as being completely unalleviated by any government relief, as witnessed by 'rural destitutes trekking into the city and dying on the streets' of Calcutta (Sen 1981: 441). He points out how colonial authorities were reluctant to impose the Famine Code in Bengal, as doing so would entail organizing work programmes and relief efforts. This only reinforced the very self-serving purpose of introducing rationing, namely, to address shortages for the creation of military, civil defence works, and strategic industries (Sen 1981: 441).

Now, we turn to the genres of the rationing documents themselves. The colonial food authorities were cognizant of supplementing the diet of certain classes of subjects, like manual and industrial workers, government employees, army soldiers and police guards, the wives of army soldiers, essential civil services personnel, pregnant women and children, among others.[14] If some of these subjects were important to feed because the colonial military effort was predicated on their labour and nutrition, others like pregnant women and the wives of army soldiers were important to support on compassionate grounds (see Figure 1.3). It is interesting that women as a rationing category taken by themselves were never accorded priority because they did not fit the description of manual worker, millhand, a soldier, policeman, or government employee.

The only exception to this rule was the certificate issued by some administrations, like the Andaman and Nicobar Islands, to the expecting mother who was entitled to extra rations after the sixth month of her pregnancy and to the nursing mother until her child turned one-year-old.[15] A separate ration scale was drawn up for some of these persons and in some instances, separate rationing documents were issued to them as well. Another wartime document that indicated the material indispensability of labour during this period was the supplementary

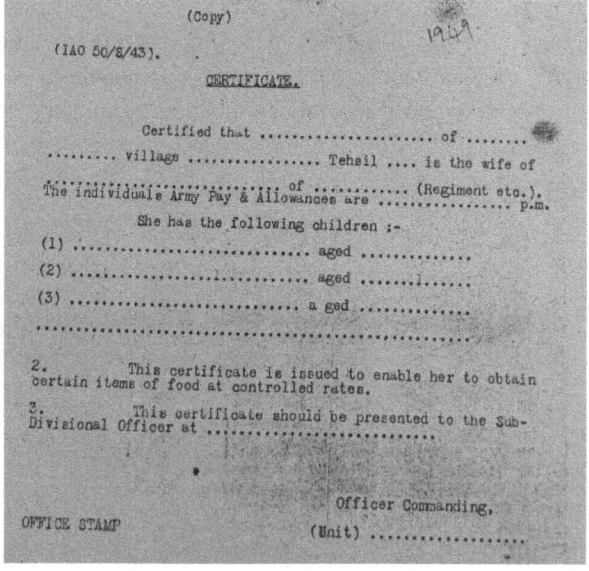

Figure 1.3 Food-based Certificate Issued to the Wife of the Second World War Soldier
Source: NAI.

ration card issued by various states and provinces (Sriraman 2011). This enabled the heavy manual worker to lay claim to rations in addition to the adult scale available through the regular channels. The manual worker's claim could not be sanctioned before it was endorsed in a paternalistic mould by his employer, who had to sign on the form for the supplementary ration card to be issued. Ajmer city, Bengal, Delhi, and Andaman and Nicobar Islands, all provided additional quotas for heavy manual workers even though not all of them came up with supplementary ration cards (Sriraman 2011: 53) (see Figure 1.4).[16] In some places, separate food and cloth ration cards were issued to children, as can be seen from the sample issued by the Government of Bengal (see Figure 1.5). These were the less common genres of rationing documents and we need to also establish the more uniform types of cards and permits that were issued.

Food supplies and cloth rations were made available to a wide cross-section of the society on the basis of a ration card and cloth permit, respectively, issued to individuals or families with or without a stable residential address. It is not possible to provide a complete list of which state and province issued what card and therefore, the discussion will be confined to the provincial city of Delhi. Where non-edible items of consumption were concerned, a major consideration, of course, was the production and the rationing of items of military need and transport: cloth, woollens, mineral fuels, chemicals, and medicines; also, continuous supplies of fuels like petroleum and coal had to be ensured.

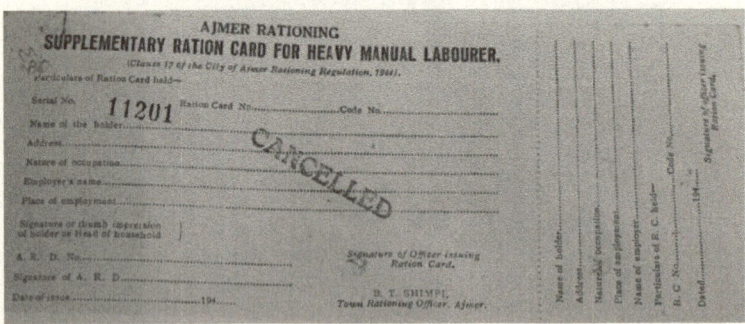

Figure 1.4 Wartime Supplementary Ration Card Issued to the Heavy Manual Labourer in Ajmer
Source: NAI.

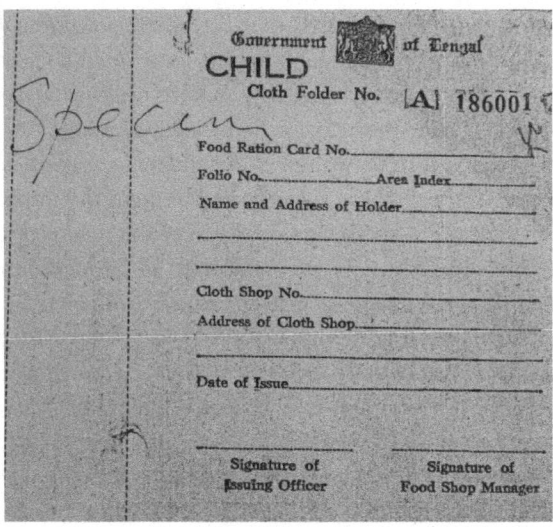

Figure 1.5 Cloth Ration Card Issued to Children by the Wartime Bengal Government
Source: NAI.

These were especially vital for 'the health of the army detachments and military labour serving on the eastern front' (Bhattacharya 2001: 84).

A Deluge of Rationing Documents: The Urban Case of Delhi

The Second World War marked a significant break in the development of the city of Delhi. Several scholars have dwelled on how the development of the city acquired a frenetic pace during the Partition owing to the flows of refugees, land acquisition and allotment, and commercial and industrial activity. While the Second World War has been acknowledged as a precursor to the Partition in the changes that it wrought upon the city, the war, and its urban and social manifestations in India have not received the same sort of attention. An elaborate comment on the wartime economy or the regulation of social life during this time in Delhi falls outside the scope of this book. The war, however, changed the landscape of the city and the social habits of its residents in large part through the instrument of law and penal regulations, in particular those which pertained to rationing. Where earlier motor cars, buses, and trucks were

used, tongas and pushbikes took their place; where government employees took their various food and fuel supplies for granted, they now had to
go to ration shops; and where weddings and festivals were special occasions for extravagance, they now called for moderation.[17] Also, where
subjects were unused to the prospect of sustained paper-based dealings
with their rulers per se, they suddenly had to incur the implications of
applying as a means of surviving. The force of the sovereign cannot be
discounted in disciplining subjects and Delhi's administration wasted no
efforts in actualizing a regime of ordinances and legislations dedicated to
rendering the colonial capital into a wartime supply base secured from
irritants of dissent and lavish or even normal consumption. Stephen
Legg (2007: 97) demonstrates how, contrary to Foucault's imagination,
the sovereign functions in colonial spaces through the modality of (and
not in opposition to) disciplinary and repressive tactics. Delhi, because
of its symbolic importance both to the nationalists and to the colonial
authority which displaced Mughal supremacy, would attract attacks. He
pinpoints the carefully thought-out stratagem of arranging pickets and
patrols either under the Police Act or the Defence of India Act in anticipation of attacks on supply lines during the Quit India Movement in
Delhi. Rohit De (2014) writes piquantly of colonial governmentality as
operating through an unexpected channel, that is, through the control of
commodities and the regulation of the economy. All the rationing orders
relating to food and clothing items as well as commodities like petroleum and tyres, or for that matter, the guest orders limiting consumption
in social gatherings, entailed applying for documents and regulated commodities, and rendered subjects vulnerable.

The Delhi food ration card, first issued in May 1944, was valid for
26 weeks and entitled individual cardholders to rice, wheat and wheat
products, including atta, *maida*, *rawa*, or *sooji*, and sugar, including
khandsari sugar.[18] At the time of introducing rationing, the population of the rationed area in Delhi was estimated to be 8.5 lakhs. On
the eve of rationing in Delhi, inquiry forms containing entries relating
to number of members, age, profession, and food requirements were
distributed among householders.[19] In enumerating people for the sake
of issuing ration cards, the Delhi administration sought to do more than
just arrange a census of its urban area: it was decided that the population of the city would be classified into classes in tandem with their
wheat requirements and that a tribunal consisting of two residents and

an official would be set up in each ward to adjudicate on the claims of people for inclusion in any such given class.[20] Within the genre of the food rationing document, there were various subcategories, like permanent ration cards (valid for 26 weeks), temporary ration cards (valid for 8–10 weeks), and visitors' cards (valid for 7 days). In Delhi, these cards were issued to individuals and not families, and they were to be presented to authorized retail distributors (ARDs) within a particular administrative jurisdiction.

Apart from this, a different class of food-based rationing documents was put in place for various establishments. 'Establishments' were interpreted very liberally to cover a bevy of places where food was served and consumed, such as boarding houses and schools; catering establishments such as hotels, restaurants, cafes, tea shops, and canteens; clubs and institutions such as orphanages, asylums, hospitals, and veterinary hospitals; manufacturing establishments such as bakeries; and chemists and *dawakhanas*. Both advertisements and articles in the *HT* are informative regarding the classification of ration permits. Those permits that were overprinted with a diagonal red line were issued to establishments which were to procure their supply from an ARD. Ration permits without such a red line meant that other establishments could obtain their supplies through an indent submitted to the rationing head office. As I will demonstrate soon, this highly differentiated typology went a long way in anticipating tactics of misappropriation and corruption in food-based commodities.

The demand for supplementary rations for heavy manual workers was made several times before it was entertained. When provincial authorities pointed out that Delhi did not have to provide supplementary rations for manual workers—because, unlike in Bombay where rationing covered all foodstuffs, only wheat and rice were rationed in Delhi, leaving the worker free to supplement his ration with other grains like bajra and jowar—bodies like the Textile Mazdoor Sabha (Textile Workers' Council) and various railway unions argued that the common food of Delhi's workers was wheat and very little of other foodgrains.[21] Even if Delhi's authorities might have indulged these demands to an extent, the administrative refusal to issue a supplementary ration card—unlike the Ajmer authorities who created one for their manual workers, for instance—to such classes was telling of the low priority accorded to them in the capital province.

... And Exceptions to the Document Regime

Unlike the food-based ration card which was issued to all individuals, the cloth permit was issued only to the head of the family, entitling him (I did not ever encounter a female head of the family in the many archives of this period) and others in such families to varieties of cloth. The coupons attached to these cards could be used to obtain coarse, fine, or processed cloth from authorized dealers against cancellation of a coupon or a portion of the coupon.[22] Fine cloth and cloth produced by the Delhi Cloth and General Mills Co. Ltd were subject to rationing. The war greatly benefited the Indian business class, especially in the textile sector: Indian cloth manufacturers received many orders from the government for shoes, parachutes, and uniforms 'and the stocks were quickly sold' (Kamtekar 2002: 201). Even though the textile business was booming in India and Delhi in particular, it was important to prevent hoarding and black marketing and so, the Textile Control Order was promulgated in June 1943—prevailing on mills, wholesalers, and retailers to declare their stocks—to impose the rationing of cloth. Under the Delhi Cloth Rationing Order, 1945, cloth was made available through a permit which was issued to the head of the family for the rest of his members, and when it was produced by the person to whom it was issued. Under cloth rationing in Delhi, each adult permit holder registered in the name of the head of the family was entitled to six units each, with one unit standing for a yard of cloth.

This ceiling became a problem, however, when the Delhi Cloth and General Mills Co. was inundated with locally produced coarse cloth, while the cloth imported from Bombay and Ahmedabad vanished from the market in no time. Very cleverly, it was decided to mobilize the cloth permit into supporting local protectionism geared to improve sales of home-made cloth in Delhi. Rationing authorities felt it was expedient to increase the ration of local cloth from 6 to 12 yards of cloth: coarse cloth quota was increased from 4 to 10 units, while the fine cloth quota remained fixed at 2 units.[23] It was not only bales of coarse cloth that gathered dust in cloth shops, fine and processed cloth, of which there was a spate, also remained untouched as the permit quota for this was too little. It was suggested that the quota of fine cloth should be increased as the demand for this far exceeded that for coarse cloth.[24] But even in the heat of these debates, the ration permit was sought to be retained as black marketing was a spectre that haunted all categories of cloth sale and distribution. All cloth after 1 August was to be stamped with the date of manufacture and orders were issued to sell all such cloth within six months of this date. Interestingly, several advertisements appeared in *HT* warning not only against the hoarder lurking among civilian subjects but also against the Japanese invader who misappropriated nationalist practices (by copying swadeshi cloth) and colonial practices (by marking it), thus profiting (see Figure 1.6). In places like Bombay and Surat, the vigil against cloth hoarders was excessive, with routine raids on shops and godowns that held unstamped cloth and counterfeit stamped cloth.[25]

As with foodgrains, requests for supplementary rations in cloth too were common for use on occasions like marriages, funerals, diplomatic

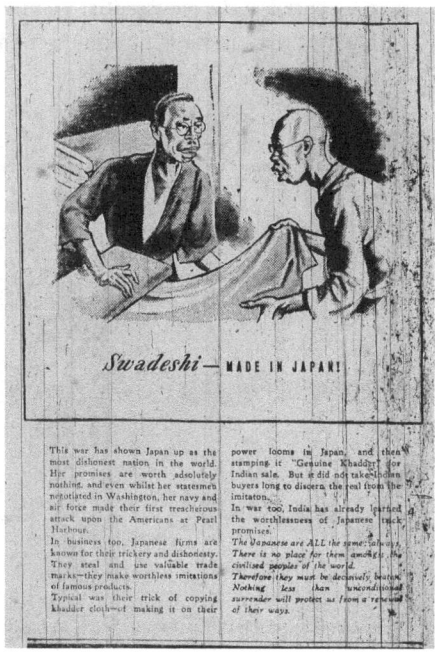

Figure 1.6   A Melange of Colonial and Nationalist War Propaganda against Japan
Source: *HT*, NMML archives.

events, and religious celebrations. While dead persons could not be
entitled to rations, an exception was made in the case of cloth rationing.
It was paramount for Muslims to procure an extra shroud of cloth in
the event of a relative's death. When a family submitted, along with the
proof of death, the dead person's ration card and his or her cloth permit,
it entitled them to a shroud of cloth which they used to cover the body
before burying.[26] Such a ration card could be, ironically enough, an
incentive to the family to report the death and procure a revised or new
ration card; but even more ironically, it could also be an opportunity for
claiming the cloth and using it for purposes other than to make a shroud.
While other historians too cite the possible theft of the rationed piece of
cloth, none are able to differentiate rumour from reality in documenting
this practice (De 2014: 288). My own archival shred of evidence vis-à-
vis such theft, supported by this fascinating Shankar cartoon in *HT* (see
Figure 1.7), is shrouded in historical speculation.

Across India, both essential and non-essential commodities came to
be rationed. In Delhi, it was the rationing of non-essential commodities,

Figure 1.7   Rumours about the Theft of the Rationed Shroud from the
Graveyard
Source: Shankar (1945).[27]

like motor spirit or petroleum, electricity, and tyres and tubes, that came to be first undertaken; and it was the Motor Spirit Rationing Order, 1941 that flagged off rationing in the capital province. The rationing of essential commodities like rice, wheat, sugar, and cloth took place only much later. Unfortunately, it is outside the scope of this chapter to offer a satisfactory comparison of the application and ration card models of essential and non-essential commodities. I do attempt this exercise partially elsewhere where I argue that the application model for non-essential commodities like motor spirit and electricity was one that was distinctively rhetorical and petition-like (Sriraman 2014). In Delhi, applications for non-essential commodities were restricted to elite representatives of the government or more privileged sections of the population, such as principals of government schools, government employees, and diplomats. The claimant interested in procuring additional supplies of petroleum or securing a temporary/permanent electric connection was to apply for supplementary coupons or a certificate, respectively. His application consisted of the form as well as a covering letter where he often ended up making a grand case for himself by appealing to the official's compassion or to the empire's civilizing mission. Alternatively, he demonstrated his own indispensability as a government employee, propagandist, contractor, or engineer to the wartime effort. A complete treatment of this model of applying within the genre of rationing documents for non-essential commodities can be found in an article titled, 'A Petition-like Application' (Sriraman 2014). As with cloth rationing, the document regime governing non-essential commodities too operated through certain exceptions. Even in Delhi, which saw an overzealous and scrupulous administration willing to cut the supplies of princes, diplomats, and other privileged classes, visiting Members of Legislative Assembly (MLAs) who made a fuss about living arrangements were able to secure permits for soft coke, firewood, charcoal, and coal (Sriraman 2014: 364). This was egregious especially considering rationing authorities' refusal to entertain other deserving candidates like dhobis who owing to the dearth of sufficient coal went on strike.[28]

Ration Card as Shaping Residential Norm

Having set up, if somewhat elaborately, the historical context in which genres of the rationing documents emerged, this section deals with the more urgent and promised task of delineating the ration card's momentous historical function in crystallizing bureaucratic conceptions of: (a) space (characterized by residential address); (b) time (of arrival and acquiring the document); and (c) kinship (family). The second function of the document, that is, setting up urban definitions of time, will be taken up for elaborate discussion in the following chapters; for the moment, it is the first and third functions that will be attended to here. If these markers of individual and familial ID came to seize and govern the very chances of compensation and resettlement of marginal subjects in the postcolonial years to come, their beginnings must be traced to the creation of rationing circles, zones, and government-approved retail shops.

It was important to configure the administrative grid of rationing, both territorially and locally. Under the Defence of India Rules, nobody could import or export rationed food without a permit issued by the chief commissioner of rationing in any given area. If states were sorted into surplus and deficit wheat and rice zones, then ARDs or the precursors of the present-day FPSs were circumscribed within specially designated rationing circles. The city of Delhi was divided into 16 circles, each with its rationing office specifying the corresponding address, as Figure 1.8 shows. Circle 16 which corresponds to the Delhi Cantonment falls in a zone which is outside the area shown in the map.

The map in Figure 1.8 was meant for educating the public as the sub-headline, 'Learn which circle you live in and where YOUR Rationing Office is', demonstrates. While ration cards were distributed at the resident's home, the Delhi Rationing Organization (DRO) strongly advised all cardholders to know which circle and which office their cards pertained to for future inquiries and complaints. Not surprisingly, most of the circles were concentrated in Old Delhi characterized by heavy informal settlements, while a couple of circles were set up for central Delhi and north Delhi each, one circle for Karol Bagh, and all of one circle for the vast and—but for a few government establishments—poorly urbanized south Delhi. In fact, the DRO bombarded *HT* with advertisement after advertisement exhorting residents to cooperate with authorities for the tremendous exercise of issuing ration cards that unfolded over many phases. More importantly, these advertisements eased residents into recognizing the inseparable coordinates of their ration card number, their circle office, and their ARD. If the first bunch

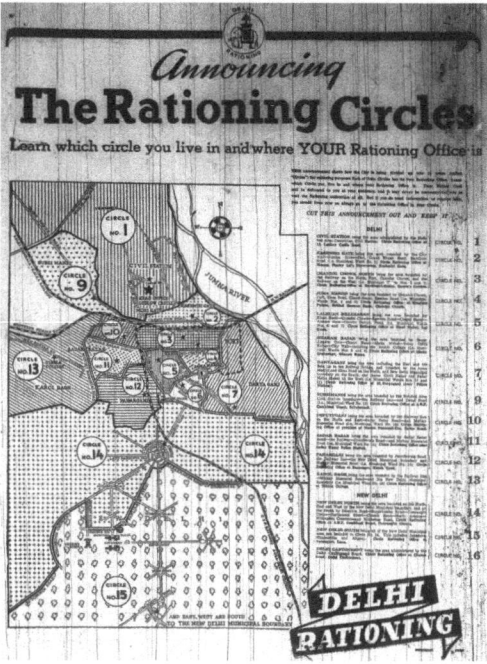

Figure 1.8   A Wartime Government Advertisement Displaying Delhi's Rationing Map
Source: *HT*, NMML archives.
Note: This map is not to scale and is provided for illustrative purposes only.

of advertisements asked residents to allow 'the rationing enumeration staff' to paint ID numbers on houses for issuing forms and later ration cards, then the next bunch publicized the days on which rationing forms were to be distributed to Delhi households in each circle.

The next bunch of advertisements alerted residents of certain specific circles to expect the distribution of ration cards on a certain date, while simultaneously asking those who somehow missed enumeration to contact their relevant circle rationing offices.[29] In the interim period following the distribution of ration cards, paternalistic instructions were issued forth telling residents to check if their food cards were in order and how holders were to use them. Simultaneously, calls were sent out to residents to visit their offices if they had not received their ration card (see Figure 1.9).[30]

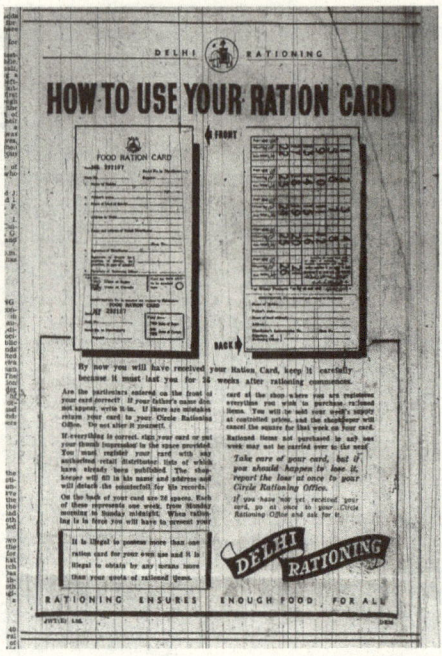

Figure 1.9   Government Advertisement, 'How to Use Your Ration Card'
Source: *HT*, NMML archives.

The elimination of widespread hoarding by householders and establishments—provoked by fears of war-induced scarcity and related to that,
shortage caused by rationing—was urgently anchored to the efficient
execution of the ration card drive. This drive could be engineered to
work well only if residential and commercial addresses were intimately
tied. Not surprisingly then, the issue of ration cards was an intensely
disciplinary drive that socialized residents into a very tightly knit system
of food distribution. If residents were to note down the addresses of
the circles they fell under for rationing inquiries, they were also to take
care not to be duped by impostors who, posing as government clerks
on enumeration duty, offered to sell them ration cards.[31] That is why a
few advertisements exhorted people to ask for the ID of the clerks who
came to enumerate residents. The number of the ration card was vital for
all official correspondence and future applications, and so residents were
asked to memorize and cite it (see Figure 1.10).[32] Though individual

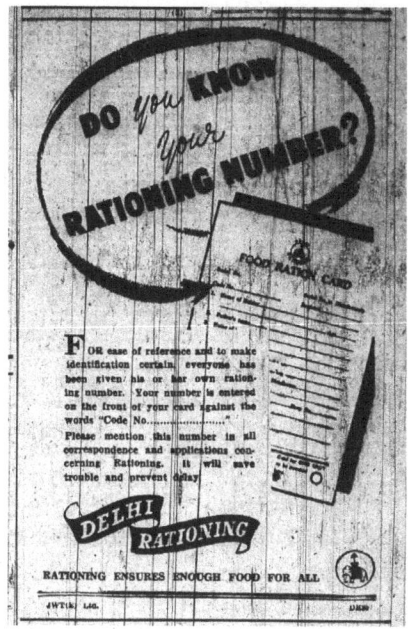

Figure 1.10   Government Advertisement, 'Do You Know Your Rationing Number?'
Source: *HT*, NMML archives.

(and not family) cards were issued to Delhi's residents, a single representative of the family was requested to be present to receive ration
cards for everybody.[33] And finally, authorities exhorted residents who
had recently changed their address to modify their ration cards, while
alerting newcomers to approach the circle rationing officer.[34]

Once the rationing drive was completed, colonial authorities never
stopped fretting about defaulters and tricksters who came in all forms,
such as the freeloader who claimed free rations in his employer's
canteen or the hotel where he stayed while drawing units from his
ration card, the ghost beneficiary, the hoarder, and the negligent
ARD who registered more cardholders than his jurisdiction allowed
(Sriraman 2011: 53). Officials sought to address their twin anxieties
of violation of jurisdiction and hoarding by mobilizing the rationing
document to spatially monitor the baker, the wholesaler, the retailer,
and those managing ARDs. Through audit and inspection services,

officials scrupulously tracked the use and misuse of food and baking
permits, licences, and ration cards. If ration cards identified individual
holders by their address and by their relation to the head of the family,
ration permits were used to identify establishments and retailers. These
permits, which were subject to examination by the rationing officer of
the area, came with various indents of the articles rationed, the units
rationed, and the number of weeks for which the establishments were
sanctioned to provide these articles.

It was not only the sale of rationed food that was responsible for the
conceptualization of a tight administrative grid consisting of a profusion of cards, licences, and permits, held together by the coordinates
of commercial address and residential location. Cloth rationing had its
part to play too. Cloth permits bore codes that correlated the document
holder to her residential address within a spatial network of authorized
suppliers, dealers, shops, and other textile establishments. The validity
of cloth permits was tied to coupons that were time-bound. Often, the
permit holders could draw rations only on a stipulated date and only
for the specified quarter on their coupons; they could not save them
to use for another quarter.[35] This administrative complex of space,
time, and commerce, however, could not be religiously enforced owing
to practical problems posed by the local economy that struggled to
dispose of surfeit cloth. When a conflict of this kind occurred, rules
surrounding rationing documents were viewed as a painful liability that
stood in the way of commercial convenience. Such rules pertaining to
dates and quarters were relaxed without remorse to allow for the quick
disposal of cloth.[36] The colonial authorities hesitated but did not shrink
away from modifying rules tying commercial addresses and residential
locations to address perplexities posed by conflicting rationalities. If it
was important to channel sovereign power to manage wartime fears of
hoarding, it was equally imperative to not lose sight of the everyday
crisis of a local economy that could easily be swamped by an over-
abundance of unsold rationed commodities. The Delhi Cloth Rationing
Order, 1945 stated that the coupons contained in the cloth ration permit for families and establishments could be presented for registration
only to the authorized cloth dealer mentioned on the permit. Cloth
dealers were authorized to sell cloth only on a licence issued under
the Delhi Cloth Dealers Licensing Order, 1944. Both these rules were
overlooked when rationing officials found themselves in quandaries of

quota management, local mill resistance, and excessive imports. Rules were relaxed to allow dealers to carry out trade in a locality even if they lacked a licence or even if the locality fell outside the administrative jurisdiction of a permit holder.

At this point, it is important to ask: was the ration card the only 'ID' genre that was introduced at the time of the war that sought to verify address in order to provide some entitlement? Not quite. A strange genre called an identity disc, which did not take on the materiality of an ID document, was also issued during this time. These discs could be bought for 1 anna from agencies like post offices, police stations, air-raid wardens, and local self-governing bodies. They bore a complex number and letter code and were meant to be worn around the wrist and the neck.[37] Vendors selling these discs were supposed to make carbon copies or prepare challans in triplicate which would be fed into the records maintained by the Civil Defence Information Bureau, while another copy could be sent to provincial authorities outside military jurisdiction. Peculiar to the contingencies of the war and the disquiet it conjured for those who were related to the fighting soldiers and other war victims, the disc was to be carried by soldiers (potential casualties of the war) and civilians (in danger of becoming air-raid victims). The number and alphabet scheme corresponded to the place of residence of the dependents of such victims who could claim compensation on the strength of this morbidly helpful evidence. Local authorities from this bureau were able to intimate relatives on the basis of the very detailed scheme of demographic information collected—this included the name and address of the person to whom the disc was issued, father or husband's name, religion, caste within religion, and name and address of next of kin.[38] While several provinces may have accepted this scheme, it is unclear how efficiently the scheme was executed or even how many people availed themselves of this possibility. Unlike ration cards whose life could outlast the war because scarcity itself never vanished, the identity disc could not be repurposed in a future context as it was anchored to the exceptional circumstance of insuring war victims. It is both owing to the lack of sufficient evidence around the actual use of this document and because, as an identity form, it did not really act to consolidate the norm of residence that I do not want to dwell on this ID any more than this.

This returns us to the question of location in matters of ration card enumeration. If this was, in general, a pressing one for colonial authorities, it was a particularly troubling one when it came to the delineation of domestic residence. In the days leading up to the enumeration of cardholders, it was important to determine the import that was to be attached to a stable residence and a fixed address. Across various states and provinces, surveys were taken of beggars and homeless persons—if necessary, by police roundup—whose particulars of identity were recorded, and in exceptional cases such as Bombay and Coorg, cards were issued to such persons. If the enumeration of homeless persons was time consuming and frustrating, so was the counting and identification of persons staying in makeshift and nondescript residences.

Historically speaking, the enumeration of those who lacked a home was never an easy affair. In Europe, the convention of marking and labelling beggars, vagrants, and nomads was enmeshed with the fortification of genteel society which feared risks to their property, lives, and children at the hands of foreign gypsies and vagabonds. At the same time, in medieval and post-Renaissance Europe, authorities were keen to exempt themselves from providing for such charges that were on the cusp of becoming liabilities. Beggars' permits, open letters (issued to gypsies), and anthropometric nomad passbooks were some of the documents that were created to recognize the exception to the rule of itinerant paupers whose movement was to be curtailed in a disparate historical milieu (Groebner 2007; Kaluszynski 2001; Noiriel 2001). Census exercises undertaken for the purpose of rationing must not be read in the same register as this history of marking homeless persons in Europe as the former entailed a different care ethic of welfare of ensuring that even such people did not starve or pose a threat to the wartime effort of securing essential supplies. Rationing censuses were not the first exercises to feature the counting of homeless persons in India. The 1901 census, for instance, saw sections of the divisional police force, steered by an overly energetic police commissioner in Bombay, responding to the request of assistance put out by census authorities by carrying out a satisfactory headcount of homeless persons during the night of the exercise. Ironically, the same officer had earned fame for his efficient handling of the nuisance of Bombay's beggars by deporting them into neighbouring princely states (Edwardes 1923).[39]

But when this enterprise of counting homeless persons was mandated for rationing purposes, the attention to detail was painstakingly

minute. It was important to distinguish residence from address and enumerators could not be lax in describing the living space. While assessing
the inquiry forms that clerks filled out within the Fuel and Kerosene
Rationing Scheme in the year 1944 in Delhi, officials were perturbed
by what they deemed lazy and conceptually fuzzy entries. The clerks
were asked severely to count the number of living enclosures and accu-
rately describe them (if a certain room doubled up as both living room
and dining room or sitting room and bedroom). These enclosures were
to be described separately from the partly enclosed spaces where someone had set up home under a tree or in a veranda. Such persons were
to be recorded separately as 'homeless' (Sriraman 2011: 54).[40] It was
also important to cite the nature of the relationship of every resident
to the head of the family (whether family member, servant, or lodger),
surnames, and the exact occupation—railway coolie or loom worker—
in lieu of 'vague entries' such as service or labour (Sriraman 2011: 54).
While such a directive to count the homeless in a meticulous manner
may have some precedent, the colonial state may have been engaged
in more than a symbolic demonstration of the power and reach of its
enumerative machinery typical to most decennial censuses to capture
people living in the most informal settlements possible. In the year
1941, the colonial government was hamstrung by war-related financial
stringencies, forcing enumeration authorities to prepare very basic
tabulations for that year's census, such as territorially classified lists of
towns, villages, cities, and towns, with their population enumerated in
the form of communities (religious, tribal, and SC) (Guha 2003: 161).
So, when it came to the 1944 Fuel and Kerosene Rationing Scheme, the
Delhi authorities may have been forced to compensate for the silences
of the 1941 census. However, they may have also anticipated that the
demographic information pertaining to stable and makeshift residences
generated from such an exercise could be mobilized into schemes other
than fuel and kerosene rationing, all of which were predicated on demonstrations of inhabited living spaces.

Fashioning Norms of Legality and Corruption

In the 1940s rationing censuses, whether of homeless persons or
householders, all those staying especially in the urban areas were to be
accounted for. The production of ID documents in this late wartime

colonial phase—while linked with narrow mandates of managing scarcity, controlling prices, and pre-empting dissent—went a long way in fashioning a discourse of legality and corruption. I would like to make a quick hop and skip at this point to reference scholarship that touches on the nested relation between documents and corruption. If a reader were to do a quick tour of literature on the history of documents (not specifically ID documents) issued in India or for that matter in Europe, he/she would be astonished by one remarkable insight shared by these scholars—separated by period and culture—that is both philosophical and ethnographic in its provenance. This insight is that if documents are formalized to mitigate venality flowing from informal conventions of writing, these very disciplinary innovations inspire ingenious methods and devious masters of manipulation. Valentin Groebner (2007) tells us the tale of how the institution of ID papers like safe conducts and letters of recommendation in medieval Europe, as a standard administrative measure to police mobility, only facilitated cheerful doppelgangers like spies and impostors. Bhavani Raman, for her part, engagingly recounts the trap of imitation, forgery, and appropriation that company officials walked helplessly into when they forged protocols of attestation and written depositions in penal processes (Raman 2012). Jane Caplan (2009) describes how conventions of handwritten signatures were casually manipulated by forgers in colonial India. Writing about a more contemporary phase in India, Emma Tarlo (2003) records the sinister abandon with which sterilization certificates—documents with no bureaucratic legitimacy—were produced and reproduced to claim housing compensation during the Emergency.

Elsewhere, while studying ID documents produced within a colonial regime of surveillance and detention tied to the plague outbreak in the late nineteenth century, I came across the genre of inoculation certificates which eased different classes of subjects into free travel that was otherwise restricted in infected areas. Colonial authorities ended up issuing these certificates quite unwittingly to unscrupulous subjects— to induce conservative Indians fearful of this strange and unfamiliar medical technology into complying—some of whom willed themselves to get inoculated as many as 30 times simply to procure monetary incentives (Sriraman 2013c: 303–4). Everywhere, the legal was its own liability and ruse. Perhaps because such authorities had become historically accustomed to a good dose of mendacity and duplicity in their paper-based dealings with such subjects, they learnt to anticipate them better over time. So, during the rationing drive, the Bombay administration—which was incidentally one of the prolific sites of the infamous faking of inoculation and exemption certificates in the early twentieth century—put in place a series of corrective measures to trace every potential crime by clerks, officials, and applicants to its veritable documentary source. They were aided in no small measure by the various control orders issued under the Defence of India Rules, 1915.

The war also put an urgent premium on such campaigns—if the Allied effort could not suffer on account of reckless spending and dissent, it could scarcely afford to lose momentum to petty thieves and hoarders. If it has been demonstrated that rationing documents willy-nilly spawned corruption, in this particular late colonial moment of documentation, they became the centrepiece of an inspired discourse where legality was fashioned as a foil to its breach. At an early stage, the Bombay Commissioner of Civil Supplies, A.D. Gorwala, mobilized administrative micro-practices, like number denominations, counterfoils, indents, changing colour backgrounds, and official logos, as well as markers of personal ID like fingerprint and bureaucratic signatures, into casting the proverbial net far and wide to apprehend every dishonest avatar (Sriraman 2011: 57). Interestingly, the fingerprint featured in these debates as one of many possible security measures, but the rationing authorities did not linger on this ID practice with purposive and long-term intent. I did come across one debate in Mysore Residency where the fingerprint was suggested as a better alternative to the signature if only because it helped mediate a better correspondence between the applicant and the information furnished in the application form. H.H. Kirby, the advisor to the Government of India, also warned of predatory writers who extracted fees from unwary and illiterate women and men who did not know how to fill out their own application forms and sign them (Sriraman 2011: 57).[41] However, long debates on the fingerprint were rarities during this time.

In this sense, the wartime prototype of the ration card must be set apart from a nineteenth century ID document like the life certificate. In her rigorous and charmingly written dissertation, 'Get a Life: Pensions in 19th Century Colonial India', Poorva Rajaram devotes substantial consideration to discussing the materialities of the fingerprint and the life certificate which she finds to be both fused and disparate in their historical functions. She writes that the life certificate is a document that certifies the status of the pensioner as a living and breathing human entity, and she traces colonial debates on procedures, place, and the hierarchies implicit in the production of the life certificate within genres of civil and military pensions. The mulish insistence on seeing the life certificate—even where its bearer is present in all his/her full-bodied glory to satisfy the pensioning authority—has become something of a farcical fable narrating the state of nature of the postcolonial bureaucracy as well. In nineteenth century colonial India, the fingerprint on the life certificate was indispensable to verify the identity of the pensioner. However, why were pensions such a rich and fertile site for nurturing the fingerprint? She suggests that this could well be owing to the fingerprint's felicity in providing anatomical detail to the colonial welfare beneficiary as well as an indispensable measure to manage what was perceived to be a burgeoning scale of pension fraud. Rajaram's work adds a lot of grist to the small but substantial cluster of scholars who have considered the cross-cultural history of fingerprinting and the colonial historiography around this ID practice across sites like indigo plantations in England and the jails of England and Scotland Yard (Cole 2001; Sengoopta 2004; Singha 2000).

One of the much-feted administrative pioneers of fingerprinting and the Chief Magistrate of Hooghly district in Bengal in the mid-nineteenth century, William Herschel, considers the fingerprint for a variety of tricky schemes desperately in need of dependable ID practices, such as the registration of land deeds and jail warrants, in addition to the disbursal of pensions. In his ambitious biographical text, Herschel endorses the British Raj by fulminating on 'the great difficulty of administration in India' and he proclaims that he has found the perfect means to ease this great burden of the colonial state. The book, *The Origin of Finger-printing*, yields Herschel's deep-seated conviction in the linkage between fingerprinting and the peculiar colonial dispensation of 'justice' (Herschel 1916). Justice here translated into ensuring that everyone fulfilled their contractual obligations even if the contract was itself cast in the most excessive and unconscionable appropriation of labour. Fingerprinting as a technology was needed to protect 'the zemindar' executing a rent roll, to verify the authenticity of 'a *kabooliyat* signed by the ryot', and to detect, say, 'a notorious convict making clay-seals of well-known landlords' (Herschel 1916: 11) and the abundance of duplicitous Indians looking to escape leases, contracts, and their conviction. Compared to this, the wartime ration card was not a site for exploring the authenticating potential of the fingerprint presumably (and here I recognize I am in the slippery realm of broad historical conjecture) because the fingerprint had distinguished itself as a technology that could yield rich results only within a limited and manageable range of comparisons. Given the exponential numbers of Indians that rationing exercises warranted and given the hurried and harried wartime deliberations, there was no time to stand and stare at amorphous and confusing clusters of 'arches, loops, and whorls' or the distinctive features of the fingerprint. Since the rationing document was intended as an emergency wartime measure intended to cut costs, this was not a prudent way to keep hoarders and impostors at bay. The clerk, the rationing official, and the dealer had to be able to quickly discern fraud and they should not have to pore over it through methods that exceeded their vocational training.

Instead of evolving universal colonial templates that would be easy to imitate or complex ones that would require unaccountable labour and 'man-hours', it was decided that states and provinces would be free to come up with their own reasoned template secured by a bevy of imaginative security measures. The only condition was that administrations unfailingly share notes both with the colonial centre and with their counterparts within the country that could inspire ingenious cross-regional counter-campaigns against corruption. Not surprisingly then, the Delhi administration fashioned its individual ration card system after the exemplary model followed in Bombay, which claimed to have saved 900,000 units in consumption after it switched over from the family ration card to the individual ration card. Clearly, the officials in Delhi were also impressed by the meticulous efforts of the Bombay administration, such as the setting up of rationing kiosks in railway and steamship booking offices where ration cards could be surrendered before departure.[42] In Delhi, the deluge of ID documents with individual ration cards, overprinted food permits, cloth permits replete with coupons, temporary cards for visitors, and motor spirit coupons was overflowing not only with security measures but also with special authorities created for each commodity rationed. This administration patted itself on the back for its incomparably severe model of rationing, marked by the abrupt introduction and withdrawal of certain document genres, the elaborate mode of applying for each document, and the over-attentive scrutiny of each application. However, despite their best efforts, the Delhi administration suffered setbacks every now and then. The *HT* pages during the war years carried reports that frequently alluded to punishments meted out to dealers and clerks who stocked and sold loose motor spirit coupons, charcoal without licence, unstamped cloth, food without permit, and sugar permits that had been tampered with, and subjects who drew rations on other people's coupons.[43]

Elsewhere, I have attempted a more elaborate taxonomy of some of these colonial discoveries of fraud (Sriraman 2011). While many of these crimes were deemed as such owing to the document's lack of an indent, mark, counterfoil, and so on, they were apprehended by various tip-offs relating to jurisdiction of who was allowed to sell and buy a commodity where. In this sense, the discourse of legality surrounding these documents was produced through norms of commercial jurisdiction and residential location. The debate on whether families or individuals posed a greater threat to the legal norms of the ration card was also productive in the sense that it informed the disparate moves of any given province to embrace either of these two units.

Debates on Norms of Family and Individual

If residential norm was important, so were the norms of the social unit of ID. Early into the rationing drive, officials were undecided about the norm most suited to the ration card. For the first six months of rationing, ration cards came to be issued universally to the head of the family rather than to individuals. Knight argues that it was important to introduce the family ration card at the very inception of rationing 'because the inquiries were less inquisitorial, and caused less anxiety among a population uneducated and suspicious of all government action affecting themselves' (Knight 1954: 206). So, if the family ration card won the trust of a rustic population by accommodating members real and fictitious, the individual ration card was embraced later by several provincial and state governments on the grounds that it allowed them to screen out ghost beneficiaries and keep tabs on each cardholder's transactions. In Delhi, under the Rationing Order, 1944, it was the individual ration card which was distributed to colonial subjects within the jurisdictions of the Delhi Municipality, the New Delhi Municipality, the Civil Station Notified Area, the Fort Notified Area, the jurisdiction of the Delhi Cantonment Board, the West Delhi Notified Area, the village sites of Shadipur and Khanpur as defined in the revenue records, and the areas defined in the chief commissioner of Delhi's Notification as extra Municipal Rationing Zone I, IIA, and IIB.[44]

The decision to issue individual ration cards in Delhi, not surprisingly, was drawn from the lessons of the Bombay experiment. After the trial period was over, provinces and states were given the autonomy to settle on the norm that was most suitable to their socio-economic requirements. Henry Knight states that the colonial authorities believed family ration cards to be prone to much abuse. Families often included fictitious names and did not report deaths and departures. The individual ration card was considered more economical and effective once a headcount was undertaken. In Bombay, when after the initial six months of rationing, a total of 1,800,000 ration cards were distributed to individual persons, they were found to yield a saving of 450,000 rations—it was believed that fewer ghost beneficiaries could now lay claim to supplies (Knight 1954: 206). Therefore, the individual ration card, once introduced, was preferred to the family ration card in the interests of reducing excess consumption.

However, the narrative underlying the debate on the family and individual norms was instructive of something else, namely, that documentary forms introduced to curb corruption often spawned it. Family members used the incentives of travel coupons and visitors' rations, but failed to report the absence (caused by death or migration) of a member. Various situations were anticipated where family members could cheat authorities by drawing rations even though they were travelling and not residing in the administrative jurisdiction mentioned in their ration card. Incidentally, this fear that the family ration card harboured all kinds of brazen tricksters never went away and a post-war survey in 1949, prompted by the need to establish this fear as fact, revealed 1 lakh bogus cards.[45]

During the war, rationing presented dilemmas of travel that were sought to be resolved by issuing special genres of ID documents such as special ration permits for subjects in transit. They were issued to ration cardholders when they undertook a journey somewhere—these permits entitled them to concessions for their meals on the way. However, these permits could be made available only if and when a cardholder surrendered his ration card and obtained a receipt.[46] Alternatively, food coupons were issued to people who were away from their homes and travelling; however, the traveller had to be registered with a food shop which agreed to give him coupons instead of a ration book. He could use these coupons to get meals in restaurants and other eating places (*Report of the Foodgrains Policy Committee*, 1943: 79). The Delhi government issued temporary ration cards for those who were permanently based outside Delhi but were visiting Delhi (see Figure 1.11). The authorities, however, entertained only those people who were related to a permanent resident and cardholder in Delhi; and in this sense, the administrative obsession with the family as a unit of ID never went away. The applicant for the temporary ration card had to cite his or her relationship to the head of the family, the date of arrival

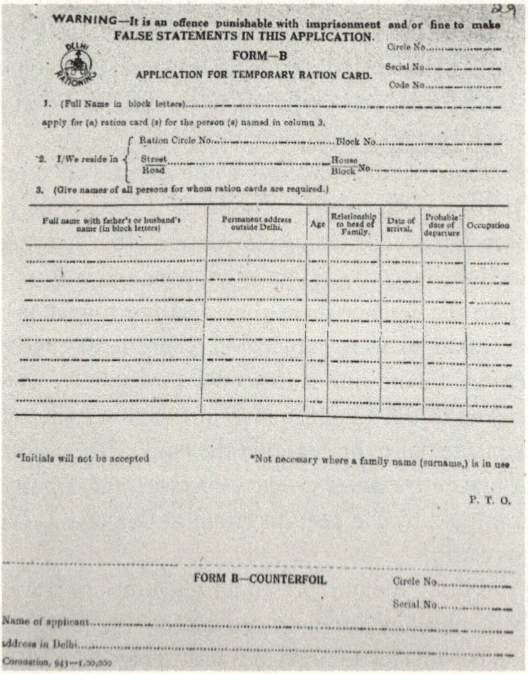

WARNING—It is an offence punishable with imprisonment and/or fine to make FALSE STATEMENTS IN THIS APPLICATION.

DELHI RATIONING

FORM—B

APPLICATION FOR TEMPORARY RATION CARD.

Circle No..................

Serial No..................

Code No..................

1. (Full Name in block letters)..................

apply for (a) ration card (s) for the person (s) named in column 3.

*2. I/We reside in { Ration Circle No.................. Block No.................. / Street/Road.................. House/Block No.................. }

3. (Give names of all persons for whom ration cards are required.)

Full name with father's or husband's name (in block letters)	Permanent address outside Delhi.	Age	Relationship to head of Family.	Date of arrival.	Probable* date of departure	Occupation

*Initials will not be accepted

*Not necessary where a family name (surname,) is in use

P. T. O.

FORM B—COUNTERFOIL

Circle No..................

Serial No..................

Name of applicant..................

address in Delhi..................

Coronation, 943—1,00,000

Figure 1.11 Application for a Temporary Ration Card Issued by the DRO
Source: DSA.,

and departure, and his or her occupation (see Figure 1.11). While individual cards were thought to be less prone to abuse, they were at the same time believed to be unnecessarily expensive. It was believed that the family ration card, though rife with potential porosity, could, if efficiently engineered, yield much more savings. However, for the moment, authorities were content with issuing individual ration cards which were complemented by other genres. By providing incentives to travelling members and visitors, and additional rations to pregnant women, the government—even as it issued individual cards—never lost sight of how families inevitably had collective food needs which needed to be monitored.

The Cultural Investment of the Ration Card

Even though Delhi issued individual ration cards during the war for very pragmatic reasons, the administration could not be indifferent to the strong cultural norms that drove family and community life. The sociality and conviviality of Indians were intermeshed with the festive habits of domestic food consumption and so, the question of what a ration card entitled an individual to could not be separated from what the family liked to eat during different festive seasons and cultural occasions that marked the year. Therefore, even though the family ration card was introduced only as late as 1953 in Delhi, cultural considerations—revolving around the family and the community—laced demands for supplementary food rations even during the war. Colonial authorities across India sought to limit the number of guests who could be invited to a wedding, funeral, or any other social gathering such as festival celebrations. In fact, the infamous guest control orders that we associate with the period of the Emergency in India had their origins in this period of war. Catering orders were also issued, requiring guests at any social gathering to use limited quantities of not only rationed items such as sugar, rice, and wheat but also sooji, atta, maida, and so on. To secure extra rations for their families, Indians were required to secure a special application, which they could naturally obtain only if they possessed a ration card.

An echo that was heard post 1943, at least centrally in the food administration, was that festivals could be no exception to the rule of wartime austerity even if certain cultural imperatives were paramount. However, a certain liberal period of supplementary rations for festivals prevailed between 1943 and 1945, before rationing authorities put a heavy foot down on this practice. In 1945, after consultation with the Food Advisory Council, the Department of Food passed a resolution valid for all state and provincial administrations—with the exception of Delhi and the province of Ajmer-Merwara—to the effect of disallowing supplementary rations even during festivals. No concessions were to be made in the allotments under the Basic Plan so that governments were left with little choice. They could either provide additional rations taking care to not let them exceed the quotas available to them under the Basic Plan or they could simply not issue additional rations at all. In spite of the embargo on supplementary rations in rationed areas outside Delhi and Ajmer, state and provincial governments encouraged claims rationalizing that they had initiated the supply much before the crucial resolution was passed. However, most of these governments were circumspect in the rationed supplies they permitted, specifying the number of men and women who could be fed and the quantities that could be supplied at any given time.[47]

Delhi may have enjoyed some leeway owing to the risks posed by strongly worded cultural assertions of various communities in the colonial capital province. However, even in Delhi, the guest control order went into force in 1944, restricting the number of guests allowed for every ration card-bearing host to 50 for all parties and gatherings barring those of an official or semi-official nature.[48] This provoked something of a furore among religious circles who read the move as being contrary to their own fluctuating cultural prerequisites of consumption. The president of the provincial Majlis Ittihad Millat, for instance, wrote urgently to the viceroy of Delhi, requesting him to sanction supplementary rations during Ramzan as sugar was indispensable for making syrup with ice which Muslims drank when they broke the fast (Sriraman 2014: 373). Acting on behalf of the Delhi Sikh *sangats*, the president of the Gurudwara Prabandhak Committee conveyed the great distress the Sikh community had to endure in the face of the refusal of the rationing authorities to sanction additional rations to mark the martyrdom celebration of Guru Tegh Bahadur. The weekly *diwan* of the Sikhs warned the British of the possibility of violent protests if supplementary quantities of rationing articles were not issued in time for preparing the langar, which was termed 'an absolutely essential right' of the community (Sriraman 2014: 373).[49]

I am tempted to take a short detour here to explore the nature of political mobilization against the ration card drive both in Delhi and British India with respect to festivals, and in general during the war; I must, however, admit the dearth of archival evidence or even secondary literature on this subject.[50] The pervasive need for fuel to fulfil ritual obligations and ceremonies definitely provoked unrest, as, for instance, witnessed by the ration strain experienced in the burning *ghats* of Nagpur and temple worship in Calcutta.[51] In Calcutta, the provincial Hindu Mahasabha severely criticized authorities for not anticipating everyday ritual routines of religious offerings to popular deities. This prompted an article in the *HT* which chronicled 'the Hindu Mahasabha's protest' against the 'rationing of deities'.[52]

Gandhi, of course, was known to have taken a principled stance against rationing (of all commodities) both during and after the war. He decried rationing as needlessly infantilizing the public who should be capable of exercising self-control (Jain 1965: 107). When he was travelling to Bombay where the wartime rationing scheme was exceptionally stringent, he refused to apply for a ration card saying that he only consumed vegetables and fruits.[53] He advised others to do likewise. He wrote in his publication, *Harijan*, counselling people on curtailing their needs and offering tips on how to do so, for example, by forgoing pulses if animal protein was available, eating dry rice with salads, or raw vegetables with chapatis. He coupled this with exhortations to cloth dealers and grain dealers to become trustees or keepers of grain and cloth for the poor.[54] While he did not outright condemn the ration card system, his disapproval of an artificial system of control was evident. His post-war views on rationing were to the effect of advising decontrol—he argued that crisis arising out of the shortage of cloth can be addressed by spinning khadi or alternatively, by nationalizing the textile industry (De 2014: 283).

Returning to the subject of supplementary rations, a unique aspect of the Delhi rationing regulations, when compared with the rules in other states and provinces, was that a special ration card was made available for those seeking additional rations to celebrate their weddings. The total supplementary rations that could be claimed were 15 seers of cereal, including, at the choice of the applicant, a maximum of 8 seers of rice and 30 units of sugar.[55] Apart from this, separate scales for supplementary rations were drawn up for different religious festivals like Easter, Ramzan, or Diwali. Prescribed forms were available for special ration that could be obtained in circle offices, and such applications were to be submitted at least 10 days prior to the day of the wedding. This application had to contain the name of the applicant, the exact relationship to the person getting married, a statement to the effect that he or she is responsible for the arrangements during the marriage, the code number on his ration card, the name of the bride and the bridegroom, the place where the marriage was to take place, the date of the marriage, and certification of the details contained within. An affidavit was to be procured to this effect which had to be attested before a judge, magistrate, or oath commissioner, or countersigned by a gazetted officer of the government.[56] Only one ration card could be issued for a marriage even if both parties of the wedding resided within the rationed area. Such applications would not be considered if parties wished to entertain guests in locations outside the Delhi rationed area. Not surprisingly, several hosts in breach of the regulations sought to escape prosecution by arguing that they had despatched invitation cards before the order was passed and that they had invited only poor people to the wedding![57]

Even as late as 1950, some of these rules were observed. Yashpal, in his novel, *This Is Not That Dawn*, invokes the cultural burden placed by the guest control order on families trying to perform weddings *dhoom dhaam se* (with fitting pomp and splendour). However, for some people organizing the wedding, the restrictions could only be a relief in economic terms because the ceiling on the number of guests naturally cut down wedding expenses. In this novel, the female protagonist, Tara, who was displaced after the Partition from Lahore to Delhi, gratefully acknowledges the guest control order, which in Delhi imposed a cap of 25 guests, when she regards her accumulating costs in getting her ward married (Yashpal 2010: 900–1). If, for a brief time after independence, Delhi seems to have allowed only 25 guests, governments of other states like Patiala and East Punjab States Union (PEPSU) and the Jammu and Kashmir (J&K) confined the number of guests that could be entertained on festive occasions to 24 persons, to be relaxed in the case of *barats* or wedding processions, where 48 persons could be invited.[58]

*

Currently, the family ration card or what is termed the household consumer card is the prevalent norm and applications for such a card require specifications of income and assets owned by the family taken as a collective unit. If the family as the unit of ration card conjures all manner of anxieties about absentee dependents or ghost beneficiaries today, it was no different during the war when ration cards were first issued. This explained the choice of the individual ration card which authorities preferred to the family ration card, at least in some parts of the colony. In Delhi, rationing documents were armed with a multitude of security measures, from the overprinting of permits, the marking of tyres, the stamping of cloth, the creation of separate authorities to oversee the application process for each commodity, to the minute correlations of ID practices like fingerprinting and signatures with the applicant, the clerk, and the bureaucrat. However, this could not entirely thwart the ingenious application of deceit and distortion by a plethora of figures in colonial society and bureaucracy. This set in motion revisions of strategy, such as the use of propaganda that played to the nationalist gallery, the institution of raids, the further decentralization of authority, and the withdrawal of certain features of the document (like the font and colour backgrounds used) and certain genres altogether (like the charcoal permit which was seen to be widely misused). Corruption was productively yoked to the unfinished business of improvising and improving document genres.

While it may appear that the postcolonial consolidation of the household as norm was predated by a wartime system of individual ration cards (at least in Delhi), this document—in the national and local imagination—was always shot through with familial affect. If during the war individual ration cards had to be fortified to support the cultural practices of family life in all its ritual and festive necessity, then the Partition with its attendant care–power ethic mandated an ID document form that could anticipate the disparate crises of displaced families. Zamindar's (2007) insightful work tells us that the Partition was not an aberrational event but 'long', in the sense that its violence was constitutive of (national) space and (postcolonial) time. By her account, documents like permits and passports were nothing short of being 'border-making practices' which were at the heart of the discourse of rehabilitation of the refugee: it was through this discourse and practices that the territorial delineation of the nation-states of India and Pakistan was accomplished. However, if passports and permits were important, so were ration cards and refugee certificates. Rohit De writes of how the Indian economy after independence assumed the proportions of a 'permanent emergency' (De 2014: 285). He points out that it is in this light that we must read the move by the Indian government to retain the ration card—as the centrepiece of centralized planning—when all other post-war dispensations had dismantled such controls. However, in addition to being an economic indispensability, rationing documents were culturally essential. Subaltern food officials responded sympathetically to middle-class families that sought desperately to circumvent ration card norms in an era of enforced commercial austerity. After the Partition, violently displaced poor families struggled to prove their blood relationships and their legitimate claims of occupation of government-owned spaces to a sceptical urban dispensation and the ration card, to a limited extent, eased administrative suspicion. It is for these reasons that my next chapter delves into the reinstitution of the ration card and its reinvention as a cultural necessity.

Notes

1. This is an extract from Henry Knight's book, *Food Administration in India* (1954: 203).
2. A fascinating archive of wartime rationing documents in America is available at www.ameshistory.org/exhibits/events/rationing.htm, accessed on 7 August 2015.
3. *Rationing in Britain*, 1944, available at http://www.youtube.com/watch?v=o9wNJ78S2GY, accessed on 4 January 2012.
4. See the advertisement, '*Swadeshi*—Made in Japan!', *Hindustan Times* (*HT*), 13 March 1944.
5. See *Report of the Foodgrains Policy Committee* (1943), as found in 165/43, Home, Public, NAI. The chairperson of this committee was Sir Theodore Gregory, who served as economic advisor to the Government of India between 1938 and 1946.
6. The food department, created in December 1942, set up the All-India Basic Plan, which was 'a ledger account of assets and liabilities which is prepared for each crop', mainly the kharif and rabi crops. Every state and province was expected to submit, in terms of the harvest of the kharif and the rabi crops, their estimates for production and consumption and whether and to what extent they were surplus or deficit. The Plan was,

therefore, the basis for allocations of foodgrains to different states and provinces, based on their surplus or deficit and on their needs of foodgrains (Planning Commission, Government of India, 2005).

7. The Basic Plan fixed: (a) quotas of exports of foodgrains that could be moved (under permit) from various surplus provinces to deficit provinces; and (b) the quantity of foreign imports that had to be supplied to deficit states and provinces. This allocation was based on the estimates of production and consumption and the extent to which they were surplus or deficit in any grain.

8. Local traders, nationalist leaders, people from the lower castes, and influential persons instigated such disobedience. Srimanjari writes that Marwari merchants assisted Congress leaders by withholding food supplies and instigating hartals. The Birla brothers, on the other hand, distributed money to beggar boys instructing them to aggravate authorities in Calcutta, while nationalist leaders exhorted people to fight the British and invite the Japanese and Subhas Chandra Bose, who would then be able to distribute rice to the starving. The posters and the anti-British propaganda might have pressured Britain into despatching 100,000 tonnes of rice to India (Srimanjari 2009: 109).

9. D.N. Gupta writes in his book, *Communism and Nationalism in Colonial India 1939–45*, that the Communist Party of India (CPI) believed that the 'Grow More Food' campaign would result in increased national production, a superior national defence, and unity amongst the kisans. These were aims that were dear to the CPI and ones that the Indian National Congress did not care for (Gupta 2008: 249–50).

10. Also see *Report of the Foodgrains Policy Committee* (1943: iv, 66).

11. 15 (176)/54, Confidential, Chief Commissioner's Office (hereinafter CCO), DSA.

12. 1023/IX, Food, Rationing, 1946–48, NAI.

13. 1023/IX, Food, Rationing, 1946–48, NAI.

14. Wherever a provision for separate ration scales and ration cards existed, it was important to furnish supporting statements by a mediating authority: a certificate by the senior medical officer in case of supplementary rations for the pregnant woman; a certificate by the commanding officer in the instance of the wife of the soldier; and so on.

15. RT-1061 (2), Food, Policy, 1946, NAI.

16. Unlike other provinces or states that issued supplementary ration cards to manual and heavy manual workers, Delhi did not issue separate rationing documents for this class but left it to employers' canteens to issue the same.

17. 'Petrol Rationing in Delhi: 25 per cent Reduction to be Effected', *HT*, 19 August 1941.

18. 14 (5)/1945, CCO, War and Civil Supply, DSA.
19. 'Delhi Rationing: Distribution of Family Inquiry Forms', *HT*, 18 February 1944.
20. 'Rationing for Delhi Likely to Be Introduced: Officials Consider Scheme', *HT*, 27 March 1943.
21. 'Delhi Rationing Grievances: Citizens' Conference Called', *HT*, 3 June 1944; 'Letters to the Editor: "Delhi Rationing"', *HT*, 28 April 1944.
22. 113 (1945), CCO, Special Press Advisor, DSA.
23. This course of increasing local rations was preferred to the derationing of locally produced mill cloth as it was feared that the measure would entail the spiriting away of local cloth outside the province. If earlier imported cloth did not come under rationing, this too was reconsidered and measures put in place to control the supply and distribution of such cloth. Amendments were carried out to disallow purchase of imported coarse cloth in excess of half the quantity of cloth prescribed under the permit.
24. 'Crowds at Delhi Cloth Shops', *HT*, 30 March 1945.
25. 'Cloth Shops Raided in Ahmedabad', *HT*, 4 January 1944; 'Police Hunt for Unstamped Cloth', *HT*, 4 January 1944.
26. Delhi Cloth Rationing, Chapter V, 38 and 41 (2) as obtained in 113 (1945), CCO, Special Press Advisor, DSA. In many ways, the cloth permit was unusual for it was the only document that entitled a dead person to rations.
27. Shankar. 1945. 'All Gone Underground', *HT*, p. 3. Delhi, 30 March 1945.
28. '2000 Dhobis on Strike', *HT*, 7 February 1945; 'Fuel Shortage Continues: Supply Position still Uncertain', *HT*, 9 February 1945.
29. See the following advertisements: 'If You Have Not Yet Been Enumerated for Your Ration Card, Call at Once', *HT*, 19 April 1944; and 'Ration Cards Are Being Distributed in Circles Nos 7 and 3 on April 19', *HT*, 17 April 1944.
30. See the advertisements: 'How to Use Your Ration Card', *HT*, 3 May 1944; and 'This Is Your Last Chance to Obtain a Ration Card', *HT*, 24 May 1944.
31. See the advertisement, 'Warning: Insist on Seeing the Identity Card', *HT*, 16 August 1944.
32. See the advertisement, 'Do You Know Your Rationing Number?', *HT*, 14 May 1944.
33. See the advertisement, 'Ration Cards Are Being Distributed in Circles Nos 7 and 3 on April 19'.
34. See the advertisement, 'Notify Your Change of Address', *HT*, 2 May 1944.
35. This was, however, variable. At some times, it was stated that these coupons could be valid for the next quarter if they did not exceed 12 units. See Delhi Cloth Rationing Order, 1945, as obtained in 113 (1945), CCO, Special Press Advisor, DSA.

36. 12 (47)/1945, CCO, Civil Supplies, DSA.
37. 'Identity Discs: People Advised to Purchase', *HT*, 11 January 1943; 'Identity Discs for People: Details of Government Scheme', *HT*, 4 May 1942.
38. 'Identity Discs for People: Details of Government Scheme', *HT*, 4 May 1942.
39. I am immensely grateful to Radhika Singha for sharing this invaluable and obscure reference with me. Descriptions of this census feature in this early twentieth century report on the Bombay city police by Edwardes (1923).
40. 27 (26), CCO, War and Civil Supply Branch, 1944, DSA.
41. 55 (7)-W, Mysore Residency Department, Bangalore Branch, 1944, NAI.
42. 'A Year of Rationing in Bombay', *HT*, 28 April 1944.
43. See, for example, 'Anti-hoarding Campaign: Delhi Police Raid Coal Shops', *HT*, 18 June 1943; 'Delhi Men Convicted under Rationing Order', *HT*, 1 April 1945; 'First Offender against Rationing Order', *HT*, 2 June 1944; 'Kerosene Mixture: Illegal Use in Motor Vehicles', *HT*, 6 January 1942; and 'Tampering of Sugar Permits', *HT*, 18 May 1944.
44. 14 (5)/1945, CCO, War and Civil Supply, DSA.
45. 9 (42)/1949, Civil Supplies, Chief Commissioner's Office, DSA.
46. RT-1061 (2), Food, Policy, 1946, NAI.
47. The United Provinces government allowed its residents one unit of cereal per day for a person related to the bride or the bridegroom and half a unit per day in the event of a funeral, both of which were subject to a maximum of 25 units. See R-1000/24, Food, Rationing, 1945, NAI.
48. 'Delhi Ban on Guests: Not More than 50 to Be Fed at a Time', *HT*, 12 January 1944.
49. 277/44, Home, Public (C), 1944, NAI.
50. We do have access to crucial administrative debates on the value of rationing after the war and I will briefly touch on them in Chapter 2.
51. 'Food and Fuel Scarcity', *HT*, 8 January 1944; 'Ration for Deities', *HT*, 18 March 1944.
52. 'Rationing of Deities: Hindu Mahasabha Committee's Protest', *HT*, 30 January 1944. If Hindu deities were one class of non-humans who were given ration card concessions, pets were not that lucky! When Calcutta's residents applied for extra rations to feed their pets, they were asked to think of alternatives which were unaffected by the rationing scheme. See 'No Ration for Pets', *HT*, 11 February 1944.
53. 'Gandhiji and Ration Card', *HT*, 13 May 1944.
54. 'Food and Clothing: Mahatmaji Advises Curtailment of Wants', *HT*, 26 January 1942.
55. Regulation 17-A, Delhi Rationing Rules, R-1000/24, Food, Rationing, 1945, NAI.

56. Regulation 17-A, Delhi Rationing Rules, R-1000/24, Food, Rationing, 1945, NAI.
57. 'Wedding Hosts Prosecuted: Breach of Chief Commissioner's Orders', *HT*, 5 February 1944.
58. RP-1085 (22)/1950, Food, Rationing, 1950, NAI.

2

EMOTIONS IN THE TIME
OF 'LICENCE RAJ'*

I felt a lot of compassion for the bride's father and I did not want his ration card to be cancelled.[1]

Bureaucracy could become positively bewitching.[2]

A crucial aspect of democracy in post-independence India was the investment of the postcolonial state apparatus in planned development and the equitable distribution of commodities like food and land. The enthusiasm for policies born out of such development and state-regulated markets saw an outburst of documentary controls and restrictions. The postcolonial years were a blur of permits, licences, ration cards, and quota applications. These documents and the information they conveyed and circulated were in dire need of interpreters, intermediaries, and officials who could set up correspondences between paper, entitlement, and identity. The intermediate official and the commercial intermediary played critical roles in the postcolonial welfare landscape. They did not simply manage the economy of arcane administrative information but they were also deeply present in the production of knowledge of welfare claimants. The postcolonial edifice was held in

* Parts of this chapter were published in a somewhat differently organized article titled 'Feeling the Rules: Documentary Practices of Rationing and the Signature of the Official', *Contributions to Indian Sociology*, 47(35), 2013: 335–61.

place by the ubiquitous intermediary, exemplified by figures such as
the food official, the dealer, the *dalal*, the policeman, and the clerk.
The existence of these intermediaries was, in turn, contingent on the
paper regimes of postcolonial India. Neither paper nor intermediary
functioned in an inert sociocultural landscape.

A bureaucracy aspires to fulfil certain organizational norms and it
is expected that a bureaucrat must act 'without anger and fondness'
(Albrow, cited in Hoag 2011: 82). But how do officials negotiate
documents in a society which is immersed in kinship ties and ritual
practices? The years of the Licence Raj were extraordinary but not
because of the surreal and tragi-comical tales of venality, and if one
were to use a facetious pun, the bureaucratic 'licentiousness' they have
now become synonymous with. The moment of postcolonial licensing
was astonishing because it gave a certain power to dull and mundane
bureaucratic objects like (ID) documents, while imbuing middling officials with a certain purposefulness and a mandate to perform. And so,
this chapter will script the role of animated documents and dynamic
bureaucrats in producing, managing, and steering the postcolonial
welfare economy. Official documents summon deep interpretive traditions of bureaucracy and enable the fluid negotiation of rules. Rationing
documents did something in addition: they unlocked emotions that
were 'culturally motivated' and 'socially articulated' (Lutz and White
1986: 409) and conjured dynamic constructions of the bureaucratic
Indian self. While contesting the parable about rationing documents as
being objects deployed by middling officials to seek petty advantage,
this chapter will argue that these documents were critical to the self-
fashioning of lower-level officials within a cultural framework. It is by
paying attention to the tangibility, materiality, and at other times, their
magical power to circulate in various spaces that 'street-level bureaucrats'—to deploy Lipsky's (2010: xi) phrase—were able to flesh out
cultural norms that were dear to them.

This chapter is indebted to the deep insights of historians and anthropologists who have delved into emotion, challenging its aloofness from
social circumstance (Gross 2006), cultural context, its lack of intelligence (Nussbaum 2001), or its priority over other choices informed by
rational instincts. The social and cultural worlds of officials shaped their
understandings of rules, and the chapter makes out a certain case for
officials 'feeling the rules' at critical moments of issuing, withholding,

or cancelling ration cards and drawing up affidavits to frame smugglers. While emotions cannot be defined as such, they are the result of deep ethical and evaluative judgements. Drawing on Martha Nussbaum, the chapter shows that officials' responses to everyday responsibilities, far from impairing their evaluative judgements, illuminated their emotions as part of their cultural reasoning. Scholars have also drawn a conceptual difference between affects and emotions. Affects have been described to invoke an 'intensity' that is not mediated through language or a history of experience. Affects do not strictly fall within the realm of consciousness; they are moments of intensity where the body responds to one or many stimuli. Emotions, on the other hand, are socially derived; they are an 'expression of our internal state' and may contain ethical evaluations based on our social experiences (Shouse 2005; also see Clough 2007).

Rather than get into the debate of how to distinguish affect from emotion, this chapter notes the operation of both. However, emotions are not merely ethical evaluations or internal states subjectively experienced. They are the result of an encounter with power structures and social hierarchies. Daniel Gross (2006) infers that our ability to feel compassion, rage, and humiliation is irrevocably tied to power relations. Sanjay Palshikar's (2005) piece on humiliation yokes this emotion, among other things, to a conception of human dignity that is socially derived. Emotions enmeshed with cultural affinities and societal norms suffuse the narratives of these officials.[3] This chapter argues that the cultural understanding of bureaucratic norms was resonant with kinship and affective ties, and social responsibility to the cardholder and the rationed public. The narratives paint a certain picture of bureaucratic self-fashioning where documents present emotional dilemmas to officials. These predicaments feature them interpreting documents in various capacities and intensities: if at times they acted subconsciously, searching out recourses instinctively, even putting documents to vindictive use, at other times, they acted emotionally, that is, out of social considerations. This chapter will thus challenge the popular normative assumptions around the Licence Raj as characterized only by venality, ubiquitous malpractices, and mercenary impulses.

While the formative Nehru years will be covered briefly in tracing the roots of the Licence Raj in the planned economy and the regulatory regime of commodity control, the chapter will dwell significantly on the Shastri and Indira Gandhi years when the era of Licence Raj reached its sublimation. This period marked a new era of socio-economic control and commercial austerity, and it corresponded with many significant events like the establishment of the Food Corporation of India (FCI), the setting up of the Delhi Food and Civil Supplies Organization, the reintroduction of rationing in urban centres, and the imposition of guest control norms. The routine duties of food officials were originally conceived to entail verification of ration card applicants, and later expanded to cover the regulation of sites of food consumption and sale, such as FPSs, hotels, weddings, and diplomatic parties, and crackdowns on hoarding, black marketing, and smuggling of controlled commodities. This chapter will lay out the framework of food distribution manifest in various injunctions, regulations, and inspections of cardholders and dealers through an ethnographic study of documentary forms and practices. These practices have been recorded to correspond to the years between 1965 and 1990 in what used to be called the Union Territory (UT) of Delhi.

Continuous with the aims of the previous chapter, this chapter too will illustrate the sustained, albeit somewhat changed, preoccupation with norms of address and household in matters of enumeration. While certain ID documents such as ration cards, licences, and permits remain central to this chapter, we will also seek to comprehend the functioning of other uncommon documents like the Daily Diary and affidavits. Such an enterprise will involve a close study of various official documents such as notifications, acts, and control orders issued in exercise of the powers of the Essential Commodities Act (ECA), 1955, which formed the template for food distribution after India's independence. The resources for this chapter have been supplied by the oral narratives of many retired and a few serving food officials who recalled their roles in enforcing rules pertaining to rationing documents within an extended social and cultural context. Such a context was composed of kinship obligation, middle-class values, and a quest for a novel bureaucratic subject position consistent with the Indian democracy.[4]

Challenging a Weberian Void of Emotions

When Weber wrote his thesis on rationalization of authority, his thoughts poignantly centred on the growth of bureaucracy, a phenomenon which he linked to the onset of modernization of states. Weber was very clear on the point that a modern bureaucracy was organized around 'the principle of official jurisdictional areas, which are generally ordered by rules, that is, by laws or administrative regulations' (Weber 2006: 49). The bureaucracy was an artifact of the legal-rational type of authority—other types being charismatic and traditional authority—that characterize modern states. In this type of authority, the assignation of duties and rights, the distribution of authority, the chain of command, the channels of appeal, and the structures of remuneration ideally allow no room for personal or social biases. This is all the more so because the 'principle of hierarchical office authority', which underlay bureaucratic structures, was universal (Weber 2006: 49). He wrote further: 'The management of the modern office is based upon written documents (the files) which are preserved in their original or draft form, and upon a staff of subaltern officials and scribes of all sorts. The body of officials working in an agency along with the respective apparatus of material implements and the files makes up a bureau' (Weber 2006: 50).

In such a dreary, mechanical routine where the bureau was managed through 'material implements' which put an onus on recording minutes, passing files, compiling data, preparing estimates, and tabulating policy decisions, there seemed very little room for matters of the heart.

Traditionally, emotions have been perceived to be alien to schemes of rationality that should guide bureaucratic actors and the only sense in which they are relevant is when officials learn to either channel or purge emotions which may deter public service (Albrow 1997: 97). However, there have been many refreshing studies that recuperate emotions in Weber's social theory. These studies show how the careful cultivation of emotional characteristics such as civility, enthusiasm, passion, and dedication mattered tremendously in the idealized exercise of authority (Albrow 1997; Graham 2002; Merton 1940; Stoler 2004). Albrow narrates the many passions of 'the maker of the modern British civil services', Charles Trevelyan, who was seized with a love for records and an antipathy to holidays. The famous sociologist, Robert Merton, hints that the reason that bureaucrats are ill-equipped to efficiently and effectively cater to clients is not a deficit of sentiments but an excess of devotion to duties. Sentiments here can be defined to mean 'socially articulated symbols' and not 'private feelings' (Lutz and White 1986: 408–9). Over time, the sentiments that make up discipline as a bureaucratic norm are no longer viewed as unimportant aims for an organization to work well. They are now present as mandated values in the official's ethic which must be fulfilled if organizational goals are to be achieved (Merton 1940: 563).

Colonially speaking, bureaucracy was eagerly propelled by emotions. The racial panics that gripped colonial rulers in India and Indonesia were resolved through engineering and calibrating the emotions of European functionaries and public servants. For instance, it was important to nurture the right kinds of sensibilities, aspirations, and loyalties to the metropolis among colonial actors who might become too attached to certain ways of life in the Dutch colony (Stoler 2004). Ann Laura Stoler writes:

> Dutch colonial authorities were troubled by the distribution of sentiment, by both its excessive expression and the absence of it; of European fathers too attached to their mixed-blood offspring, of Indies-born European children devoid of attachment to their (Dutch) cultural origins, of European-educated children who, upon return to the Indies, held sympathies and sensibilities out of order and out of place. (Stoler 2004: 5)

Dutch 'political rationalities' were deeply invested in techniques to mould 'the affective states' of such figures such that they were more appropriate to the desired 'social membership' of the colonial order, she writes. In colonial India, bureaucratic moves to peruse applications or entertain petitions were met with emotional gestures from applicants, petitioners, and officials (Cody 2009; Hull 2012b; Sriraman 2014). The plague outbreak of 1896, for instance, saw a string of distraught petitions from colonial subjects in Bombay who were dismayed by regulations that sought to ban fairs, impose quarantines and detentions, and carry out inoculations and intrusive inspections of the body (Sriraman 2013c). These emotions were bureaucratically managed through the creation of ID documents such as detention and exemption certificates, plague passports, and inoculation certificates such that epidemic measures did not disproportionately upset Indians. During the Second World War, certain classes of privileged applicants requesting the sanction of supplementary rations for commodities like petroleum, tyres and tubes, and electricity in late colonial India fell back on curious genres of bureaucratic rhetoric. They argued that their roles and they as educators, administrators, propagandists, and war industrialists were 'essential' and 'prior' to the wartime effort. The application process saw them attempting to stoke favourable emotional responses such as compassion, pity, and pride from the rationing authorities while making requests for petroleum coupons, tyre permits, and permanent electric connections. Ironically, rationing authorities responded with a contrary order of emotions such as contempt and derision, when they perceived that the war conditions in the 1940s warranted much more commodity-based restraint on the part of these applicants (Sriraman 2014).

Partha Chatterjee's oft-cited article titled 'Development Planning and the Indian State' (2000) shows how postcolonial planning was visibly constituted as a domain that fell outside of politics and how, as an enterprise, it was supposed to signify the unified and rational will of the nation as a whole. Planning (and not just national self-determination) was envisaged as the means through which the postcolonial state would exercise and legitimize its power—this was because such planning was wedded to national development as opposed to the colonial state's warped approach to development which was a necessary means to appropriating indigenous wealth and resources (Chatterjee 2000: 120–1). However, planning, by its very instrumental definition, would have to be a disputed and self-destructive enterprise owing to the obdurate insistence on precisely working out the demand for commodities, the exact estimations and allocations of priorities, consistencies between different objectives, and the capacities of the implementing agencies. Nothing short of 'omniscience' (Chatterjee 2000: 124–5) was then required to plan effectively and meaningfully; and because this was often not available, one imagines that the domain of planning, far from being a straightforward and civil business, was often a heavily contested one where passions, hot opinions, and violent disagreements ensued.

If, so far, it has been discerned that bureaucracies are no strangers to emotional expression and what is more, that emotions are very pertinent to the fluid and shifting spaces of rule and governance, then it is important to stop short of committing an egregious mistake. A study of emotions in bureaucracy may not be possible without a genealogy of emotions. A genealogy in the sense that Foucault uses the term would imply various discursive and layered formations lurking behind systems of knowledge and power operating not only at the conscious but also at less discernible and less conscious levels. So, Foucault goes in search of effects, mistakes, accidents, disparities, and emotions. Foucault alerts us by asking us to regard history as shaped in 'unpromising places' such as 'sentiments, love, conscience and instincts' (Foucault 1984c: 76). But emotions, while they shape history, must themselves be the subjects of history; and never can we commit the fallacy of regarding emotions to be historically stable. In other words, once we consider the possibility of emotions as shaping history, we must know also that no single emotion has remained a constant in history. Foucault suggests that emotions do not illuminate history or unveil history as constituted by actors stirred by each other's humanity; instead they serve to disguise, edify, and camouflage domination and violence. An emotion like compassion has served several historical functions. If at one point it may have had little place in penal regimes that iterated punishment in the most absolute and cruel register, its sudden emergence as a norm had to do with the modernist impulse to more productively discipline persons and to render certain kinds of domination more unassailable.[5] If compassion is couched in certain legal assurances such as peace, rule of law, norms of probity and conscience, accountability, and constitutional safeguards of liberty, it exists only to carry out historical impulses of violence contingent on space and time and helps replace one form of domination with another. Indeed, 'the universe of rules' and law itself is needed 'not to temper violence, but rather to satisfy it' (Foucault 1984c: 85).

While, of course, one cannot fully contest the disciplinary nature of emotions in the self-fashioning of the bureaucratic figure, this chapter traces only in part the effects and rituals of a newly instituted and modern domination (read democracy). It concerns itself predominantly with effects and rituals which fall outside a Foucauldian consideration, namely, affinities and kinship obligations birthed by the shared postcolonial matrix of family, region, religion, and cultural sociality. While the task—to show how emotions were disparately at work in moulding different bureaucracies—is impossibly beyond the scope of this chapter or book, I would like to suggest that the sentiments and emotional formulations in the period during the Licence Raj were quite distinctive and peculiar to this period in many senses.

The Everyday Mobilization of Documents during Licence Raj

If the documents issued during this time owed their lineages to a wartime colonial establishment struggling to enact legal norms at a time of intense scarcity, the patchwork of ration cards, licences, permits, and certificates acquired a new meaning and mobility in a postcolonial network of state planning, bureaucracy, business interests, and electoral politics. The meagre but immensely significant scholarship concerning the period of Licence Raj as well as the substantial body of work centring on the everyday state (Fuller and Harriss 2001) must be mobilized and critiqued to secure new perspectives on how documents, bureaucrats, and their emotions interacted with each other.

In theorizing the rich interactions or the relations between state and society, scholars have shown how everyday forms of democracy and local idioms of community and kinship are thickly enmeshed in institutional forms of the Indian state, such as police stations, government schools, secretariat offices, city magistrate, and rural record offices (Chatterjee 2004; Gupta 2012; Hansen 2001; Harriss-White 2003). These scholars use the sites of corruption and communal violence, and within such sites, the popular importance assigned to codes of reciprocity, social identities, and the informal economy, to illuminate the fuzzy and porous boundaries between state and society. In this narrative corpus of scholarship on the everyday state, land requisition certificates are forged, permits illegally secured, ration cards issued in the names of imaginary persons, and SC/ST certificates are faked by people who cast wide and porous nets of kinship and mutual obligation which officials and claimants alike are caught up in (Brass 2011: 214; Gould 2010: 124; Parry 2000: 32, 42). Bureaucrats figure in such analyses as metaphors for the everyday state which is differently shaped and socialized by cultural forces. The rare and immensely valuable scholarship around Licence Raj, which abounds in the writings of historians like William Gould and political scientists like Paul Brass and Stanley Kochanek, supports these views. In his excellent historical exposition on the nature of state–society relations in late colonial and postcolonial India, Gould points out that it was not just cultural forces that moulded the forms of corruption during the Licence Raj era: 'political networks', 'business–Congress links, used to finance elections, power bases and factional loyalties' facilitated 'the black money of licences and permits' (Gould 2010: 130). While the links between businesses and Congress date back to the early twentieth century—when the Birlas and Singhanias, for instance, provided material support for party activities and party workers' families—they are revitalized at a time of intense regulation and commodity controls after independence. Businesses recognize that applications for any given genre of licences (for imports, securing commodities such as cement, steel, and sugar, setting up new industries, and so on) take forever to process. Anticipating some of the peculiarities of the Indian bureaucratic process such as formalism, red tape, casteism, and nepotism, businesses seek to cultivate political contacts through multiple channels (Kochanek 1974).

Within such an action-packed screenplay plotting the life of Licence Raj, there seems little space to discuss the emotions of officials, much less their emotional responses unleashed by documents. It may be useful to grasp certain emotions like compassion, resentment, and emotion-laced codes of hospitality as flowing from discourses of rituals, social hierarchies, and community within a normative cultural framework. Emotions taken out of their social context may tell us nothing about how certain sentiments interacted with the mandate to enforce rules related to this period. But anthropologists and historians studying emotions point us in the direction of ritual systems, which show how indigenous systems of cultural beliefs, morality, and feelings dovetail in the making of a person's self (Lutz and White 1986; Rosenblatt et al. 1976; Rosenwein 2002). Emotions are then much more than evaluative judgements containing elements of cognitive expression (Nussbaum 2001).

In presenting and framing the officials' actions, I will be doing much more than demonstrating how documents triggered officials' emotions manifest as ethical actions. Given how the Licence Raj was encoded with power relations, modes of striving for and achieving social recognition, aspirations towards intimacy with well-placed functionaries and leaders, and the craving for political and economic mobility, our anti-hero, namely, the lower-level official, experienced a gamut of emotions related to these pursuits. It is critical to tie an analysis of bureaucratic emotions to social hierarchies, power relations, conceptions of dignity, humiliation, compassion, and rage within a cultural matrix. This is where I would like to differ from the scholarship around the everyday state. Enactments of emotions did not necessarily blur the boundaries between public servants and private citizens in ways that are suggested by this scholarship: for instance, it did not necessarily follow that 'the modern sector' was being 'legitimated in pre-modern terms' (Chatterjee, cited in Fuller and Harriss 2001: 24). Emotions that were supported by kinship norms and a ritualistic society were enacted in contemporary terms and in ways continuous with the temporally specified foibles of the Licence Raj. Following Gould, who writes that customs of interaction and transaction that involved rituals anchored to social expectations were not the manifestation of pre-modern relations but the 'products of colonial and postcolonial governance' (Gould 2010: 14), I show how culturally manifest emotions were coded in starkly bureaucratic languages of norm and procedure, and they were not vestiges of some timeless Indian tradition. This passage of socially anchored emotion into the bureaucratic self was made possible by the presence and circulation of certain kinds of ID documents like ration cards and other genres of the rationing document like permits and licences. At the heart of our discussion is the bureaucratic self-fashioning of public officials and the movement of documents in an indigenous context.

A Brief Note on Oral Narratives

The ethnographic material for this chapter is drawn hugely from interviews that I conducted over five months (January–May 2011) with officials of different ranks—joint commissioners, assistant commissioners, food and supply officers (FSOs), food inspectors, and clerks—as well as government-approved commercial players such as FPS dealers. But the most relevant ones are the interviews which I held with retired food officials, most of whom were inspectors and FSOs between 1965 and 1995. Some of these officials had joined the food and civil supplies department in Delhi when it first started functioning in 1965, while others joined the department later. I have changed the names of all the retired officials, the sources and offenders they cited, partly because these officials wished to stay anonymous and also because some of the stories shared can be unfavourably construed and even misappropriated. These oral narratives of food officials are relevant vis-à-vis certain moments of transition constituting major shifts in welfare discourse, such as the first few Five Year Plans, the austerity measures of 1965, and rationing and the establishment of the PDS in the same year.

Before I narrate some of the stories told to me by these food officials, it may be fitting to revisit the timeless and still daunting debate on the reliability of oral narratives. In his historical inquiry into industrial planning and its capitalist moorings, Vivek Chibber pertinently points out how the archive for postcolonial India is not simply scattered, it is also exasperatingly elusive, not least because of the erratic practices of bureaucratic record-keeping and the even more shocking practices of record destruction (Chibber 2003: xi–xii). Where the haystack is almost as elusive as the needle, the researcher is truly confounded. It is for these reasons that oral accounts are such a rich cache of historical meaning, and therefore the interviews with these lower-level bureaucrats were invaluable to me because they straddled the distinction between official and popular narratives. Even though it is assumed otherwise, oral narratives are needed not merely to tell the history of the strictly 'non-hegemonic classes' (Portelli 1998: 66), they are equally necessary for telling the history of the lesser privileged 'ruling classes' whose claims to history in this case have all the momentousness of being an important footnote to the corruption of these years. In relying on such narratives, I am fully mindful of how they render somewhat obscure any meaningful distinction between 'the factual and the artistic', 'events and feeling', what concerns the individual and what concerns the group (Portelli 1998: 66). That said, it must be pointed out that the subjects of these interviews prided themselves on their sharp memory of their serving years. What makes these oral narratives so compelling is the subjects' intense desire to be acknowledged by their stories if not by name and face, their beliefs that their bureaucratic subject positions shaped and disrupted the flow of the Licence Raj years, and their reliance on personal archives of their making, comprising personal and official letters and diaries. This chapter will not be relying on these narratives to merely gaze into the official's worldview, or the consciousness of the bureaucrat, or to get another glimpse of history. These narratives will instead aid us in comprehending how subjects move within networks of information (Marcus 2005: 17) constituted by the media, the political economy, and their own cultural contexts, and how certain documents came into their hands and enticed them with new possibilities of defining their quotidian roles.

'One Hearth, One Home, One Family'

Let me start with a particularly captivating story told by Jadeja, which occurred sometime between 1984 and 1985 when he was FSO. This involved an applicant for a food card named Surinder who was the son of a Congress politician. Surinder was working in a smallish office near Jantar Mantar in Delhi where he had installed a gas stove but he was not living there. Surinder tried to intimidate Jadeja into issuing him a ration card by informing the latter of his political connections. A somewhat affronted Jadeja proceeded to make his own personal inquiries before taking a decision on the matter. He looked up the Mahanagar Telephone Nigam Limited (MTNL) telephone directory of Delhi to see if Surinder's father owned a separate residence in Delhi and found an entry marked in the name of the father staying in Janakpuri. Next, Jadeja requested his counterpart in whose jurisdiction Janakpuri fell to send him a copy of Surinder's father's ration card. Jadeja noted, with some satisfaction, that the card listed Surinder, clearly establishing what Jadeja had suspected all along, that Surinder was applying for a second ration card. He then turned down the request for a ration card, though he admitted to me somewhat mischievously that he may not have turned detective or gone to these lengths had Surinder not intimidated him by citing his influence. Jadeja told me he would have bent a rule or two to issue a card even though it was not due had Surinder been civil to him.[6] This was because Jadeja understood how impractical it was for ration cardholders to always be living, working, and eating within the same space. It was Surinder's absolute lack of regard for Jadeja's position and the *tariqa* that should accompany special requests that prompted Jadeja to act with anger and outrage bordering on what he described himself to be 'a state of vindictiveness'.

It is essential to emphasize a few pertinent conceptual distinctions that lie, historically speaking, at the heart of the food distribution policy as it was enacted over the decades. The distinctions that have been sustained are those between offices and domestic residences, commercial establishments and homes, those residing permanently in a house and those visiting the house, and finally, between a family residing in the house and a group of unrelated persons living together. The Delhi Rationing Regulations of 1965 specified that ration cards were meant for household consumption and ration permits for bulk consumer establishments. And the same regulations also emphatically stated, clearly establishing Surinder's transgression, 'No person shall apply for a ration card in respect of a rationed article if he has already

obtained a ration card in respect of such rationed articles' and that
'no person shall apply for a ration card in respect of any person who
is already included in a ration card'.[7] A household was defined in
1981 as:

> a family unit living together in one building or portion of the build-
> ing held in possession by any member of the family as common resi-
> dence and maintaining a common kitchen and includes persons so living
> together whether or not dependent on the holder of the consumer card
> or the person in whose name the application for the issue of consumer
> card is made.[8]

A very coherent description of 'home' appeared in the *Manual of
Instructions* for food officials in Delhi, published most probably in the
year 1986 as the introductory note indicates.[9] It stated that permanent
food cards may be issued subject to certain conditions: the applicant
should be actually residing in a pukka house; the applicant should be
actually residing at the address given in the application; there should
not be any evidence of illegal occupation; and the applicant should
produce one of the following documents to substantiate the claim that
he is actually residing at the given address—rent receipt, electricity
bill, water bill, telephone bill, house tax receipt, gas connection, or no
objection certificate from the landlord. Each official I spoke to, high
and low, testified time and again that a home can be so termed only if
it contains a kitchen or a hearth and a family in continuous occupation
and that it could not be used for official or commercial purposes. These
various ideas within these distinctions were compressed by Jadeja in an
elegant phrase, possibly of his own coinage, 'one hearth, one home, one
family'. Jadeja harboured the conviction that if this principle was valuable to ensure that wrongful claims on government largesse were not
made, exceptions could be made if the rule was, in spirit, not violated.
Having visited the office space that doubled up as a home, Jadeja was
convinced that even if it lacked a kitchen, there was enough evidence
to believe that Surinder lived there. But Surinder's middle-class sense
of entitlement offended Jadeja and he decided to put a fine point on
the rule. Jadeja believed that when 'suitable attitudes both towards the
services they receive and towards the street-level bureaucrats' (Lipsky
2010: 11) did not accompany application requests, they could be selectively entertained.

Choosing between Licence and Ration Card Norms

If enumerating families to issue ration cards was part of the lower-level food official's job description, monitoring the functioning of FPSs to ensure that dealers did not violate licence norms was also part of their stipulated routine. As in the previous story, officials found that social purpose and context mattered, this time in weighing what was more important, that is, respecting licence norms or ration card norms. Before recounting officials' narratives of such a dilemma, let us take a cursory glance at some of the various rules regarding the location of an FPS shop and the conditions under which an FPS dealer may obtain a licence. The rules state very clearly that dealers should sell only rationed items, should not run a *chakki* or a flour mill, and should run a shop only in certain premises accessible to heavy vehicles and located in a busy commercial area.[10] Badrinath, an FPS dealer who ran his shop from 1972 to 1997 in Krishnapuri in west Delhi, told me the other legal criteria of eligibility: all sites of applicants who wished to open FPSs had to be inspected based on their capacity or storage space; and the official had to check if there were other shops already functioning in that *ilaqa* and if so, how many, and also the financial liability of the applicant, that is, whether he could afford a shop or not.[11] He too spoke of the rule that the licence to run an FPS could not be misused to sell any other non-rationed items. However, he added, in all seriousness, 'But my father, sister or brother can sell rationed items in an adjacent store, and it won't count as abusing the licence, right?'[12]

Let me now recount the story of Jadeja's encounter with an FPS dealer where Jadeja had to commit an indiscretion and save the dealer even though he was riled by his attitude. Jadeja states that in either 1968 or 1969, he remembers having an altercation with an FPS dealer who had a licenced shop to issue rations to cardholders opposite Odeon cinema in Connaught Place (CP). Here, it would be useful to know that the ARD, later termed FPS in the Delhi Specified Food Articles (Regulation of Distribution) Order, 1968, could not register more than a certain number of cardholders depending on the number of units already registered with him. In 1965, when each cardholder 8 years and above was entitled to 2 units, the maximum cereal and sugar units for every distributor were fixed at 5,000 and 3,000 units, respectively.[13] So, even if a person fell under an FPS dealer's jurisdiction, he could not register him if he was already catering to a sufficient number of cardholders covering this value. This meant that there was a great demographic pressure on FPS dealers, but it also meant that cardholders counted themselves lucky when they could be registered in an FPS of their choice and in their location.

Jadeja said that the particular FPS dealer, instead of respecting his licence to run an FPS and an FPS only, also sold groceries like soap, Coca Cola, and cigarettes and was therefore treating, for all practical purposes, the ration shop as a sideshow. 'When I confronted him about it', he adds, the FPS owner responded callously, 'Ration cardholders here want matchboxes and soaps as well as rations. If I don't offer them groceries, they will not come simply for the rations. But if I don't offer them rations, they will still turn up for the soap. I care two hoots about your licence, take it back even now if you want.'[14] Hanging his head low as he concluded the story, Jadeja said he just could not bring himself to cancel the licence because of where the shop was located. His sense of compassion for a clientele who potentially depended on this shop for their everyday needs prevailed ultimately. Had it been located anywhere other than CP, he would have immediately revoked the licence, but because there were very few FPSs functioning in that area, he could not have forced the FPS to close down without causing a lot of inconvenience to the few residents in and around CP who really needed the rations. Even though he felt bad about it, in his reckoning, Jadeja was not flouting norms. He was weighing which administrative norm was more important to protect in the present event of a conflict: a rule that sought to ensure the integrity of FPS dealers or the unwritten one that sought to ensure the proximity of FPSs to (possibly unprivileged) ration cardholders.

But some officials were either not aware of some of these rules regarding the licence of an FPS at all or found the rules to be fraught with inconsistency. For instance, Madanlal Mehta, who served as food inspector first and later as FSO between 1965 and 1980 in Delhi, conveyed undisguised confusion: 'But where was the contradiction? Non-rationed items were not in conflict with rationed items. How did it matter that an FPS dealer sold a broom or masala powder? These were not rationed, anybody should be able to sell them. I don't remember any such crisis.'[15] The clever tactics employed by both the FPS dealers—I mean here, Badrinath and the one in Jadeja's story—in bypassing rules regarding licences and Madanlal Mehta's bewilderment convey, on the one hand, the equivocal nature of rules surrounding ration cards, and on the other hand, the permeability of documents to cultural interpretation. Rules about documents were to be culturally construed in order to uphold practical and popularly beneficial criteria.

Postcolonial Debates on Rationing

Food officials like Jadeja and Mehta served at a time of extreme austerity in national consumption when institutions like the FCI and the Agricultural Prices Commission (APC) were being set up. Many of the stories they narrated must be read in this context of political intervention in food distribution and other welfare measures. These officials were expected to enforce measures of austerity, regulate eating establishments, and ensure minimal consumption in public gatherings.

Nehru threw his weight behind commodity 'controls and regulated distribution', defying not only Gandhi—who felt that free citizens should not be disciplined—but other contemporary figures such as the formidable Congress President, Purushottam Das Tandon, who made an impassioned argument for free market and private capital (Jain 1965: 119). The overwhelming thrust to Nehru's food policy was provided by the move to purchase sizeable imports, implement controlled distribution, and exercise caution against black marketeers. Nehru's stand was also cemented by the views of the Planning Commission and the Parliamentary Committee on Commodity Controls. Both these bodies argued the need to curb the designs of powerful interests on the economy, 'ostentatious consumption', and the mandate to protect 'the minimum consumption standards of poorer classes' (*Planning Commission Report 1951*, cited in De 2014: 287).

The food policy to counter rising prices in the 1950s evolved in lieu of capital allocations to agriculture. These allocations were redirected to industry, which was accorded a high priority in the first few Five Year Plans. This was in keeping not only with the various ideas of progress floated in the Bombay Plan but also with those later expressed by Nehru and Prasanta Chandra Mahalanobis,[16] who designed a four-sector model where agriculture was lumped together unceremoniously with cottage industry. While Nehru did not assign that much of a priority to agricultural production, he did not ignore it altogether. Nehru

was keen to extend the land under cultivation through investment in
irrigation and fertilizers. Minimum support prices were announced and
credit assistance to help farmers manage capital costs was offered by
setting up 'cooperatives, land development banks and other institutional agencies' (Vaidyanathan 1983: 960). Nehru declared in a speech
addressed to the Lok Sabha: 'We dare not weaken our food front. If our
agriculture becomes strongly entrenched, as we hope it will, then it
will be relatively easy for us to progress more rapidly on the industrial
front, whereas if we concentrate only on industrial development and
leave agriculture in a weak condition we shall ultimately be weakening
industry' (Nehru 1954: 89).

Nehru, even as he stresses the importance of agriculture, speaks of
it only in relation to industrial development. Besides, Nehru's government relied heavily on imports and price controls to address scarcity
and inflation. The acceptance of large-scale imports under the US
Public Law 480 facilitated continuity of the PDS within urban areas
and enabled a hugely effective manipulation of prices that benefited
consumers (Mooij 1999: 70). Wheat imports from all international suppliers, which averaged 6.67 million metric tonnes for the year 1964–5,
accounted for '54 percent of domestic production and 35 percent of
overall availability of wheat in the country (domestic production plus
imports)' (*Report of the High Level Committee on Reorienting the Role
and Restructuring of Food Corporation of India* 2015). However, a food
policy that turned to imports was too provisional and tenuous, given
the risk of sudden interruption or termination, to allow for sound and
controlled planning of food distribution. Owing to his policy preferences, Nehru was not adequately attentive to the related long-term
needs of centralized food production and food provisioning even if he
recognized an immediate crisis of food scarcity.

There prevailed a brief interim period of decontrol which was
widely believed to have been the consequence of Rafi Ahmad Kidwai's
interventions as Food and Agriculture Minister and the bumper crops
in the early 1950s (Jain 1965). A significant departure in food policy
came at the behest of Lal Bahadur Shastri for whom agriculture and
agricultural production was not just another sector but a talisman that
promised to lift India out of its morass. Shastri's decision to privilege
this sector was also informed by predictions of famine and proposals for
new agricultural technologies in the Ford Foundation report published

in 1959 (Guha 2007: 325). He spoke voluminously and imploringly in many of his addresses to chief ministers and other dignitaries of the need to motivate his 'kisan brothers' who were to 'produce more, market more'.[17] So high was internal agricultural production in his view that he conceived of 'farms to strengthen arms'[18] and spoke of the agricultural initiative in no lesser terms than the military effort.

It is no small matter that the FCI and the APC were both set up during the tenure of Shastri, who tried to impress on the population their civic roles in managing the shortages that bedevilled the food distribution establishment in India. It is also no coincidence that these organizations emerged at a time when rationing was introduced again in the country. When Shastri chose to impose rationing for the third significant time in India (the first time being in the 1940s; the second time being in the early 1950s), it was backed by an entirely different rhetoric of self-sufficiency and a different modus operandi. If the first time rationing was introduced by colonial authorities to protect the urban settlements because they were such a strong link to the war effort, it was justified differently in 1965. This time, Shastri stated unequivocally that rationing was an interim measure to be backed by central procurement of foodgrains, planned growth of the agricultural sector, and a large buffer stock of imports. Shastri saw in food planning a Gandhian imperative of *swarajya*, though he did not, unlike Gandhi, shy away from food controls as an ad hoc measure. Gandhi had said on rationing: 'Controls give rise to fraud, suppression of truth, intensifications of the black market and to artificial scarcity. Above all, it unmans the people and deprives them of initiative, it undoes the teachings of self-help they have been learning for generations. It makes them spoon-fed' (Gandhi, cited in Jain 1965: 107).

In stark contrast to this reasoning, Shastri sought not simply to impose rationing controls but also to impart to the trader, the housewife, the restaurant-owner, and the farmer an education about their significant roles in regenerating the food economy. Hotels and restaurants were asked to cut down rice and wheat in their meals and limit the number of courses served; and non-vegetarians were asked to curtail cereal consumption. In the letter, 'Increased Production only Solution', from Lal Bahadur Shastri to the chief ministers, dated 8 August 1964, places like Punjab, Delhi, Uttar Pradesh, Rajasthan, and Madhya Pradesh were asked especially to observe austerity as they were not in such dire shortage of foodgrains (Shastri 1974: 96). A dramatic consciousness of the situation was imparted to the public with Shastri exhorting the populace to observe a night's fast during a week. In response to his call, Bombay's restaurants remained closed every Monday night. Festivities and ceremonies were frowned upon as inopportune and legislations regulating the same were imposed. He declared in a speech:

> Parties, dinners and lunches are not in tune with the times at all. At weddings, there should be no exhibition of ostentation. There is no need for many dishes to be served. Hotels and restaurants also have to keep in line with present day requirements. Austerity is the need of the hour and it must be encouraged by strong public opinion.[19]

All these regulations, be they directed at catering establishments or at consumers, were carried out through documents such as ration cards, licences, and applications for parties or functions. These injunctions had the legislative force of the Delhi Guest Control Orders and the Delhi Catering Orders that were issued from time to time under the ECA, 1955. If these orders were originally introduced by the colonial authorities, they were a definitive feature of the 1960s food regime with its pillars of austerity, agricultural productivity, and rationing controls. While these control orders sought to regulate gatherings of all kinds—official parties, funerals, and festival gatherings—they were, however, mainly aimed at the opulent displays, lavish hospitality, and the unrestrained social impulse to invite hundreds of guests at Indian weddings. The central administration in both the 1960s (when the Delhi Guest Control Order and the Delhi Food [Restriction on Service of Meals by Catering Establishments] Order were issued in 1968) and the 1970s (when the Delhi Guest Control Orders were put in place again, once in 1972 and then in 1976) looked to its lieutenants—the food inspectors—to report overindulgence at social gatherings.

A Metaphor for Corruption: Guest Control Orders

From my conversations with retired food officials, it emerged that lavish weddings with numerous or more than the stipulated number of guests indeed took place, even during the days of the guest control orders of the 1960s and the 1970s. Let me first outline some of the requirements of these orders that were renewed from time to time. The

Assam Guest Control Order, 1966, which became the model for the Delhi Guest Control Order, 1968, was addressed to caterers, catering establishments, hosts, institutional establishments, and residential establishments[20] (see Tables 2.1 and 2.2). The guest control orders usually defined these terms and forbade caterers, hosts, and so on from preparing or distributing 'prohibited foodstuffs' or those foodstuffs containing cereals. The Delhi Guest Control Order, 1976, added 'cereals or pulses and all sweets including gram and its products' to the list of forbidden items for more than a stipulated number of guests.

No person was to be allowed to accept or consume prohibited foodstuffs at any social gathering that included 'party, entertainment, social or other function, marriage, or funeral',[21] where more than a stipulated number of guests were invited. The Assam Guest Control Order, 1966

Table 2.1   A Timeline of Significant Control Orders Regulating Food Consumption in Delhi

Name of the Order	Year in Which It Was Passed
Delhi Rationing Order	1944
Delhi Specified Articles (Regulation of Distribution) Order	1945
Delhi Guest Control Order	1945
Delhi Rationing (Limiting of Guests) Order	1946
Delhi Rationing (Meals in Establishments) Order	1946
Delhi Rationing Regulations	1965
Delhi Guest Control Order	1968
Delhi Food (Restriction on Service of Meals by Catering Establishment) Order	1968
Delhi Specified Food Articles (Regulation of Distribution) Order	1968
Delhi Guest Control Order	1972
Delhi Guest Control Order	1976
Delhi Guest Control (Third Amendment) Order	1977
Delhi Specified Articles (Regulation of Distribution) Order	1981

Source: Compiled by the author based on an archival reading of the Delhi Gazettes published from 1944 to 1981.

Table 2.2   A Timeline of Significant Guest Control Orders in Other States

Name of the Order	Year in Which It Was Passed
Uttar Pradesh Food Consumption Restriction Order	1948
Assam Guest Control Order	1966
Rajasthan Guest Control Order	1972
Mizoram Guest Control Order	1972
Jammu and Kashmir Guest Control Order	2004

Source: Compiled by the author from newspapers and popular online resources.

was more liberal in the number of guests it allowed, setting the limit at 25 guests for ordinary parties and 100 guests for marriages and funerals. The Delhi Guest Control Order, 1976, significantly issued during the Emergency, set the number for all parties at 25, whether it was a social function, marriage, funeral, or any other.[22] Equally significantly, the Delhi Guest Control (Third Amendment) Order issued in 1977, the year the Emergency was lifted, raised the number of guests in both categories—of ordinary functions to 50 and those who may be invited to marriages or funerals to 100.[23] Anybody wishing to throw a party had to submit an application form, stating the purpose of the function held and the number of guests invited, along with a copy of the ration card and a copy of the invitation card.

In the recent past, media interest in the infamous control orders of the 1960s was revived in the context of the proposed Food Security Bill. Food Minister K.V. Thomas stated in 2011 that a lot of food could be saved by regulating the number of guests invited to weddings and by capping the number of dishes served. Food thus saved could be distributed to the poor and the needy, as the Food Security Bill envisaged. This spurred a debate in various political parties and media circles about the efficacy of reviving guest control orders and bringing back the Licence Raj. Some party representatives argued that such proposals only hid the incompetence of the ruling establishment to manage rotting food supplies and what is more, that these control orders would only lead inspectors astray, putting the temptation of petty bribes in their line of duty.[24] In the words of one opposition leader: 'Even in the days of Guest Control Order, there were lavish weddings and functions.'

So how will it be any different now? There is a greater chance that this could lead to greater corruption as conspicuous wealth has only gone up in the last decade or so.'[25]

This angst about conspicuous wealth and flamboyant consumption, packaged in so many policy avatars, has now been rearticulated and proposed as a bill to regulate weddings. Termed the Marriages (Compulsory Registration and Prevention of Wasteful Expenditure) Bill, 2017 and proposed by the Congress Member of Parliament (MP), Ranjeet Ranjan, this draft bill seeks to place a cap of Rs 5 lakh on all weddings. Where families decide to spend more than Rs 5 lakh, they should declare the excess in expenditure and be ready to contribute 10 per cent of the expenditure to a government-created welfare fund that will enable the marriages of poor girls.[26] These new policy overtures have prompted journalists to direct their historical gaze towards the 1970s yet again, to indicate how these rules were poorly observed and cheerfully bypassed even then. One such journalist, Bhavya Dore, writes that restaurants like Delhi Darbar in Bombay city flouted guest control and food rationing norms by preparing meals after the clock struck midnight and seeking permissions to remain open after 'the official deadline' of 11.30 p.m. She also describes, in this article, the public perception as manifest in social media of 'the Inspection Raj' in these terms:

> Some people on social media envisioned a return to the days of food rationing when the Indian government advised people on what to eat and how to cut over-consumption, when it even dictated how much ration shops and restaurants could source. It was a time when hoarders could be penalised, and food inspectors had a field day, while a black market for goods flourished on the side.[27]

Statements about the era's propensity to corruption and the petty temptations it yielded to among officials are hardly unusual and have dominated the political discourse on development and welfare distribution in post-independence India. At the heart of such statements are assumptions that informal practices of bribe-taking are embedded in local conditions where there is an intermingling of vernacular discourses and local power networks of dalals, pradhans, FPS dealers, and lower-level officials. Such a construction misses many subtle interactions. First, bribe-taking is rendered into a structural effect of state practice (Mitchell 2006: 180) and a 'fundamental transaction of the Indian state' (Visvanathan and Sethi 1998: 6). It is considered a demon that possesses all officials who perform homogeneous roles as disembodied brokers of power in local spaces of opportunity and petty advantage. Such an act of reading does not account for officials' sentiments that spring from kinship ties and cultural affinities. Second, this construction decontextualizes individual responses to legal norms and prescriptions of official duty from the social worlds they inhabit and suggests that all officials in various situations and spaces, when tempted with bribes, will react similarly. Most importantly, this construction assumes that officials' indiscretions are the outcome of a narrow discourse of corruption, where officials are willing to bend rules only when offered pecuniary inducements and not for anything else.

The point made here is not one about various shades, hues, and intensities of corruption—what one scholar has described 'painting black what is in reality a variety of colours' (Ruud 2000: 273–4)—ranging from citing and misusing influence to gift giving, nepotism, and misappropriation. While this is a valid point and an especially apposite one as the period of the Licence Raj was undoubtedly characterized by a colourful miscellany of unethical and corrupt behaviour, I am interested in showing something altogether different. Needless to say, there are ample examples to demonstrate Ruud's point: one official came up with a delicious irony when he declared, 'I was vindictive but I never took bribes—*Ek pachas ya sau rupaya zyada kamane ki bhavna nahin thi*' (I never wished to make an additional 50 or 100 rupees).[28] But I am not arguing that officials selectively interpreted rules, violated rules, and were thus unethical and mildly corrupt. Rather the questions animating this chapter are: how did officials shape their bureaucratic selves by affectively identifying themselves with a cultural practice?; and how did the document help them do this?

Compassion, Kinship, Cultural Affinity, and Status

In painting the classic picture of the bureaucrat as Weber modelled him, Robert Merton speaks of the bureaucratic 'pride of craft'. He writes, 'as we have seen, bureaucratic officials affectively identify themselves with their way of life' (Merton 1940: 565). This makes them resist change in their routines, but this also makes them cling to certain 'bureaucratic symbols and statuses' (Merton 1940: 565). Merton was alluding to the bureaucratic tendency to insist on the fulfilment of certain norms (related possibly to the movement of files, observance of hierarchies and jurisdictions, and so on) because officials derived moral legitimacy and a sense of importance from them. But this purely bureaucratic pride mingled freely with another sort of amour propre.

The inspector who was, generally speaking, a relatively low-ranking food official, nevertheless enjoyed a mighty status contingent on such occasions as inspecting a wedding or issuing a card. William Gould, writing on the role of town rationing officers and district rationing officers in Uttar Pradesh of the 1940s and 1950s—roughly the counterparts of the FSOs in my story—gives us a sense of their tremendous local power manifest in their authority to suspend and cancel dealers' licences. If their temporary, non-statutory appointments made them vulnerable, they were often confident in the knowledge that court cases that held them responsible for reckless or vindictive acts of discretion would be legally drawn out such that they could 'mobilise political defence' (Gould 2010: 126). In Delhi, such was the power of inspectors and FSOs in the two decades between 1960 and 1980 that these officials enjoyed the aura of the *annadata*, which was nothing less than the supreme power to give *and* take away food. Their administrative power and occasionally their enjoyment of political privilege, not surprisingly, translated into cultural capital. Deepak Gupta, a retired food inspector, told me, 'Inspectors *ki badi izzat hoti he; ek* Inspector *ya* FPS dealer *annadata maana jaata he, unke bachchon ko bauhut saare* marriage proposals *aate hein*' (Inspectors are respected a lot [in our society], an Inspector or FPS dealer is regarded as food-giver and their sons or daughters receive a lot of marriage proposals).[29] He said this in the context of the power such officials wielded over various commercial establishments and agents such as *halwais*, hotels, and boarding homes, all of whom had to apply for permits to get their monthly or weekly rations, and FPS dealers whose stock registers were inspected by the food inspector. The site of applying for licences and permits, whether they were for sugar, cement, or tyres, may be one of visible corruption but it was also one that carved out the official's cultural status. Bakeries, establishments, FPSs, and various classes of citizens had to follow due procedure in order to be able to run shop or to obtain ration cards. Such power was relevant in the context of various injunctions applying to catering establishments implicit in control orders, such as the Delhi

Food (Restrictions on Service of Meals by Catering Establishments) Order, 1967. This control order stipulated that no proprietor of a catering establishment was to supply for consumption and that no one was to obtain or consume at such an establishment 'for the purposes of a meal more than two courses'.[30]

The cultural significance of the inspector was relevant in the context of everyday ritual, sociality and festivity as manifest in weddings and funerals, and in the context of official exhibitions of ceremonial power, such as official parties and embassy functions. This was a status that could not be trifled with as this official could reduce even an industrialist or a top-level minister to a whimper. Jadeja remembers with fond pride his role in inspecting an official party attended by Indira Gandhi and V.K. Krishna Menon, who asked him deferentially if there were any violations. Yet, this perception of cultural eminence of an inspector, for Jadeja, dissolved to give way to a painful encumbrance on occasions when he had to report the bride's parents who struggled and failed to cap the number of guests at a certain wedding. Jadeja explained his predicament through this pithy exchange between him and one Brigadier Kalra who pleaded with him when Jadeja went to inspect Kalra's daughter's wedding, '*Aap bhi to ek Punjabi hein, aap kya karte agar aap mere jageh hote aur aap ko bhi apni beti ki taraf se meheman bulane padhte?*' (You are a Punjabi too, what would you do if you were in my place and you had to invite guests on your daughter's behalf?).[31] An appeal to his compassion within the mould of kinship and regional solidarity weighed Jadeja down even further.

Other officials too felt anguish at the prospect of inspecting the catering arrangements in wedding parties and carrying out a headcount of the guests who attended a function. Madanlal Mehta tells us this story: Sometime during the Emergency, a person came to Mehta to tip him off about a violation that in all likelihood would occur at a wedding hosted by a man who ran a crockery shop in Karol Bagh. Mehta sized up the complainant to be a relative or someone close to the family. Mehta dragged himself unwillingly to the site of the wedding at Kirti Nagar to inspect the catering arrangements and the guest list. On arriving there, he came to know that the bride's father faced eight different complaints in connection with the wedding: someone had come to press charges against him for using electricity illegally; someone else to question his unauthorized use of the garden; and so on. Mehta, in explaining his decision not to report a violation where clearly more than the stipulated number of guests were invited and rationed items were cooked indiscriminately, said: 'I felt a lot of compassion for the bride's father who was under a lot of pressure on so many fronts. So I shouted at him and pretended to be angry. But I gestured to him to simply give me the samples which I inspected and reported as revealing no violation'.[32] Clearly, Mehta too loathed the food inspector's duty of inspecting marriage ceremonies because he felt it interfered with his perceptions of kinship and familial obligation. He went back to his office and made an entry in his Daily Diary that there was no violation at the wedding. Mehta felt vindicated when he later came to know what happened to the bride's father. He told me, *'Mujhe baad me pata chala ki apni ladki ko sasural bhejne ke baad ek ghante ke andar hi woh bechara mar gaya'* (I came to know later that the poor man died within one hour of sending his daughter to her in-laws' place).[33]

Jadeja's Daily Diary was marked by a conspicuous dearth of violations at the wedding parties he inspected. Thus, many of the entries the food inspector made in his Daily Diary were 'paper truths'[34] (Tarlo 2003: 62), which contained compassionate lies but assumed a certain legitimacy because they were transcribed in the form of official record. The Daily Diary of the food inspector was a quotidian record of the food inspector's dealings with the public (cardholders and applicants) and his field visits. The food inspector was required to mention which houses he visited for inspection, issue of cards, to inquire into complaints, and so on. William Gould suggests that guest control orders were wantonly breached in Uttar Pradesh high society: families that could draw on political influence got away with throwing lavish parties that were graced by the presence of prominent politicians (Gould 2010: 126). Middle-class families in Delhi that could not dream of such luxury resorted to more modest contestations by resorting to tactics such as breaking up the wedding party and holding it in more than one place at the same time such that violations of ration card norms were not easily detected.[35] In hosting such weddings during Indira Gandhi's tenure, such families presumably became vulnerable to malicious neighbours and rivals, as the famous Urdu writer Ismat Chughtai suggests in one of her stories about an ordinary Muslim family and its rise to wealth and fame through an opportunistic politician.[36]

Unlike the previous narratives of food officials—where officials' emotional responses were legitimated by the contradictions posed by ration card and licence norms—this particular cultural conundrum presented a more serious case of bureaucratic misconduct. However, officials quite conscientiously contra-distinguished their lack of willingness to persecute marriage parties with their alacrity in apprehending and bringing to the book food and oil smugglers who hoarded, on a massive scale, rationed articles in their godowns, illegally disposed of them, or spirited smuggled goods into other neighbouring states. Lower-level food officials may not have been seized with a drive to conform to all the impersonal norms that the political lords during the Licence Raj imposed, but definitely honoured the ones that they considered representative of the founding ideals of the predecessor Nehruvian 'service state' and the Shastri-driven mandate for austerity.

The Magical Power of Documents

The Licence Raj in India was an artifice created by the widespread commodity controls imposed in a post-war and postcolonial state. Such controls—which were conceptualized as an emergency measure to address wartime shortages and consumer distress—were to become a lasting feature because planners believed that 'the Indian economy was in a permanent state of emergency' (De 2014: 277). Nehruvian state socialism and centralized planning routinized such controls, and gave them the backing of penal law and bureaucratic authority such that managing the economy was significant from the vantage point of everyday governance. Rohit De writes that many of the penal injunctions that were a part of the Defence of India Act, 1939 were replicated in the ECA, 1946, and later with the ECA, 1955 (De 2014: 284). This ECA gave blanket powers of 'regulating by licences, permits or otherwise the production or manufacture of any essential commodity'.[37] Several control orders came to be passed to aid the enforcement of this act in the production and sale of commodities as diverse as coal and its derivatives, automobile parts, cotton and woollen textiles, iron and steel, paper, tyres and tubes, petroleum products, and foodstuffs such as sugar and different kinds of wheat flour.

The burgeoning corruption and black money of this era cannot be imagined purely in terms of the proliferation of bureaucratic power that occurred through these commodity controls. It is imperative that we consider the rising opportunities that the licence and permit system presented for competitive electoral politics, settling political scores, and the politicians who sought legitimacy through exposing corruption. Through their exciting archival and ethnographic work, scholars have demonstrated how this period supplied incentives for generating political propaganda and publicity and forging political networks, in addition to prospects of making money (Brass 2011; Gould 2010; Kochanek 1974; Parry 2000). Paul Brass documents how the law itself became the shield for ensuring the diminishing line between patronage and corruption such that this period heralded 'a republic of privilege' for small yet influential actors like newspaper editors, 'rival traders, journalists, touts and politicians' (Brass 2011: 214, 219). Ironically, the multiplicity of the systems of control put in place to prevent corruption served not only to facilitate and spawn but also to mirage and disguise its various forms such that even the smallest of small actors were not culpable. The Santhanam Committee Report (1962–4), which recommended measures to fight corruption, observed, 'The sudden expansion of economic activities of the government with a large armoury of regulations, controls, licences, permits provided new and large opportunities for corruption' (cited in Visvanathan 1998: 27). Even a renowned journalist of yesteryears, Dilip Chitre, writing for the once-famous *Quest* magazine, remarked with great dismay on the disproportionate avenues of income and power that bureaucratic controls gave to the large class of differently ranked employees of central and state governments. These avenues seemed all the more disproportionate because they inhibited even small businesses and prevented 'a managerial revolution that alone can pull India out of a static rate of growth' (Chitre 2011: 291).

The sparse scholarship on Licence Raj has given us refreshing insights into, and exciting ways to understand, this period. I would like to complement this scholarship by remarking on how licences and permits, not unlike passports (Zamindar 2007), assumed amplified powers when officials used them to cast the net of anti-corruption. I have no intention of contradicting the existing scholarship by arguing that officials were valiant and incorruptible gatekeepers of the documentary edifice of licences, permits, and ration cards. Instead, I will illustrate how officials were swayed by the magical power of the documents of

this era such that their enforcement of control orders was chimerical and shadowy rather than lawful and rule bound. Once again,
we will see how documents brought cultural premises and emotions
to the fore and aided officials in fleshing out and fashioning their
bureaucratic selves.

In Delhi, as in other states, control orders under the ECA, 1955 were
issued from time to time, whenever the government felt that there was
scarcity of any commodity. Apart from food commodities, such as rice,
wheat, wheat flour, sugar, and kerosene, other articles of commercial
use, such as coal, cement, bricks, and tyres and tyre tubes, were regulated through licence regimes and rationing controls. Applications for
licences and permits to trade in and acquire tyres, bricks, and cement
were issued under the control orders pertaining to the commodity in
question. These articles were controlled not simply for commercial use
but also for private or domestic purposes. And in this sense, my fieldwork too bore out the insights of scholars who testified to the everyday repercussions of commodity controls for middling and struggling
classes such as traders, dealers, and vendors.

The retired officials I interviewed indicated that control orders did
not regulate but spawned corruption, which in their imagination was
hydra-headed. To them, there was no better illustration of this point than
the ocean of dubious applications for permits that the Tyre Tube Branch
of the food department in Delhi saw in the early 1970s. This feeling of
pervasive corruption in this branch was voiced not only by middle-level
food officials like the food inspectors but also by clerks. Rajnath, a clerk
who worked for this branch in 1973–4, snorted in derision when asked
about the functioning of this branch. He said that more tyres were sold
in black within this department than through unofficial channels. He
also stated his belief that whatever commodity is controlled, that commodity is black marketed, not the other way around. He added that
black marketing occurred because the permit holder was free to use
his permit to claim a certain quota of tyres in any given year, though he
did not have to use all of them in the same year.[38] All he had to do was
produce his registration certificate and permit and walk away with the
tyres. This information was borne out by the rules governing the issue of
tyre and tubes in the control orders. He, along with other food officials,
indicated that the experience of tyre and tube rationing spoke for the
history of rationing through the Licence Raj in India.

The rationing of tyres and tubes, unlike that of foodgrains, was relevant only for certain kinds of customers like automobile owners and truck owners, many of whom applied for tyres and tubes for inter-state movement. The opportunities and temptations to smuggle and sell these tyres in other states were far too great, especially in the face of provisions that allowed permit holders to apply for and obtain a certain number of tyres even if they had no need for them. The late 1960s saw order after order being passed in Delhi on the control of the movement and sale of tyres and tubes.[39] The Delhi Automobile Tyres and Tubes Control Order, 1969 covered various vehicles, such as scooters, scooter rickshaws, autorickshaws, motorcycles, cars, trucks, buses, jeeps, vans, as well as tractors and tractor trollies. A few regulations should be mentioned here to make sense of the officials' narratives around tyre and tube control. First, any dealer could 'obtain, attempt to obtain, or store for sale or distribution or offer for sale or sell automobile tyres and tubes' only after he applied for and obtained a licence.[40] The licence could be used by the dealer only for the premises for which it was granted and the dealer would have to acquire a separate licence for another place of business.[41] All licencees were to display 'at a conspicuous place' in their premises, the prices of the varieties of tyres and tubes at their disposal. Most importantly, licenced dealers could not sell automobile tyres and tubes at prices exceeding those fixed by the central government, the lieutenant governor of Delhi, or by the manufacturers of automobile tyres and tubes. At any rate, the price could not exceed that which was reached by adding 7.5 per cent to the billing price, if prices had not been fixed by any of these authorities.[42] The last clause gave some extraordinary leeway to dealers to fix arbitrary and exorbitant prices, and automobile owners who did not know the exact percentage could always be duped. The tyre and tube rules, therefore, were fraught with ambiguity—the last clause was unlike the rules governing any other commodity. Rationing of other commodities was undergirded by firm and clear stipulations that the chief commissioner would notify the prices from time to time; this gave FPS dealers very little scope for interpretation.

Another significant rule of the Tyres and Tubes Control Order was that any vehicle owner was eligible to receive only a certain number of tyres and tubes (of first quality and second quality) depending on the scale of issue for that particular vehicle in a calendar year.[43] Nylon tyres

meant for public carrier trucks may be sold only to those holding permits
for inter-state routes issued by the Directorate of Transport, Delhi, and
only four Nylon tyres could be supplied for any such truck in a calendar
year. Another crucial detail was that the permits had to be signed by one
of the following officers: the deputy commissioner, Food and Supplies;
civil supplies officer; or the inspector, Tyres and Tubes Branch.

Retired food official Madanlal Mehta recalled with distaste that
the Tyres and Tubes Branch was 'swarming with drunk and coarse tyre
dealers'. He added that he wanted to 'exit' the branch quickly, but the
commissioner of Food and Civil Supplies was adamant that he stay
there. When asked to explain his aversion to the branch, he narrated
this story:

> In January 1972, a somewhat handsome fellow, a Muslim in all likeli-
> hood, came to the Branch on behalf of the UAE Embassy. He wanted a
> special permit and brought an application form that bore the signature
> of an Embassy representative called Al-Fateh. I told the food and supply
> officer (FSO) who was in charge of the Branch that he could not issue a
> special permit even for the embassy without orders from above (with-
> out the permission of the commissioner of Food and Civil Supplies). I
> also smelled something fishy, I don't think the Embassy would send a
> man just like that. The FSO-in-charge told me not to interfere in diplo-
> matic matters. But I was stubborn and so, the FSO said, go to the deputy
> commissioner (DC) and take his opinion. I told the DC my story, he
> agreed with me—if any permit is to be given, the Embassy representa-
> tive should have the permission of the commissioner. I reported this to
> the FSO and he said, okay, let's investigate the matter before issuing the
> tyre. We (Mehta, the FSO, and another official) called up the Embassy
> and asked them if the vehicle numbers mentioned in the permit appli-
> cation were registered with the UAE Embassy. He retorted, how am I
> supposed to know the vehicle number, we have so many vehicles. So
> then, I (Mehta) asked the Embassy person on the phone, is Al-Fateh
> working with you? I got the reply, No, he was working with us five years
> back, not now. He went abroad after that. Next, we contacted the Delhi
> Transport Department and asked them to tell us about the vehicle's
> provenance by giving them the vehicle number. They told us the vehicle
> was sold to someone many years back and that the vehicle number was
> presently not valid. We also verified this information by checking the
> Embassy's registers containing the numbers of vehicles used by the staff.
> And so it was established that it was a bogus application.[44]

The FSO in this story was not keen to verify the applicant's credentials or create a fuss. According to Mehta, if it had been up to the FSO alone, the latter would have issued the tyres even though a colleague had expressed doubt about the authenticity of the application. From various conversations with Mehta, Jadeja, Gupta, and the clerk, one could gather that officials in this branch accepted the porous legality of rules: officials working here believed that the tyre and tube rules did not require them to be meticulous, but at the same time, they knew that they were expected to issue permits only to strictly eligible applicants. After the FSO gave him permission to look into the matter, Mehta could have simply told the Embassy representative who brought the application that he should come back with written permission from the Embassy and the commissioner of Food and Civil Supplies, but he instead wanted to implicate the man in the act of wrongful representation. Interestingly, the technique Mehta improvised to expose the man was one of his own creation. This technique drew on the imagined materiality and the magical power of documents and signatures. So, he told the man:

> Your permit is ready. Please show us your Embassy ID. When the man failed to show me any, I said, please write on this paper that you are authorised to collect the permit on behalf of the Embassy and sign your name. He immediately signed and wrote a statement that he was authorised by the Embassy to collect the permit. Meanwhile, the police, who we had called, arrived on the spot. I told the police, here is your culprit. This (addressed to the researcher) was how I started my career in that Branch.[45]

By dangling the permit, Mehta lured the impostor into creating a legally acceptable document inscribing his guilt. Mehta fashioned his tactics of apprehending the impostor through his acquired understanding of documents as objects of imagined material significance. Signatures clinch identity and written statements become affidavits in the legal world of culpability and proof. He was aware of the narrative force of a document which turned suspicion into evidence and speech into confession. A penal document or a document embodying punitive force had to be one that even the 'stentorian state' would be forced to accept as juridically credible (Guha 1987: 140–1). Mehta had also been nurturing a surfeit of pent-up frustration with existing administrative guidelines that exhaustively inventoried forms of corruption but were useless in helping food officials pin down offenders. If the permit was anyway a shadowy document, why not conjure another document, this one being purely mythical? Mehta felt that he needed to make a difference and stand out from the rest of the casual corruptible herd, and the situation replete with possibilities of invoking documents (both existing and imaginary) allowed for the resolution of his teeming disgust with his colleagues.

Madanlal Mehta recalled another story where he had heard from someone that a man named Kishanlal was impersonating him and forging his signature on tyre permits issued in Delhi. Mehta further shared: 'He used to print application forms resembling the original with serial numbers similar to those issued by the Tyre Branch. I came across 2 to 3 permits that were issued bearing my signature. We in the Tyre Branch filed an FIR with the police and we even went to the CID and asked them to investigate.'[46] Following up on this lead, Mehta and other officials from the tyre branch approached various dealers in Delhi warning them that the police wouldn't spare them if they were found to be entertaining Kishanlal. Later, with the help of other dealers and in a dazzling climax that involved using code words, duping Kishanlal, and getting him to confess, the case was drawn to a close.

Mehta's stories were not aberrational. These narratives supplied by interviews with food officials throw up feelings of bureaucratic anxiety vis-à-vis the world of smugglers, impostors, and forgers who were emboldened by malleable licences and permits. This anxiety could only be countered by drawing on the power of other kinds of enchanted ID documents—affidavits, declarations, undertakings, and notes of confession. These could be manufactured at a moment's notice and belonged to a certain genre of state documents whose legal claims to truth are dubious but may be inscribed as substitutes for non-existent evidentiary and punitive forms of ID. If affidavits have been known to fulfil this function for purposes of recording domicile, date of birth, statements containing information about ration card applicants, property transfers, and so on, then they could be readily mobilized into framing and implicating suspicious sorts. There was a rough equivalence between the legally permeable genres of licences and permits and the shadowy genres of declarations and affidavits as far as these officials were concerned. Where smugglers and impostors could easily procure permits, they could be thwarted only through enticements of leniency and demonstration of threats in the form of affidavits and declarations.

Another food official, Deepak Gupta, was able to act on a tip-off and hit upon the cleverly concealed godown of a food smuggler.[47] Reflecting on the best means possible to proceed, he devised on the spur of the moment a strategy which involved enticing the smuggler to perjure himself and to write a note stating that he (the smuggler) had in his possession various goods that had been illegally procured. Deepak Gupta assured the smuggler that such a note would give him reprieve and he may be able to get away with merely surrendering his ill-gotten goods. The smuggler wrote the note but suddenly realized what the document could do to him. He crumpled and threw away the document in a fit of rage. The official had to use his instincts to simultaneously retrieve the note and to soothe the smuggler. He put his foot inconspicuously over the crumpled note almost as a reflex while he told the smuggler reassuringly that he needn't give a note in writing after all. This incident reflected the power of the document to transmit affects or momentary intensities where the smuggler and the official were responding in a barely conscious form to certain threats, risks, and temptations posed by the document. The official's instinctive actions, however, conceal his cultural appreciation of the potential of documents to draw out desired responses among criminal figures.

The finest schemes of governmental intervention are tinged with illegality in urban sites. And ironically, if it is documents that are meant to uphold public purpose or enact processes of modernization—in this case, by ensuring austerity and commercial propriety in keeping with the planning ambitions of a developing country—they are also the sites in which these norms can be easily subverted. This paradox must be juxtaposed with another: public agents inevitably enforce rules through their circumvention and extend protection by reiterating threats (Fawaz 2009). In countries like Mexico, Brazil, and India, there have been other researchers who have documented how regulation in informal settlements proceeds through state-appointed juntas, private developers who have an understanding with state officials, political leaders who enjoy state patronage, and so on. Such arrangements are formalized through documents like application forms, deeds of adverse possession, titles recognizing subdivision of land, and building permits, all of which enable the bypassing of rules within a legitimate framework (Fawaz 2009; Hoag

2011; Holston 2009; Varley 2002). In India, documents like *tehbazari* permits and *hafta* slips are issued by state actors to marginalized groups such as hawkers and rickshaw pullers, such that their entitlements hinge on constant jeopardy. If ID documents suspend actors between 'threat and guarantee' (Poole 2004), they also unleash, mediate, and manipulate emotions. Scholarship remarking on this relation between documents and emotions talks of how subjects experience a 'political haunting' (Navaro-Yashin 2007: 83) through spectres of the state, such as the flimsy passport issued by the Government of Northern Cyprus to its residents, the tenuous registration certificate issued by the Indian government to Tibetan refugees, and the colour-coded identity cards issued by the Israeli government to Palestinians (Kelly 2006; McConnell 2013; Navaro-Yashin 2007). Possessing these ID documents makes holders uncertain of their legal statuses as refugees, secondary citizens, or citizens of a clandestine state, and renders them terrified about how they will be read in critical spaces of these subjects' marginality. While the smuggler in our story is not quite comparable to these subalterns, he too is subject to the same immense and systematic power of quasi-legal or 'make-believe documents' to manipulate emotions (Navaro-Yashin 2007). Smuggler and official alike are tantalized by the subversive potential of documents: if, in a stroke, these papers could be utilized to forge, mimic, and impersonate, they could be repurposed to trap the devious offender into admitting his heinous deeds.

*

Modern states resort to various documentary practices to shore up 'administrative power' and political legitimacy or, alternatively, they resort to writing practices as a discursive strategy to create an illusion of legality even where there is a conspicuous absence of the same (Das 2006: 162–3). The agents of such deception are often the faceless officials working in the lower rungs of the bureaucracy. They are often tasked with the interpretation of rules that are too abstract to allow faithful conformity in local settings, and thus they end up working in the interstices between policy and practice, objective and subjective, legal and illegal, public and private, dispassion and passion (Hoag 2011: 82, 84).

Such a job description facilitated delicious hybrid roles, such as the food official taking on the garb of annadata and *sarkari* goonda. I came

across this not so edifying sketch of sarkari goonda in one of my interviews with the charming albeit slightly eccentric Jadeja, who sorrow-
fully identified with this label in the context of his dealings as a food
inspector during the Emergency era. In their brushes with quotidian
authority in a non-idealized setting, the food officials, sometimes will-
ingly and at other times inescapably, succumbed to the gap between
the rule and its execution, or the legal form and what it signifies (Das
1998: 176; 2006: 162). The rules spelt out in a bureaucratic document were often not helpful in particular contingencies which require
situated knowledge and cultural sympathies. This was a gap which was
often exploited by lower-level and middle-level officials to frustrate or,
at times, even defraud poor rural subjects (Gupta 2012: 20, 135), but
at other times, to subvert the designs of criminal figures and to open
out welfare spaces. The emphasis on writing as a bureaucratic norm,
coupled with the inability of the rule to communicate to the official,
enabled various fictions to be normalized on paper. But these food officials were able to do all this only because the documents of the kind
that were discussed in this chapter were imbued with the capacity to
evoke a host of emotions, ranging from anxiety and insecurity to compassion and empathy. It was within this matrix of documents, emotions,
the bureaucracy, and cultural belief systems that the street-level official
was able to fulfil various mandates to protect the steel frame, ensure its
relevance to certain ritual practices, and attend to the serious business
of enforcing austerity and preventing large leakages of state resources.

Notes

1. A retired FSO remembers how he refused to implement guest control
   norms at a wedding during the Emergency; interview by author with
   Madanlal Mehta, 25 March 2011.
2. See Clifton Crais' article, 'Chiefs and Bureaucrats in the Making of Empire'
   (2003: 1039).
3. I am not trying to argue that food officials were given to corrupt behaviour
   and that their emotional selves came in the way of complying with document controls and the norms associated with them.
4. These interviews were held over five months in the year 2011, and later
   over a month in the year 2013. Some of them were held at the Department
   of Food and Supplies in Delhi; and others at the residences of retired
   food officials who graciously talked to me for whole days over lunch and

evening snacks. I spoke to 12 retired officials, one of whom was posted in Haryana and the others in Delhi. Some of these officials were initially food inspectors and later became FSOs. Other than this, I interviewed nine serving officials across different ranks in the food and supplies department in Delhi. I spoke, in addition, to two erstwhile FPS dealers and a few clerks in the food and supplies department. This chapter relies on a total of 47 interviews, some of which were held with the same official or clerk.

5. I thank the LassNet Delhi Conference participants for aiding my understanding of Foucault's 'Nietzsche, Genealogy, History' (Foucault 1984c).

6. Interview by author with Jadeja, New Delhi, 28 January 2011.

7. No. F.6(2)/65-CCR, Delhi Rationing Regulations, 1965, *Delhi Gazette, Extraordinary*, 7.

8. No. F.23(2)/78-81-F&S (P&C), Delhi Specified Articles (Regulation of Distribution) Order, 1981, *Delhi Gazette, Extraordinary*, Part I, 12.

9. *Manual of Instructions*, Department of Food, Supplies and Consumer Affairs, Delhi. A copy of this manual was obtained with much difficulty from the Department of Food and Supplies, Delhi, in February 2011, owing largely to the kindness of R.T.L. D'Souza, the then additional commissioner-cum-additional secretary of the same department. Though the Directorate of Consumer Affairs, Delhi is mentioned in the manual, it bears no year of publication.

10. No. F.23(2)/78-81-F&S (P&C), Delhi Specified Articles (Regulation of Distribution) Order, 1981, *Delhi Gazette, Extraordinary*, 1981; see Form A, which is the application form for grant of authorization, and Form C, which is called terms and conditions of the authorization. While I was not able to procure any document that corroborated this rule for the decades starting from 1960 to 1980, food officials insisted that it held even back then. This was also corroborated by an FPS dealer who ran a shop at that time.

11. This information was borne out by the statutory rules thereof for FPS dealers as stipulated in 3(E) of the Delhi Specified Food Articles (Regulation of Distribution) (Amendment) Order, 1976, No. F.2(4)/68-75-F&S (P&C)/30089, *Delhi Gazette, Extraordinary*, Part IV, 1976.

12. Interview by author with Badrinath, New Delhi, 30 March 2011.

13. Delhi Rationing Regulations, 1965, Paper II, 20. As for how much each unit stood for, 'The value of each unit in terms of quantity of the rationed article or in terms of the rationed article in combination shall be notified by the Chief Controller in the Official Gazette from time to time'; see Paper II, 17 (2).

14. Interview by author with Jadeja, New Delhi, 15 March 2011.

15. Interview by author with Madanlal Mehta, New Delhi, 7 February 2011.

16. As a member of the Planning Commission, he played an influential role in designing the Second Five Year Plan.

17. Broadcast to the nation titled, 'Produce More, Market More', 10 October 1965 (Shastri 1974: 113).

18. Broadcast titled, 'Young World Mobilisation Appeal', 17 October 1965 (Shastri 1974: 117).

19. Broadcast to the nation titled, 'Produce More, Market More', dated 10 October 1965 (Shastri 1974: 115).

20. Assam Second Guest Control Order, 1966, *Assam Gazette, Extraordinary*, 2, available at http://aasc.nic.in/acts%20and%20rules%20%28goa%29/ Food%20&%20Civil%20Supply%20Deptt/The%20Assam%20Guest%20 Control%20Order,%201966.pdf, accessed on 27 April 2012; No. F.27(2)/76-F&S (P&C), Delhi Guest Control Order, 1976, *Delhi Gazette, Extraordinary*, Part IV, 2.

21. Delhi Guest Control Order, 1976, 3 (3).

22. However, the 1976 order did allow the bride's side to invite any number of guests if only 'liquid refreshments, beverages, potatoes and/or preparation thereof without any admixture of any cereal or non-cereal other than condiments, *chatni*, sauce or ketchup are served' to the said guests who will have to be excluded from those to whom prohibited foodstuffs are served; Delhi Guest Control Order, 1976, 3 (3).

23. No. F.27/(2)/76-F&S (P&C)/11362, Delhi Guest Control (Third Amendment) Order, 1977, *Delhi Gazette, Extraordinary*, Part IV, 3 (1) and 3 (2).

24. All these objections were raised by Brinda Karat, Prakash Javadekar, and other opposition leaders as part of a debate spurred by the many statements made by K.V. Thomas. One of these statements was that 15 per cent of all foodgrains and vegetables were wasted through extravagant functions. See A.M. Jigeesh, 'Food Security: Government finds Lavish Menus Unsavoury', *India Today*, 22 February 2011. The Assam Control Order, 1966 was cited as a model in which a limit of 25 persons for ordinary parties and 100 persons for marriages or funerals was stipulated to avoid wastage in social functions; 'Government Panel to Control Food Wastage at Social Functions', *The Indian Express*, 19 April 2011.

25. See A.M. Jigeesh, 'Food Security: Government finds Lavish Menus Unsavourly', *India Today*, 22 February 2011.

26. Nandini Rathi, 'Proposed Lok Sabha Bill to Prevent Extravagant and Wasteful Expenditure in Weddings: Pros and Cons', *The Indian Express*, 17 February 2017.

27. Bhavya Dore, 'No Rice on Wednesdays and only Two Courses per Person: When Food in Indian Restaurants was Rationed', *Scroll.in*, 25 April 2017.

Also see her article, 'No Band and No Baaja: When Indian Restaurants were Legally Required to be Austere', *Scroll.in*, 27 February 2017.

28. Interview by author with Jadeja, New Delhi, 28 January 2011. Other officials too came up with illustrations of how they were not easy to corrupt, though they were not above showing 'compassion' where necessary. One official, Mehta, sought to explain how he was a clean government officer, 'I used to go on my beat to field sites on a cycle, and when I say I go on a cycle, you know what kind of official I was, if I took bribes or not' (interview by author with Madanlal Mehta, New Delhi, 2 April 2011).

29. Interview by author with Deepak Gupta, Delhi, 4 February 2011.

30. No. F.22(46)/67-DCS (P), 3, Delhi Food (Restrictions on Service of Meals by Catering Establishments) Order, 1967, *Delhi Gazette, Extraordinary*, Part IV, Schedule appended to the order.

31. Interview by author with Jadeja, New Delhi, 28 January 2011.

32. Interview by author with Madanlal Mehta, Delhi, 25 March 2011.

33. Interview by author with Madanlal Mehta, Delhi, 25 March 2011.

34. My usage of this term coined by Emma Tarlo must be read at a single remove from the context in which it originally surfaces. Writing at the time of Emergency, Tarlo was alluding to the insidious genre of sterilization certificates which helped state and DDA authorities to normalize the family planning and eviction drives in Delhi—considering that they put in motion a series of illegal actions, these papers contained half-truths. While 'paper truths' (Tarlo 2003: 62) in the context of this chapter do not quite satisfy such sinister aims, their effects are similar in that the Daily Diary too contained only a semblance of legality and official truth. The official may have visited the wedding site but may not have reported the violation as such in the Diary.

35. Interview with members of a Punjabi family, New Delhi, 18 August 2011.

36. In this story called 'The Survivor'—set partly in Nehru's time as prime minister and later his daughter's tenure—about the frail Maulvi Saheb and his unholy alliance with the politician, Bachchan Babu, Maulvi Saheb holds a lavish wedding for his daughter where 'the number of guests exceeded by ten times the legally permissible limit. The miscreants counted the number of cars and the guests and complained to the police. Maulvi Saheb suffered great humiliation. He contradicted the facts published in newspapers under oath, but there was quite a bit of fuss over it' (Chughtai 2009: 123).

37. Essential Commodities Act (ECA), 1955, 3 (a), *The Gazette of India*.

38. Interview with Rajnath, New Delhi, 15 January 2011.

39. There were separate control orders passed on these tyres and tubes depending on the vehicle or class of vehicle in question: the Delhi Cycle Tyres and Tubes Control Order was passed in 1967; the Delhi Car Tyres and Tubes

Control Order pertaining to taxis and tractors was passed in the same year; and apart from this, the Delhi Automobile Tyres and Tubes Control Order was passed in 1969.

40. No. F.22(13)/69-F&S (P), Delhi Automobile Tyres and Tubes Control Order, *Delhi Gazette, Extraordinary*, Part IV, 1969, 4.

41. Delhi Automobile Tyres and Tubes Control Order, 1969, 5 (5).

42. Delhi Automobile Tyres and Tubes Control Order, 1969, 8 (3).

43. The scale of issue was specified in the Schedule of the Control Order. Private cars could be issued only 5 tyres and 5 tubes; taxis, 8 tyres and 8 tubes; trucks, private carriers, and public carriers, 12 tyres and 12 tubes; and so on in a calendar year as per the Schedule, Delhi Automobile Tyres and Tubes Control Order, 1969. The number was different for vehicles registered in a state other than Delhi.

44. Interview by author with Madanlal Mehta, Delhi, 25 March 2011.

45. Interview by author with Madanlal Mehta, Delhi, 25 March 2011.

46. Interview by author with Madanlal Mehta, Delhi, 25 March 2011.

47. Interview by author with Deepak Gupta, Delhi, 4 February 2011.

3

REFUGEES AND THEIR DISPLACED
DOCUMENTS OF IDENTITY

In any event, will you take a census of the refugees here, particularly of the petty hawkers and vendors so that the authorities may know who are not refugees?[1]

These people from Kalkaji stated that the Delhi state authorities were requiring production of evidence which was not practicable for them but they could produce other evidence which would establish that they fulfil the condition. I have no doubt that you will give consideration to this aspect of the matter and will also take steps to ensure that unnecessary rigidity in the acceptance of evidence is not enforced as long as it can be established that in fact the person fulfils the condition.[2]

These are the persons who have burnt their boat and have centered their hopes and aspirations on free India. In the absence of the Refugee Cards, no one can reveal his identity of being a refugee and no one admits us as refugees.[3]

Some of the most remarkable Partition fiction and scholarship (for example, Hasan 1995; Manto 1997; Reza 1994; Yashpal 2010) have dwelled on the memory and emotional claim-making of refugee subjects who have tried to conjure up imaginary homelands that they may no longer be able to 'corporeally inhabit' (Malkki 1992: 24). In contrast to such scholarship, which has reflected on narratives of displacement, loss of home, and a yearning for community, there has been another wave of scholarship, old and new, that has looked at claim-making in the more literal sense of the term (Dutta 2000; Kaur 2007; Kidwai 2011;

Rao 1967; Rao and Desai 1965; Yashpal 2010). This story of claim-making broadly prefigures the paternalistic enterprise of state-driven rehabilitation of a class of aspiring 'bona fide refugees' who overflowed, to alter Dipesh Chakrabarty's phrase, 'the waiting room' of citizenship (Chakrabarty 2008: 8). It was important to establish them as citizens of either this or that postcolonial and post-partitioned nation—for upon this was predicated their prospects of unencumbered travel, right to franchise, education, employment, and housing. Corresponding to this sea of humanity that deluged both countries, ministries were formed and replaced, legislations enacted and improved upon, definitions of refugees and displaced persons (DPs) fashioned and adjusted, and urban landscapes and administrative dispensations forged. This fostered a visual image of the rehabilitation effort resembling a phoenix that rose only to die and be reborn in new provinces of material need.

Much of this story of claim-making and welfare distribution is replete with urban implications consequent to the refugee influx in Calcutta, Chandigarh, Delhi, Islamabad, Karachi, and Lahore overtaking administrations. In the years following 1947, refugee camps and later resettlement colonies, townships, markets, and businesses in these cities came to be demarcated and defined by the figure of the refugee or the Partition DP. With the exception of the remarkable book by Vazira Zamindar, *The Long Partition and the Making of Modern South Asia: Refugees, Boundaries, Histories* (2007), certain momentous questions have not been asked—questions that straddle the philosophical and the feasible, the material and the intangible, and all of which touch upon the underlying instruments for enumerating, identifying, and in a poignant sense, 'knowing' the refugee dwelling in urban spaces. So, this chapter asks the question: what role did refugee knowledge play in the fashioning of ID documents issued in the aftermath of the Partition? Given that refugees frequently inserted themselves into urban processes of their own ID, it would be fitting to single this aspect out for examination.

Owing to the fraught situations in which refugees had to cross borders, it was not merely their persons and effects but also the ID documents that were issued to them prior to migration that suffered from a sense of displacement. The various actors, that is, the Ministry of Rehabilitation, the housing agencies of Delhi, the Delhi administration, and the refugees themselves, acted in concert to fortify the process of rehabilitation from the chaos of displaced documents of identity. A tendency to embrace alternative norms and protocols of evidence drawn from the itineraries, narrations, and narratives of refugees during the post-Partition rehabilitation phase became evident. Whether they moved to fashion refugee certificates, carry out their own inquiries, or to reimagine evidentiary markers of time and space, refugees unhinged traditional theories of the state monopoly of inscription by impelling governmental authorities to privilege evidence that sprang from their lived experiences. They were able to do so largely because enumeration and the issuing of ID documents were activities that unfolded in urban spaces where the sovereignty of laws, ordinances, and policies was poorly defined and the infrastructure of evidence was tenuous. This argument is, however, enabled by paying attention to the process of claim-making itself rather than its possible failures.[4]

This chapter does not simply seek to show that disparate sets of refugees were precluded from this state move of welfare distribution which was rather generous to upper-caste, property-owning, middle-class Hindu and Sikh refugees. This chapter's task is rather to argue how, within the process of rehabilitation, the form of the survey and the aspect of claim-making, the form of the ID document and forms of refugee knowledge were interwoven. The infrastructure for identifying people and assessing evidence, and even the laws which defined the DP, were shaped by the subjects in question: the refugees, refugee associations, and their demands. In this sense, this chapter suggests that instead of seeing the Partition merely as a moment of disaster and loss, we also see it as enabling in several material and performative senses of staking out claims and fashioning modalities of proving the prolonged fact of refugee-ness.[5]

This was also a moment marked by intensified official predicaments of how to count, whom to count, and what evidence to deem important. While raising questions about the miscellaneous nature of initiatives that entailed enumerating, certifying, and verifying refugees at large, this chapter will focus its inquiries, for the most part, on a smaller universe of those who have been disparagingly referred to as 'refugee squatters' or 'DP squatters' in Delhi. These subjects had to make claims on a scale that ranged from the grand to the miniscule—this included proving their nationality, their date of arrival in the city, their date of occupation of government land or their date of squatting in government-built quarters, and their continued stay in the same space. Within the amorphous urban spaces of a city like Delhi, town planning and health officials worried that the masses of the poor might defy any sanitized taxonomies of displaced and non-displaced squatters, refugee hawkers and non-refugee hawkers, leave alone distinctions between those refugees who arrived within state-ordained datelines and those who came afterwards. Given the onslaught of 'refugee squatters' from West Pakistan, those who came directly to Delhi and those who came to Delhi from different states, and considerations of who came when, urban authorities could hardly resist the temptation to enumerate endlessly. Subsequently, several surveys came to be taken up. Resettlement projects were split over which survey to deem as the benchmark, given that migration across borders and the occupation of contested urban sites were not coeval. Alongside state-issued ID documents, like the refugee registration certificates (RCs), ration cards, and slips from the squatter census, authorities were forced to consider an unconventional bevy of ID documents forged from the telling journeys of refugees. To avoid a dangerous situation where large pools of refugees would have to be neglected simply because they could not produce standardized ID documents, authorities were willing to routinize community moves of self-enumeration. That said, exercises of enumeration devolved into discriminating acts of ID. While refugee associations strove to blur the differences between applicants in order to secure universal housing for their members by using common templates, declarations, letterheads in their petitions and application forms, governmental authorities were tenacious in their search for self-contained familial narratives and the nuclear refugee family. So, while a scholar like Ian Hacking (1982) understandably regards enumeration and collection of statistics to be hallmarks of a modern state, what I would like to belabour in addition is that enumeration's successes would be diminished in the absence of well-defined infrastructures of ID.

   To get a sense of all this, I will start with a picture of the refugee capital of India at the time of the Partition and the infrastructures of evidence it desperately needed. At this juncture, a caveat is in order. Unlike Zamindar whose inquiries into Partition-displaced families too pivot on documentary claim-making, the framing material for this chapter is not evacuee property or travel across borders, but contestations around the ID of poor refugee subjects who laid claim to different schemes of government housing and regularization of accommodation loosely in the period between 1947 and 1960. Another caveat is in order here. This chapter may well disappoint readers who would be justified in feeling that it says nothing about the processes of settling claims around evacuation property. I can only say in response that the evacuee claims aspect of Partition rehabilitation has been the more common subject of discussions on this period and I am rather keen to dwell on the non-propertied poor refugee in search of urban housing who is designated in official files as the DP squatter.

The Chaotic City

The official reports that document the demographic upheaval in Delhi during the period in question gesture at a disproportionate number of Hindu and Sikh refugees who entered Delhi in comparison with the Muslims who left Delhi: by one such estimate, in the four years between 1946 and 1951, 3.29 lakh (0.329 million) Muslims moved out of Delhi while 4.95 lakh (0.495 million) Hindu and Sikh refugees entered Delhi such that its population increased by 1.66 lakh (0.166 million) entirely as 'a consequence of the population movements resulting from Partition' (Rao and Desai 1965: 56). The population of Delhi, according to another estimate, saw a 157 per cent increase from what it was in the year 1941 (0.7 million) to what it came to be in the year 1951 (1.8 million) (Rao and Desai 1965: vii). These statistics were not out of character with the communal trends in the movement of population groups in other northern cities and towns within Rajputana and United Provinces, which were also affected by the Partition. The imagination of the Partition in numerical terms was common to fiction too: a Partition short-story writer remarked that in the town of Dharampore, the number of incoming refugees recorded in the register outnumbered the total Muslim population of the town (Singh 1995: 103).[6] However, Delhi surpassed all other urban centres in the infrastructural and spatial changes it imbibed and allowed as a consequence of the colossal rehabilitation initiative. As petty businesses in Old Delhi's *katras*, tiny retail and merchandise outlets, bookshops and catering establishments, hawkers and vendors, all drawn from the class of refugees and more specifically Punjabi refugees (Dutta 2000: 279), sprang up, the city was faced with a mass of informal settlements.[7]

But perhaps not so well-documented in this scholarship is the arrival of other refugee figures from parts that constitute Pakistan-administered Kashmir into Delhi. Also, the post-Partition resettlement of East Pakistan refugees did not significantly impinge on Delhi; if refugees from East Pakistan came to Delhi at all in any sizeable numbers, this occurred in the aftermath of the creation of Bangladesh and not before that.[8] The East Pakistan refugees were resettled mostly in West Bengal after the Partition; and outside this state, in places like the Andamans, Bihar, United Provinces, Orissa, Madhya Pradesh, Assam, and Tripura.

The planners, autonomous urban agencies, and municipal authorities had to reimagine the built model of the city with due consideration to the unique housing, commercial, and business needs of the incoming heterogeneous potpourri of DPs. To cite Narayani Gupta, Delhi's most prolific historian, the occupation of 'the echoing empty monuments, the stretches of rocky uncultivable land, the open areas west of the Ridge and east of the Yamuna, the houses in Mehrauli and in Shahjahanabad' abandoned by fleeing Muslim families and claimed by other refugees spawned a housing crisis (Gupta 2000: 158). The occupation of open and enclosed spaces by refugees only prompted the growth of government offices, which, in turn, had the effect of inciting fresh in-migration and squatting (Gupta 2000: 158). Lawmakers and administrators could not simply proceed on the assumption that the infrastructure of ID practices that was needed to ease all these refugees into colleges, universities, industries, offices, housing colonies, and commercial outlets would create itself over time. This early hour of state formation and city re-formation had to grapple with a breakdown of infrastructures of evidence. This was because the inherited legal and bureaucratic frameworks were simply no good in stipulating norms for a crisis of ID of a people so alien to the memory and form of the colonial state. The processes to know the many-shaded refugee that were set in motion had to inquire into the residues or the remnants of life as they had been retrieved in the journey from Pakistan to India. And for this, new norms, forms, and parameters of enumerating claimants and verifying their identity had to be devised. It is in this context that we must revisit the epic tale of inscription to note the salience of indigenous forms and habits of knowing, testifying, and stipulating within a novel evidentiary regime of welfare distribution. The insights of Simone (2004), who has theorized that people were present as infrastructure in fragmented cities where dense and unlikely networks across ethnicities and traditional solidarities were forged to make things work in a place like Johannesburg, are relevant, in an altered sense, in the post-Partition Indian context where infrastructures of administering urban welfare regimes were shaped by more conventional networks of refugees.

Definitions of 'Refugee' and 'Displaced Persons'

Before getting to the contestations around refugee ID as they feature in the housing debates that are so salient to this chapter, it is vital to sift through early evidentiary debates around the very definition of refugee as they feature in certain sites of rehabilitation such as education and employment. The chapter will also show how the RC, while initially favoured as proof of the refugee's identity, came to be officially diluted. While refugees were resettled in Punjab, PEPSU, Delhi, United Provinces, Saurashtra, Madhya Bharat, and Rajputana Agency, this chapter will dwell, for the most part, on the story of enumeration, ID, and rehabilitation in Delhi alone.

The Ministry of Relief and Rehabilitation was the most memorable of the protagonists in the rehabilitation story. To get a sense of its far-reaching mandate and the influence it wielded over the other ministries in all matters pertaining to evacuation, property claims, employment, housing, and vocational assistance imparted to the Partition refugees, the reader may refer to *The Story of Rehabilitation* (1967), written by U. Bhaskar Rao and widely cited by all Partition scholars. It comprehensively chronicles the activities of this ministry but does so in a nationalist voice sadly lacking in nuance. The Ministry of Relief and Rehabilitation was set up, in the words of Nehru, as 'a special emergency ministry'; it was re-christened the Ministry of Rehabilitation on 25 April 1949 and wound up all its operations by 1965.[9] It hosted a paraphernalia of secretariats, boards, corporations, offices, bureaus, and sections that emerged and folded up within the larger organizational structure. In the different phases of rehabilitation, boards and corporations like the Rehabilitation Housing Corporation and the Displaced Harijans Rehabilitation Board, which functioned within governmental purview, were allowed a fair deal of autonomy. Recognizing the social welfare credentials of institutions like the Jamia Millia University and private bodies like Gandhi Ashram and the Nai Talim Association, the government roped these bodies too into the effort. These institutions were tasked with momentous missions like fact finding and searches for missing persons, the recovery of abducted women and children, the registration of refugees and their evacuee property claims and compensations, education, industrial employment, agricultural land and housing allotment, regularization of occupied accommodation, and eviction and resettlement. The ministry's interventions were often shortchanged by its severe temporal restrictions and developmental conflicts with other provincial and central ministries. The ministry did not, curiously enough, foresee the indispensability of the RC in the many realms of rehabilitation struggles. In its lieu, it ended up accepting alternative forms of evidence from refugees who demanded that it intervene to either undercut the value of the certificate altogether or issue it universally.

For functional purposes, it was decided that the various offices and bureaus considering refugee candidates for employment in Delhi should respect the definition of refugee as it featured in the Delhi Refugees Registration Ordinance, promulgated in the year 1947. This ordinance defined a refugee as 'any person who has since the first day of March 1947, entered the province of Delhi having left his place of residence elsewhere on account of civil disturbances in that place or the fear of such disturbances'.[10] While this definition did not per se exclude any category of the DP from registration, it was very clear from the date of March 1947—which concurred with the communal riots in Rawalpindi and Multan—that this temporally construed figure of the refugee was constituted entirely by the West Pakistan refugees. Such a definition was hotly contested by those persons who considered themselves refugees and who had their homes and property in parts that fell under West Pakistan, but were 'temporarily' based in the Indian Union where they were 'following some occupations' but 'where they had no homes'.[11] The Ministry of Relief and Rehabilitation had to contend with several accusations of discriminatory definitions whether it was the term 'evacuee' or the term 'refugee'.[12] But the ministry stood its ground and stubbornly defended the ordinance's original definition by showing how legal categories cannot have their basis purely in emotional suffering but must simultaneously convey economic loss:

Widening of the definition of the term 'refugee' would undoubtedly be welcome to many persons who have suffered directly or indirectly as a result of the Partition. But with the limited resources of the country, such widening cannot be contemplated. Unlike the men who come within the present definition, those who have remained in the Indian Union or a foreign country, have not suffered from an interruption in their economic life, and have remained gainfully employed.[13]

So, despite several petitions addressed to the Ministry of Relief and Rehabilitation, it was decided that temporary retrenched employees whose families may be legitimate refugees, government servants whose homes may have been in West Pakistan but were serving at the time of the Partition in the Indian Union, and so on, could not be registered as refugees and correspondingly taken up for consideration by the Transfer Bureau.[14] Curiously, a loss of home, in the enduring sense of the term, which all these refugees may have suffered was not construed to be an interruption in their economic life that was worth compensating. So, even as home remained a constant that had to be documented in most applications in the form of place of residence, its loss was not worth compensating. This is manifest in the statement, 'we should not undertake to register any discharged personnel even if they do not have homes to go back to'.[15] As far as Hindu and Sikh refugees went, the move to define refugee to include only those who 'suffered from an interruption in their economic life', 'those who entered the province of Delhi', or in another description, those who have suffered from 'disturbances', must be read also in terms of a certain information panic given the huge numbers that registration centres, refugee camps, the Transfer Bureau, employment exchanges, and the multitude of registrations agencies already had to handle.

Muslims who may have been desirous of remaining in the country, who suffered just about every kind of loss ranging from economic to psychological, material to cultural, were turned into refugees residing in camps at monuments, mosques, barracks, and the homes of Muslim ministers. Muslims in Delhi who sought relief in refugee camps within the country were not given refugee status. These subjects did not pass muster as far as the legal definition was concerned. Anis Kidwai, the patient chronicler of the stories of Muslims who managed to survive in Delhi, hints that if any paperwork was at all undertaken in the two camps that were set up for them—in Purana Quila and Humayun's Tomb—it had to do with permits to go to Pakistan (Kidwai 2011: 38). This was because the government would have nothing to do with their safe return or rehabilitation in India. Registration of these figures as refugees in India was out of the question. Nehru was alone in terming them refugees and pleading with the Ministry of Rehabilitation to recognize them as such in matters of sealing their shops and confiscating their homes and lands; however, he could not even succeed in getting a special officer appointed within the ministry to look after their affairs.[16]

If Mushirul Hasan and Gyan Pandey have written to document the communal style of the functioning of this ministry and the Delhi administration at large, other scholars have indicated that Muslims were perceived to be evacuees rather than refugees (Hasan 1997; Pandey 1997; Zamindar 2007).[17] The government turned its back on Muslim inmates of relief camps in Purana Quila—it refused to set up peace committees for them, and supplies to these camps were borne by the Muslim League, the ulema of the Jamiat ul-Ulema, and ironically, the Pakistan government (Kidwai 2011: 42; Pandey 1997: 2265). These scholars incisively show how the constellation of acts worked to benefit and award non-Muslim refugees at the cost of the disenfranchisement and the criminalization of the Muslim who wished to return to India, the Muslim who wished to claim compensation for evacuee property, and even the Muslim who wished to remain in India. Even as evacuees, they were cheated of their properties owing to discriminatory laws that redistributed their lands and houses to the incoming Hindu and Sikh refugees.

Another definition of the term 'refugee' was put into effect through a notification of the Ministry of Home Affairs (MHA) on 4 September 1948, published in the gazette. This notification was issued in the name of the powers sanctioned by the Census Act, 1948, in the interest of undertaking a census in various provinces and states, including Delhi, and the definition employed here was: 'any person who has entered India on or after 1 March 1947 having left or been compelled to leave his home in West Pakistan on account of civil disturbances there or the fear of such disturbances or on account of the setting up of two dominions of India and Pakistan'.[18] In stark contrast from the stifling category of refugee in India, Vazira Zamindar notes that the term muhajir was more expansively and liberally defined in the 1951 Pakistan census to accommodate any person who had entered Pakistan 'as the result of or fear of disturbances connected with Partition, no matter from where, when or how long a stay they have come' (Zamindar 2007: 48). The Indian

definition blatantly left out, for purposes of enumeration and rehabilitation, those classes of refugees regarded to have their homes in East
Pakistan. To assuage the sentiments of those East Pakistan refugees who
felt discriminated against by such a definitive and definitional exclusion,
certain rules pertaining to domicile were relaxed where applicants from
these areas sought education and employment after the Partition.[19]

Eventually, the term 'refugee' fell into disuse, yielding way to the
term 'DP' that had fewer resonances of an international crisis. Within
the establishment, there was pressure to perceive Hindus and Sikhs
as internally displaced people rather than as people who belonged to
another state. Besides, the term 'refugee' did not really carry any binding
legal obligations as India had not signed the 1951 Refugee Convention
(Das 2003: 107). According to the new definition, a DP was:

> any person who, on account of the setting up of the Dominions of India
> and Pakistan, or on account of civil disturbances or the fear of such dis-
> turbances in any area now forming part of Pakistan, has, after the 1st day
> of March, 1947, left, or been displaced from, his place of residence in
> such area and who has been subsequently residing in India and includes
> any person who is resident in any place in India and who for that reason
> is unable or has been made unable to manage, supervise or control any
> immovable property belonging to him in Pakistan.[20]

While it may appear that this definition of DP accommodates both
the East and the West Pakistan refugees, such an assumption is belied
by the exclusion of the East Pakistan refugees implicit in acts like the
Administration of Evacuee Property Act, 1950 and the Claims Act,
1950. In these acts, it was made very clear that East Pakistan refugees
could not claim compensation for evacuee immovable property.

The Refugee Registration Certificate

It is time to consider the more important part of the Delhi Refugees
Registration Ordinance, 1947. The term 'registration' in this ordinance
must not be confused with the term 'registration' as it features in an
act like the Claims Act, 1950. The former entailed registration of the
refugee per se, while the latter implied registration of claims in getting
compensation for lost movable and immovable property. This chapter
does not concern itself with registration as it features in the disputes
around compensation for evacuee property.

This ordinance, which came into effect on 11 October 1947, prescribed that refugees register themselves, if not at a camp, at the registration centre of the area within a stipulated time frame, namely, within 15 days from its commencement or within 7 days from the date of arrival in the province, whichever is later. The same piece of legislation specified the protocols for registration, issued the form for applying for an RC, and contained a sample of the certificate itself. Even though this legislation stipulated that refugees must register themselves within a very tiny window offered to them, in practice, they were given more time. As it turned out, the last date for registration for DPs from west Punjab was 10 December 1947, and for DPs from other places in West Pakistan, it was 29 February 1948.[21] If, largely owing to critical feminist scholarship (Butalia 2000; Menon and Bhasin 1998), we have a deep understanding of the patriarchal narrative of post-Partition rehabilitation, as revealed through state moves such as the recovery of abducted women, it may be useful to look for this in the mundane elements of the bureaucratic artifact as well. The ordinance specified the need to identify a male head of the family who alone could register all members of the family 'for the time being with him'. He was to be held responsible not only for all the adult men in the family but also for any person who was 'a female, a minor, a lunatic, an idiot or a person incapable by reason of some physical infirmity of attending at the registration centre'.[22] This shocking move to describe women in the same coin as children, lunatics, and idiots must not be dismissed as a perfunctory linguistic lapse of the archaic officialese used in the ordinance. In the debates on rehabilitation of refugee squatters, we will see how, performatively, the voice and the signature of the female refugee were denuded of powers of agency (to undertake her own registration) and representation (to register the names and claims of others).

The form for the registration of refugees operated in several demographic, historical, experiential, and pastoral registers. In the routine factual and demographic information it sought, this form was like any other in that it asked questions about the name of the refugee, original place of residence, and size of the family. The nature of the enumerative exercise, however, also required refugees to classify present and missing family members within the form (in depersonalized columns, such as members at present 'with the refugee', 'at original domicile', and 'missing'), with complete details relating to each member's relation to the head of the family, his or her literary education, occupation, and monthly income. If all this information was fitted into a section called 'personal data', another section bearing the head of 'resettlement data' inquired into moveable and immoveable property held (in intricate detail pertaining to urban and rural aspects, value that assets added up to), present occupation and desired employment, choice of destination, and whether the refugee was open to travelling anywhere within the country. This section clearly signalled what Foucault would deem the pastoral aspects of power in that authorities tried to render refugees into civil collectives comprising enumerable subjects of governmental care and welfare. The RC that was eventually issued was sparser in the number of entries it contained. The only prominent details that featured in the certificate were the name of the refugee and the head of the family, address before evacuation, and signature or fingerprint (see Figure 3.1).[23]

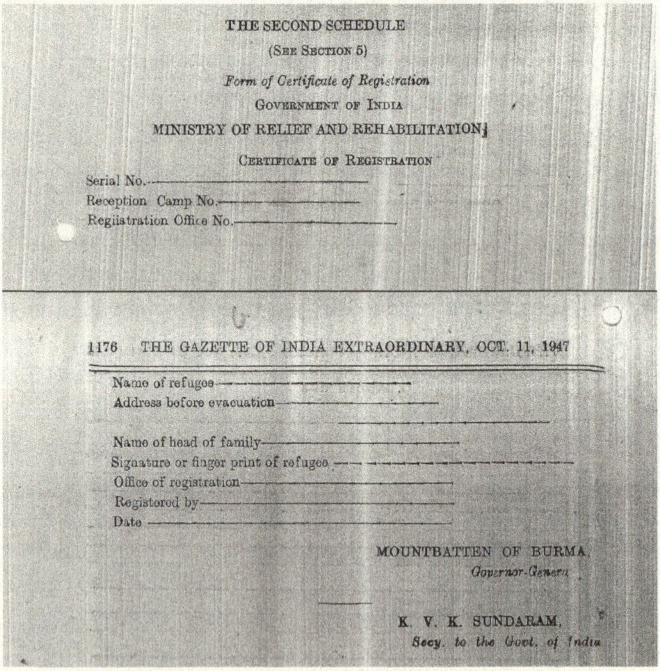

THE SECOND SCHEDULE

(SEE SECTION 5)

Form of Certificate of Registration

GOVERNMENT OF INDIA

MINISTRY OF RELIEF AND REHABILITATION

CERTIFICATE OF REGISTRATION

Serial No.

Reception Camp No.

Registration Office No.

1176 THE GAZETTE OF INDIA EXTRAORDINARY, OCT. 11, 1947

Name of refugee

Address before evacuation

Name of head of family

Signature or finger print of refugee

Office of registration

Registered by

Date

MOUNTBATTEN OF BURMA,
Governor-General.

K. V. K. SUNDARAM,
Secy. to the Govt. of India

Figure 3.1 RC Issued Briefly in the Wake of the Partition
Source: NAI.

A system of classification of refugees was also undertaken—not supported by the ordinance—which went like this: able-bodied men who were capable of finding rural or urban employment; women who could be employed in work centres or who needed to be accommodated in special homes for single women; and the old or disabled who had to be treated as 'permanent liability' and placed in permanent liability camps (Chakravarty 2014: 74).[24] Ravinder Kaur documents how refugees arriving at the Old Delhi railway station were ushered into the refugee registration office located in the nearby building called the Wavell Canteen, where they were issued numbers and then sent through a dubious system of sorting (of the poor to Edward and Outram Lines) camps and (the rich to Hudson and Reeds Lines) barracks (Kaur 2007: 99).

In the early days, registration was deemed compulsory and basic relief could often be denied to those refugees who were not registered.[25] As part of her extensive ethnographic project researching the citizenship claims of Delhi's Punjabi refugees, Kaur makes another interesting observation. Decades after the Ministry of Rehabilitation wound up, the claims process was still kept alive by refugees who thronged resettlement offices, often bearing their RC or card. This card itself came to be assigned different meanings of dependence, helplessness, and self-reliance depending on the subaltern location of the refugee subject (Kaur 2009: 442–3).

While this chapter by no means contradicts these arguments of how such ID documents carried different significations, it advances a different theorization about the popular construction of documents. Documents other than the RC were assembled, contrived, and presented to governmental authorities and refugees sought to control which pieces of evidence came to represent them in a process that blurred categories of the enumerator and the enumerated.

Early Contestations around Refugee Identification

Several petitions were presented to the MHA, the Ministry of States, and the Ministry of Relief and Rehabilitation in the aftermath of this ordinance, for these definitions hardly clarified any matters on the point of the bona fide refugee who needed to be clothed, housed, educated, and recruited, and for all these reasons needed to be 'recognizable' as such. The MHA and the Ministry of Relief and Rehabilitation did feel that the RC was special in that it summoned refugee status like no other document could. However, they found that fewer and fewer people could produce it in the many sites of rehabilitation. So, concessions were made and other documents accepted as 'collateral evidence' in lieu of the RC.

Provisions were made for recruitment of refugees through the Transfer Bureau[26] and in its lieu, employment exchanges. It was decided, after much heartburn and intense debates around equal opportunity, that certain age and fee concessions could also be made for refugee candidates who applied for bureaucratic posts through the open competitive exams held by Federal Public Service Commission (FPSC), which later became the famous Union Public Service Commission (UPSC). From the various petitions addressed to the FPSC, its responses to the same, and its correspondence with the MHA, it was all too clear that this body prided itself on being autonomous; however, given the various classes of concessions it was forced to consider, the FPSC found itself weighed down by the imperative of consulting the MHA if only to secure interpretations of the evidentiary kind. In response to queries from one Harcharan Singh and the FPSC on who a 'bona fide refugee' was, the MHA issued clear instructions through a press note that such a figure was to be identified through RCs or, in their lieu, certificates from responsible gazetted officers of the central government or the district magistrate of the same area where they reside.[27] The same note also stated that for permanent appointments made through FPSC-held open competitive exams, the age limit could be relaxed up to three years (the same as SCs) for refugees. As for the definition itself of the refugee, the MHA simply reiterated the same definition as provided in the 1947 Delhi Ordinance but replaced 'migrated to Delhi' with 'migrated to the Indian Union' (Table 3.1).[28]

Despite these clear guidelines, the ministry had to deal with pleas from desperate petitioners on the grounds that the FPSC recognized RCs but not necessarily certificates issued by gazetted central government officers or the district magistrate. One petitioner, P.M. Advani, proved to be a spot of trouble for the FPSC as he sought to expose the patent incompetence of the commission in failing to recognize the certificate he submitted from the Executive Engineer, Planning Circle of Central Public Works Department (CPWD) (a central gazetted officer). Advani complained first to the FPSC and later to the MHA

Table 3.1   An Illustrative List of Conventional and Makeshift ID Documents Required from Refugees for Employment in Delhi*

Proof of Refugee Status	Proof of Age	Proof of (Previous) Employee Status	Proof of Domicile in India/Proof of Address**
Refugee registration certificate.	Refugee registration certificate (useful while applying for age concession).	Employment letter from Pakistan.	Domicile certificate in India (usually not possible to get because refugee did not enjoy domicile).
Certificate issued by a central gazetted officer.	Certificate issued by central gazetted officer (useful while applying for age concession).	Salary statements/slips.	Declaration of eligibility (issued by the Government of India waiving the domicile rule for refugees).***
Certificate issued by the district magistrate of the area (ideally having 'intimate personal knowledge of the refugee').	Certificate issued by the district magistrate of the area (useful while applying for age concession).	Letter terminating services.	Letter notifying change of domicile due to communal disturbances.
Registered claim of evacuee property.	Matriculation certificate.	Letter from employer who was also a refugee.	Correspondence received at place of residence.

Source: Compiled by author upon close scrutiny of NAI files.

Notes: * Not all these kinds of proof were demanded by any single agency. The emphasis on any given combination of proof varied depending on whether it was the Transfer Bureau, employment exchange, or the FPSC handling the recruitment. The list is also not comprehensive.

** The domicile certificate was usually demanded in eastern provinces like Assam, West Bengal, and Tripura. A declaration of nationality (by birth/domicile/birth and domicile) had to be furnished as part of the application form.

*** Only those who had migrated to India before 30 September 1948 could be treated as domiciled in India.

that he was refused admission to one such exam conducted by the
FPSC (the Survey of India Class II Services Exam) in 1949 on the
grounds that he was too old and he was not able to submit his RC in the
original. However, not all refugees were issued RCs, and alternatives
were issued by the ministry to prove bona fide refugee status in the
absence of the RC. This time, Advani added, he would be appearing for
another exam, the Engineering Services Exam, in 1950, and he wished
the FPSC to accept the certificate he had secured from the CPWD
officer.[29] After much note passing and a few timely interventions by
the MHA, the FPSC deigned to accept a certificate from the district
magistrate of the area but not a central gazetted officer. A bemused and
angry Advani wrote to the district magistrate asking him for a letter
certifying him thus and giving as proof the same certificate from the
CPWD officer. However, the district magistrate's office then asked him
to produce his RC. Advani reacted to his catch-22 situation, typify-
ing so many Indians' frustrated encounters with the bureaucracy, by
writing animatedly, 'thus, it has proved to be a merry-go-round affair.
I have already taken the examination (Roll No. 298) but the Sword of
Damocles hangs over my candidature till this dispute is resolved.'[30]

In the site of education too, workarounds were common.
Recognizing that certificates or even duplicate copies of diplomas and
degrees were going to be impossible to secure in a process of migration
that put life, limb, and property at risk, it was decided to accept, for
admission purposes in schools, colleges, and universities, whatever the
candidates could put together in the form of 'collateral evidence from
responsible government servants', provided it had a ring of credibility and a documentary aura of authenticity.[31] Certain ID documents
acquired bureaucratic acceptability because they were imbued with a
unique congealing of knowledge that was in the possession of certain
individuals or those in situational proximity to them. Within critical
ethnographies of documents, it has been shown that there is a certain
affinity between the artifacts and 'knowledge practices of actors' such
as bankers, auditors, accountants, bureaucrats, and officials; university
officials and hospital officials; and researchers, anthropologists, and ethnographers (Holmes and Marcus, cited in Riles 2006: 7). In the edited
volume called *Documents*, these authors rise marvellously to the call
for comparative ethnographies of field notes, hospital medical forms,
fellowship application forms, jail intake forms, and researcher ethics

and consent forms within a study of dispersed bureaucratic models. The contingent moment of post-Partition rehabilitation threw up its own categories of privileged yet marginal, unprivileged, and marginal knowledge producers (Table 3.2).

Table 3.2   An Illustrative List of Conventional and Substitute ID Documents Required from Refugees for Education in Delhi*

Proof of Refugee Status	Proof of Age	Proof of Educational Qualifications
Refugee registration certificate.	Matriculation certificate.	Copies of self-attested degree certificates.
Certificate issued by a central gazetted officer (who should ideally have 'intimate personal knowledge' of the refugee).	A copy of the matriculation certificate sent directly by the college or university to India (through special arrangement between the Governments of India and Pakistan).	Copies of certificates sent directly by the college or university to India (through special arrangement between the Governments of India and Pakistan).**
Certificate issued by the district magistrate (same rule applies).	Declaration of age or affidavit before a first class magistrate.	Provisional certificate issued by the university.
		Affidavit signed in the presence of a first class magistrate.
		Certificate from the principal (also a refugee) of the college the candidate studied in Pakistan.
		Certificate from a teacher (also a refugee) of the college where the candidate studied in Pakistan.***
		Certificate from the registrar of a university in India (who should

(Cont'd)

Table 3.2 (*Cont'd*)

Proof of Refugee Status	Proof of Age	Proof of Educational Qualifications
		ideally have 'intimate personal knowledge of the refugee'). Certificate from the member of a senate (same rule applies). Certificate from a high gazetted officer of provincial or central government (same rule holds).

Source: Compiled by author upon close scrutiny of NAI files.
Notes: *These workarounds or options to submit substitute documents were also common to the process of admitting refugee children to school.
** This channel of recovering displaced documents (especially from universities in west Punjab) was given up by the Indian government soon after tentative attempts in the direction.
*** This certificate by a college teacher was less acceptable than one by the principal of the college, but where the principal had not made it, authorities were forced to accept this 'collateral evidence'.

While refugee status itself became easy to certify owing to this leeway granted, it was relatively difficult to establish age and birth, and the substitute documents could not be stretched to testify to these aspects of the candidate's biography. The same issue persisted when candidates sought even petty employment as clerks or typists as illustrated by the case of one Bachan Talwar residing in Delhi whose application faced a setback. Though she was able to produce a certificate from a college professor (bearing the attestation of the principal) regarding her educational qualifications, she could only produce a certificate signed by her father (a first class magistrate) regarding her age.[32] And so it was that the RC was conspicuous in the critical sites of claim-making and rehabilitation by its absence as well as its presence. While refugee status was not mandatory to prove through the genre of the RC, other intractable imperatives of certification destabilized expansive gestures of allowing 'collateral evidence'.

Registered DPs and Bona Fide DPs

The discussion so far has made one thing clear: officials were often divided on whom to deem bona fide DPs, persons who were registered or persons who merely possessed credible evidence. By the year 1954, the thought of a DP as being only a registered DP perished, at least at the centre. To understand why this came to be, we need to discern how different states approached registration. For the short time that it was undertaken, registration was compulsory in Delhi, United Provinces, and Rajputana Agency, while it was voluntary in Punjab, PEPSU, and Ajmer-Merwara. In the eastern provinces that received refugees, the policy varied in that West Bengal, Assam, and Orissa rendered it voluntary; Tripura required compulsory registration for a considerably long period of time; Bihar promulgated an ordinance for registration briefly; while Manipur and Andamans did not require registration at all.[33] While most states were averse to the notion of reopening registration after it had wound up in the critical years, a couple of them, namely, West Bengal and the United Provinces (which became Uttar Pradesh), did wish to continue it afterwards. Interestingly, in the NAI files on governmental housing for Delhi's refugees, several applicants were able to cite their registration number, a few were able to produce their RC, but many others were unable either to produce their RC or to cite their registration number. Those DPs from West Pakistan who could not register themselves for various reasons, foremost of which was their late arrival in Delhi, could not however be cut off from rehabilitation schemes. The interminable flow of DPs from East Pakistan arriving in West Bengal could not be afforded the luxury of registration over the decades. Knowing fully well that this would cut off a very sizeable proportion of people from compensations and benefits altogether, the Ministry of Rehabilitation made a wise all-India policy decision to do away with nuanced distinctions between registered and unregistered DPs wherever such doubts could potentially arise.

Rehabilitation benefits were many. They included:

1. financial assistance to displaced students;
2. vocational and technical training;
3. housing loans and plots for house building;
4. allotment of agricultural lands and grant of rural loans to allottees;

5. small urban loans for business and industry;
6. allotment of evacuee property other than evacuee land; and
7. allotment of shops and industrial concerns.[34]

If, initially, benefits under (3), (4), (5), (6), and (7) were reserved only for those who had registered themselves, this distinction was done away in all states and provinces by the ministry's fiat. These and many other rehabilitation benefits like pensions and maintenance allowances were recognized in the interim compensation plan. This plan integrated such general benefits with compensations and made them available to all DPs from West Pakistan, registered or not. The first two benefits were eventually made available to other DPs too from East Pakistan and Pakistan-administered Kashmir. However, registration was 'not a condition precedent for the grant of compensation' or rehabilitation benefits for any DP.[35] While there were some objections, especially from the Uttar Pradesh (which was earlier called United Provinces) government, on the question of retaining this distinction for purposes of disbursing loans, the ministry instructed all states to accommodate as many DPs as possible while giving precedence to registered DPs.

It is evident that though, in the initial years, states sought to reserve welfare schemes for registered DPs, over time, this policy could not be sustained for long. The notion of the registered DP as the ideal subject of welfare gave way to the concept of the bona fide DP. In the year 1954, the Ministry of Rehabilitation felt strongly against the idea of allowing refugees to register for an indefinite period of time: 'All that was deemed necessary was that in order to get the rehabilitation benefits, the DPs should establish their bona fides ... to keep uniformity throughout India, we should adopt one principle so that any group of DPs may not have any grievance.'[36] It was deemed unfeasible to continue registration in any given state owing to trends of inter-state movement and fears of double registration. So, this gave birth to the category of the bona fide refugee who needed only to prove his refugee status and not the fact of his registration. However, in the absence of the RC, how could this be accomplished?

Ration cards were also a possible means of documentation, though not certification, of the refugee. It was important to print them in all regions that received refugees in substantial numbers. In Partition fiction, these documents are recognized as a motif of rehabilitation.

For example, Yashpal, in his magnum opus, *Jhootha Sach* (the translated book is titled *This Is Not That Dawn*), writes that in Jullandhar, the first bulk order a printing press received was one for ration cards (Yashpal 2010: 506). In Delhi, these cards came in three forms, namely, ration cards issued in refugee camps, temporary ration cards issued on a monthly basis, and permanent ration cards (which replaced the temporary ration cards). The ration cards issued in camps were short-lived, much too short-lived, so much so that the meagre welfare gesture that they embodied was criticized by refugees. Yashpal signals this in his novel by rendering his characters in a Delhi refugee camp so helpless that they had to borrow ration cards belonging to other families (Yashpal 2010: 616). Temporary ration cards were renewed on a monthly basis and issued to individuals. The permanent ration card replacing the temporary ration card was issued to families and introduced in the year 1953, and then discontinued within a year owing to the imposition of decontrol. Where permanent cards were concerned, it was not until some time had passed that the refugees could lay claim to them, and given the reports of rampant fraud in the ration cards issued in a camp like Kingsway,[37] ration card as proof of refugee status (in the absence of the RC) was somewhat tenuous. The DRO sought to keep tabs on the permanent ration cards that needed to be issued and cancelled by printing notices in a newspaper like the *HT*. Here, it asked outgoing Muslim refugees and incoming Hindu and Sikh refugees to surrender and apply for these cards (Kaur 2007: 92–3). The unpredictable rhythms of the Partition could hardly validate such an expectation and the ration card itself could only constitute a very flimsy claim to the status of the bona fide refugee. In the debates that ensue, we will see how several other substitutes to RCs and ration cards were suggested, disputed, and eventually accepted.

The Census as a Mode of Rehabilitation

The famous economist V.K.R.V. Rao describes the First Five Year Plan as having favoured the strategy of correcting an economy riddled with war-induced inflation and Partition-related shortages over any grand scheme for the economic reconstruction of the country. Having to deal with the economic and political aftermath of the Partition through the effort of providing relief and rehabilitation thwarted the impulse to do

'anything spectacular or significant ... by way of economic development', he writes (Rao 1952: 6). The First Plan then would appear to
slow down the developmental state as it took stock of its humanitarian
crisis such that it sought to justify everything as a cost of rehabilitation. The gargantuan rehabilitation effort was to entail the supply of
temporary relief in the form of rations and doles, the conversion of
relief camps into work centres, creation of jobs, and ultimately, the
provision of housing and the construction of townships and other
urban settlements where camps existed.[38] The Ministry of Relief and
Rehabilitation sought to regulate the batches of incoming refugees in
different states such that no state got more than its manageable quota
of refugees and that surpluses were not incurred.[39] An all-India conference of the heads of rehabilitation departments of all states was held in
July 1948 to decide provincial quotas (Rao 1967: 59). To ensure that
no state or province was forced to face a spate of refugees, the ministry
suggested that refugee censuses be undertaken in each such place that
receives refugees and added that the 'cost of taking the census should
be considered an expenditure on rehabilitation'.[40] Such an operation
was to be conducted by the census commissioners and census officers
and the compilation of these censuses could be undertaken under the
powers bestowed by the Census Act, 1948.

As Foucault would have it, insofar as they desired to make spaces,
people, and assets visible to governments, censuses captured the historical turn from the government of things to the science of government (Foucault 1991). The census has been universally acknowledged
to be an 'instrument of knowledge' in that it relays information that
may be purposed into taxation, revenue extraction, conscription, and
the management of disease and mortality (Cohn 1987; Mann 2007).
This practice of information gathering has simultaneously alerted us to
the possibilities of creating enduring categories of power through the
census' ingrained habits of codification and classification of populations
into communities and collectivities (Cohn 1987; Dirks 2001). The enumerative modality of the state has been regarded as a vital function of
its scientific rationality and the census has been termed 'a scientific
undertaking' (Mann 2007). A few lone voices in this gallery of scholarship, such as Sumit Guha, Rebecca Jean Emigh, and Norbert Peabody,
have challenged the tendency of historical speculation in assuming that
states undertake enumeration of ostensibly integrated societies that

are regarded 'passive on-lookers' or 'unwitting imperial praetorians' (Peabody 2001: 820) who, at best, coax authorities to represent them in accordance with their desired social ranking. Sumit Guha then urges us as scholars to look at censuses less as insulated quantitative enterprises and more as collaborative ones. We need to be asking how societies are politically involved in each historical stage of numerical representation without becoming reduced to be 'creatures of the colonial or postcolonial imagination' (Guha 2003: 163). This is not true of India alone. As Emigh writes, even early modern European societies contributed to state enumeration. Through an interesting analytical move, she regards states as drawing on the pre-existing numeracy (or the number-literate habits of populations) of various sections of society like shopkeepers, tenants and landlords, and religious institutions. Exercises in enumeration could be present as 'interactive social process' (Emigh 2002: 655) and not always as 'scientific undertakings' (Mann 2007).

This chapter deals with a profusion of surveys and censuses of refugees, very few of which have been acknowledged in social science scholarship. If some of them may be read with a capital 'S' and 'C', being nationwide information-gathering initiatives, urban exercises in enumeration have occupied a more innocuous space in the postcolonial imagination. The urban refugee surveys and censuses taken in Delhi demonstrate Sumit Guha's point amply in that authorities decentralized and democratized these exercises not only to involve a bevy of local authorities but also to admit a range of unusual modes of gathering information. Refugee communities were asked to provide declarations of their identity, to be present at public hearings where individual depositions were heard and evidence examined, and identity cards printed by refugee associations were considered. These bodies were told to collect and collate information in bulk about members, and private institutions were charged with undertaking micro surveys of orphaned refugee children, squatters, and hawkers.

The rehabilitation authorities were forced to be inventive and think of different means to accommodate the swelling numbers who came in waves to Delhi in the years following the Partition. Not surprisingly, one of the early Ministers of Rehabilitation, Mohanlal Saksena, admitted quite openly that land policy was so fraught that even with state assistance, refugees and especially those with low income could scarcely afford the 'soaring' costs of construction.[41] The chosen courses of rehabilitation had to be such that they did not alienate the city's planners and key municipal figures seized by a keen developmental vision and an urban manifesto for Delhi. The city's housing authorities were forced to take not one or two but several surveys and censuses to identify potential refugee beneficiaries for allocation. The decennial 1951 census included a definition of the term 'DP' and included questions like, 'Are you a displaced person from Pakistan? If so, when did you arrive in India from Pakistan and what was your original district in Pakistan?'[42] A special refugee census was to be undertaken in Delhi in October 1948 featuring the most comprehensive range of questions probing place of residence and details of family dwelling, rural and urban immovable property owned in Pakistan, place of accommodation in India (allowing for details like house, refugee camp, dharamshala, and in the open), rehabilitation benefits received from the Indian government, and property and business owned in India.[43] But neither of these important forays into refugee enumeration served the hybrid forms of housing compensation that had to be devised for these classes of persons. In their place, more modest and improvised surveys came to be undertaken, necessitating a set of information-gathering practices that blurred the lines between the enumerator and the enumerated, the sovereign and the governed. Enumeration may have found its ultimate disguise of governmentality as a benign cost of rehabilitation, but such a cost was to be dispersed across a wide cross-section of society. However, even in a democratized form, how effective was it? To know this, I turn my gaze next to the story of housing for the poorer refugees in Delhi who had to be evicted, allotted minimal plots, have their houses regularized, and for all these purposes, to be enumerated, identified, and known.

De-camouflaging the 'Refugee Squatter' through the Survey

Let us start with a telling story of the deep anxiety surrounding refugees that had taken hold of the Ministry of Health, which wielded considerable power and jurisdiction in matters pertaining to the Delhi Improvement Trust (DIT).[44] I use the term 'squatter' self-consciously as I do not wish the subjects being talked about here to be reduced to the term's disparaging attributes—not unlike the term 'slum dweller' (Menon-Sen and Bhan 2008: 3)—but I rather employ it to refer to the visual imaginary of poverty, squalor, congestion, and a tendency to indiscriminately occupy vacant spaces with which official writings equate certain classes of persons. I also use the term squatter here not simply to refer to slum residents but very loosely to correspond with the way this figure was invoked in the myriad stories of encroachment considered in its many forms, that is, the unauthorized occupation of all kinds of public, private, and housing agency-held land, government-built quarters, and plots developed for refugees. Formed in the year 1937 in the wake of the very influential report that A.P. Hume wrote about the imperative need to decongest Old Delhi, the DIT was conceived 'as a coordinating agency, well equipped to develop different kinds of land in the city, government and private, while enforcing building bye-laws scrupulously' (Sharan 2014: 132). However, more importantly, it also tried to undertake slum clearance and improvement alongside the development of extension areas, link displacement of poor residents to the provision of resettlement (Hosagrahar 2005; Sharan 2014: 131), and in this sense, sought to impart a certain humane vision to the amelioration of the city. Its failure to do so and the reasons for that failure as elaborated by the Birla Committee Report (1951), as well as the various initiatives to improve and supersede this city improvement body in the report's aftermath, such as the DIT Enquiry Committee (1950), the Town Planning Organisation (1955), the Delhi Development Provisional Authority (1955), and later the DDA (1957), have been widely documented elsewhere (Hosagrahar 2005; Sharan 2014; Sundaram 2010).

What interests us here is how the DIT responded to the frustrating mandate to house refugees and refugee squatters in Delhi. While it was conceived as an objective and impartial agency, free of 'the ponderous sub-committees' of the Delhi municipality, that would be 'working midway between government and the local body',[45] it failed to escape the moorings of wilful municipal actions. The DIT was also not able to secure any relief from the blanket assurances that the Ministry of Rehabilitation and the political establishment made to refugees. The fact that land was made available to both the DIT (for city improvement) and the Ministry of Rehabilitation (for refugee housing) incited friction. By the end of 1954, more than 2,250 acres of land, including 174 acres of developed land belonging to the DIT, was transferred to the Ministry of Rehabilitation.[46] The DIT had to wait for the ministry to give them various lists of refugee allottees before they could proceed with slum clearance schemes. At a certain point in time, officials of the DIT also complained that they could not carry on their slum clearance schemes even when those did not interfere with the housing of refugees in rehabilitation colonies by the Ministry of Rehabilitation.[47] The DIT's petulant responses smacked of its refusal to admit the city planning problem to be overlaid with a more human predicament of creating infrastructure for refugees.

To get a sense of this, I will dwell very briefly on the rhetoric of the eccentric, if somewhat well-meaning, health minister, Rajkumari Amrit Kaur, concerning the figure of the (refugee) squatter. Kaur is remembered for the pioneering role she played in inviting the Ford Foundation to help in creating a Master Plan for Delhi, steering various committees around town planning, and the prominent linkage that she drew between the control of epidemics, sanitation, and the decongestion of the city at large (Sundaram 2010: 36–7). In her 'Foreword' to the *Interim General Plan for Greater Delhi*, she wrote, 'if the "matter of sanitation" was already overdetermined by the "promiscuous buildings and lay-outs", "over-crowding everywhere and miserable slum areas, miles of ribbon developed hut-shops", the inflow of refugees "has also entailed endless difficulties for the proper development of the metropolis"' (Ministry of Health, Government of India, 1956: 1 [?]).[48]

Greatly exercised by the dubiously massive scale of unauthorized construction on what she regarded as sacred DIT land, Kaur first wrote to Mohanlal Saksena, the Minister of State for Relief and Rehabilitation, on 16 March 1949:

> I am getting more and more perturbed about the refugee situation in Delhi. I am in charge of local self-government and also responsible for health. It is difficult to serve Delhi in either of these spheres under the existing circumstances. It seemed to me during my last drive through Old Delhi and the shopping areas of New Delhi that, far from a decrease, there would appear to be an increase in the number of refugee hawkers and unauthorized constructions. I enclose a note left to me by the Chairman of the DIT from which you will see that, in spite of the generosity with which DIT land has been made available for permanent construction, there has been illegal encroachment on the part of refugees to the tune of the best part of 5000 acres of Trust land. These unauthorized structures are not always temporary, indeed some of them are

semi or altogether permanent and the sad part of it is that they are not according to any plan and not in accordance with the municipal bye-laws. Even some of the permanent structures, in Northern Extension area for example, will eventually have to be treated as slums. I understand that a fair percentage of the pavement-hawkers does not belong to the refugee population, but of course, all such take cover under the plea that they are refugees.[49]

Kaur believed that the state of sanitation in Delhi had taken a turn for the worse and she attributed this deterioration in no small part to the congestion of Delhi caused by the unauthorized construction and the indiscriminate hawking practices of the refugees. Not trusting the Ministry of Rehabilitation to act without an instruction from the MHA, she addressed the Home Minister, Sardar Vallabhbhai Patel, in a separate letter. In this correspondence, she informed him that the municipality's and the DIT's hands were tied and pointed out that these subjects had been emboldened by the presence and the stance of the Ministry of Relief and Rehabilitation that 'their (refugee) structures will not be demolished for three years' until alternative accommodation is given to them. Those guilty of unlawful construction and the forcible occupation of buildings were not hindered so that 'an impetus is being given, as it were to people to flout the law'.[50] In extending the suggestion of satellite townships to accommodate refugee squatters as well as many other professional classes, she felt that 'Delhi itself cannot and should not really be expected to give permanent rehabilitation to more than a very few'.[51] In this, she was supported by no less a figure than Nehru himself. In one of his letters, Nehru suggested the decongestion of Delhi through the possible construction of satellite townships at a distance of 20–5 miles around Delhi.[52] The DIT took this proposal seriously, as evidenced by the emergence of several townships in Faridabad, Sheikh Sarai, Tihar, Kalkaji, and Mehrauli.

While writing to Mohanlal Saksena, Kaur expressed the collective desire (felt by her, the chief commissioner of Delhi, and also the DIT) for a census, which alone would help authorities identify the refugees who were camouflaged by their squatter-like garb of poverty. Observe the following statement, 'in any event, will you take a census of the refugees here, particularly of the petty hawkers and vendors so that the authorities may know who are not refugees?'[53] She pleaded that the rehabilitation effort must not unfold in a wanton fashion unmindful

of the larger problem of congestion and even if it did, it could not take
a generous stance on all refugee squatters. Distinctions were sorely in
need of being made; and though she does not refer to it anywhere, it is
clear that Kaur was not satisfied with the refugee census of 1948 as it
did not meet the very special needs of fashioning some order out of the
burgeoning chaos of a squatter-dotted Delhi. While a squatter survey
did indeed take place in 1952, this survey may have been the result
of Kaur's exhortations, though I cannot corroborate this. It may be
felicitous to mention here that such a deep conundrum of telling apart
poor refugees from refugees in general was common to other provinces
too. Rao writes about the 'responsibility of separating genuine refugees
from others who had sneaked into the Sealdah station premises' (Rao
1967: 152). Not surprisingly, such a conundrum was greeted with the
issuing of tokens to DP squatters in Calcutta and slips or identity cards
to refugee families in Delhi.

The Decade of the Survey: A Quick Overview of Squatter Enumeration in the 1950s

Between the years 1947 and 1960, there were at least five exercises
of enumeration in which squatters figured (see Table 3.3). In the year
1950, a sensational set of assurances was given to refugees who were
branded squatters because they had set up 'unauthorized constructions'
on government, DIT, *nazul*,[54] and private lands and had taken possession of government-built houses meant for other DPs. These were
popularly termed the Gadgil Assurances, named after N.V. Gadgil, the
Minister of Works, Housing and Supply, who chaired the committee
that devised them. It would not be amiss to point out that the term
'unauthorized constructions' was not only jarring for such persons but
was also empirically contested by refugee associations largely because
their houses were constructed on typically 'a waste, arid stony tract
used mostly as a convenient common open latrine'.[55] How could
construction on what was wasteland be 'unauthorized', argued such
associations. However, these assurances enabled refugee associations
formed by these people to stand their ground firmly in the face of
eviction and even resettlement to places that they did not wish to be
removed to. But the same set of assurances became an albatross around
the neck of housing and town planning authorities, especially the DIT,

Table 3.3 A List of Censuses and Surveys in Delhi between 1947 and 1960 in which 'Refugee Squatters' were Counted*

Year of Survey or Census	Nodal Authority in Charge of the Exercise	The Category of Refugees Enumerated	The Act Guiding the Survey or Census	Bounded Area of Enumeration	Number of Refugee Squatters (as cited in official records)
1948	Ministry of Home Affairs and the deputy commissioner, Delhi.	A refugee census in Delhi undertaken as part of a special refugee census in select provinces and states across India.	Census Act, 1948	The urban limits of Delhi taken as a whole.	Figure not specified.
1951	Ministry of Home Affairs	Refugees were counted as part of the larger exercise of the decennial census.	Census Act, 1948	In all regions that saw a refugee influx.	Figure not specified.
1952 (technically late 1951 and early 1952)	Ministry of Rehabilitation (but more specifically, the Department of Rehabilitation, Delhi).	Refugee squatters alone were counted in this survey.		In all areas (government land, Trust land, nazul land, and private land) within the urban limits of Delhi where refugees squatted.	27,700 families.

(Cont'd)

Table 3.3 (*Cont'd*)

Year of Survey or Census	Nodal Authority in Charge of the Exercise	The Category of Refugees Enumerated	The Act Guiding the Survey or Census	Bounded Area of Enumeration	Number of Refugee Squatters (as cited in official records)
1957	Delhi Development Authority	All squatters, refugees included.		Nazul land in Delhi where refugees squatted.	6,744 refugee squatter families out of a total of 11,864 squatter families.
1960	Ministry of Home Affairs, and the chief commissioner, Delhi in particular.	Construction labour, local squatters, and DP squatters.		All public land (including but not limited to government land) where unauthorized constructions were set up.	45,000 families in all (number of refugee squatters unknown).[56]

Source: Compiled by author upon close scrutiny of NAI files.

Note: *Quite apart from these surveys, a wealth of localized small surveys of refugee squatters in satellite townships and rehabilitation colonies came to be undertaken in the 1950s by the housing and rent officer, Delhi.

every time they tried to clear unauthorized constructions in a sector. When the Delhi Premises (Requisition and Eviction) Act, 1947 was sought to be amended in the year 1950 through the passing of a bill in the Parliament, it evoked objections on questions like the recovery of rent arrears and the resettlement of refugees in places removed from their businesses and livelihood. By substituting the term 'government premises' with 'public premises', this bill sought mainly to strengthen the DIT's legal position as an authority that could, in its own right, evict people from land and buildings that fell under its possession. This was an important move, as far as the DIT was concerned, given that its land did not qualify strictly as land belonging to the municipality or the government.

A select committee was formed, composed, among others, of representatives from the local administration; and it was in the light of the recommendations of this committee that Gadgil announced several assurances that became a touchstone for rehabilitation policy in this decade. While these assurances were manifold, the most important of them had to do with extending preferential treatment in the form of alternative accommodation to a streamlined, 'original' set of refugees who set up unauthorized constructions in Delhi before 15 August 1950. Beyond this, those DPs who occupied public land or constructed a whole or a part of a building between 15 August 1950 and 1 January 1951 were to be evicted with three months' notice without any compensation. Finally, those refugees who were squatters in the same category in the period after 1 January 1951 could be summarily evicted after just 10 days' notice. The original set of DPs were to be resettled 'as far as possible' in places close to their business and employment. The DIT, though mandated with 'the responsibility of having a well ordered plan for the city of Delhi', was to modify it so that there would be very little destruction of such constructions.[57] And so, especially in the matter of dealing with the original set of refugees, what were deemed unauthorized constructions could even be regularized especially where they could be made to comply with municipal requirements and town improvement plans. After an assessment of the value of the land, squatters were to be given the option of buying such land, on a no-profit, no-loss basis, in easy instalments. Those families who figured in the survey were either handed plots, or government-built houses, or were allowed to remain in their houses if they were eligible for regularization.

Eligibility chits were given to those whose houses were demolished to pave way for resettlement and it was these chits that sheltered the claims of squatters who called themselves 'allottees'.[58]

All this, of course, begged the necessity for a survey that came to be undertaken by the Delhi Department of Rehabilitation in the late months of 1951 and the early months of 1952. Following these mandates, the Ministry of Rehabilitation was roped in to prepare a sector-wise plan to monitor the clearance of slums in each sector to ensure that no bona fide refugee, who now devolved into a bona fide refugee squatter, was left behind. These assurances and the survey itself would not have materialized had it not been for the powerful demands against eviction made by refugee associations that had set themselves up in the wake of the rehabilitation effort. These associations demanded a census or some information-gathering exercise that would result in guarantees on paper for all those considered DP squatters. However, that was not all; it may well be that the form of the survey itself was shaped by refugee associations. While I do not have information about the specific questions that were asked during this survey, this exercise would have had to depend on crucial bits of proof showing that a refugee was a squatter on land prior to 15 August 1950. While sifting through the survey information, DIT even decided to take into sympathetic consideration those who had arrived after 15 August 1950 but prior to the date of the survey. It sorted this set of refugees into a secondary category.[59] The memorandums of refugee associations suggest that their leaders in different localities were influential in collating information about residents for the survey.[60] These developments are an important precursor to the more recent, post-2000 phenomenon of the Delhi government relying on resident welfare associations of unauthorized colonies to prepare maps of their localities for regularization. All this, as we will see, will go to show a tendency for enumerated subjects to insert themselves into genres of evidence for their rehabilitation.

However, this 1952 survey, which, by official estimates, counted 27,700 squatter families in all (20,500 families who 'squatted before 15 August 1950' and 7,200 families 'who were found squatting on the date of the survey'), was criticized for various exclusions. In the later years of this decade, other claimants pressed their case against their omission. Some of them were DPs who were present before the survey dates but were not counted. There were others who squatted later but had to be compassionately included because they had suffered the consequences of rain—such squatters were often labelled 'rain sufferers'; and so it was that the demand for a survey itself was framed as a case for compassion for DPs. However, the spectre of discerning them from the ubiquitous masses of squatters in general persisted and the last survey that I mention here came to be undertaken in 1960.[61] By this time, it was decided that the DP squatters, barring a few concessions under the Gadgil Assurances, would simply be subjected to the Delhi Slum Clearance Act, 1956 applicable to all slum residents. If this was the time that the Ministry of Rehabilitation was winding up its operations for West Pakistan refugees, this was also the time that the DIT was being replaced by the Delhi Development Provisional Authority (in 1955) and later the DDA (in 1957).

The DDA, which was responsible for creating the first Master Plan for Delhi (1960–80), was given a vast mandate for 'large-scale acquisition, development and disposal of land' (Jain 1990: 78). If this housing authority shouldered a responsibility to 'prevent bad layout and haphazard construction of buildings' (Jain 1990: 77), it was not supposed to neglect the all-important business of handing houses and plots to slum families at select resettlement sites. Not surprisingly, it did not live up to this mandate, pleading lack of financial resources and land (Kundu 2004: 260–1). The DDA, in the year 1957, held a survey but this was mainly confined to counting those who had set up constructions on nazul land. The last enumeration exercise I refer to here was termed a squatter census; it was held in 1960 and it was by far the most interesting experiment of them all because it engendered the creation of an identity card for all those enumerated (see Figure 3.2).[62] This survey was needed to get a picture of all squatters (including refugee squatters) on all public land and not just nazul land or government land considered separately. Owing to its ambitious mandate to count all such residents who fell under the jurisdiction of disparate housing agencies and municipal bodies such as the New Delhi Municipal Council (NDMC), the Municipal Corporation, and the DDA, it was decided that no less an authority than the MHA and the chief commissioner of Delhi would oversee the census. It was ordered as an exercise that would pull-off various stunts: to paint a picture of all the residents squatting on land that the DDA needed for development; to ensure that new encroachments could be policed in the light of the Master

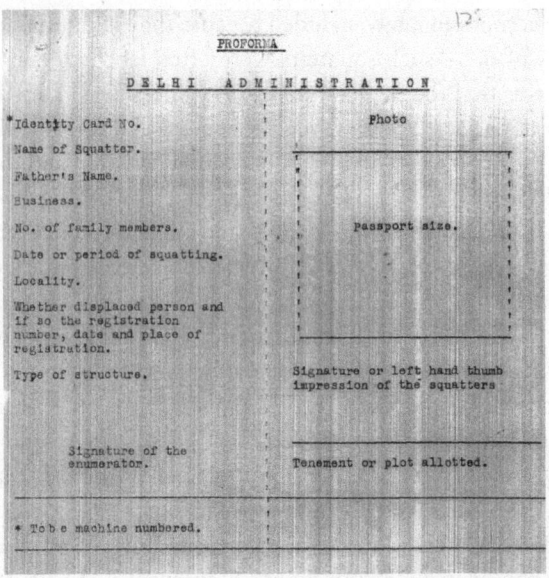

Figure 3.2　ID Card Issued as Part of the 1960 Squatter Census in Delhi
Source: NAI.

Plan; and to extend a minimum of preferential treatment to the DP squatters who were to be distinguished from the others (construction labour and local squatters). The census was eventually conducted in June–July 1960, and it was followed by a sweeping clearance drive of slums in several areas across Delhi—like the surveys before it and the ones that followed, this one too, futilely, sought to distinguish between those who came before and those who came after the date of the survey (Sivaramakrishnan and Agrawal 2003: 154; Tarlo 2003: 72).

Perhaps because this census was cast within the narrative of the 'Greater Plan' for Delhi, it concerned itself with all kinds of squatters and not just displaced squatters. Consider, for instance, the request of the Assistant Architect, DDA, to the Ministry of Rehabilitation for information about the exact location of all unauthorized constructions in rehabilitation colonies so that the Master Plan could either reflect them or account for them in some way.[63] It was in this context of the slow disappearance of the Ministry of Rehabilitation and the overarching anxieties of the Master Plan that the survey was held and

ID cards issued to squatters. This would also explain why authorities took a hardheaded and cold approach to evidence after the 1960s. A heap of still-ongoing court cases accumulated in the Delhi High Court over the Gadgil Assurances featuring the DDA pitted against DP slum residents who sought regularization. The DDA was able to confound these petitioners with a frustrating tendency to hinge its arguments on minutiae such as the non-correspondence of successive ration cards issued to the same person, the unavailability of the RC or any other document, smudged dates and serial numbers, and questionable signatures.[64] Substitute ID documents and a general latitude in considering evidence held no water here.

This census was to be carried out in a single day across the urban areas of Delhi—but the tabulation and the issuing of identity cards that followed the exercise may have taken two months all told. It required enumerators to fill out a form with answers to multiple questions that, among others, asked 'whether the occupant is a registered Displaced Person and is entitled to certain benefits in terms of Gadgil Assurances'.[65] This proforma was to be printed and bound within several consecutive registers. This census also incorporated astonishing features of photographing the squatter on the spot. If this early use of photography in ID was not interesting enough, the head of each squatter family was made to carry on his chest a slate which bore his name and the chalked-in serial number allotted to him in the register containing the proformas (see Figure 3.2).[66] And so when the ID card was issued, a correspondence between the document and the register would be hard to fudge. A record of squatters complete with a primitive form of de-duplication was achieved.

If one were to modify Appadurai's famous phrase of 'number in the colonial imagination' slightly, it would be possible to dub moves such as this one as an attempt to inscribe the number in the postcolonial imagination. Appadurai, in considering the colonial turn to enumeration, deemed the enterprise to count Indian caste-based communities as one that produces hitherto non-existent congealed entities of the collective self (Appadurai 1993).[67] In this, Appadurai was complementing the work of others like Bernard Cohn and Sudipta Kaviraj who regarded the colonial census to objectify and reify caste as a category and create 'enumerated communities' of the Indian self (Cohn 1987; Kaviraj 2010). In his famous writing on the census and the objectification of caste, Cohn writes that the colonial census, in collaboration with pandits and other Sanskrit scholars, which created ranking orders of social hierarchy among the castes of India led to newfound aspirations of status, privilege, mobility, and prestige. Where earlier caste was a free-floating entity embedded in 'a whole matrix of custom, ritual, religious symbol, a textually transmitted tradition', region, and period, it was now abstracted into a singular and distinctive identity (Cohn 1987: 229). Building on this scholarship, Appadurai writes, 'the huge diversity of castes, sects, tribes, and other practical groupings of the Indian landscape were thus rendered into a vast categorial landscape untethered to the specificities of the agrarian landscape' (Appadurai 1993: 327).

Unlike the number in the colonial imagination, the number in the postcolonial consciousness was not so much about socially transforming groupings of subjects into fixed and immutable collectivities. It was rather about inscribing numbers and individuals within a tightly configured relational grid of information such that they would defy understanding except in correspondence to each other. It was to be played out in other moments of documentation, like the creation of the corresponding number in the muster rolls and the job cards issued to workers under the famous Mahatma Gandhi National Rural Employment Guarantee Scheme (MGNREGS) (Mathur 2012: 171). Over time, as newer and newer technologies of classification entered the governmental realm, it became commonplace to strive for more complex computed correspondences of questionnaires, biometrics, numbers, and faces with a single individual. However, whatever may be the latest preoccupation with techno-fantasy in the realm of enumeration, number in the postcolonial imagination was carried out through 'a negotiated order achieved by a vast system of forms' (Bowker and Star 1999: 26), certificates, earlier officials, and later, computers and softwares. While new theorizations of what number denotes in the hyper-informatized networks of welfare are under way (Bowker and Star 1999; Lampland and Star 2009), they may have to rework older formulations specific to the history of enumeration in certain parts of the world.

Housing Schemes for Refugees

The Partition rendered the state a powerful actor and 'the largest owner of real estate' in Delhi largely owing to its prerogative in disposing of evacuee properties or immovable properties in the nature of houses, workshops, factories, shops, and agricultural lands (Kaur 2007: 96). In the telling of the multi-sited story of rehabilitation, the role of local authorities—the Ministry of Health, the DIT, and later, the DDA— who had to reconcile the impetus to provide housing compensation with the grander plan for Delhi (which in time would be christened the Master Plan) has been generally ignored. The DIT and the DDA have featured as protagonists in various stories of town and city planning but not so much in stories of rehabilitation in Delhi. It has been quite rightly pointed out how the DDA, as an authority that was empowered to dispose of the vast swathes of agricultural land that it acquired, squandered its great privilege to resettle the poor in developed plots (Dupont 2008: 79). A sizeable proportion of this urban poor who fell by the wayside were refugees whose cases were advanced by refugee associations and political leaders, and considered minutely by the Ministry of Rehabilitation.

As the housing needs of the many refugees who came to Delhi could not all be addressed by the allotment of evacuee property that the Ministry of Rehabilitation came to handle, other options were then explored: the acquisition of agricultural land; the creation of colonies and townships; and the allotment of plots. Four modalities of housing refugees were eventually proposed and accepted. These were the development of ready-to-inhabit plots by the government, the construction of built quarters by the government, the creation of colonies through private developers such as the Delhi Land and Finance (DLF), and the building of accommodation through cooperative housing societies (Sengupta 2007: 80–1).[68] One scheme within this framework was the cheap housing scheme meant for low-income refugees that entailed the creation of plots (ideal for building houses) measuring 100 square yards. Though this scheme was not intended for squatters primarily, the Ministry of Rehabilitation was impelled—if only in order to get them to move—to extend it to those who squatted on government land, on DIT land, on nazul land, and in townships. These plots were to be distributed on a nominal lease for 99 years and distributed along with a building grant of up to Rs 500 to be used as construction aid. Another scheme involved the allotment of plots (and shops) in colonies that were specially created for refugees through government funding and initiative in areas like Lajpat Nagar, Patel Nagar, Rajendra Nagar, and

Kirti Nagar. In this scheme, several concessions were offered ranging from loans and provision of building material to the permission to set up cooperative housing societies. In many such cases, a government agency called the Rehabilitation Housing Corporation Limited supervised the applications for the sale of such plots and it was decided that a certain percentage of plots would be reserved for refugees.[69]

An ordinance passed by the government, called Resettlement of Displaced Persons Land Ordinance, 1948—which later took the form of an act in the same year—enabled the government to acquire land needed for exclusive rehabilitation purposes from farmers who were rather unwilling to part with it.[70] This ordinance was used especially for the construction of townships with fully built houses. Among the flourishing government schemes for refugees, one of the most celebrated ones was the satellite township scheme—several 'full-fledged townships' (Rao 1967: 61) came up in Delhi, with the more famous ones being located in Faridabad, Nilokheri, and Kalkaji. As pointed out earlier, these townships were strategically located in areas where camps had been set up, and many of them in places that were at a significant distance from the centre of Delhi. The DIT, which played a significant role in developing these townships, issued a notification in this regard in January 1948.[71] These townships were meant to be self-sufficient in that they came with schools, hospitals, shopping centres, and industries. The construction of these townships was heavily contested not simply by the agriculturalists but also by those residing in the camps who feared that they would not be considered in the final reckoning.[72] Allotments in these townships were disputed by those who came to squat in the built quarters and it is with this last category that we will concern ourselves.

'Legible' and 'Illegible' Allottees and Non-allottees

Let us start with one of the bulky files at NAI which bears the title, 'The Unauthorized Occupation of Homes in Kalkaji (township)—Request for Regularization', and deals with the subject of the squatters in the homes built in these townships. When the township in Kalkaji was constructed and ready for occupation in the year 1956, the Government of Delhi, acting upon the instructions of the Ministry of Rehabilitation, ordered an auction for all the houses except a small number of (one-room) tenements whose value did not exceed Rs 10,000. There were several residents (roughly 120) who, without authorization, occupied these houses in the township—many of them before the year 1955—and who protested when they were sent notices by the housing and rent officer (HRO) to vacate. Anticipating a situation like this, the distinctly poor (Hindu and Sikh) refugees who had occupied these houses in Kalkaji and formed an association with a curiously literal name, the Refugee Society for Non-Allottees, swung into action. After holding a dharna at the prime minister's residence for 33 days, they were able to procure a promise that their 'illegibility shall be verified and they shall be informed and that no eviction shall take place until the verification is complete'. They claimed the right to appeal to 'the legibility and illegibility committees'.[73] The word 'illegibility' is instructive—while the refugees in question meant 'eligibility', perhaps in the ordeal that followed it was their illegibility that really was at issue.

Matthew Hull writes that, often, misspelled words can be more accurate than their proper or original version. And so, the villagers in Pakistan who were evicted from their homes and lands were often called 'effectees', rather than the original 'affectees', in newspaper and official writings. However, this misspelled word was more illuminating in that it cast light on these people's attempts, through the use of 'fraudulent documents', to influence the actions of a powerful bureaucratic organization that shaped the future of planning and development in the city of Islamabad. He writes that the term 'effectees' was more effective 'in capturing the peculiar mix of agency and subjection that has characterized the owners of expropriated land in the last decade' (Hull 2008: 503). Legibility and illegibility, as misspellings of eligibility and ineligibility, can similarly be helpful analytical moves to better comprehend how these people sought to steer the operation of the welfare process. They captured the residents' keen knowledge of the working of bureaucratic forms that represented them in writing. These terms indexed their deep awareness of the power of inscription that rendered the most opaque of transactions legitimate as long as they bore traces of 'the legibility of the state' (Das 2006; Tarlo 2003). Knowing all this, their task was to render the state's legibility favourable to their condition, which implied that they clothe the lists and representations they submitted in the fictions of transparency and relationality.

Following up on the dharna, the refugees also wrote to several authorities, including the Minister of Rehabilitation himself, the Prime Minister's Secretariat, and political leaders, asking for the auction to be stalled and the notices to be withdrawn until their situation stabilized. In these letters, they made themselves out to be lawful and not illegal occupants of the township by citing notifications issued by the Ministry of Rehabilitation, especially to the effect that refugees may not be evicted unless provided substantial alternatives. They demanded one of many such alternatives: that they be allowed to stay back in those tenements ('C' type one-room tenements) and those block quarters ('G' block quarters costing not more than Rs 7,000 rupees) should not be auctioned because they did not exceed the value of Rs 10,000; or that they should be given the option to apply for the 1952 cheap housing scheme which entitled refugee applicants to a plot of 100 yards and a building grant of Rs 500.[74] This barrage of letters and protests bore some fruit and they were able to prevail on the Ministry of Rehabilitation to form an ad hoc committee which would look into their individual cases and take a decision on the regularization of the occupation of these houses.[75] This committee, comprising members from the Ministry of Rehabilitation and the Delhi Relief Rehabilitation Department, and the HRO, Delhi, invited members of the non-allottees society to meet them, produce declarations of their identity, and submit the relevant proof to show that they had satisfied two of the stipulated criteria and ideally, the third criterion, though the last one was not insisted on. Those found eligible would be granted regularization of their houses provided they paid arrears of the rent due by them to the HRO under terms equivalent to the interim compensation scheme of 1953.[76] The committee put in place these criteria, which were advertised in a press note dated 4 June 1955:

1. Only those persons who were registered as refugees in India (and preferably in Delhi).
2. Only those persons who occupied accommodation prior to 1 April 1954 were entitled to regularization of such houses.
3. Among the DPs, only those who had arrived in Delhi before 15 August 1950 were entitled to rehabilitation benefits in Delhi.

If the first two criteria dealt with proof of refugee status via registration in Delhi and proof of occupation of the quarters before a certain date, the third sought to determine when the refugee came to Delhi. The fourth criterion discussed was continuous residence in Delhi since the date of arrival before 15 August 1950, but, given the immense political pressure that the ministry felt from all sides, it was decided to overlook the fourth one.[77] This date of 1 April 1954 was chosen so as to enable the HRO to undertake a survey in the year 1955 and ask pertinent questions to ascertain if these persons were present before that date. Such a survey should not be confused with the various enumerative exercises that took place in Delhi. As shown earlier, a refugee census was undertaken in 1948, followed by a comprehensive survey of DP squatters in 1951–2 where all those enumerated were given eligibility slips. This survey was neither of those exercises. It was instead one that concerned itself with the narrow case of establishing the township's unauthorized occupants. However, the date of 1 April 1954 was imbued with significance in another sense too: ration cards—first, temporary individual ration cards and later, permanent family ration cards—were being issued in Delhi until the year 1954.[78] As decontrol was made effective in 1954 and the DRO wound up its operations in the same year, the ration card was an authoritative document proving the presence of a family in a specified area.[79]

De-fetishizing Proof: 'Latitude in the Acceptance of Evidence'

The non-allottees society, worried that these criteria may be restrictively implemented in terms of evidence, decided to submit a list of 33 persons, all of whom they considered eligible, and their declarations (see Figure 3.3, which gives the sample of one such declaration) to B.N. Kaul, Principal Private Secretary to the Prime Minister. Kaul, who had been consistently supportive of their predicament, forwarded this list to the Ministry of Rehabilitation, with the result that the ad hoc committee set to work to carry out a thorough inquiry to establish their eligibility for regularization. Soon afterwards, the Prime Minister's Secretariat sent another list of 63 persons, also occupying the quarters of Kalkaji. The committee held several sittings where it invited the individuals concerned to produce in person the relevant proof. It then examined all cases and found only 17 candidates from both lists eligible. However, before they could examine these claims, Kaul wrote to the ministry asking it to bring 'a certain amount of latitude' to the inquiry. He wrote:

This is a matter that can be dealt with either very rigidly or with a certain amount of latitude in acceptance of evidence. These people from Kalkaji stated that the Delhi state authorities were requiring production of evidence which was not practicable for them but they could produce other evidence which would establish that they fulfil the condition. I have no doubt that you will give consideration to this aspect of the matter and will also take steps to ensure that unnecessary rigidity in the acceptance of evidence is not enforced as long as it can be established that in fact the person fulfils the condition.[80]

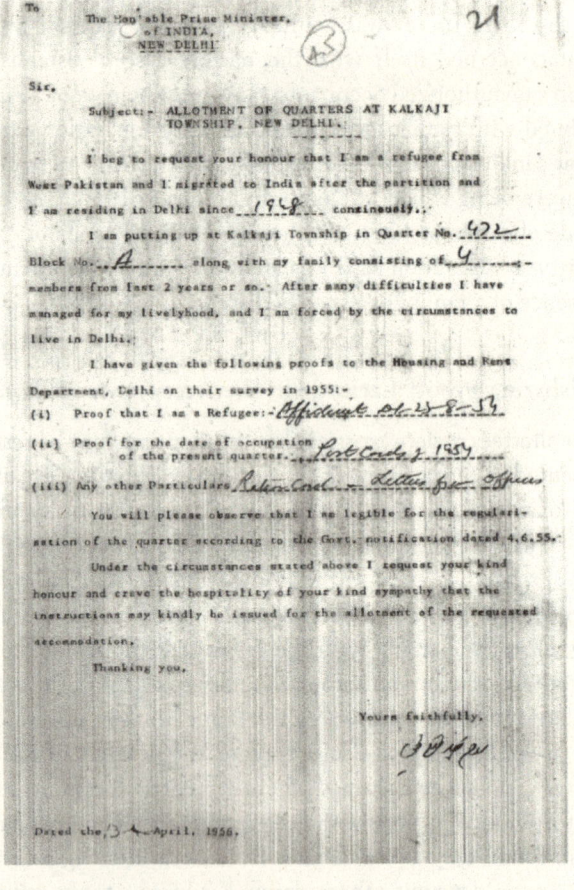

Figure 3.3 Declaration by a Refugee 'Non-allottee' Squatter
Source: NAI.

It is perhaps in the spirit of Kaul's sentiments (which, in turn, were inspired by the letters of these refugees) that the committee considered, to its credit, an unstinting range of such evidence. What merits mention and is vital to the argument of this chapter is that such an inquiry was *not* close-ended but one that was closely linked to what the occupants themselves desired. This inquiry very liberally admitted into consideration any evidence that legitimately sprang from the day-to-day life of these occupants, as well as their itinerary as refugees in Delhi's relief camps and other locations where they may have temporarily dwelled. The fact that, despite this very sweeping gesture, many applicants failed the test goes only to show that the lapses of welfare distribution are not so much the consequence of top-down unilateral state policies and schemes as much as the preservation intact of rubrics of nationality, place of residence, and date of entry.

The committee considered both the survey information collected by the HRO and the declarations produced by these refugees. These declarations, possibly drafted by the non-allottees themselves, were of a standardized template (see Figure 3.3). They featured a certain narrative refrain of how the refugee squatter started staying in a certain block at Kalkaji quarter along with his family.

I say 'his' because all but two of the 33 representations found in the NAI files were by men—and the two women applicants were extremely suspect simply because they submitted their own ration cards and not their husband's ration cards. This plaintive testimony of migration was followed by three columns showing that he was 'legible': proof of a refugee; proof for the date of occupation of the present quarter; and any other particulars. It was here that the representations varied. For the first column, if several declarations cited the refugee registration number issued to them, it was only very few that stated 'attested copy of the refugee registration certificate is attached' or registration card of Delhi 1947. A few others also simply stated 'office letter', or 'certificate of government by gazette officer', or 'a certificate to the facts from MLA Duljit Singh'—for if any such letter was tendered by a recognized official or political representative who was also a DP, then such an ID document was as good as a refugee certificate. It was not only educational institutions that de-fetishized refugee certificates and college degrees, rehabilitation officials in their capacity as housing authorities too did the same by recognizing other alternatives. For the second column about proof of date of occupation of present quarter, applicants mentioned postcards, ration cards, the shopkeeper's bill, railway employee at Delhi since 24 April 1944, proof taken by housing authority (read HRO), bank account number showing continuous transactions from 1950 to 1952, document showing admission of child in school, a letter from the Senior Superintendent of Delhi, a certificate from the local MLA, Duljit Singh, or simply 'letter from office'. As can be seen, in the absence of any restrictive mandates of what such proof regarding date of occupation of quarter should consist of, refugees exercised their own common-sense understanding of which daily transactions (bills, employment letters), what benchmarks marking time (school admission certificate), what notions of address (postcards), or whose speech acts (letters from officials and political representatives) were privileged to have the aura and material aspect of evidence.

In considering this evidence, the committee members prepared six columns in their official inquiry form (see Figure 3.4). The inquiry

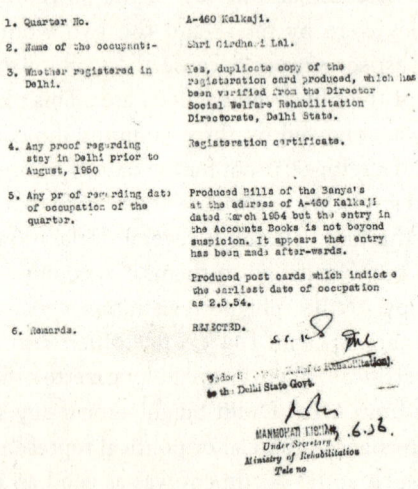

Figure 3.4   An Inquiry Form Prepared by the Kalkaji ad hoc Committee
Source: NAI.

form was tinged with all kinds of considerations regarding the material aspect of the document, notions of nuclear family, continuous presence of the husband in the city, and a strong conception of the head of the family as male. For the third column in the inquiry form that committee officials filled—'whether registered in Delhi'—the officials made entries for some occupants stating that they had registered in Jullandhar. Though registration in Delhi seems to have been preferred by the officials, this was not held against the occupants as much as the failure to give satisfactory oral and written evidence to the fourth and fifth questions, namely, any proof regarding stay in Delhi prior to August 1950 and any proof regarding date of occupation of the quarter. In the year 1956, all the applicants were invited to appear before the committee, which held hearings at the Ministry of Rehabilitation situated in Jaisalmer House. A close perusal of the 33 inquiry forms (pertaining to the first set of non-allottees) that are available in the NAI file throws up a few important things.

The committee took a very liberal view of what constituted proof of refugee status and they accepted in lieu of the RC other credible documents like the discharge certificate of a refugee in military service in Pakistan (as in the case of one Dewan Chand) before he came to Delhi. Also, when non-allottee applicants were not able to submit any such reliable proof, they were still given a little time to prove the same. Even the responses to the question pertaining to proof of stay in Delhi prior to August 1950 were not written in stone—the sketch pen markings that overrule a 'rejected' or 'ineligible' typewritten entry in favour of an 'eligible' decision show that officials, though divided on the point of stay in Delhi prior to August 1950, relaxed this consideration too if an applicant was able to efficaciously prove that he was a refugee who occupied a quarter before 1 April 1954. However, anyone who came to Delhi and then went back to Jullandhar, for instance, and returned to Delhi was immediately suspect, as was evident from the case of one Ram Narain. In this sense, even those who shifted from one quarter to another quarter because they were evicted were not selected unless they showed proof of having occupied both quarters. So, while one applicant (Bhim Sen) made the cut because he notified his employer at the time of moving from one quarter to another within the township, most others were unable to prove their occupation of either the old or the new quarter that they lived in and were hence declared ineligible.

In these cases, those who submitted temporary ration cards only for a couple of months (as in the case of Ram Narain) before the year 1953 when the permanent ration card was issued were again not credible. In this sense, postcards, even though they had no sanction of official authorities (unlike ration cards which were issued by the DRO), were accepted without questioning as long as their date of dispatch corresponded with the date of occupation of the quarter. Interestingly, the material aspect of the document mattered a lot because bills produced by the 'fuel merchant' or 'the *banya*' were rejected if they appeared to be fudged or where the entry of date in the account book seemed to have been tampered with (see Figure 3.4).[81]

Gendered Processes of Reading Evidence

Two women appeared before the committee; and the entries in the inquiry form relating to them were disparaging, to say the least. In the column asking for the name of the occupant, the official entry read, 'Shrimati Shakuntala Rani, wife of Shri Lekh Raj'. Whether the officials regarded Shakuntala Rani to be appearing in lieu of her husband who was not present or whether they believed that no female non-allottee could really represent her family is unclear. A gender bias may have been reinforced by the introduction of the family ration card in 1953 and the consolidation of the male as the head of the family. In the column marked 'remarks', the typewritten entry read, 'Ration cards are also in the name of the lady'. These ration cards could have been the temporary individual ration cards issued on a monthly basis before the permanent family ration card was issued. Her husband's maddening tendency to move in and out of the city and the country, caused by his visits to Calcutta and Iran, was also something that attracted the officials' eye. That 'the lady', considered in her own right, may have been present right from the beginning was not a good enough reason to hand her the regularization. Several other things also went against her, such as her inability to prove her refugee status and her date of arrival in Delhi prior to August 1950.

The second female applicant's name did not even feature in the application since the column only bore the entry, 'Shri Bikramajit', and in other columns, she was mentioned as his wife. The husband's presence at Jodhpur at the time of reckoning and his employment with the railways were both matters for concern—if the former implied the head of the family's absence, the latter raised the question of why he did not seek alternative accommodation with his employers. This precluded any inquiry into the wife's continued presence in the city or her desire to remain in Delhi. Was she able to submit documents of her own which were not regarded by the committee? The files are not revealing on this point. Ultimately, 17 non-allottees from a total list comprising 96 applications, after several rounds of consideration as borne out by the multiple typewritten, pen, and sketch pen entries in the inquiry form, were sanctioned regularization of the built quarters in the Kalkaji township. So, what we see from all these survey exercises is a dogged and obsessive need on the part of rehabilitation authorities to unblur and disentangle the collective claims of any given refugee association such that an application form of a family stands apart and speaks for itself and itself alone.

Caste and Caste-ness

The housing schemes that were created for lower-caste families from West Pakistan were bound to feature elaborate and even more complex exercises in ID. Apart from their anxieties about caste, which will be shown later, authorities wished to satisfy themselves on the point of displacement of Dalits. Upon the repeated advice of the Displaced Harijans Rehabilitation Board, the Ministry of Rehabilitation did take up the question of accommodation for squatters and petty traders among Dalits. Such applicants, not unlike the ones we saw, were to furnish proof that 'squatting' had taken place in the early stages of migration and that the squatters were DPs.[82]

The authority that was given jurisdiction over urban housing for Dalit refugees, the Displaced Harijans Rehabilitation Board, enjoyed greater autonomy than did its predecessor, Harijans Section, that worked within the Ministry of Rehabilitation. The Harijan Sewak Sangh (HSS), an organization that Gandhi founded in 1932 and which later acquired the status of an autonomous agency of the central government, and its various regional committees, attended to the work of collecting statistics about displaced Dalit refugees, alongside its more traditional work of undertaking reform in temple entry, land, scholarships, and gram panchayat representation across India.

Rameshwari Nehru, who was simultaneously the Chairperson of the Displaced Harijans Rehabilitation Board and the Vice President of the HSS, went to some lengths to glean information about these refugees, where especially many of them had been left out of the 1952 survey. If some Dalits were not counted, others may have been included but not listed as lower-caste refugees in need of special assistance. The government offered cheap plots to some of the Dalits who worked as sweepers and scavengers, but the latter could not accept them because they were remotely located from the middle-class houses they worked in. Petitioners from the Young Men Balmiki Association, for instance, wrote to Rameshwari Nehru asking that they should not be removed from the dilapidated barracks in Vinay Nagar for these reasons.[83]

But how did caste and caste-ness or the verification of caste identity figure in the rehabilitation of Dalits? As Ravinder Kaur demonstrates, rehabilitation processes were not aloof from intense caste discrimination in the provision of basic relief in refugee camps and compensation in the form of housing resettlement. Stories of segregated spaces within relief camps and even the denial of entry into these camps, as documented by Ambedkar in one of his letters to Nehru (cited in Kaur 2007: 176, 178), would axiomatically mean that the government neglected to ensure universal registration of these refugees and the creation of RCs for them even in the initial days. As the correspondence between Nehru and Mehr Chand Khanna (first, advisor to the ministry and later, minister of rehabilitation, and himself a refugee) shows, nearly 5,000 refugees from Dalit communities faced all manner of restrictions in merely securing registration.[84] Without registration, this community of refugees, for a considerable period of time, would have been reduced to the structural neglect of authorities and a complete denial of compensation. Reports of the denial of ration cards to Dalits who approached relief quota shops abounded in Delhi and elsewhere.

Thankfully, by the 1950s, rehabilitation came to be decoupled from registration and Dalits were able to secure housing allotments in Delhi. The allotments—which accounted for nearly 31,000 Dalit families—made by the government (as against the Displaced Harijans Rehabilitation Board) were not ideal because the houses were intended merely as appendages to the neighbouring upper-caste and middle-class colonies.[85] The Board and Rameshwari Nehru, in particular, were instrumental in ensuring that the government parted with some rural evacuee land, and where it was not possible, 'waste culturable land', for allotment in Delhi's villages. The Board also undertook the construction of single-room tenements in urban parts and provided Dalit refugees with loans to be repaid in easy instalments. The number of houses built for Dalits in Delhi amounted to 500 around the year 1950.[86] Both Rameshwari Nehru and the HSS wrote that the Planning Commission's estimate of 18 crores for Dalit rehabilitation (that was to include land allotment and urban construction) came abysmally short as their numbers were in the proximity of 5 crore or a 15 per cent of the general population that was a little over 35.5 crore.[87] But to understand the conundrums of identifying Dalit urban claimants, it is imperative that we sense the intense rural denials that surrounded Dalits at the time.

A good percentage of the lower-caste refugees were agriculturalists. While trying to cross the border, Dalit refugees faced enormous and disproportionate hardship, compared to upper-caste refugees, because 'they had neither the means nor the resources to compete with the other migrant groups'.[88] This was owing to Pakistan's resistance to the migration of Dalits on grounds that they constituted a good percentage of the sweeper and the manual working class. The Pakistan government sought to block their movement by passing the Essential Services Ordinance and many Dalits in Sind and Punjab were left behind. Even so, Rameshwari Nehru writes that 6 lakh (0.6 million) Dalits were able to leave west Punjab, Sind, and NWFP.[89] But, being tenants and sharecroppers, their chances of rural rehabilitation were thin because they were either landless or because they had lost their pattas while escaping massacre.[90] While they tried to procure this evidence from the *jamabandi* after reaching India, Dalit refugees argued that the Pakistan government did not entertain such requests. Since the Ministry of Rehabilitation was primarily interested in compensating farmers for the land that was demonstrably lost, such refugees became a lesser priority. What bears understanding here is that across the villages of Rohtak, Alwar, west Punjab, and Delhi, there was immense resistance to land reform, with erstwhile zamindars appropriating Dalit-owned *shamlat deh*, forcing them to work as bonded labour, while the district boards in these places levied professional taxes on the few Dalits who owned land.[91]

Where there were food scarcities and imminent dangers of starvation, Dalits living in Delhi's villages sought desperately to secure ration cards and petitioned rationing officials repeatedly, only to be denied the same, and eventually, they turned to the HSS for assistance.[92] This was not a stray incident but one that has to be framed within an overarching caste history of gastronomic privilege. In Delhi's ration shops just before the Partition, news reports abounded of dealers and shopkeepers not selling necessities like grain, salt, gur, and kerosene oil to Dalits. In post-Partition Rohtak, Dalits complained that their quantum of rations was drastically reduced.[93] These Dalits who had remained on the Indian side of the border were either in danger of being evicted or had been already evicted by *Jat* landlords from the rural parts of north India. Correspondence of the HSS documents the futile efforts of Dalit refugees who went from Alwar to west Punjab in search of land for cultivation only to return empty-handed.

It is against this vitiated rural landscape of Dalit distress that the ID of Dalit urban claimants must be seen. A 1957 socio-economic survey undertaken by the HSS in Bhangi colony in Delhi's Reading Road (a scavenger and sweeper colony) showed that the majority of the 3,000 odd residents used to be villagers in Punjab, United Provinces, Rajasthan, and Delhi.[94] It was owing to unyielding upper-caste and official denial of everyday life in rural spaces that Dalits in general, and Dalit refugees in particular, came to the urban parts. It was out of a sense of unavoidable historical guilt that the Displaced Harijans Rehabilitation Board addressed the question of urban housing for Dalit refugees, and eventually both the government and the Board set up colonies and cooperative housing societies for them in Lajpat Nagar, Karol Bagh, Moti Nagar, West Patel Nagar, Ramesh Nagar, Tihar Nagar, Kilokri, Rameshwari Nagar, Vinay Nagar, and Kasturba Nagar.[95] Citing the example of the Dalits living in Regharpura near Karol Bagh, Kaur writes that lower-caste communities were subjected to 'socio-spatial exclusion' in that they were made to inhabit 'untouchable colonies' where they could practise their traditional occupations (Kaur 2007: 169, 173). Given, however, that the Displaced Harijans Rehabilitation Board was a little more thoughtful in the setting up of its cooperative housing societies which were intended to be self-sufficient, unlike the government-built houses which were constructed to complement the needs of the more wealthy middle-class urban migrants, it would also be useful to see how this translated into practices of ID.[96]

Within this analysis, it is imperative that we heed a timely warning that rings out repeatedly in Dalit literary writing and scholarship. Injustice against Dalits is hardly confined to rural spaces and it is only the most complacent who believe that caste is solely visible in land ownership, village rites, and rituals (Rege 2006: 2). Caste is not alien to everyday urban life then or now, and it must be read as 'a form of power and of economic, social and cultural capital in the contemporary world' (Tharu and Satyanarayana 2013: 14–15). The chances of applying for urban compensation depended on a debilitating insistence on proof. Added to this was the fraught question of representation of Dalits in the very bodies that decided their fate. It repeatedly came to light that Dalits were poorly represented in the HSS committee both in the city and in the countryside. The important clause in the constitution of the committee, stating that some posts in the HSS should be reserved for Dalits, was deleted in the year 1955. Thakkar Bapa, the General Secretary of the HSS, commented glibly that untouchability was practically gone by 1950 owing to reservations, and that if one were to compare the status of 'Harijans, the hill tribes and other touchable Hindu and Muslim backward classes, the Harijans may be the best off'.[97]

In his seminal essay, 'Caste and Castelessness', Satish Deshpande writes that the Madras High Court, while hearing a question of whether reservations violated the fundamental right to equality early into the birth of the republic, ruled in the year 1950 that caste could be invoked as 'a liability and a regrettable and hopefully short-lived exception to the meritocratic norm' (Deshpande 2014: 407). The passage of the upper-caste subject who did not seek reservation into citizenship was smooth and unmediated and left him unmarked (while, in reality, such a subject was clothed as an upper-caste Brahmin) (Deshpande 2014: 407–8). The Dalit subject, on the other hand, had to mark himself/ herself at every turn to claim the citizenship that the new republic bestowed. Deshpande writes that the new republic 'perpetuates and intensifies the compulsory marking of the lower-caste identity' (Deshpande 2014: 408). In the matter of imbuing the compensation process with legitimacy by ensuring the representation of the Dalit DP in the bodies that carried out this work, Dalits were regarded to be unmarked and somehow less lower caste. However, when it came to granting Dalits welfare, their lower-caste status was to be anxiously performed. In this sense, norms of justice left the Dalit subject 'marked' in some senses (by placing the burden of ID on them), while unmarking them where their agency mattered the most (by refusing to valorize them as lower-caste partitioned people).

There was an unmistakable onus on Dalit refugees—termed 'Harijans' in official files of this era—to produce documents that substantiated their caste. So, they had to struggle to prove their caste, in addition to their refugee status, in order to be eligible for housing that was earmarked for them. Here, the Displaced Harijans Rehabilitation Board was emphatic on the point that housing should be given only to *pakka rakka* Harijan refugees from Sind and Punjab—such terminology was used in considering the construction of cheap tenements for Dalit refugees in Shahdara within the Rs 1 lakh (0.1 million) grant issued by the central government.[98] These houses, to be built at a cost of Rs 1,000, were to be scrupulously given to Dalits 'of character' and one way to ensure that was to collect a deposit of Rs 25 from them. The loans were to be recovered over a period of 20 years and the money left over from the central government grant was to be utilized for creating amenities for Dalits. While such pakka rakka Harijan-ness was established in evidentiary fact, authorities may not have stated that only a caste certificate be accepted for these purposes. Here too, authorities, while they were emphatic on Harijan-ness, could not insist on the form which that identity should take. If one were to examine some of the petitions then, different demonstrations of caste-ness emerge. One Dalit sweeper, Gagan Ram, who belonged to the Balmiki community and was living in Rameshwari Nehru Nagar, wrote to the Displaced Harijans Rehabilitation Board asking to be considered for housing in the cooperative society set up in the same area. He explained painstakingly that he was employed as a sweeper in the colony and that he was now staying in an unauthorized house near the colony. However, since he was an employee of the colony, he wrote that he should be accorded prior consideration in the colony which had one house vacant for a long time. In order to demonstrate his bona fide caste status, he wrote in the letter to the Board that he had registered himself with the old Harijan Section of the Ministry of Relief and Rehabilitation. He added, 'I have paid share money and my name stands on the live register of the members of the Shrimati Rameshwari Nehru multipurpose cooperative society, Karol Bagh, Delhi.'[99]

The Construction of Evidence and the Role of Refugee Associations

Conundrums of ID and verification of squatters and poor refugees were bound to feature in the housing schemes on offer. What is revealed in the narrative so far through all these schemes is a body of evidence that emerges from life events, traumatic incidents in the past, and mundane occurrences. It is not strung together by the officials or enumerating authorities but is forged from the itineraries of the refugee subjects. Indeed, scraps of official and non-official paper in the refugees' personal archives were mobilized to tell the story of places inhabited and deserted, professions abandoned, new trades undertaken, spaces and buildings occupied, temporary absences, and surveys attended and missed. The Kalkaji township squatters willed authorities to take cognizance of their personal archives consisting of proof that they constructed by themselves and through their refugee associations as mediator. The president of the Refugee Society for Non-Allottees in Kalkaji township, both in his capacity as a member of the Socialist Party and as an affected resident, helped the squatters collect evidence and handle declarations which in all likelihood would have seemed baffling. He even tried to ensure that official inquiries into each declarant's credibility occurred through the offices of the association. However, he failed in these efforts as the ad hoc committee insisted that each non-allottee appear in person before it and speak for himself and in the case of the women applicants, in lieu of their husbands.

The intercession of these refugee associations, who played their part as invaluable mediators in securing housing allotments, evacuee property, and assorted compensations from the government, has been underplayed in most scholarly accounts. A cursory knowledge of the names of the refugee associations in Delhi is enough to get a sense of the rich filters of occupation, caste, religious affiliation, and region through which they operated: the Hawkers and Vendors Association; Evacuee Press Association; Refugee Lawyers; All India Refugee Students' Committee; Delhi Sindhi Association; Frontier Pursharthi Jirga; Bhartiya Khudai Khidmatgar Jirga; and Arya Samajist Refugees, to name a few (Kumari 2013: 65).[100] The squatters associations themselves—examples being Self-Rehabilitated Displaced Persons Association, Karol Bagh, the Jawahar Refugee Quarters Association,

Jhandewalan 'E' Old Patel Nagar Association, Cheap Plot Holders Association, and allottees and non-allottees associations of this or that area—appear to have been more synchronous with their location as localized communities occupying a realm of marginality and risk of eviction from different government bodies. One of the rare scholars to document the role of these associations, Amita Kumari, mentions how evacuee property allotments to Sindhis were undertaken in consultation with the Delhi Sindhi Association (Kumari 2013: 65). Nehru hints that some of these refugee associations were communal in character and that their links with the Hindu right-wing Rashtriya Swayamsevak Sangh (RSS), sympathetic to displaced Hindus, were well known.[101]

Pallavi Chakravarty, in her rigorously researched dissertation on the rehabilitation of refugees from East and West Pakistan, indicates that the reach of these associations was so immense that a law on evacuee property (Administration of Evacuee Property Act, 1950), framed initially to temporarily make available abandoned property for housing refugees, was rewritten to accommodate unreasonable and self-centred demands that discriminated against the Muslims.[102] In this twist of a singular bureaucratic tale, the Indian government conceded several demands made by refugee associations, foremost among them being that evacuee property across India be made available for refugees. What perhaps is most shocking is that this Act also authorized Hindu and Sikh refugees to notify evacuee property and provide testimony about the Muslim evacuee. Despite Nehru's alarmed entreaties to not deem it as such, evacuee property legislations ended up soliciting 'the evidence supplied by outsiders' and outside agencies in deeming a certain piece of land, house, or shop to be evacuee.[103] A parallel phenomenon may be observed in another realm of rehabilitation. The squatter refugee associations sought to influence how the large and small surveys counted refugees and what evidence was admitted into the final record. However, unlike the former trend which was patently discriminatory in that it allowed some (Hindu) refugees to proffer evidence against other (Muslim) refugees, the admission of refugee self-identification into surveys was much more progressive in that the government allowed refugees to count and inscribe themselves.

It is time to consider an extraordinary story involving another refugee association, even if it is one that does not, strictly speaking, feature them as squatters. These refugees came from Mirpur, the largest city and one of the districts in Pakistan-administered Kashmir, a region that is either dubbed Pakistan-occupied Kashmir or Azad Kashmir depending on which side of the nationalist fence you find yourself in. Following the conflict between India and Pakistan over Kashmir, in November 1947, the Hindu and Sikh residents living in the areas of Mirpur and Muzaffarabad within this region found themselves at the receiving end of a tribal raid involving mass slaughter, abductions, destruction of property, and looting. This induced the flight of an estimated number of 1.35 lakh (0.135 million) people, of which 87,000 people migrated to J&K and the rest to other parts of the country.[104] The story I am about to tell relates to the struggles of a few of these refugees to get themselves enumerated, registered, and issued identity cards and certificates. The Ministry of Rehabilitation did take cognizance of this category of refugees and even appointed a special officer to inquire into their needs.[105] Refugees from Mirpur spent considerable time in the camps of J&K, and from there, some of them traced their journey to Delhi. Once they found their feet in Delhi, they formed an association called the Mirpur Displaced Persons Association and set up an office in Lajpat Nagar. None of them was able to register themselves as refugees, or register their claims of evacuee property, or procure RCs either in J&K or in Delhi. In its prolonged negotiations with various ministries around the issues pertaining to their status as DPs, this association placed, on the top of its agenda, the question of securing identity cards or RCs. They traced to their paperless predicament their many quandaries of being unable to access their deposits in the J&K Bank, secure loans from the Indian government, apply for jobs through employment exchanges, secure places in colleges and universities, and get cheap housing on par with the West Pakistan DPs.[106] As Nehru pointed out, a few resettlement schemes may have been conceived for them but most of them hit a wall.[107] Many of them did not dare to squat on government land for fear that the laws that shielded the bold DPs of West Pakistan occupying government-built quarters and the special assurances meant for the DP squatters occupying nazul land did not apply to them. Indeed, this was the crux of their stand-off with the Government of India and the Delhi government, which refused to treat them on par with the DPs of West Pakistan.

It was the Ministry of States and not the Ministry of Rehabilitation that became the nodal agency in their negotiations. This had to do

with the classification of states in the post-independence era and the
allocation of administrative control over Part A, B, C, and D states to
different authorities. Jammu and Kashmir fell under the Part B states
that consisted of former Indian states, or the Union of States, including Hyderabad, Madhya Bharat, Mysore, PEPSU, Rajasthan, Saurashtra,
Travancore, Cochin, and Vindhya Pradesh—all of these states as well
as the Part C states[108] were placed under the purview of the Ministry
of States. Insofar as the Mirpur refugees' case threw up delicate tussles
between the states of J&K and Delhi, the Ministry of States became the
vital authority. The Ministry of Rehabilitation could not be bypassed
altogether as they had to be consulted on decisions as drastic as the
creation of refugee identity cards. The perseverance of the Mirpur
Displaced Persons Association was not entirely in vain and their untir-
ing representations helped them secure tentative status as DPs, as well
as concessions such as financial assistance for the general education of
their children and vocational and technical training.[109]

From the year 1952 onwards, this association brought to bear a
steady stream of pressure on the Ministry of States and the Ministry
of Rehabilitation on the question of ID documents. In placing this
demand over all others, the association made a strategic choice, as they
felt their many disappointments in the allied walks of rehabilitation
sprung from this void. In one of his letters, the President of the Mirpur
Displaced Persons Association describes their dispossession through
the prism of ID documents: 'These are the persons who have burnt
their boat and have centered their hopes and aspirations on free India.
In the absence of the Refugee Cards, no one can reveal his identity of
being a refugee and no one admits us as refugees.'[110] Through their
concerted efforts, they were able to prevail on the Ministry of States
to arrange for the publication of a list of all the Mirpur DPs who had
come to Delhi before 1 July 1949. The ministry, however, felt that they
could not do even this without first verifying and getting in one place
the particulars of all such DPs; and the association rose magnificently to
the task by placing advertisements in newspapers and getting credible
information about 211 of their members. Subsequently, a formal letter
of recognition issued by the Ministry of Rehabilitation containing 211
names was published and sent to all those included in it. However, this
letter failed, in the stated experience of the members of the association, to produce any desired results in their disparate attempts to claim

refugee status. They resolved that they would stop at nothing short of an RC or in its lieu, an identity card.

Realizing, however, that they were on a weak wicket as it was pointed out to them that RCs were not being issued either in Delhi or anywhere else anymore[111] and that registration itself was not compulsory everywhere, they took an innovative if somewhat audacious measure. This association, on its own, borrowed important features from the template of the RC as it was issued, and printed out 300 identity cards for all the Mirpur refugees of Delhi and sent them to both the ministries requesting formal recognition of the same. Tragically, when I eagerly scoured the file for copies of these ersatz identity cards, I did not find any! They prefaced their extraordinary request with the explanation that unless they were given these cards or some other refugee certificates, they would not be able to claim basic support in the form of assistance for vocational training, work through the employment exchange, or secure allotment of houses on a rental basis—concessions which, to a limited extent, were made available to them. The Ministry of States was sympathetic to their deeply emotional pleas, recognizing 'the practical inconvenience in the absence of concrete evidence'[112] that these people faced. This ministry wrote repeated letters to the Ministry of Rehabilitation asking them to recognize these cards and issue them formally with an official seal. The latter was visibly perturbed by the notion of special cards for Kashmiri DPs, especially considering no such thing was being circulated for the other DPs. They also felt that this would pave the way for marking the Mirpur refugees out for preferential treatment and even their inclusion under the Claims Act, a move that would be disastrous given that even the East Pakistan refugees were not legitimately covered under this Act. Upon their refusal to act, the Ministry of States wrote to the President of the Mirpur Displaced Persons Association stating that the formal letter containing the list should be 'considered as sufficient proof to enable Kashmiri displaced persons settled in Delhi to claim rehabilitation benefits'.[113] The association wrote back sharply that this flimsy list would not have any value as universities, colleges, and courts would have little patience with a displaced Kashmiri if he was to present it as a demonstration of his identity. A representative of the association asked despairingly, 'Of what avail is this mere inclusion of names in the list lying on the files of the Ministries of States, Rehabilitation and this Association?'[114]

At some point, the Ministry of States floated the idea of an ad hoc or very basic bona fide certificate for the 211 Kashmiri DPs in the form shown in the box below.[115] This would not be the same thing as an identity card or a refugee certificate. The government could, by issuing some such document, concede the Mirpur refugees' demand for some form of ID, while at the same time avoiding the dreaded pitfall of issuing a piece of paper that would mark them out for 'preferential treatment'.

> Certified that Shri _____ is a bona fide Kashmiri displaced person and that his name is included in the list of Kashmiri displaced persons who are eligible for rehabilitation benefits in Delhi.

The file ends with the Ministry of States seeking the final approval of the Ministry of Rehabilitation as it felt that it would be better if the certificates were issued by the latter.[116] It is not evident if the Ministry of States was ultimately able to prevail on the Ministry of Rehabilitation to issue this basic certificate.

If, so far, I have told a story of registration, enumeration, and verification that was distinguished by its generous aspect of latitude in considering evidence tendered and even fashioned by the refugees of West Pakistan and Pakistan-administered Kashmir, it was one that precluded the East Pakistan refugees. Every leitmotif of the story of migration and rehabilitation was different for, and mostly detrimental to, the East Pakistan refugees, be it the exodus of refugees, the definitions of refugee, the registration of refugees, the nature and duration of the relief camps, the governmental resettlement initiatives, the treatment of evacuee property, the refugee struggle for housing, and the provision of alternatives in the face of eviction of squatters. Since this chapter, and the book, tell a sited history of ID practices within the urban spaces of Delhi, it cannot do justice to narratives of post-Partition East Pakistan refugees who were rehabilitated in West Bengal and other parts of India but not in any sizeable numbers in this city. From a reading of secondary work on this subject, it may well be that a reflexive culture of enumeration and ID that we associate with the bureaucratic treatment of West Pakistan refugees was not extended to their East Pakistan counterparts. The reader can, for a cursory understanding of ID practices as they feature in West Bengal's rehabilitation policy, consult a few other sources.[117]

The Monopoly of Inscription Reconsidered

This chapter does not seek to question the operation of governmentality but constitutes an inquiry into the set of conventionally assumed historical conditions that make such an operation possible. In what is now regarded as a biblical text for scholars (at least for reasons of citation) working on ID documents, *Invention of the Passport*, John Torpey writes that the story of the emergence of this document was one of modern states very gradually learning to monopolize the legitimate means of movement. This feat could be accomplished by nothing less than an 'extensive administrative infrastructure', that consisted of 'censuses, household registration systems and passports', put in place by states that separated 'their own' citizens from others (Torpey 2000: 7, 14, 13). Torpey strongly suggests that such a monopoly of movement could be possible only through another monopoly, namely, the state monopoly of inscription, especially where they are antecedent to the distribution of welfare benefits, taxation, and conscription. Torpey's insights are, no doubt, of immense value in understanding how paper works to codify and institutionalize distinctions that have been central to nation-state membership. However, this parable of the consolidation of the state as a political entity by making exclusive certain modes of writing discounts 'the volatility and precarity' (Das and Randeria 2015) of enumerating, identifying, and governing poor, poorly documented, and marginal subjects dwelling in liminal spaces of legality, administration, and sovereignty. In a late postcolonial sense, the work of Tarlo (2003), Eckert (2004), Anjaria (2011), Das and Randeria (2015) serves to illuminate exactly these in-between modes of dwelling and belonging that are implicitly sanctioned by the state itself to support the poor's chances of survival. If law is not always a stable category, enumeration of refugees served only to eclipse purely state-driven processes of gathering information and classifying subjects. Veena Das demonstrates how law and administrative procedures will themselves to undergo slow momentums of change to enable the poor to live; her observations bear out what has taken place not only in the contemporary urban spaces but also historically situated ones (Das 2011: 325).

So, instead of thinking about the state as enjoying an unchallenged monopoly of inscription, it could be more useful to pay attention to: (a) how state power is uniquely particularized in urban locations; and (b) how in the life of a state, situations of flux and uncertainty would imply a complete breakdown of existing techniques and infrastructures of gathering information and power. If much of the anthropology and historical sociology around the bureaucracy (Hull 2012a; Raman 2012; Singha 2000) shows how discretionary practice came to be translated into protocols of attestation, certification, and verification through colonial moves of documentation, what I am arguing is slightly different: urban regimes sought not so much to appropriate as to accept and enable popular notions of ID momentarily in order to better enumerate and govern them.

In a poignant and rich story called 'The Dog of Tetwal', Manto (2001) signals the absurd crisis in imagining the identity of a dog that strays alternately into Indian and Pakistani sides of the border. Yet this story was prescient in that it gestured at the utter necessity of stipulating identity not only during the momentary occurrence of massacre but also in the extended phase of rehabilitation, where too people's identities could not be second-guessed.[118] If a turban, a beard, vermilion, a scarf, or a skullcap held more valence as proof of identity at gunpoint, it was people's documents that had to be administratively salvaged in the long Partition that ensued, to use the title of Zamindar's (2007) book. In the hybrid local settings of Delhi, the post-Partition urban dispensation of the state welcomed, and even occasionally solicited, moves of persons and collectives to write themselves into survey forms and ID documents. Insofar as it sought narrations, narratives, and itineraries that were then altered and routinized as ID documents, this particular avatar of the state was in dire need of alternative norms and notions of evidence. This unstable regime could not help but seek claims, demonstrations of identity, and constructions of evidence because the templates that already existed were either of no use or had to be reworked. It is paramount that we do not dub the rich popular practices around ID documents that followed the Partition to be some sort of a counter-revolution of 'the people writing back' or 'the people unleashing resistance' against an intractable state. ID documents wove in and out of welfare processes within which the administration had to immerse itself in the everyday affairs of rehabilitation with all its unsavoury criss-crossing claims and counterclaims. The semblance of an orderly administration rested on the ability of people to produce verifiable claims of identity, and this moment was all about enabling some sorts of claims (of those people who had the backing of strong refugee associations) while disabling others (those of Muslims).

While this did constitute a special and exceptional moment of assembling evidence, certain sediments of this reflexivity remained within administrative cultures of governing urban spaces. Debates around notary attestation and self-attestation often dogged the post-Partition years. The Kejriwal government, renowned for its popular modes of governing characterized by mohalla *sabhas* (neighbourhood councils), responded enthusiastically to a central directive from the Modi government to privilege self-attestation over notary attestation. While the political milieu of the Kejriwal move is entirely different as it falls within a new post-2000 era of legalism in housing discourse, it carries a distant and faint echo of the 1950s which saw unconventional forms of assembling information.[119]

This moment of post-Partition ID of refugees can also be likened to the aftermath of the manifold disasters in India like earthquakes, floods, and the tsunami which mercilessly wiped out evidentiary traces of people's lives. These crises had to be met with equanimity and a coalescing of administrative and popular notions of claim-making. The post-tsunami compensation process in Tamil Nadu, for instance, saw the acceptance of lists of dead fishermen and destroyed catamarans prepared by the fish workers' panchayat. These documents had to be accepted in place of ration cards, death certificates, ID cards issued by the fisheries department, and slips reflecting that the catamarans were registered (Tata Institute of Social Sciences [TISS] 2005).[120]

This chapter does not seek to argue that the material culture of the Indian bureaucracy is a flexible people-friendly one. That would militate against the very reasonable truisms about the self-referential, circular, 'merry-go-round' (as a character in this chapter puts it) gloom of the 'Documents Raj' that still hangs over India. During this period, the unreasonable demands placed on Dalit refugees to satisfy criteria of caste-ness and the ineffective administrative response in assisting these families with acquiring the template for claim-making is a sobering revelation. As Emma Tarlo's (2003) work on documents that bordered on the illegal and the criminal contrived during the Emergency only goes to show, governmental forms can lend themselves to a terrifying rigidity as well as a disabling reflexivity. The chapter shows that the 'Documents Raj' of ID in its present living and breathing avatar is distinguished by a bureaucratic and political impetus to let people inscribe bits of their selves, stories, and journeys into official forms of ID. What perhaps is remarkable is that the bureaucratic treatment of applications militates against poor persons despite these expansive and progressive trends writ large across the history of evolution of ID documents in India.

Notes

1. Rajkumari Amrit Kaur (Minister of Health) to Mohanlal Saksena (Minister of Relief and Rehabilitation), 16 March 1949, 51/147/49, Home, Public, 1949, NAI.
2. B.N. Kaul (Principal Private Secretary to the Prime Minister) to Dharma Vira (Secretary, Ministry of Rehabilitation), 23 April 1956, HI/6(6)/56, Ministry of Home Affairs (MHA), Rehabilitation Division (Housing Section I), 1957, NAI.
3. The President of the Mirpur Displaced Persons' Association to the Secretary (Kashmir Affairs), Ministry of States, Letter No. MDPA/C/(268), 19 August 1953, 7 (94)—K/53, Ministry of States, Kashmir Section, 1954.
4. This chapter is indebted to Awadhendra Sharan for this and many other constructions, as well as for his characteristically sharp conceptualizations of the various shifts in Delhi's urban housing discourse. Ravi Sundaram was, as always, indispensable to my writing process. Special thanks must also be expressed to Hilal Ahmad for pushing me to think of 'a political science of the archive'. I would also like to thank all the participants in my Cornell University SAP fellowship seminar, as well as those who attended my CSDS end-of-fellowship seminar—their intense engagement helped me revise drafts.
5. I am very grateful to Usha Ramanathan for belabouring this point.
6. Khushdeva Singh's story, 'Love is Stronger than Hate', features in a 1995 anthology of Partition fiction, edited by Mushirul Hasan.
7. There is quite a bit of scholarship that inventories the reasons for the pronounced preference that Punjabi refugees felt for Delhi in particular. They list, among others: the presence of relatives and contacts; the urban demographic profile of these refugees who were raised in big cities and towns of Rawalpindi, Multan, and Lahore; the concessions offered by

the Delhi government for their rehabilitation; and the vast number of properties abandoned by the evacuee Muslims (Dutta 2000; Kaur 2007; Rao 1967; Rao and Desai 1965; Sengupta 2007).

8. A small exception to this story is the East Pakistan Displaced Persons Association (EPDPA) in Delhi, which successfully negotiated with the government in the 1950s and procured plots of land in forested and deserted parts of southern Delhi. This colony, which today popularly goes by the name Chittaranjan Das or CR Park, may trace its origins to the initiative of the EPDPA, but it is now home to only very few people from East Pakistan. The larger majority staying here migrated in later days from West Bengal. It is also important to mention here that the original few residents were civil servants and relatively affluent and were consequently able to secure a generous strip of land that was broken down into blocks.

9. Letter from Jawaharlal Nehru to Mohanlal Saksena, 17 April 1949, *Selected Works of Jawaharlal Nehru* (hereinafter *SWJN*), in S. Gopal (ed.), Vol. 10, 1997, p. 285.

10. Section 2, Delhi Refugees Registration Ordinance, 1947, *The Gazette of India, Extraordinary*, as found in 117-P147, Office of the Regional Commissioner, Abu, Rajputana Agency, 1947, NAI.

11. 51/134/49–Public, 1949, Memo No. RH-521 (31), 7 March 1949, Home, Public, 1949, NAI.

12. The definition of the term 'evacuee' underwent several changes, most of which were overshadowed by the urgent imperative to sanction abandoned Muslim properties to incoming Hindu and Sikh refugees. All Muslims, whether they stayed or left, had legitimate cause for fearing the ever-widening scope of this definition. See Chaudhri (1957) and Schectman (1951); in particular, see Chakravarty (2014).

13. Memo No. RH-521 (31), 7 March 1949, 51/134/49, Home, Public, 1949, NAI.

14. Here, it is worth noting that the Transfer Bureau was created to cater to government employees recruited in Sind, North West Frontier Province (NWFP), and Baluchistan. Refugees from East Pakistan could not register their names with this bureau and the bureau catered purely to West Pakistan refugees; 30/61/48, Home, Appointments, 1948, NAI.

15. Private Note No. D.S. (AN), 4/3/1948, filed by H.J. Stooks (Director of the Transfer Bureau), 30/61/48, Home, Appointments, 1948, NAI.

16. Letter from Jawaharlal Nehru to Mohanlal Saxena, 19 May 1949, *SWJN*, Vol. 11, p. 73.

17. See also Chakravarty (2014).

18. Notification No. 2/14/48, Public (I), Home, Public, 1948, NAI.

19. Central and provincial authorities were, however, greatly reluctant to waive considerations pertaining to residence in a certain area over a long period of time—in some cases, these concerns took the form of insisting on a domicile certificate. The Governments of Assam and West Bengal were known to make a fuss in this regard when dealing with East Pakistan refugees, with the result that antsy applicants in this category cite how such bureaucratic actions violated MHA's rules relaxing domicile rules for them. Several NAI files document the frustration experienced by refugees from this region when employment exchanges refused to register them unless they produced either an RC or a domicile certificate. For example, see Atul Ranjan Deb (one such refugee applicant in Assam) to the Secretary, MHA, 43/48/49, Home, Appointments, 1949, NAI.

20. Section 2 (b), Displaced Persons Claims Act, 1947, *The Gazette of India, Extraordinary*.

21. Note for Supplementaries, Starred Question No. 489, RHA-2 (21)/54, Ministry of Rehabilitation, Rehabilitation Section, 1954, NAI.

22. Section 4, Delhi Refugees Registration Ordinance, 1947, *The Gazette of India, Extraordinary*, as found in 117-P147, Office of the Regional Commissioner, Abu, Rajputana Agency, 1947, NAI.

23. See *Form of Registration* appended in the First Schedule and *Form of Certificate of Registration* in the Second Schedule, Delhi Refugees Registration Ordinance, 1947.

24. Chakravarty writes that in Delhi, this classification does not appear to have entailed the creation of disparate border slips of the kind that were issued in West Bengal. In the latter, refugee families headed by able-bodied males, women, and those who denoted permanent liability were sorted into different categories and issued colour-coded border slips. See Chakravarty (2014: chapter 2, fn. 28).

25. Letter from Nehru to Mohanlal Saxena, 20 March 1949, *SWJN*, Vol. 10, p. 277.

26. Office Memo No. 13–Admn (21)/49, as it appears in 51/122/49–Public, Home, Public, 1949, NAI.

27. Office Memo No. 60/94/48–Ests, Home, Establishments Sections, 1948, NAI.

28. The undersecretary to the Government of India, MHA, to Harcharan Singh. Office Memo No. 60/94/48—Ests, Home, Establishments Sections, 1948, NAI.

29. Advani to the undersecretary to the Government of India, MHA, 26 September 1949. Office Memo No. 60/94/48—Ests, Home, Establishments Sections, 1948, NAI.

30. The FPSC ultimately allowed him to attend the viva voce and through this move, conceded to him the relaxation of age limit that Advani sought. Advani to the undersecretary to the Government of India, MHA, 4 May 1950. Office Memo No. 60/94/48—Ests, Home, Establishments Sections, 1948, NAI.

31. A provisional certificate issued by the university in Pakistan, a declaration signed in the presence of a first class magistrate in India, or a certificate from the principal of the college in Pakistan where the candidate studied (who may have also had to migrate to India after the Partition); or even a certificate from the registrar of a university, a member of a university senate, or a gazetted officer working for a provincial or central government were some of the alternatives laid out for refugees. 53/31/50–NGS, Home, NGS Section, 1950, NAI and 60/209/49, Home, Establishments, 1949, NAI.

32. 60/209/49, Home, Establishments, 1949, NAI.

33. In West Bengal, which received refugees sometimes in 'trickles' but at other times in 'surges' (Chatterjee 2002: 74), registration of refugees was introduced in April 1948 and the practice continued until 15 January 1949 when camps were wound up; RHA-2 (21)/54, Ministry of Rehabilitation, RHA Section, 1954, NAI.

34. RHA-2 (21)/54, Ministry of Rehabilitation, RHA Section, 1954, NAI.

35. RHA-2 (21)/54, Ministry of Rehabilitation, RHA Section, 1954, NAI.

36. In response to a starred question posed by an MP in the Rajya Sabha, S.N. Dwivedy, asking about the continued need for registration, the Minister of Rehabilitation replied, 'it is considered neither necessary nor feasible to restart registration'; RHA-2 (21)/54, Ministry of Rehabilitation, RHA Section, 1954, NAI.

37. Article appearing in *HT*, 7 May 1948, cited in Kumari (2013: 63).

38. 8 (72)–G (R)/48, Ministry of States, G (R) Branch, 1948, NAI.

39. F.2 (15)–G (R)/49, 1949, Ministry of States, G (R) Branch, 1949, NAI. But even with such a measure, Delhi exceeded its quota, presenting a problem of civil supplies provisioning (Kumari 2013: 62).

40. Mehr Chand Khanna, rehabilitation adviser to the Government of India, to all provincial governments and chief commissioners, F.2 (15)–G (R)/49, Ministry of States, G(R) Branch, 1949, NAI.

41. Mohanlal Saksena to Rajkumari Amrit Kaur (Minister of Health), Individual Correspondence–A1, 23 February 1956, Mohanlal Saksena Private Papers, NMML.

42. Definition of DP in the 1951 census, cited in the *Census of India, 1961* (1966: 127).

43. Notification No. 2/14/48–Public (II), Home, Public, NAI.

44. The DIT Enquiry Committee was constituted under the Ministry of Health in the year 1950.
45. Hume, *Report on Congestion*, Vol. I, pp. 67–8, cited in Sharan 2014: 133.
46. 14-27/54-159, Part I, Ministry of Health, LSG Section, NAI.
47. Given that the Ministry of Rehabilitation could simply not accommodate masses of those deemed squatters in its various housing schemes, many of them had to be coaxed into the slum clearance schemes floated by the DIT in Ajmeri Gate, Jhandewalan D and E Blocks, Nehru Parbat, Patel Nagar, Ahata Kidara, and Moti Nagar areas, to name a few. 14-27/54-159, Part I, Ministry of Health, LSG Section, NAI.
48. Report of the '*Interim General Plan for Greater Delhi* prepared by the Town Planning Organisation', Ministry of Health, Government of India, attributed to the year [?] 1956.
49. Rajkumari Amrit Kaur to Mohanlal Saksena (Minister of State for Relief and Rehabilitation), 16 March 1949, 51/147/49, Home, Public, 1949, NAI.
50. Rajkumari Amrit Kaur to Sardar Vallabhbhai Patel, 17 March 1949, 51/147/49, Home, Public, 1949, NAI.
51. Rajkumari Amrit Kaur to Mohanlal Saksena (Minister of State for Relief and Rehabilitation), 16 March 1949, 51/147/49, Home, Public, 1949, NAI.
52. Letter from Nehru to Mehr Chand Khanna (at this point in time, Advisor to the Ministry of Rehabilitation), 27 June 1949, *SWJN*, Vol. 12, p. 107.
53. Rajkumari Amrit Kaur to Mohanlal Saksena, 16 March 1949, 51/147/49, Home, Public, 1949, NAI.
54. Nazul lands refer to the local territories which came under the possession of the Mughal emperor of Delhi.
55. Memorandum of Self-Rehabilitated DPs Association, Faiz Road, Karol Bagh, 14-27/54 LSG, Ministry of Health, Local Self-Government Section, 1954, NAI. The Ministry of Rehabilitation was flooded with representations from associations like the All-India Refugee Association, the Jhandewalan 'E' Old Patel Nagar Refugee Association, and Vasudev Nagar Refugee Association, Andha Mughal, which stated that houses that could have been regularized were unkindly demolished.
56. This figure is cited in Bhargava (1981: 134).
57. 'N.V. Gadgil's Statement made on the 29th September 1951 in the Parliament of India in Connection with Delhi Premises (Requisition and Eviction) Amendment Bill', 14-27/54—LSG—Part II, Ministry of Health, LSG Section, 1954, NAI.
58. Very few regularizations occurred because the DIT claimed that 95 per cent of such constructions were almost always in blatant breach of municipal bye-laws and pre-approved layouts for parks and open spaces.

In addition, the DIT argued that encroachment was always in crowded and congested areas that could not accommodate such collectivities. Besides, unless it was given additional land to develop, how could the Trust possibly cater to the non-refugee squatter and the DP squatter population simultaneously unless it compromised the needs of any one group?

59.   The DIT did not dismiss those who were present before the date of survey but were unable to prove that they had set up constructions before 15 August 1950. These people were allowed to apply for a plot of land measuring 100 square yards along with other cash or material grants. However, those who moved in before 15 August 1950 were entitled to choose between the plot and built accommodation.

60.   See, for instance, the Memorandum of the Self-Rehabilitated DPs Association, Faiz Road, Karol Bagh, 14-27/54—LSG—Part II, Ministry of Health, LSG Section, 1954, NAI.

61.   'It was not possible to check whether the squatter was a DP', argued an official of the Delhi Development Provisional Authority. HI/6 (40)/57, MHA, Rehabilitation Division (Housing Section I), 1957, NAI.

62.   Memorandum No. 26/1/59-Acc, issued by the Ministry of Works, Housing and Supply, 21 January 1959, NAI. This memorandum stated that 'a systematic census of all unauthorised constructions on public premises in the urban areas of Delhi has to be conducted through the Chief Commissioner, Delhi.'

63.   D.O. No. SC/GP/Genl/55/716, 25 April, L.B. Mathur, Settlement Commissioner (GBP), to M. De Mello (Technical Adviser to the Government of India, Ministry of Rehabilitation), HI/6 (40)/57, MHA, Rehabilitation Division, Housing Section I, NAI.

64.   ID documents that had to be produced by squatters who applied under the Gadgil Assurances were: RC; receipts for payment of damages assessed by the authority; ration cards; electricity, water, telephone bills from the year 1950; slips or ID cards of the squatter census of 1960; the voter list of 1951; and any other letter addressed to the squatter at his place of occupation prior to 15 August 1950. Please see Basu (2014: 102–3). To get a sense of how many applicants' claims were frustrated owing to intricate details corresponding to ID documents, see, for instance, the following judgements in the Delhi High Court: 582/03/00, Darshna Lal vs DDA on 17 December 2007; and 142 (2007) DLT 474, Darshna Devi and ANR vs DDA on 20 April 2007, Ashok Kumar vs DDA on 10 August 2007.

65.   Other questions included queries about the receipt of alternative accommodation; payment of rent to the government; and reasons for continued occupation to squatters in general. The DPs had to satisfy other questions like whether they had secured verified claims (of evacuee property)

against the Ministry of Rehabilitation. See 'Draft Proforma for Carrying Out Census of Unauthorised Constructions in Delhi', HI/6 (40)/57, MHA, Rehabilitation Division (Housing Section I), 1957, NAI.

66. At least 25,000 identity cards were sought to be printed. It was proposed that 1,000 enumerators and 250 supervisors be drafted for the task. These cards were to be machine numbered, and start with letters of alphabet representing zones of enumeration. Such a stupendous exercise needed manpower drawn from across the board of the Delhi administration. The Directorate of Education, CPWD, the DDA, the Municipal Corporation, the Land and Development Office, and the NDMC were all required to pitch in. See the minutes of a meeting held on 20 February 1959 in the Office of the Deputy Secretary, Ministry of Works, Housing and Supply, HI/6 (40)/57, MHA, Rehabilitation Division, Housing Section I, NAI.

67. Elements of the thesis of the number in the colonial imagination have been contested in the writings of Guha (2003) and Peabody (2001).

68. Those who were allotted plots were classified on the basis of their financial liability into: (a) those who could invest their own funds and those who could manage with the mere provision of building materials at controlled rates—they were supposed to construct within the framework of 'an approved plan within a prescribed period'; (b) those who could afford to pay only a part (one-third or one-fourth) of the cost of the building and who needed to be urged to form cooperative housing societies—financial assistance to this group could be supplied through a Rehabilitation Housing Corporation; and (c) those who had no resources of their own and who could be given interest-free loans not exceeding Rs 500. F. 8 (72)–G (R)/48, Ministry of States, G (R) Branch, 1948, NAI.

69. See Chakravarty (2014: 99) description of the process of applying for a plot in Kirti Nagar.

70. For instance, many of them made representations to Nehru against the acquisition of their lands in Faridabad where a township came up. See Chakravarty (2014: 102–3) and 'Meeting of the Faridabad Development Board', SWJN, Vol. 11, p. 110.

71. Annexure VII: Notification in regard to Satellite Townships, in F. No. RDB/B/53, 'Satellite Towns around Delhi' in NAI, cited in Chakravarty (2014: 102).

72. Consider the protesting residents of Faridabad camp outside Nehru's house who sought to stall the construction of the township. Letter from Nehru to Mehr Chand Khanna, 8 August 1949, and 'A New City at Faridabad', addressed to refugees at Faridabad camp, 10 August 1949, SWJN, Vol. 12, p. 124.

73. The Secretary, Refugee Society for Non-Allottees, Kalkaji to the Rehabilitation Minister, HI/6 (6)/56, MHA, Rehabilitation Division (Housing Section I), 1956, NAI. This letter was written on 15 January 1956.

74. Yet another option proposed by the Non-Allottees Society was that they be allowed to set up a cooperative housing society and be made eligible for a plot and loan assistance in one of the colonies that was being set up for the refugees.

75. One individual official figure, B.N. Kaul from the Prime Minister's Secretariat, was very supportive of the non-allottees society's demands. He exchanged a series of letters with Dharma Vira, Secretary to the Ministry of Rehabilitation. He told Dharma Vira in no uncertain terms that when the ministry takes up the inquiry to regularize such occupied houses, they should not leave out any eligible candidate 'as the whole stand in this matter is likely to get weakened'. Letter No. 29/51/56—PMO, 18 April 1956, HI/6 (6)/56, MHA, Rehabilitation Division (Housing Section – I), 1956, NAI.

76. The interim compensation scheme that was finalized in 1953 did not merely consist of plans to materially compensate refugees who had lost movable and immovable property; it was also devised to include all kinds of rehabilitation benefits like loans for housing, business, industry and pensions and provident fund payments. All distinctions between regis-tered and unregistered DPs were dismantled for receiving benefits under this scheme. RHA-2 (21)/54, Ministry of Rehabilitation, RHA Section, 1954, NAI.

77. Press Note, 4 June 1955, and signed by P.N. Thukral, the Secretary (Relief and Rehabilitation) to the Delhi state government.

78. The individual ration cards were replaced by family ration cards in February 1953. 14 (23)/52, Civil Supplies, CCO, 1952, DSA.

79. 15 (176)/54, Confidential, CCO, 1954, DSA.

80. B.N. Kaul to Dharma Vira (Secretary, Ministry of Rehabilitation), 23 April 1956, HI/6(6)/56, MHA, Rehabilitation Division (Housing Section I), 1957, NAI.

81. See copies of inquiry forms attached in HI/6(6)/56, MHA, Rehabilitation Division (Housing Section I), 1957, NAI.

82. RHB/27/50, MHA, Rehabilitation Division, RHB Branch, 1950, NAI.

83. Petition from the Vice President, Young Men Balmiki Association, to Rameshwari Nehru, 19 February 1952, F. No. 1 (9) 1936–1955, Rameshwari Nehru Private Papers, NMML.

84. Letter from Nehru to Mehr Chand Khanna, 4 June 1949, *SWJN*, Vol. 11, pp. 78–9.

85. Chakravarty (2014); also see 'Foreword' by Rameshwari Nehru, 8 December 1957, F. No. 1, Vol. 2, 1956–60, HSS correspondence, Rameshwari Nehru Private Papers, NMML.

86. Subject File No. 12, Rameshwari Nehru Private Papers, NMML.

87. Letter from Rameshwari Nehru to Gulzarilal Nanda (Minister of Planning, Irrigation and Power), F. No. 1 (A), 1936–55, in Subject File No. 1, Part 3, Rameshwari Nehru Private Papers, NMML; and Short Memorandum to the Chairman, Planning Commission, F. No. 1 (9), 1936–1955, HSS, Rameshwari Nehru Private Papers, NMML.

88. Foreword by Rameshwari Nehru, 8 December 1957, Speeches and Writings on the Harijan Work, S. No. 121, F. No.1 (9) 1936-1955, Rameshwari Nehru Private Papers, NMML.

89. F. No.1 (9) 1936-1955, Rameshwari Nehru Private Papers, NMML.

90. Letter from A.V. Thakkar to Rajkumari Amrit Kaur, 15 December 1949, F. No. 1 (A), 1936–55, Part 1, HSS, Rameshwari Nehru Private Papers, NMML.

91. Rameshwari Nehru to Rajendra Prasad (President of India), 12 April 1951, F. No. 1 (A), 1936–55, in Subject File No. 1, Part 2, Rameshwari Nehru Private Papers, NMML.

92. DO No. WAS/P/30, Rameshwari Nehru to Johnson (Director of Rationing and Civil Supply), 10 September 1951, F. No. 1, Vol. 3, Part 2, HSS correspondence (1947–60), Rameshwari Nehru Private Papers, NMML.

93. L.M. Shrikant, Commissioner for SCs, MHA, to Rameshwari Nehru, F. No. 1, Vol. 3, Part 1, HSS correspondence, Rameshwari Nehru Private Papers, NMML.

94. F. No. 1, Vol. 2, HSS correspondence, Rameshwari Nehru Private Papers, NMML.

95. See Chakravarty (2014: 111).

96. Rameshwari Nehru Papers and Jaglal Choudhary Papers, cited in Chakravarty (2014: 111).

97. A.V. Thakkar to Nihal Singh, 26 May 1950, F. No. 1 (A), 1936–55, in Subject File No. 1, Part 1, HSS correspondence, Rameshwari Nehru Private Papers, NMML.

98. A.V. Thakkar to Sevakram Karamchand (Working Secretary, Displaced Harijans Rehabilitation Board), 14 February 1950, F. No. 1 (A) ,1936–55, in Subject File No. 1, Part 1, HSS correspondence, Rameshwari Nehru Private Papers, NMML.

99. Gagan Ram, Rameshwari Nehru Nagar, Karol Bagh, to the Chairman, Displaced Harijans Rehabilitation Board, 27 May 1952, F. No. 1, Vol. 3, Part II, HSS correspondence (1947–60), Rameshwari Nehru Private Papers, NMML.

100. Chakravarty (2014: 114).
101. Letter No. 241—PMO/54, Nehru to Ajit Prasad Jain, 20 June 1954, Ajit Prasad Jain Private Papers (1950–54), NMML.
102. To accommodate the housing demands of the Hindu and Sikh refugees from West Pakistan, the government passed a new law replacing the old one, enabling it to acquire evacuee property not simply in the parts of the country where migration was excessive but across the country. This ended up making it impossible for Muslims to leave their homes even temporarily for fear of arbitrary seizure.
103. Letter from Nehru to Mohanlal Saksena, 8 September, 1949, *SWJN*, Vol. 13, p. 101; Letter from Nehru to Mohanlal Saksena, 13 September 1949, *SWJN*, Vol. 13, p. 108.
104. Letter from Nehru to Mohanlal Saksena, 19 May 1949, *SWJN*, Vol. 11, p. 73, fn. 2 (S. Gopal).
105. Letter from Nehru to Mohanlal Saksena, 19 May 1949, *SWJN*, Vol. 11, p. 73.
106. Pamphlet titled, 'Mirpur Displaced Persons' Association: Demands for Justice', 7 (94)—K/53, Ministry of States, Kashmir Section, 1954, NAI.
107. Letter from Nehru to Mohanlal Saksena, 19 May 1949, *SWJN*, Vol. 11, p. 73.
108. Part C states, consisting of the areas falling under the chief commissioners' administration such as Bhopal, Bilaspur, Cooch-Behar, Himachal Pradesh, Kutch, Manipur, and Tripura, were also placed under the Ministry of States. Though Ajmer, Coorg, and Delhi too qualified in the description, they were excluded from the purview of the Ministry of States and instead placed under the administrative control of the MHA.
109. K.N. Channa (Deputy Secretary, Ministry of Rehabilitation) u.o. Note No. D.8917/RHA/0/1953 to the Ministry of Rehabilitation, 10 March 1954. The state government of Delhi, however, wanted special funds to undertake even these minimal schemes; 7 (94)—K/53, Ministry of States, Kashmir Section, 1954, NAI.
110. Letter No. MDPA/C/(268), President, Mirpur Displaced Persons Association to the Secretary (Kashmir Affairs), Ministry of States, 19 August 1953, 7 (94)—K/53, Ministry of States, Kashmir Section, 1954, NAI.
111. Letter No. F. 7 (94)—K/53, K.N.V. Nambisan (Undersecretary to the Government of India, Ministry of States) to the Honorary Secretary, Mirpur Displaced Persons Association, 7 (94)—K/53, Ministry of States, Kashmir Section, 1954, NAI.
112. K.N.V. Nambisan (Undersecretary to the Government of India, Ministry of States) to K.N. Channa, 7 (94)—K/53, Ministry of States, Kashmir Section, 1954, NAI.

113. K.N.V. Nambisan (Undersecretary to the Government of India, Ministry of States) to the President, Mirpur Displace Persons Association, Letter No. F. 7 (94)—K/53, Ministry of States, Kashmir Section, 1954, NAI.

114. Letter No. MDPA/C/(46), Honorary Joint Secretary, Mirpur Displaced Persons Association, to K.N.V. Nambisan, 7 (94)—K/53, Ministry of States, Kashmir Section, 1954, NAI.

115. K.N.V. Nambisan's Private Note No. D.8310-K/54, 23 September 1954, 7 (94)—K/53, Ministry of States, Kashmir Section, 1954, NAI.

116. 7 (94)—K/53, Ministry of States, Kashmir Section, 1954, NAI.

117. Joya Chatterji has peripherally addressed procedures of registration of East Pakistan refugees in West Bengal which she characterizes as being rigid. She writes poignantly that a desperation index was mobilized in determining who a refugee in need of state support was; and where refugees did not register, it was believed they were not 'genuinely interested' to receive benefits and could be safely discounted as refugees (Chatterji 2001: 82). Pallavi Chakravarty (2014)'s unpublished thesis deals generously with ID documents. Apart from writing of the classification of refugees underlying rehabilitation policy into able-bodied men, women, and those who constituted a permanent liability, she too reinforces Chatterji's observations about the culture of rigidity surrounding practices of ID. Rehabilitation benefits were organized around citizenship certificates, migration certificates, the RC, the border slip, border ration slip, and a certified copy of the national census register in relatively inflexible terms. The migration certificate figures in the rehabilitation of the East Pakistan refugees in a big way—this is a document that amounts to an abdication of all welfare responsibility by the state. The migration certificates were issued only to those who signed declarations that they do not want any assistance from the state. See Chakravarty (2014).

118. I thank Ravikant for pointing me in the direction of this story. I relied also on the idiom-rich translation of Manto's story, 'The Dog of Tetwal', by Ravikant and Tarun K. Saint in the collection called *Translating Partition* (Manto 2001).

119. 'In Paradigm Shift in Government Work, AAP to Introduce "Self-attestation"', *The Indian Express*, 12 September 2015. I thank Ravi Sundaram for nudging me to explore the connections herein.

120. Freny Maneckshaw, 'Restructuring Society Post-Tsunami', 3 June 2005, available at www.indiatogether.com, last accessed on 14 February 2016. I am very grateful to Awadhendra Sharan for pushing me to think of how the Partition moment of bureaucratic latitude may by impelled by compulsions similar to those experienced during disasters such as earthquakes and floods.

4

MAKING PROOF IN A SLUM

A jhopadpatti is not an address. The law says ration cards can only be issued to people with real addresses.[1]

So what if he (V.P. Singh) did not give us concrete houses? He gave us laminated ID cards.[2]

Previously, he used to sell vegetables and today, he sells ration cards.[3]

On the first day of the New Year of 1990, V.P. Singh, the then prime minister of India, arrived at Navjeevan camp,[4] a squatter settlement located in south Delhi. On this day, V.P. Singh announced to a cheering crowd that every slum resident in Delhi would be issued, within three months, a ration card, an identity card, and a metallic token bearing a number. This was a relatively obscure enumeration initiative—associated in popular memory with a progressive leader—which constituted a historic and implosive moment in the city's urban ordering. This drive was impelled by unconventional arguments of urban poor entitlement that ran counter to the established administrative norm termed the factum of residence in postcolonial food and housing policy. This moment of urban poor enumeration is remembered, above all else, for its startling move to do away with residence and identity proof as prerequisites for receiving identity cards. Since they could not demand to see proof in order to issue ration cards and identity cards, food officials anchored their search for enumerable homes to extra-documentary markers of residence, such as the *chulha*, the charpoy, and the *gadda*, and kinship ties organized around these objects. In the decades that followed this exercise, slum residents were faced with the implementation of measures of raw distributive justice where they were classified into communities of housing eligibility on the strength of the ID documents issued in 1990. While the initiative did embody a thoughtful and conciliatory gesture towards slum residents, the new forms of proof simultaneously enabled consecutive administrations to carry out elite forms of urban planning and slum resettlement. This chapter dwells on the micro-practices of enumeration during the initiative as well as the anguished political struggles of slum residents around these ID documents after the initiative.

Through ethnographic and archival work, this chapter re-enacts the book's argument of how identification documents take on alternative popular forms in certain spaces thus rendering possible the administration of the people living in them. This moment of enumeration was marked by a whole constellation of unusual modalities of creation, circulation, and the subterranean reproduction of ID documents that were unique to marginal spaces. The official practices of enumeration were also remarkable in that they were imbued with deeply affective and sensory modes of recognizing beneficiaries. In fact, through the instance of this initiative, the book suggests that ID documents will themselves acquire traces of marginality in sync with the residents whose everyday lives they impinge on. By taking on such signs of marginality, these ID documents allowed urban poor subjects to mobilize a diverse range of material and emotional claims on welfare (mostly housing) benefits. The chapter also takes on a certain significance as it crystallizes a time in the history of ID regimes in India that, on the one hand, coincides with neo-liberal reforms and, on the other hand, precedes the electronic era. Given that the decade from 1990 onwards saw deregulation and cutback of benefits, this initiative was aberrational in the welfare-based consideration that its authors, and this leader in particular, showed to slum residents in the capital city. However, given that the ID documents that were issued were not backed by an electronic record, they took on colourful lives in popular and official schemes. ID documents issued as a part of this initiative became the basis for determining the criteria of eligibility in schemes of resettling slum residents. The date of issue distinguished the ID documents created during this initiative such that residents were classified on grounds of who came before and who came after the date of the survey of these residents and the issue of these ID documents. Under these circumstances, the

date became a metaphorical document which residents had to negotiate using the actual ID documents that were issued to them. This
chapter demonstrates the ambivalent nature of all drives of ID which
can be distinguished as benign and compassionate—insofar as ID documents valorize a date and an address, they can only eventually result
in administrative legalisms of deep denial. If these ID documents were
counterfeited with abandon for many years after the initiative, such
popular habits were impelled by an 'emergent citizenship' (Das 2011,
2012) and a necessity to secure themselves against evolving legalisms
of denial.

The analytical thrust of this chapter consists in demonstrating
that an alternative governmentality was at work in the enumeration
and ID practices in the slum. When makeshift ID cards were issued
to residents of marginal spaces, these practices were mediated not by
the individual but by the family, its perception and its affects. Here,
unlike in the previous chapter, it will be shown how enumeration did
not devolve into document-based proof-seeking; the survey exercise
was embedded in other distinctive modes of establishing residence and
family. Certain emotional categories of family (for example, those who
came before the initiative, those who came after the initiative, those
who rented their house to tenants, and those whose children moved
out) as well as tactile practices of living as a family were critical to
claims and counterclaims around 'the date' and the ID documents that
were created in this regard. Enumeration and ID do not always imply
each other and in this case, enumerators had to grapple with the sweet
irony of surveying families without demanding to see proof and yet
their efforts were to result in the creation of new identity cards for
them. The ethnography in this chapter draws on three years of fieldwork involving Govindpuri's residents; interviews with retired food
and housing officials who participated in this initiative; food and housing policy documents; newspaper archives; and information procured
through the filing of RTI applications.

The Marginality of ID Documents in Slums
and Subaltern Realms

Before presenting this intricately knit narrative of proof issued in
a slum, I would like to start by asking perhaps the most befuddling

question of them all: why do slum residents need a different order of ID documents? The hint of an answer can be found in this rich fictional exchange that dwells on the marginality of the subaltern subject's application process for a ration card. In the novel, *A Fine Balance*, by Rohinton Mistry (1996), the two main protagonists, Ishvar and Om, approach the rations officer with their application form for a ration card. They both live in slums which, in Hindi, go by various names such as *jhopdi*, *jhopadpatti*, and jhuggi jhopdi (JJ). The rations officer greets them by offering them the services of a writer who could fill out their application form for a fee. However, Ishvar declines this offer as he knows how to write. He fills out the form and hands it over. The officer smiles with an air of superiority as he views the cluttered application and asks Ishvar to explain 'the rubbish' that he has written in the address column. Ishvar had entered the name of the road leading to their place of residence but had left empty the column that asked for building name, flat number, and street number. When the officer disapprovingly presses them for more details, they plot their address with painstaking detail by listing landmarks such as adjacent streets, a train station, neighbourhood cinemas, a hospital, and a fish market. The conversation ensues in this manner with the rations officer putting a label on their place of residence:

> 'Stop, enough,' said the Rations Officer, covering his ears. 'I don't need to hear all this nonsense'. He pulled out a city directory, flipped a few pages, and studied a map. 'Just as I thought. Your house is in a jhopad-patti, right?'
> 'It's a roof—for the time being'
> 'A jhopadpatti is not an address. The law says ration cards can only be issued to people with real addresses.'
> 'Our house is real,' pleaded Ishvar. 'You can come and see it.'
> 'My seeing it is irrelevant. The law is what matters. And in the eyes of the law, your jhopdi doesn't count.' (Mistry 1996: 176–7)

The rations officer ends the conversation by saying that Ishvar and Om can get a ration card through other means, such as getting a sterilization operation done and producing a family planning certificate. A novel that unfolds partly during the Emergency, *A Fine Balance* is, among other things, an unsparing indictment of the insidious informal forms of power set in motion by the era's administrative schemes. The various events that spill over into each other owing to these administrative schemes amount to the unravelling of the life chances of India's rural and urban poor. However, what I would like to take away from this surreal exchange is something more rudimentary: the slum resident's address serves to embody the lack of an address. Framed in illegality and liminal in nature, slums can be seen and reported but not acknowledged. The existence of slums has prompted taxonomies such as real addresses and narrated addresses. Whenever slum residents wished to be identified and issued documents to the effect of residence and identity proof, they had to resort to practices that could only be characterized as furtive, shady, clandestine, and murky. By their choices of residing in a slum—the alternative often being homelessness—such residents open themselves to a world of makeshift documentation. They would have to get sterilized, enter into negotiations with brokers, politicians, and pradhans, and depend on the largesse of governments. It is necessary to dwell on the unusual meanings, fuzzy functions, and stark compromises that have surrounded ration cards taken as proof of residence in the margins of urban existence. Doing so will allow us to regard how marginal subjects become the bearers of a different order of ID documents in alignment with a differentiated legality of urban existence.

There have been a modest number of articles which have deeply reflected on the spectral legalities and the contingent potencies of ID documents in subaltern spaces. Yael Navaro-Yashin writes that residents in Northern Cyprus experience a 'political haunting' through the spectres of the state apparatus which hover over them in documentary form. Northern Cyprus cannot claim legitimacy as a state and yet, it tentatively enjoys the status of one through the 'make-believe papers' it issues (Navaro-Yashin 2007: 80, 83). Subjects from Northern Cyprus are required to implicitly arrange their everyday mobile practices of entry and exit around a set of papers which have a legal currency only within this state. The people of Northern Cyprus hold a make-believe passport, but also strive to possess the legitimate passport issued by the Republic of Cyprus. For those who have to wield and juggle the different genres of ID documents, these material forms unleash 'affective energies' (Navaro-Yashin 2007: 81) which correspond to the subjects' fears of their liminal legal statuses. In his work on semantically rich ID practices at Israeli checkpoints on the border, Tobias Kelly signals that document holders can never be sure of the determinate meanings of a Jordanian passport, Israel-issued colour-coded cards, or Palestine National Authority-issued identity cards. The startling taxonomy of orange, green, and blue identity cards issued by the Israeli state only point to an ideological policy where authorities could assign varying categories of restrictive rights of travel, residence, and political rights to keep the legality of Palestinian subjects in abeyance. Here, too, ID documents cannot take on settled political meanings or be present as 'reifying abstractions' (Kelly 2006: 90). Instead, they produce a 'doubling of subjectivity' (Kelly 2006: 91) that is borne out through the entities of the physical and the legal person, the known and the unknown aspects of the ID document.

In her article on the citizenship claims of the urban poor in Noida, Uttar Pradesh, Veena Das captures the tenuous legality that is accorded to ration cards issued to those living in *kabza* land (Das 2011: 328). The practices around both the application for the ration card and its creation are deeply rooted in a legal marginality that is cut from the same piece of cloth as the legal ambiguity of the spaces they dwell in. Das writes that through the offices of the pradhan, the people of this area contributed to the locality's acquisition of ration cards by paying for its regulariza-tion. However, the ration cards that they eventually secured were valid only for three months (thus setting them apart from the ration cards which are usually valid for six months). However, though the card was to expire in 2004, the record of transactions indicated that residents were using it for a long time afterwards. Das conveys that though slums are deemed illegal, their residents still enjoy a status as legal subjects as evidenced by liminal ration cards and rations. This chapter thus acknowledges the operation of this alternative governmentality, but explores how it is made possible by an affective and familial politics of bureaucratic recognition and self-representation. It traces a politics of recognizing beneficiaries using *saas* and bahu, chulha and gadda, and other idioms of class belonging, kinship ties, and domestic materiality. Though administrative practices of issuing ID documents by overlook-ing the factum of residence and invoking extra-documentary criteria were deeply unusual, we will see how the enumerative imaginary was still deeply conventional in its middle class-ness.

We will see how a certain initiative was able to mobilize these administrative classifications of legality to set up an urban regulatory discourse. Such a discourse set in motion an emotional economy of welfare claims. The slum residents' ration card claims were fraught with intense anxiety for one's immediate family; and their innovations, such as counterfeiting and RTIs filed against counterfeiters, demolished traditional distinctions between family and household, enumerable space, and the lived space of home. To unpack the V.P. Singh initiative, I picked Govindpuri cluster as my ethnographic site for one very important reason. The choice of the field site— sometimes referred to as Govindpuri cluster and at other times as Kalkaji cluster—was informed by V.P. Singh's decision to inaugurate the historic initiative there.

The Field Site

V.P. Singh chose to inaugurate his layered policy decision on slums in Navjeevan camp which was one of the settlements in Govindpuri cluster, the other two being Nehru camp and Bhumiheen camp, all of which were divided into different blocks. In the years between 2011 and 2013 when I visited this cluster, memories of this initiative as much as its after-effects were surprisingly fresh, even though a few decades had elapsed since the man stepped in Govindpuri and pledged his administration would move heaven and earth, or at least the mammoth food bureaucracy in Delhi, to get the cards issued. This chapter is organized around how resident, official, politician, and NGO figures alike have witnessed, remembered, and narrated this initiative and its implications. The profiles and the points of entry of Govindpuri's residents into the 1990 initiative were dazzling in their range. *Anganwadi* and *balwadi* workers (pre-school government teachers), erstwhile unelected slum leaders (pradhans), political party workers, social welfare workers, domestic helps, drivers, construction labourers, petty grocery, eatery, and meat shop owners, lower-level employees in garment export companies, women who ran small commercial setups from their homes, and fully unemployed men and women were only some of the profiles I came across. I spoke to many more women than men in the belief that their stakes in the slum and their narratives of identity cards would be much more layered owing to their engagement with social institutions such as caste and patriarchy in addition to bureaucratic offices. Even though the residents gave me full permission to quote them and narrate their stories, I have decided to err on the side of caution and change all the names of the people I interviewed in Govindpuri in order to protect them from any undesirable consequences of their candid conversations with me. Despite this, it may be possible to deduce the identities of the people interviewed here, especially where I am referring to specific episodes and views expressed. In these places, I have taken care to ensure that the information is not of the kind that gravely compromises the resident.

The slum cluster in Govindpuri is not a notified slum area as defined by the Slum Areas (Improvement and Clearance) Act, 1956. Notified slum areas are those which are eligible for legal benefits such as water and ration cards even though they are deemed unfit for human habitation. While the government is not obliged to provide any benefits in slum areas that are not notified, it often cannot avoid the official provision of ration cards, and also ends up overlooking the private supply and 'theft' of electricity in these areas. Non-notified slums are also acknowledged at the time of demolition and there have been norms issued from time to time to provide resettlement options to them too. Govindpuri has been classified as a jhuggi jhopdi (JJ) or a slum cluster: JJs are listed as illegal 'encroachments on public or private land'.[5] This slum cluster is located in south Delhi and consists of three squatter camps popularly and administratively termed as Navjeevan, Nehru, and Bhumiheen camps, inhabited by migrants who came to Delhi from different parts of south, east, and north India since the 1970s (see Figure 4.1). A long, straight, slightly narrow central road prone to heavy traffic leads to the slum cluster in Govindpuri. This road met, without contriving to, the consumer needs of the DDA flats that rubbed shoulders with the cluster, and the cluster itself. It is dotted with a profusion of temples, Reebok and other footwear stores, flower shops, sweet shops, garment stores, and bank automated teller machines (ATMs) that catered to all classes. Closer to the cluster, a more distinct commercial topography was evident. A fish market, a bamboo market, tiny masala stores, a veritable deluge of abattoirs, spare tyre carts, petty beauty parlours, a makeshift furniture market, lubricant oil outlets, matchbox-sized medical stores, and Municipal Corporation of Delhi (MCD)-run toilets were all on offer. Though middle-class residents of Govindpuri may have succeeded, in a literal sense, in constructing boundary walls to forestall proximity to these slums, they still could not create an island owing to the sprawl of this commerce.

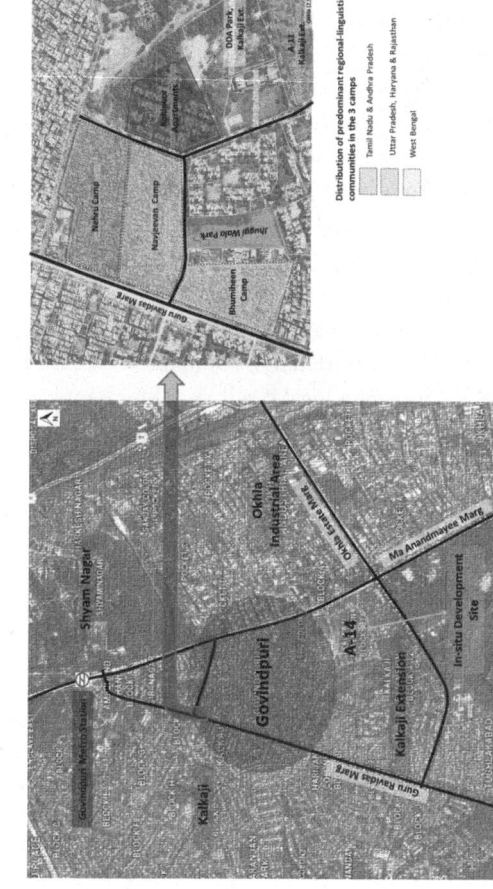

Figure 4.1 A Map of Govindpuri Showing the Three Camps in the Area

Source: Courtesy Vandana Solanki.[6]

Note: This map is not to scale and is provided for illustrative purposes only.

The cluster is organically dependent on the neighbouring industrial area of Okhla, which served as an overbearing constant for the residents. Many of the residents in the cluster were employed with various glass and steel factories, garment exporters, and as domestic helps and drivers in this area. Alternatively, they had to go there when their rationing office shifted briefly to Okhla. Residents assert that the character of each of these camps is distinct in linguistic and regional terms: Navjeevan camp was chosen as a location by migrants from Uttar Pradesh, Haryana, and Rajasthan to signal its difference from Bhumiheen camp which was predominantly inhabited by Bengalis both from West Pakistan and erstwhile East Pakistan. Nehru camp, on the other hand, was tucked away in a corner of Navjeevan camp and was home to migrants from north India as well as those from Tamil Nadu and Andhra Pradesh. A road was all that separated Bhumiheen from Navjeevan and Nehru camps. In caste terms, this cluster was predominantly inhabited by Dalit and backward-class communities—60 per cent of the families in the cluster came from Dalit and backward class communities like *Chamars*, *Bhangis*, *Valmikis*, *Jatavs*, *Kahars*, and *Namasudras* in the estimate of a local pradhan. This chapter draws on qualitative interviews with 80 families spread across all 3 camps over the course of 3 years.

This cluster underwent many phases of evolution and saw several developments, such as the initial occupation of the barren wasteland that was Govindpuri in the early 1970s, the flow of Bengali residents into the cluster after the 1971 war, and the regional demarcation of camps in the 1980s. This was followed by the issue of a bundle of identity cards (ration cards, identity cards, and number-bearing tokens) during V.P. Singh's administration in the 1990s, and the many DDA housing surveys in the late 1990s and the 2000s. These surveys neatly classified potential beneficiaries into different brackets of prospective resettlement based on who moved into the cluster prior to 1990 and who occupied government land after 1990. The means to substantiate the temporality of occupation was supplied by the ID documents issued in the 1990 initiative. This classification had considerable potential to govern residents' resettlement chances as it entailed differential entitlements in plot size. The plot scheme was, however, jettisoned in favour of an in situ plan in 2013 to resettle residents of all three camps in built houses across two sites, namely, A-14 Kalkaji Extension and in Govindpuri itself. This project was conceived to unfold over three phases, with the first phase anticipated to be finished within the next three years.[7] A project like this was conceived to accord with the blue-print of the latest Delhi Master Plan, which favours resettlement plans to include mixed land use, the involvement of community-based orga-nizations and NGOs, and an invitation to the private sector to develop land. With the exception of the last feature, the in situ rehabilitation plan involved all of the above. 'Land as a resource', it was believed, was best served through private sector investment and involvement—yet this wisdom was partially abandoned in favour of a fully government-funded and operated resettlement scheme for this cluster (DDA 2010: 21–2).[8]

Very few families interviewed actually believed that the relocation would happen saying that they had lost count of the number of times they were surveyed. Multiple surveys notwithstanding, there were no organized demolitions in the heart of the cluster since its inception and this sowed scepticism that resettlements would actually take place.[9] In this scheme of things, identity cards were immensely treasured; for though they were disbelieving, Govindpuri's residents could never stop fearing that, in the event of the actual transition and the move, they might not feature in—what was perceived to be the under-enumerated—the figure of 8,000 families as the core beneficiaries of resettlement. A Congress politician and an active member of the DDA, Subhash Chopra, took credit for a progressive move under this resettle-ment scheme to ensure that the housing agency, in its survey, counted at least 30 per cent tenants too.[10] Many of those interviewed—tenants and landlords—reported that they were not beneficiaries of the full survey which involved door-to-door verification and the biometric exercise of capturing the resident's fingerprints.

The Scene Unfolds

V.P. Singh's visit to Navjeevan camp was a visit that very few of those present on the occasion could easily forget. On account of being the adopted son of one king and the real son of another, V.P. Singh was pop-ularly called Raja *Saheb*, an epithet that I repeatedly heard the people in the settlement use to refer to him. He unveiled his government's decision that every slum resident in Delhi would be issued a ration card

by the end of three months. The scene of the prime minister's address
unfolded in the large open area of what was disparagingly termed the
Jhuggi-wallah Park (Slum Park), which lay in intimate proximity to the
slum cluster near Govindpuri (see Figure 4.1). One newspaper article
called the enumeration initiative 'V.P. Singh's New Year gift to the
lakhs of JJ dwellers and others belonging to the economically weaker
sections of the capital',[11] while another declared that 'the wretched of
the earth could not have had a rosier dawn' than the day on which the
prime minister extended his 'New Year gift'.[12] The popular media's
metaphor of the gift in discussing the V.P. Singh drive does not suggest
that the leader was corrupt. Far from it, the newspapers allude to his
paternal impulses and his benevolence. Scholars writing on patronage
politics in South Asian societies discuss the gift as a mutual 'socially
and politically constitutive' bond (Piliavsky 2014: 9): the card initiative
may have rendered V.P. Singh and the urban poor in hierarchical and
rhetorical terms of mutual obligation. It must be noted that South Asia,
and particularly India, has a deep tradition of viewing welfare schemes
in populist and, by extension, moral terms of gift giving. In erstwhile
Andhra Pradesh under the late N.T. Rama Rao regime, ration books
were presented as *anna-varam*, which translated mischievously into big
brother's gift and food gift in Telugu (Olsen 1989: 1598). Even a document like the FIR, whose place in the penal world of court procedures,
police norms, and criminal justice is undisputed, has a currency in
discussions of patronage and local cultural power structures (Jauregui
2014). I bring up these invocations of gift and patronage only to show
that it is not only laptops, bicycles, and foodgrains that stand out as
the objects of populist exchange; ID documents are equally potent
as channels of political leverage. Their legal properties are permeable
to local moral idioms of munificence and they inflate the patron-like
capabilities of officials and politicians.

Witnesses to this pivotal, yet scarcely remembered,[13] moment of the
urban history of Delhi were many officials and ministers who accompanied V.P. Singh.[14] The day was special for V.P. Singh as it was his first
(and what was to turn out to be his only) New Year as the prime minister of India. It was, however, also a day when V.P. Singh was going to
endear himself politically to the urban poor population of Delhi residing in slums in a way that few politicians had done before. With what
appeared to be a magician's sleight of hand, he rendered that day the

first of an incredibly short three months at the end of which every surveyed slum resident in Delhi came to possess, apart from a ration card,
an identity card and a metallic plate or token on which was inscribed
a number or an identity for every home. What did these documents
translate into? They set up a tenuous legal infrastructure of identity
which was to extend, among other things, an insurance against arbitrary
eviction, a fixed ration contingent on a fixed residence, a postal address,
and assurances of resettlement on the strength of occupation in Delhi
prior to 1990. V.P. Singh did something unusual when he announced
this initiative: he argued that welfare eluded the poor owing to their
scanty access to ID documents and ration cards in particular. Slum
residences were marked by a dangerous fragility because they were not
borne out on paper, he indicated. In his speech, as reported in *HT*, on
the same day when he visited the slum cluster, he stated that while, on
the one hand, there was always a lot of talk of removing poverty, on the
other, nobody bothered to address the plight of lakhs of needy people
who were not provided ration cards.[15] He added that if the annual
financial budgets had 'paid attention to the actual needs of people, then
lakhs of JJ dwellers would not have been without ration cards'.[16] In
the days that followed, a comprehensive survey was undertaken in the
months between January and March 1990 of all the JJ clusters in Delhi
based on which ration cards were issued. It is recorded that in the first
phase, 694 slum clusters with a population of 2.26 lakh families were
identified and cards issued to families that were residing in slums.[17] A
reported number of 120 teams were deployed across slum clusters to
issue ration cards, each team consisting of an inspector from the food
and supplies department, a volunteer from the Urban Basic Services
Programme, a clerk or a patwari, and an attendant.[18]

V.P. Singh's Enumeration Drive: The Identity Card, the Token, and the Ration Card

Every representative of a family was issued a ration card and simultaneously, an identity card and a metallic token. The ration card bore the
names of the head of the family as well as the other members of the
family; the identity card carried only the number of family members
and a single representative's name and signature; and the metallic token
contained a number. These various ID documents were intended to

meaningfully lift the stigma of illegality around urban poor occupation in government land. One of the aberrations of this rationing and ID exercise, and a point on which the government prided itself, was that it did not place any demands on slum residents to produce the usual documents, like gas or electricity bills,[19] birth certificates or any residence proof, or for that matter, the surrender certificate of the previous ration card. Nor was an affidavit stating that the applicant had surrendered his previous card demanded from any slum resident. This rendered the whole exercise remarkable in the urban history of ID document production. Previous to this exercise, some form of documentary evidence was absolutely essential to all regional initiatives involving enumeration and rationing of residents. Officials and slum residents alike remarked on the extraordinariness of the enumeration drive where all existing documentary protocols were set aside for the purpose of issuing these ID documents.

The previous chapters in this book have demonstrated how food officials were deeply present in the knowledge economy of food distribution which was predicated on practices of enumeration and verification of identities. The employment of emotional filters such as compassion, anger, and resentment was common among these middling 'everyday state' figures. These officials sported aesthetic considerations—that spoke to their class positions—of what enumerable homes should look like. Such notions translated into distinctive yardsticks of counting families in the slum. These figures mobilized these aesthetic norms in identifying a house which needed to be enumerated. In explaining how homes and families were located for the 1990 exercise, the food officials reasoned that they could not weave their way through the winding and jagged paths that were so typical of squatter camps, and therefore they had to solicit the help of local pradhans or political leaders active in the area. *Itni gandgi me hum saare ghar nahin dhoondh pate* (We would not have been able to find all the houses in the midst of all the filth) and 'this is why we needed to take the help of insiders,' said one food official.[20] Apart from the coarse dichotomy this draws between the middle-class 'us' of a figure like the food official and the 'them' of the urban poor, such a construction underlines the intrinsically different or the distinct topography of colonies inhabited by the poor where dirt and squalor interfere with a natural sense of direction. This class-inflected administrative stance also emphasizes the need to trace enumerable units of home and household through the performative mould. Such a mould was composed of urban poor self-knowledge and sociality manifest in neighbourly relations and quotidian practices of mutual recognition.

The Identity Card or the V.P. Singh Card

In the months following 1 January 1990, tents were set up in the open area of the park located at the intersection of Bhumiheen and Navjeevan camps where forms were scrutinized and photographs were taken. Here, photographs were meant not for the ration card but for the special laminated identity card, which was issued for a price of Rs 5 along with the ration card. These photographs were to be taken either at the site of the cluster or at some convenient point near the food and supplies office.[21] This card issued to slum residents—one card per family along with the ration card—was popularly called the *lal* card because it was shot against a *lal parda* or a red colour background, and more often, V.P. Singh Card, named after the leader at the helm of the initiative. The card is still demanded and accepted by DDA officials in housing surveys (see Figure 4.2).

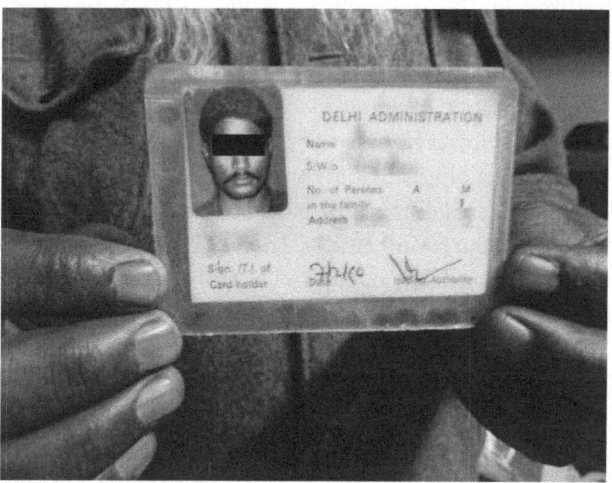

Figure 4.2 A Govindpuri Resident Shows His V.P. Singh Card
Source: Author.

Govindpuri's residents fondly remember V.P. Singh's many slum-related promises, such as the single-point bulb and concrete houses. *Pukke makan nahin depaya par pukka card zaroor diya*, goes one refrain. In other words, resident after resident spoke with warmth of the leader who gave pukke (laminated) cards to the dwellers of jhopadpatti even if he was not able to deliver on his promise of pukke makan. The V.P. Singh Card is understood to have many uses in this cluster: some residents spoke of using it in lieu of their voter identity card to cast their vote, while others said they showed it to get a voter identity card in the first place. Some others told me the card was useful to get their children admitted in MCD schools.[22] Their possession of this laminated card denoted for many residents their wholeness as political subjects and the dignity that went with it.

This card also conjured up pride of residence among many who considered its possession to be an irrevocable proof of their continuous occupation in the city. Such a response was prompted by the housing policy implemented in the early 2000s when both the ration card and the identity card instituted 'the datelines' of eligibility (Tabassum and Sarda 2010: 65), where the DDA assigned plots of different sizes to residents who were in occupation of a slum on government land prior to 1990 and those who came to Delhi after 1990.[23] A housing policy was approved by the DDA on 4 February 1992 with retrospective effect from 1990. A new strategy—which coincided with the setting up of the urban improvement department in 1990—laid down that there could be no relocation of slum residents in case of fresh encroachments on public land. However, past encroachments could not be removed without providing alternative accommodation. The planning department instructed officials to assign plots of 18 sq. m to those possessing ration cards with the cut-off date 31 January 1990, while those possessing ration cards post-1990 and up to December 1998 were to be given plot sizes of 12.5 sq. m.

The Metallic Token

There was one other document issued in this initiative which lacked the material form of a card. Metallic plates or tokens were to be affixed to the doors of slum homes. They signalled that families had been counted and the survey of the slum household was complete. Some slums still bore these tokens on the doors of their house even if they appeared somewhat worse for wear, having oxidized over time (see Figure 4.3). Over the years, the token receded into the background as other colourful markings denoting serial numbers of various housing and census-related surveys became prominent.

In the first few years after the initiative, this number or the token bearing this number extended to residents the convenience of a postal address. Paroma, who used to be a resident of C Block in Navjeevan camp, told me how before 1990, her post used to find its way to another Paroma staying in E Block in the same camp. However, with these token numbers, the mix-ups stopped and the postman promptly delivered all her post to her house. This was a story that demonstrated how such artifacts accomplished both the correct ID and the de-duplication of the postal recipient.[24] However, this postal efficiency

Figure 4.3 Metallic Token Issued during the V.P. Singh Initiative
Source: Author.

was probably very short-lived as most households did not wish to leave their tokens unguarded owing to thieving incidents in their camp. Not all these pilferers were malicious, for tokens often wound up in children's games who relished vexing residents of the cluster by stealing the tokens on their doors when the latter were not looking. 'Children pluck this token from the door and dash away,' explained a Tamil migrant, Saira.[25] This bad experience of some became a lesson for others who learnt to safeguard their tokens (by removing it from their doors and preserving it in their almirahs) so as to keep in census authorities, DDA, and other surveying authorities and keep out playful children, malevolent neighbours, and other mischief-makers. Postal delivery went back to being unreliable in the cluster in the last decade since some families lost these tokens or kept them inside, and those families which did display the token on their doors did not ensure that the number remained visible.[26]

This token was demanded by housing authorities who believed that the V.P. Singh Card could be forged: the token had a tactile feel which rendered it difficult to counterfeit and if residents could produce it in addition to the V.P. Singh Card, their claims were more credible; or at least, this was the imagined rationale behind the token in the narratives of slum residents. It was thus that ID documents had a contingent albeit spectral quality relative to different situations and they must be seen in comparison with other genres. In this sense, this artifact shared certain resonances with other ID documents in the history of postcolonial India that too have animated unlikely uses and imaginings outside their prescribed mandate. Passports, for instance, are commemorated not merely for their citizenship functions, nor are they used mechanically to apply for travel. Zamindar writes that in the wake of the formation of the postcolonial states of India and Pakistan, passport regimes born out of the imperative to discipline mobility across the border rendered the ID document into a phantasm. Faced with situations where the passport could restrict their movement and block their struggles to reunite with their families, holders would attempt to throw them away, destroy them, carry them without a visa, and use them in unauthorized spaces (Zamindar 2007: 191–5). Something similar can be observed about both the V.P. Singh Card and the metallic token, whose circulation escaped the political and administrative rationality assigned to them in this initiative.

The Ration Card

In slum spaces, ID and verification exercises could only be pale imitations of what was legally mandated because those squatting on government land could not be entitled to permanent ration cards.[27] The ration card—which was issued alongside the identity card and the token—had many uses in the slum. It was an assurance of food security; it extended the tenuous promise of resettlement; and it could be utilized right up till the year 1999 to bail out friends and relatives in jail. Some of the women I interviewed narrated the process of acquiring the confidence and the know-how to cautiously enter the discriminatory and male-dominated world of bail, policemen, and FIRs. In these circumstances, the ration card was stamped in a thana or in a court: in the former instance, it was called *kachchi zamanat*; and in the latter case, it was called *pukki zamanat*.[28] I describe elsewhere the gendered specificities of using the ration card to secure bail and how women in slum spaces were able to counter hegemonic spatial norms of masculinity in police stations through performative invocations of paper and ration cards in particular (Sriraman 2014).

Another unconventional use of the ration card, which was marginal to the legal gaze of the state, was the practice of pledging it. This was something that helped insure the poor against indebtedness (Gulati 1977; Mooij 1999; Sriraman 2011). This habit was observed in certain squatter colonies in south India where residents would offer the card as a surety against loans from friends or relatives who were able to use these cards and claim rations that they were legally not entitled to. The latter were, in addition, able to charge arbitrary rates of interest for the cash they lent. Residents in the cluster used the Hindi expression *girvi dena* to describe the practice of mortgage in this cluster. Interestingly enough, every person who was asked if they pledged their cards shook their heads in shock and disbelief as if they had heard someone utter a profanity. The common view expressed here was that the ration card was worth much more than anything anybody could lend. 'When people are ready to give Rs. 1000 or Rs. 2000 as commission [read bribe] to make a new ration card, why would anybody want to pledge the ration card?,'[29] asked one resident. Some residents expressed their outrage at the question in the light of their struggles to trace their lost ration cards in different offices. One of them said emphatically, 'We can mortgage our gold and silver but never our ration card.'[30] While no resident admitted to having pledged her card in the cluster, a couple of them did say that they claimed the rations on their card not for themselves but for somebody else. One such resident, Babita, had no use for the coarse grains that were issued to families in the 1990s because she did not want her children to have substandard food. Back in the early 1990s, when Babita worked as a domestic help, she always remembered to collect her PDS foodgrains from the FPS dealer. Babita would spend all her savings on purchasing good-quality rice and she would give away the coarse grains to her neighbours, who gladly took it. This account turns on its head notions of middle-class charity (to their maids or helps) where PDS foodgrains could only be consumed by the poor. This also contradicts the prevalent notion of middle-class charity that is predicated on their unique possession of alternative resources and purchasing power.

In various housing policy documents, the ration card is alone acknowledged as constituting proof of urban residence in the year 1990. This is perhaps because the original list of V.P. Singh cardholders was (rumoured to be) lost and officials had no way of determining the truthfulness of the V.P. Singh Card. A photocopy of the ration card issued in 1990 yielded more reliable evidence. However, very few slum residents had photocopies of their then-issued ration card. This was because the ration card was an ID document that was issued, cancelled, and renewed from time to time. Since residents had to submit their ration cards to get them renewed for fresh rations, they could not afford to preserve them. Photocopies were rarely treated on par with originals by such families and they were often lost in the sea of paper. Residents often presumed that the V.P. Singh Card, since it was issued once and only once, bore a more immediate link to resettlement. Officials, while they were loath to accept V.P. Singh Cards as proof, were forced to acknowledge them because ration card copies from 1990 could rarely be produced. The common practice of counterfeiting V.P. Singh Cards was responsible for the official aversion to these cards as proof. However, why was counterfeiting attempted and what purposes did it serve?

The Date as Document: Narratives of the Counterfeit

Unlike the ration card, the V.P. Singh Card was issued only once in 1990 and never again. Therefore, this card cast on its holders the halo of urban time and triggered an intense politics of claim-making. The 'temporal' features so prominently as an administrative signifier in slum spaces across India that the 'date' warrants discussion as a 'document' all by itself.[31] There are any number of instances of the date being valorized in postcolonial historical milieu in India, all of which add up to a damning indictment of the deep legalism of denials endemic to welfare dispensations. For example, rights to travel freely were accorded selectively to only those Tibetan refugees who could produce RCs dated between 1959 and 1979 (McConnell 2013: 972–3). Similarly, in order to secure concessions in education and healthcare facilities, squatters in Mumbai were expected to demonstrate the time of their occupation through electoral rolls issued by the Maharashtra government in 1995 in order to be eligible for a resettlement scheme (Dupont and Vaquier 2013: 317).

The date's ability to recast urban politics of resettlement and the very claim of belonging to the city conjured up an emotional and moral economy of welfare claims in housing. The date became a performative signifier of self-embodiment and forged new forms of political subjectivity. Here, the mere possession or absence of the card was not the only thing that provoked suspicion, pride, and resentment among residents and officials. It was also how, when, where, and who got cards made. The 'when' implied the date of the V.P. Singh Card, which placed residents in brackets such as who resided before and who resided after 1990 in the city. It was necessary to ask the question, 'who were the rightful holders of this card', in order to establish whether the owners of this card resided in the same place at the time the card was made, that is, in the first three months of the year 1990. The 'who' and 'when' were, therefore, integral to the 'how' and the 'where' of the card, that is, if a resident got a card made through a dalal. This word means a middleman, but it was often used in a pejorative sense not only by officials but also by residents to mean a petty crook who exploited the dearth of services and residents' fear of being excluded for lack of proof. The date as a document was thus at the heart of narratives of the jaali and the naqli.

Before I present narratives of the counterfeit in the slum, it is important to address the following question: why was a document like the V.P. Singh Card, issued in 1990—and in this sense, a dated document— counterfeited after all these years? To do this, it is necessary to pierce the official silence that enshrouds this ID document. One housing official closely associated with the 1990 enumeration initiative stated that the V.P. Singh Card was no longer relied on owing to its notorious reputation of being 'duplicated' in the slum cluster.[32] However, this document was, in practice, demanded in various housing surveys as marking dependable proof of occupation. In 2011, I saw a DDA official in Govindpuri cluster reject a V.P. Singh Card on the grounds that it looked too new. The survey of 1990 could not be erased from the administrative imagination of Delhi's housing policy. The last DDA survey that took place after 2010 in Govindpuri was necessitated by the new in situ project to resettle families to Kalkaji. In this survey, there was no mandate to follow the old guidelines which specified the datelines of 1990 and 1998. In its stead, the officials simply asked for identity cards corresponding to the year 1990 to establish continuous residence. Apart from the fact that this card continued to be actually demanded in survey practice, there was another important reason for counterfeiting it. Given that housing policies were so mercurial such that plots were replaced by flats in housing entitlement and datelines also kept changing, there was no knowing what additional or new restrictive eligibility criteria would be enforced in resettlement schemes. In slum spaces, the ration card was important to obtain because it contained details of the family as a whole—details that were indispensable to lay claim to resettlement in housing schemes. As has been already established, resettlement was incumbent on the date of entry into the city. Though the V.P. Singh Card did not mention individuals by name, it did carry the photograph of the head of the family and list the number of family members. In the last DDA survey, this document, presented along with the present-day ration card, gave the official an idea of the number of people present in the year 1990, how many members left the family, and who joined the family. When a family had lost its ID document or had no ID documents to prove the date on which they came to the city, it became important to counterfeit the V.P. Singh Card which could serve as proof of occupation in urban time. Govindpuri's residents were also aware that elsewhere in the city too, these cards were considered vital to resettlement. Slum residents were given plots in Bawana and Savda-Ghevda resettlement colonies on the strength of the V.P. Singh Cards, as they attested to these subjects' urban presence in 1990 (Menon-Sen and Bhan 2008: 10; Tabassum and Sarda 2010: 243).

Narratives of the counterfeit had everything to do with the enumeration of families in slum spaces. Family as an extended concept organized everyday life in slums and mediated residents' negotiations of government agencies, welfare schemes, and community relations in India after independence. In urban discourses of migration and forced displacement, arbitration of marital disputes, and local nuisances of gambling and drinking by samitis and *mahila mandals*, there is some operative definition of family and an associated normative tangle of commitments, violent relations, and betrayals. However, even outside these institutions and the roles they played, residents often sized up their short-term and long-term commitments in familial terms. While resettlement and the thought of it conjured all manner of apprehensions, the family was never far away from the horizon where one imagined the future. We will now see how familial affect came to structure narratives of the counterfeit in the accounts of residents who were either witness to the phenomenon, benefited from it, or partook of it.

Owing to the high stakes involved, counterfeit cards were sought, made, and transferred. Tarang, a resident and one-time slum leader (pradhan) of one of the camps, admitted to getting this card made through a dalal in a bold, courageous, and somewhat troubling account of the role she played and the influence she enjoyed in the cluster. Tarang got the V.P. Singh Card counterfeited for her daughter who got married and eventually moved out of the cluster. The fee she paid to get the card made was a whopping Rs 6,000. She was able to afford this fee through an income earned in a dangerous career as a rough and tough pradhan. Tarang had, back in 1990, a family of two sons, one daughter, and a husband, who was a contract employee who was away most of the time. She was a pradhan, an informal title that certain individuals in each camp earned for themselves through the personal assistance they rendered to residents. She got pukki jhuggi made for residents, helped people get married, and got men out on bail. She told me that she would take a little money after tendering such risky help in the fraught political environment of the slum. Tarang once helped her neighbour, a blind woman, who had lost a relative in an accident involving a rash bus driver. It became a police case and Tarang had to help with getting the body back from the police and in arranging the funeral. She was able to arm-twist a local leader into helping to get the body from the police. Her success had to do with knowing the deep stakes that the leader had in the upcoming election for the municipal councillor. Having helped her bypass formal procedures of postmortem, Tarang took Rs 1,000 from the neighbour. Tarang had to ease herself into the hurly-burly of slum life where she learnt to handle policemen, negotiate with politicians, rough up residents, and take on a whole lot of people. It was through such a career that she was able to afford the counterfeit V.P. Singh Card. In short, her struggle to get this card made entailed finding the courage to transgress the presumptive urban boundaries of morality that was bound up with discourses of femininity. She had to step 'out of bounds' (Nair 2009: 88) to partake of the risky business of *dalali*, which was inimical to female orientations towards infrastructure in public spaces (Niranjana 2001). She narrated her journey of securing a counterfeit V.P. Singh Card through a performativity of politics inherent to the cultural roles she played as pradhan in the slum.

But why did this card entail so much for her? She saw a need to take the necessary steps to secure her daughter's future in the slum. Tarang was convinced that the DDA survey-wallahs would give her daughter a plot or a flat someday on the strength of the V.P. Singh Card and that the card held out a promise of better housing for its holders. However, since she was not sure of the security she (her daughter) would enjoy outside the cluster, she wanted her daughter to be able to enjoy the same prospective privilege that she (Tarang) enjoyed. It was unfair that the government could deny her daughter a housing entitlement on flimsy administrative grounds. Her daughter was her blood and did not cease to be so when she got married. The V.P. Singh Card's protection in the sense of being an insurance against demolition would extend to her daughter only as long as she remained unmarried. This was why it was important to get a counterfeit card. Though no demolitions had taken place at the time of speaking, Tarang had to prepare herself for all eventualities. She was willing to take this immense risk to fortify her daughter against the all-too-likely discrimination between near and distant family, that is, those who were present during the initiative and continued to stay with their family in the slum on the one hand, and second-generation beneficiaries who left the cluster on the other.

For those who made counterfeit cards, this was a 'side business' which supplemented their actual income as a grocer or vendor. It was, however, important to charge a lot of money as this was a risky affair.

'If you ask me why dalals take so much money to make the cards, I would say, if the dalal gets caught, he can at least arrange for his own bail!,' said one resident.[33] This card was not hard to replicate because the materials needed to fabricate it—such as ink, cameras, and even forgers—were plentifully available. Photographing persons against a red background to imitate the lal parda of the identity card was quite facile. To give the card an old look, dalals advised their customers to squish the card in the folds of a sari or to toss it about a little in mud.

Counterfeiting was seen as a gamble within everyday life in the cluster which was intrinsically violent. Both the maker and the seller of the card may be driven by what Veena Das (2012) terms 'the gambler's faith'. Colin McFarlane (2011: 216) and Veena Das (2012) suggest that slum residents preserve certain urban materials such as corrugated iron and brick, tyres and rubber, in the hope that they may yield unpredictable future uses in the ecology of the slum. Writing about the slum dwellers in Delhi and Mumbai, respectively, Das and McFarlane consider urban poor relationships with commodities as accruing from the uncertainty of their future aspirations and the deep presence of certain materials in urban poor spaces.[34] Counterfeiting of cards only carried the gambler's future orientation to an extreme where residents were seized by the trepidation that their children would not benefit from resettlement. Pace Veena Das, these piecemeal actions would characterize an 'emergent citizenship', where people preserve all manner of commodities and refashion and repurpose all sorts of ID documents such that they become oriented towards an everyday future full of tentative promises (Das 2012). In his ethnography of fake ID documents in Delhi's slums, Sanjay Srivastava writes that these practices of trickery are 'produced by being in the city' and they, in turn, 'produce certain kinds of relationships and ways of being in the city' (Srivastava 2012: 79). He suggests that those who live in conditions of precariousness undertake a panoply of measures to protect themselves from being tricked out of benefits even as they themselves seek to trick their way into getting benefits. He records slum residents in east Delhi as carrying laminated photocopies of ID cards if only to ensure they do not fall into the hands of thieves and others who submit fake cards in order to get genuine ones. The slum also allowed for people to gain a modicum of stability by fostering certain transactions of buying and owning houses and forging ration cards. Srivastava points out how buyers have been successful in getting their names added as relatives in ration cards of house sellers, for instance. This scholarship indicates that these 'topographies of deception' (Srivastava 2012: 79) allowed the delicate negotiation of the arbitrary legalities and illegalities of the slum. However, what has perhaps gone unnoticed is the deep investment of counterfeiting—to be associated with the desire to counterfeit and the impulse to police the counterfeiter—in familial affect.

Not surprisingly, the invocation of jaali cards elicited angst-ridden responses from many residents. These responses bordered on tensions existing between families around their dates of arrival in the slum. Bharati, who told me her son was issued a V.P. Singh Card in 1990, said in emphatic tones, 'I have been staying here from 1980, why would I need a dalal? Only those who came here after 1990 would need to approach a dalal and get a card made!'[35] All these constructions contained an emotional assertion of what constituted a just familial entitlement. However, a just entitlement was not simply morally defined, it turned on the 'date as document'. To explain this point better, let me now turn to the example of Raj Gandhi, one of the oldest and more litigious denizens of Govindpuri cluster.

Raj Gandhi was an ex-serviceman who many decades back was part of India's artillery regiment in the India–Pakistan War in 1965. Today, he was applying himself industriously to various causes in the cluster, such as filing court petitions, FIRs, and RTI requests, and making complaints to the MCD. With the MCD, for instance, he took up the matter of public toilets in the cluster stating in the complaint how the caretakers in charge fleeced residents even though MCD had extended this service free of charge. Raj Gandhi was, however, most vociferous in his activism against those who had obtained jaali[36] ration cards or V.P. Singh Cards. He was hugely concerned that when the time came for housing officials to identify genuine families, there would be injustice done to those who possessed legitimate cards issued in 1990, while those with counterfeit V.P. Singh Cards would walk away with flats in hand. He was indignant about one dalal in the cluster and he proclaimed, '*Pehle sabji bechta tha, aaj ration card bech raha hai, pehle apne liye jaali ration card banvaya tha, aajkal yeh aadmi do number ka kaam kar raha hai*' (Previously, he used to sell vegetables and today, he sells ration cards. First, he made himself a jaali ration card and now he is doing this shady work for others).[37] In order to expose the counterfeiter, Raj Gandhi

fell back on a cultural premise of how the card was issued only to those
with family. He also prided himself in being one of the oldest residents
of the cluster. The counterfeiter was young, in his forties, he said. He
continued:

> I know every family who stayed in the cluster before 1990. This *dalal*
> came to the cluster after 1990 and bought a plot from a resident here
> who sold it and went away. If he came after 1990, how come he has a
> V.P. Singh card? He has *no family here*. You see, it is only those people
> with a father and mother residing for a long time who could have been
> issued a ration card or a V.P. Singh card in 1990.[38]

Unlike some of the other residents in the cluster, Raj Gandhi had
no great nostalgia for the V.P. Singh Card. In fact, his activism set him
apart from a few other residents who displayed a fierce sense of loyalty to V.P. Singh. Their attachment to the card and their aversion to
counterfeiters were born out of deep love for the leader. One such
resident told me that he would treasure the card for as long as he lives
and he would ask his children to keep the card in his memory and V.P.
Singh's memory. Raj Gandhi's activism against counterfeiting was not
sentimental. He believed that cards had a sacred purpose within an
order of legality, outside of which they were suspect and exploitative.
The document was not a commodity that could be procured in an
informal market pandering to desires and everyday struggles, according to this activist. The V.P. Singh Card was all the more important to
secure from counterfeiters because though it looked and performed all
the functions of an ID document, it was unlike other cards in that it
was solely responsible for crystallizing the date of 1990, thus imbuing
resettlement claims with legal morality.

In her work on the housing and sterilization drives of slum residents
in Delhi during the Emergency, Tarlo (2003: 11) remarks that the poor
in Delhi relate to the state through the market. Her point was that basic
amenities such as electricity, water, and roads, as well as welfare benefits
such as land and jobs, are not provided but purchased in exchange for
votes, money, or in the instance of the Emergency, sterilization certificates. Counterfeiting in the slum would seem to fit within this scheme
of things as people purchase cards in the local market to secure housing
entitlements. It is hard to theorize these practices of alternative legalities without acknowledging Partha Chatterjee's descriptions of political

society and his telling of the tale of governmentality (Chatterjee 2004). Partha Chatterjee uses the term 'political society' to encompass residents with intersecting identities, such as squatters, refugees, landless people, and day labourers, who mobilize themselves into a community. This community is born out of a collective need to cope with the precariousness of their civil and political rights, the foremost of which are their mode and place of residence. The space of political society is marked by paralegal arrangements and an absence of the conception of law in general. The terms of association in political society stand in stark contrast to civil society; the latter deals with the government in the language of law and rights and engages, rather than negotiates, with the government. It has, however, been pointed out contra Partha Chatterjee that the legitimate struggles for citizenship need not take shape within hegemonic state formations. Julia Eckert, for instance, argues that even though they may act in an extralegal terrain, subjects such as slum residents are desirous of moulding 'good order' (Eckert 2004: 46; Chatterjee 2004).

As the actions of Udai Bhan and the case of a few other litigious residents demonstrate, the language of law was not alien to the politics of the slum. Govindpuri's slum residents were willing to counterfeit but also file petitions, RTIs, and seek other legal remedies.[39] They were able to use a rich repertoire of legal and extralegal practices in an everyday context to forge recognition for citizenship claims. It has furthermore been argued that the legal and the illegal, those who govern and those who are governed, cannot be distinguished so sharply (Das 2011). Let me add another category here: the distinctions between those who enumerate and those who are enumerated cannot be so well-defined either. The food officials' heavy reliance on pradhans' knowledge of the slum and the location of houses illustrates the fuzzy nature of this distinction. If Veena Das also writes that governmentality cannot be the only modality of administering subjects, this chapter's description of affective and tactile practices of counting families and verifying identities amounts to a subversion of the Foucauldian as well as a Chatterjee-ian interpretation of governmentality. Das (2011) writes of the operation of kinship networks that have their roots in caste and region as also serving to mobilize slum residents. While this chapter does not trace kinship networks organized around these categories, it does, however, look at how neither officials nor residents could treat family as a strictly 'enumerated category'. Instead, they reconstituted it as an affective, lived, and gendered reality. If, on the one hand, this chapter shows how residents sought to use their cards to insure their familial futures, on the other, it will also demonstrate how they sought to rearrange domestic objects such as curtains, floors, and stoves to make a persuasive case for a card.

The Performative Mould of Enumeration

If the 1990 initiative has been noted in urban poor scholarship (Batra and Mehra 2008; Kundu 2004: 263) as benefiting slum residents in the kind of entitlements it made possible for them, what has been less visible is how easily these forms of proof slid into liabilities that threatened residents and jeopardized their claims. This liability to sudden loss was all the more severe owing to egregious lapses of record-keeping, where it was rumoured that the list of original V.P. Singh cardholders was lost, thereby foreclosing chances of its replacement. The striking survey exercise of 1990 did not insulate slum residents in its aftermath from loss of documents incurred in everyday mobility or for that matter, the routine recurrence of fires (Dupont and Vaquier 2013: 318). A fire in one of the three camps engulfed several homes soon after this initiative, taking lives and obliterating ID documents in its wake. One resident, Rajendra, let the embers settle down and then retrieved delicately from the scorched remains of his house a fragment of the V.P. Singh Card in order to be able to communicate this involuntary documentary loss. He preserved this fragment by pinning it along with other ID documents on a piece of cardboard (see Figure 4.4).

Yet another resident, Babita, spoke of the bribe she paid to a policeman to get an FIR to serve as a tenuous signifier for the card her son had lost on his way to some office.[40] In Govindpuri cluster, these anguished improvisations were all the more fraught because it had seen repeated housing surveys though no demolitions, at least in the heart of the cluster. Fear, hope, and despair were all writ large on Babita's face in narrating all this to me for she did not know if this was good enough in the case of the V.P. Singh Card which was a one-off business, there being no precedent or antecedent. She articulated to me her worst fears: who was to know if the DDA people would accept the FIR as a substitute for the lost card?[41] Also, considering that there were so many

Figure 4.4   A Fragment of the Burnt V.P. Singh Card along with Other ID Documents Attached to a Piece of Cardboard ... or a Mobile Personal Archive
Source: Author.

DDA surveys and no real attempt to actually issue plots or flats, was Babita's money wasted?

As I have already argued, ID documents can be regarded to have spectral qualities in the way they insinuate themselves into the everyday struggles of slum residents. Gupta records the intimate foreboding that certain subjects have of the mediating power of files: 'in a protest against globalization', farmers made sure they burnt all the files in the possession of a Monsanto office (Gupta 2012: 214). It is not merely their salience to making entitlement claims that made it so vital to manipulate, replace, or present documents in a certain way. Identification documents can be patently unreadable in the sense that they can be projected in so many ways to make a case against the claimant. 'How do we know you are saying the truth?' 'How do we know your card is not new?' These were all questions that were posed to Govindpuri's slum residents. However, conditions of loss or damage of the document presented other predicaments altogether because the object had to materially enact and bear residual traces of its ideal representation. The FIR can enact the loss of the V.P. Singh Card but would fail in setting up a material correspondence to the card. The burnt fragment of the card looked like a diminished form of its ideal representation and in this sense, it could work. However, administrations were often unconvinced by the argument of the irreplaceability of cards or its deterioration. This initiative thus exemplified, both in its immediate execution and its aftermath, the systemic production of arbitrariness on various administrative scales, like the suspension of the mandate for proof, the search for spatial markers of household, and a heavy reliance on discretionary markers of authenticity. Determining whether an FIR or a burnt fragment was credible as a legal artifact too constituted such a call of codified discretion.[42]

The mobilization of identity cards was embedded in affective and gendered ties. A ration card or an identity card for every nuclear family was critical in the face of gender hierarchies and patriarchal domination. Vidya, a migrant from Tamil Nadu, told me about how she would guard the identity card that was issued by the V.P. Singh government with her life because it was an insurance against harsh eviction by her husband's second wife, a prospect that seemed very real to her. She said, 'If she chases me away, it is this card that will help me in the future.'[43] She explained that her husband alternated between staying with her in the slum she resided in and the second wife's house constructed behind the first. She was very keen to get the identity card made in her name as the other wife had got one made in hers. ID documents, in this sense, extended this fragile yet indispensable protection to women compromised by unkind patriarchy. This initiative helped trace tenuous distinctions between the enumerable space of the household and the affective space of the family. Let me explain this by delving into one of the most vital parts of the 1990 exercise.

Drawing Fault Lines: 'The Factum of Residence'

When the administration was ordered by fiat that ID documents as a genre of proof could not be consulted for purposes of issuing ration cards and identity cards, food officials had to anchor their searches for enumerable homes and households to something tangible. 'We cannot

give any man a ration card by selling our conscience,' proclaimed a
food official;[44] and an official's conscience suffered when he had to
issue household consumer cards without being able to count, classify,
and draw fault lines. This particular initiative, which exempted slum
residents from having to produce proof, was very perplexing for food
officials. These officials could not be indifferent to where and how families resided or what was termed the factum of residence. This prosaic
refrain which had its echo in legal parlance was to be scrutinized when
an official crossed the slum resident's threshold. However, before we
regard how the factum of residence found its way into the micro-legal
worlds of food officials, a few words about the bureaucratic framework
of household enumeration in the 1980s and the 1990s and their slum-
related caveats will be in order.

In official narratives, slum spaces in India were not only characterized
by the administrative delineation of incoherent land use but also by the
aesthetic and functional aspect of houses spilling into each other and
rooms blurring into each other in terms of commercial space, dwelling
space, and cooking space. Such lived spaces did not translate into ideal
enumerable units. There was a certain sense of accord between census
and food policy norms for the purposes of defining a household. In
food policy, there were fortifications against urban chaos in the form
of strictures related to informal housing arrangements. A food-related
control order issued in Delhi in the year 1981 to regulate rationed food
articles defined 'household' to mean:

> a family unit living together in one building or portion of the building
> held in possession by any member of the family as *common residence* and
> maintaining a *common kitchen* and includes persons so living together
> whether or not dependent on the holder of the consumer card or the
> person in whose name the application for the issue of consumer card
> is made.[45]

The 1981 census outlines the difference between 'family' and
'household', specifying that a family comprises persons related by
blood but a census household is 'a group of persons who commonly live
together and would take their meals from a common kitchen' (*Census
of India, 1981: Delhi, a Portrait of a Population*, 1989: 171).[46] Even in
the last decade, the decennial census featured enumerators delineating
census houses not on the basis of distinct housing structures but on
that of actual use and habitation by a group of persons.[47] The rationing

policy was also keen to disentangle families and households, as well as institutional/commercial and residential households. If food policy and census norms regarded the definition of residential household to be based on the kitchen and its presence, interviews with food officials too featured these men stressing the *rasoi* as sacrosanct to ration card enumeration. The operative metonym for kitchen was the chulha which had to be located in slums where there were no delineated living, cooking, and sleeping spaces.

If the chulha was an important motif in food policy vis-à-vis issuing ration cards, its mere presence did not attest to a household and a home. The ration card application was evaluated in performative terms to yield proof of long-term habitation and family size. A couple of food officials who were part of this exercise said that they expected the stove to be found either against the wall, in a corner, or in a tiny adjunct to the house which served as a kitchen (see Figure 4.5). If a family was using a stove, then the wall against which it was placed should be stained by grime. If the family was cooking using firewood or kerosene instead of liquefied petroleum gas (LPG), then officials should look for these items in the house and check whether the bricks bear streaks of

Figure 4.5   An Enumerable Home in Present-day Govindpuri
Source: Author.

soot. Dissembling families which placed a stove merely to persuade officials of their ration card eligibility could thus be easily found out. It was believed to be common among slum residents to demand additional ration cards by separating their houses cosmetically, namely, by placing curtain partitions, by building floors, and so on. This was why an official could not be careful enough. *Baltis*, charpoys, and gaddas were reinforcing visual markers of the number of family members, it was believed.

Another erstwhile food inspector told me that he found these rules of thumb to be unrealistic and even uncompassionate. It was not possible to compute the number of people living in a house based on the number of charpoys in a cramped one-room jhuggi. This was because the space taken by charpoys would infringe on the room available for kitchen utensils. However, even this official wished to rule out mischievous and deceptive attempts to weave a tapestry of family where none existed. Cloth partitions and a jhuggi over another jhuggi were ration card frauds which could not be indulged. Moreover, this food official insisted, it was important to determine material evidence of familial affinity. If in a jhuggi, there was only one charpoy, but the mother-in-law was sought to be included in the ration card, such a claim had to be dubious, given the cultural animosity between mother-in-law and daughter-in-law. The size of the house had to be correlated with the number of persons and the affective ties between those reasonably thought to be staying in a slum.

In enumerating any household or counting members for issuing a ration card, food officials had to be scrupulous. This was not really because negligence in counting a household would result in ration leakage. In the 1980s and the 1990s, variable ration quotas were issued to households depending on the number of family members. It was only post 2000 that ration card quotas became standardized across families and remained so until the passing of the Food Security Act, 2013.[48] Thus, at the time of the initiative, the quotas varied from household to household depending on their size. This meant that, going by the incentive of food entitlement alone, there was no reason for slum residents to bifurcate a household in order to get two ration cards instead of just one. If considerations of food entitlement were not so salient to household enumeration, then what was? The food administration was given to believe that ration cards, if combined with identity cards, made a concerted political case for resettlement. Two ration cards translated into two housing claims. Housing policy has always discounted first-floor jhuggis for resettlement purposes. This sometimes forced the residents to demonstrate their atomistic familial status by setting up cloth partitions within a house. This practice, in turn, triggered suspicion around material objects like the chulha and the charpoy and whether they really told the truth about the number of families present.

All instrumental reasons (of food entitlement and resettlement) aside, food officials believed that if they did not count and classify, they opened themselves up to charges of being venal and unprincipled. This was because enumerating households could never be a random administrative exercise. Handelman writes that, faced with the 'diffuseness and indeterminacy of much of daily life', bureaucracies were often spurred to cluster 'their taxonomic and systemic notions' in 'certain locations and contexts' more than others (Handelman 1981: 12). The systematic 'idea of the bureaucracy' was imposing in that it 'awaits instructions to name, to place, to exhaust, and to classify virtually every phenomenal domain to which it is attached' (Handelman 1981: 9). Administrations were no different: the space of the slum where households were not distinct and the context of the initiative where food officials could not ask for proof aggravated the need to draw fault lines by whatever means possible. These officials took the mandate to turn 'political questions' into 'technical problems' seriously (Hoag 2011: 83; Scherz 2011: 35). Owing to 'the lack of guidelines' in this initiative where food policy norms relating to ID documents were temporarily suspended, food officials had to improvise on notional norms. What I am arguing is that certain administrative but also deeply cultural norms of counting the household by gauging kinship ties and noting visual markers such as the chulha and the charpoy were always a part of ration card enumeration in postcolonial dispensations. However, this initiative may have presented an overwhelming necessity to do so owing to a void of ID proof and the impending need to substitute it with extra-documentary modes of ID and verification.

The Delhi Master Plan: Populism and Class Contestations

The chapter, so far, has attended to how ID documents in this initiative circulated in the slum and how officials issued them in the first

place. In particular, we saw how family and its affects ordered both
official practices of counting slum residents and popular practices of
counterfeiting ID documents. Let us now turn to the effects these ID
documents had in class narratives and the class discourse around the
Delhi Master Plan.

This enumeration initiative illustrates how governments had to constantly move from one kind of politics to another, and from politics to
administration in the everyday. If the initiative was prompted by populist impulses to win the slum resident's vote, it also wished to order the
residential spaces of the urban poor in Delhi. A squatter settlement
spends much time in relative invisibility until there is a perception of
a boundary having been crossed, the city having been breached. V.P.
Singh's enumeration initiative may not have been very different. For
four years from 1986 to 1990, not a single ration card had been issued
in the slums of Delhi and nobody had noticed.[49] The initiative followed
reports of an outbreak of cholera and gastroenteritis in 'the city's resettlement colonies and the illegal slum settlements' which threatened to
spill over into middle-class localities owing to 'accumulated garbage,
and the water in the newly paved drains [that] now flowed backwards
in some areas, flooding open spaces nearby' (Chaplin 1999: 155). Less
than a month after V.P. Singh's government unveiled the enumeration
initiative, it made another announcement—that the Delhi administration would not remove any existing slums before providing alternative
housing. However, the administration would make sure that newly
constructed slums were razed to the ground.[50] The survey of slums in
1990, as part of the ration card drive, would enable officials to leave
out illegitimate candidates. A press note of the government stated that
'the administration has the responsibility to safeguard public land and
to maintain the norms of the Master Plan and municipal regulations'.
At the same time, it had to be 'sensitive to human considerations, partly
in relation to the most disadvantaged section of the people residing in
jhuggi clusters'.[51] Ironically, the V.P. Singh government was accused by
newspapers of triggering an epidemic of slum construction in the city
where owning one illegally on public land could yield future compensations provided the slum resident was able to procure an identity card
or a ration card.[52] The government tried to neutralize such accusations
by showing how scrupulous officials had been in issuing ration cards. In
the clusters of Shahbad, Daulatpur, and Kalyanpuri where 'large-scale

construction of fresh jhuggis' was reported, ration card operations were 'suspended' pending an inquiry.[53]

The first two Master Plans of Delhi (1961–81 and 1981–2000) sought to segment land, create green belts in the city, demarcate land zones, bring down the population of the city, and address geographical imbalances by shifting what was deemed the surplus population to ring towns in neighbouring states (Batra and Mehra 2008; Datta 1983; Thynell et al. 2010). At the same time, they also consisted of designs to provide housing to the poor in certain resettlement sites (Kundu 2004). In chastising the V.P. Singh government for not complying with planning norms, the middle classes of Delhi recalled the Master Plans to benignly perform the first set of aims (create green belts and so on) but not the latter (resettle poor households). In their various debates on jhuggis and their place in the urban spaces of Delhi, newspapers often referred to ration cards in relation to the Master Plan, and to both of these in relation to illegal migration. Various editorial columns in *The Statesman* spoke of the ration card initiative as playing into the hands of opportunistic policemen, greedy slum-dwellers, speculators, and land grabbers. The threat of illegal migration was always looming large in these reports—migration both of labour from other states and of the Bangladeshi immigrant looking for means to get an Indian passport.

Many of these reports, while seeming to send out very mixed messages, are ideologically straightforward. One journalist writes that there are many things that attract migrants to Delhi, most of all its 'open-door policy' to them: 'For, Delhi cares for them. It gives them water, electricity, sanitation, medical facilities, alternative sites or dwelling units, night shelters, television, soft loans and eventually ration cards that confirm citizenship and entitles the holder to so many other facilities.'[54] The present policy of allotting 25 sq. m plots to jhuggi residents who can prove with their ration card that they were residents of Delhi before 1990 would involve 'handing over village after village till such a time that Delhi becomes a veritable concrete jungle'.[55] Migrant labour should be sent back to where they belong, otherwise, 'Masterplan or no plan, Delhi can never be remodelled on modern lines,'[56] writes one journalist. Another laments that 'Delhi's personality and topography had never been destroyed so mercilessly as during these last 13 years' of 'political chicanery' where politicians wooed JJ residents presumably through ration cards.[57] Many reports concur that unless civic amenities

are provided in the resettlement colonies soon after they are set up,
the new settlements will continue to congest Delhi and blot its landscape. A few middle-class readers, however, applauded the initiative
because they perceived it to perform the largely overdue surveillance
of slums.[58] It was at the same time argued that the many fires that mys-
teriously engulfed the city—many of which were reported the same
year—rendering residents eligible for compensation, only legitimized
the encroachment and by extension, the allocation of compensations in
the form of ration cards and plots.[59]

Such anxieties also deepened in the face of DDA's poor housing
drives. In Govindpuri, middle-class colony residents reacted hysteri-
cally to the initiative when DDA's JJ or slum wing constructed flats
in the middle of the park located near the cluster, thereby 'slicing the
park by half' and flouting zonal plans.[60] Many residents of this cluster complained bitterly that they moved into Pocket A-14 of Kalkaji
Extension based on a promise stated in a DDA brochure dated 9 March
1981 which showed lots of open space and a neighbouring park which
they had hoped would be developed, though not into an adjunct of
the cluster. The move to enumerate ration cards to slum residents was
projected by journalists and readers as one made by a populist government that would go to any lengths to jeopardize the idyllic middle-class
neighbourhood so central to the sanctioned plans of Delhi. Intriguingly,
if the overarching middle-class's charge against the V.P. Singh government was that its ration card initiative threatened the Master Plan of
ordering the city, sanitizing its spaces, and grooming its residents, the
latter responded by showing that this initiative actually embodied the
Master Plan by its twin attempt to enumerate slum residents and to
ensure that no new jhuggis were constructed.

Policies and measures for slum residents are nebulous, mercurial, and
unreliable, as evident by the fact that the ration cards issued during this
initiative were valid for only five years. After this initiative, the ration
cards were, once again, issued erratically to those residing in slums.
Invitations for ration cards were not always issued at the same time
that they were due for renewal. In the years after the initiative, successive governments evicted slum residents without alternative housing.
Ration cards and identity cards notwithstanding, these governments
paid scant regard to the cardinal policy norms adopted by the erstwhile
V.P. Singh administration that placed a freeze on all demolitions unless

they were backed by resettlement. 'It is owing to V.P. Singh's crusade against arbitrary eviction that we have a rudimentary framework for housing the urban poor,'[61] said Jai Bhagwan Jatav, who co-founded with the former prime minister, V.P. Singh, an NGO called Jan Chetna Manch, which fought legal battles and participated in protests on matters pertaining to the urban poor in Delhi. However, this framework was conspicuous by its absence until the emergence of the Aam Aadmi Party (AAP) in Delhi: in his post-prime minister days as an activist, V.P. Singh was left to protest the callous violation of demolition norms adopted during his tenure.[62]

*

All enumeration exercises require performative inquiries into the categories they are rooted in. These categories could vary in scale—the kitchen, the family, the slum. Officials sought the help of pradhans and politicians in locating slums. They looked for cultural markers of lived household space and they cast about for the operational kitchen in the form of the chulha and its telltale presence. Following scholars like Matthew Hull and Bruno Latour, this chapter is attentive to the mediating artifacts which are necessary for measurement, classification, and enumeration. Hull writes with insight that 'The more abstract the scheme is the more mediators are required to link it to empirical objects' (Hull 2012a: 166). This initiative was definitely very abstract in the sense that it gave poor guidelines to the enumerating authorities to conduct the survey and issue ID documents. When certain conventional mediators like ID-based proof are not available to verify the empirical object of the household, other modes of discretionary authority are privileged. Bhavani Raman suggests that instead of looking for a veritable discord between rule and discretion, it would be more felicitous to consider how the 'concentration of discretion went along with the official faith in writing' (Raman 2012: 17–18). The move to look for tangible but unwritten objects was not inconsistent with an abiding belief in proof of the documentary variety. The survey of enumerable households tried to steady itself against the material void of bureaucratic currency through markers that visually reinforced the urban factum of residence. While certain practices like looking for the chulha were implicitly endorsed in food policy, others like looking for the grime on the wall had a valence only in a footloose scheme of administrative legalism.

The temporary suspension of proof could be tolerated in order to create a comprehensive legal architecture and infrastructure for the urban poor that conformed to Delhi Master Plan sensibilities. In this sense, this initiative did not simply wave away proof. It also created proof in the form of the V.P. Singh Card and the metallic token. These forms of proof corresponded minutely to urban frameworks where time was an important element in housing discourse. In housing policy, datelines are set, revised, and reset: while these datelines are universally acknowledged as crucial to claim-making, the ID document as the mediating artifact that sets up datelines is not so well-established in existing scholarship. In other cities and other poor housing schemes too, ID documents like ration cards and electoral rolls created datelines of eligibility. These other schemes too involved surveys of the urban poor. However, the 1990 initiative was a rare moment in the history of urban time-making because it involved creating new proof like the identity card or the V.P. Singh Card for slum residents and not merely mobilizing existing ones like ration cards.

But these ID documents cannot really be called 'weapons of the weak' (Scott 1985) because they do not clinch entitlements in a wholesale manner, anywhere and everywhere. The genres of each ID document and their small-scale spatial practices can set a lot of trapdoors of urban poor entitlement that these subjects can easily fall through. These trapdoors may be better understood if we were to consider an ID document as a witness to many bureaucratic truths. It sometimes serves as a proof of nationality; at other times, it is a narrative proof unto itself where it is a testament of the cardholder's veracity; and at yet other times, it is a proof of the minutely urban. The ration card and the V.P. Singh Card may have been performing similar functions but it was important to gauge their contingent salience across varying urban situations. It was important for subjects to be able to read the unique resources of an ID document in relation to genre and built urban form.

It may be wrongly deduced that such an exercise was anomalous because of how it privileged forms of discretionary authority. The next chapter will show the fallacy of such assumptions—some of the insights of this chapter can be carried over to the next chapter where I analyse an ID project called Aadhaar which prides itself in its technological efficiency and institutional capabilities for proof-making. In enrolling subjects for the Aadhaar, the footmen of this new-age enterprise had to resort to self-assigned practices of establishing eligibility and notional norms of verification. The analysis of the Aadhaar will be framed in the urban space of a bus terminal in north Delhi where transport authorities issued quasi-legal identity cards and metallic badges to a porter community. Whether we are dealing with the slum resident or the rural migrant, the ecosystem of urban housing documents is eerily similar, especially when one regards official tendencies to issue tenuous documents that resemble their bearers' in-between zones of belonging. Here, too, the footmen of the always-unfolding Aadhaar enterprise stood to benefit from a deep immersion into local proof-making.

Notes

1. This is an extract from a conversation between one of the protagonists, Ishvar, and the rations officer in Mistry (1996: 177).
2. A Govindpuri resident remembers the V.P. Singh initiative in these words; interview by author, New Delhi, 3 February 2011.
3. A Govindpuri resident held great disdain for counterfeiters in general, and this one in particular; interview by author, New Delhi, 4 April 2013.
4. Squatter settlements in Delhi are called camps and a grouping of camps is called a cluster. In Hindi, a single house in a squatter settlement is termed a jhuggi or a *jhopdi*.
5. Available at http://delhishelterboard.in/main/?page_id=128, accessed on 1 July 2014.
6. This map corresponds to the urban geography of Govindpuri and its vicinity as I witnessed it in the years between 2011 and 2013. Much has changed on the ground since then.
7. The first phase involved relocation to A-14 Kalkaji Extension where a community centre used to exist. It is in its place that the new multi-storied building complex housing the resettled residents is being constructed. The inauguration of this resettlement plan coincided roughly with the other in situ project in Delhi which involved the relocation of the slum residents of Kathputli colony. See 'Delhi CM Sheila Dikshit briefs Sonia Gandhi about Kalkaji JJ Cluster Rehab Plan', *The Economic Times*, 23 October 2013; and 'Kalkaji Jhuggi Residents meet Sonia', *The Hindu*, 24 October 2013.
8. I say 'partially' because DDA does plan to sell the land that is expected to be freed by relocation to private players.

9. Demolitions were recorded to have taken place in the fringes of the slum cluster where slums or shops spilled on to the road. The most memorable of these demolitions was the drive to remove slums to construct a wall between a middle-class colony and the cluster. I was able to confirm this through a response secured to an RTI filed to DUSIB. Preeti Jha, 'Great Wall of Kalkaji', *The Indian Express*, 6 April 2008 and RTI Response No. D-239/DD (SUR)/DUSIB/2011.

10. Subhash Chopra, former Congress MLA, interview by author, New Delhi, 4 March 2014.

11. 'Ration Cards for Slum-Dwellers', *HT*, New Delhi, 2 January 1990.

12. A.R. Wig, 'Ration Cards for Slum-Dwellers: Norms Need to be Drawn Up', *HT*, New Delhi, 7 January 1990.

13. The biographical note on V.P. Singh by Wikipedia does not even mention the enumeration initiative. Interestingly, not even the collection of V.P. Singh's selected speeches and writings includes speeches given during this initiative or his writings on slum resettlement. See *V.P. Singh: Selected Speeches and Writings 1989–90* (1993).

14. Among those present on the occasion were Commissioner of Slums and the JJ Department, Manjeet Singh; Urban Development Minister, Murasoli Maran; MP and Delhi BJP Chief, Madan Lal Khurana; MP from the Janata Dal government, Chaudhary Tarif Singh; Minister of Labour and Welfare, Ram Vilas Paswan; and Delhi Janata Dal President, Viresh Pratap Chaudhury. See 'Ration Cards for Slum-Dwellers'.

15. He said, 'It is a matter of shame that the JJ dwellers have not as yet been given ration cards'; see 'Ration Cards for Slum-Dwellers'. However, was V.P. Singh really the leader to have recognized the lack of access of slum residents to documents? Madan Lal Khurana, the BJP Chief, present with V.P. Singh on that day, was keen to claim credit for the BJP when he 'thanked' V.P. Singh for the ration card initiative which, he said, was a very old demand of the BJP conceded by the National Front government. 'Khurana hails PM's Decision', *HT*, New Delhi, 2 January 1990. Khurana was acknowledged in an *HT* column as having inspired the initiative by bringing to the notice of V.P. Singh the fact that since 1986, not even a single slum resident had obtained a card from the Delhi administration. Wig, 'Ration Cards for Slum-Dwellers: Norms Need to be Drawn Up'.

16. 'Ration Cards for Slum-Dwellers'.

17. Official reports state that all slum settlements, except the makeshift ones on footpaths and pavements, in Delhi were covered in this survey. By the end of the survey period, it was estimated that 2.60 lakh jhuggi families were enumerated as residing in 929 JJ clusters. A survey after this was undertaken only in 1994 when the Slums and JJ Department drew up a list of 1,080

JJ clusters as on 31 March 1994, with 4,80,929 slum-dwelling families in Delhi. Available at http://delhiplanning.nic.in/Write-up/2002-03/volume-II/Urban%20Development.pdf, accessed on 8 July 2011.

18. 'Ration Cards issued to Jhuggi Dwellers', *HT*, New Delhi, 28 March 1990. The slum clusters were to be divided into five zones and clusters were distinguished zone-wise by assigning different numbers to all jhuggis. The number plate contained details of zone, cluster code, and jhuggi number. 'Process for JJ Ration Cards', *HT*, New Delhi, 1 February 1990.

19. Such bills were irrelevant and producing them was implausible as, more often than not, electric connections were illegally acquired and gas cylinders were bought from the black market.

20. Erstwhile food official, interview by author, New Delhi, 10 June 2011.

21. 'Process for JJ Ration Cards'.

22. The EPIC was introduced in 1993 by the EC of India with a view to inject more authenticity into voter verification as the voter's face could now be compared with her photograph. In the years following the introduction of the EPIC, the EC tentatively allowed polling officers to accept other documents such as permanent account number (PAN) cards, driving licences, and property documents as ID proof as long as they contained the photograph of the voter (Banerjee 2013: 136). There may thus be some truth to the claim that the V.P. Singh Card was used to exercise franchise, though I would not wish to labour this point.

23. *Annual Plan 2004–05*, Vol. 2, Planning Department, Government of NCT of Delhi, RTI Response No. D-239/DD (SUR)/DUSIB/2011.

24. I am grateful to Usha Ramanathan for noting this effect of the metallic token.

25. Saira, resident of Govindpuri, interview by author, New Delhi, 11 February 2011.

26. In 2009, a new national ID project was unveiled which went by the name of the UID project and was given the mandate to roll out 12-digit national ID numbers for every resident in India. While these numbers can be downloaded, they are meant to be delivered by the postman. In recent times, residents said they had not received their UID numbers, or their Aadhaar cards, which were languishing in the post office. Eventually, the elected municipal councillor in the Govindpuri ward, Chandra Prakash, arranged for the delivery of some of these cards to their homes. See the next chapter for a more detailed analysis of the Aadhaar project.

27. Ration cards for slum residents are renewed or issued afresh from time to time rather than automatically extended. In the 2000s, the introduction of the category 'below the poverty line' (BPL) and the distribution of variable rations for different demographic groups complicated things

as it has entailed subscribing to new estimates of poverty by the Planning Commission, fresh surveys of income and other poverty indices, and biometric reviews.

28. For more on the ration card as a bail resource, see 'Enumeration as Pedagogic Process' (Sriraman 2013b).

29. Taramati, resident of Govindpuri, interview by author, New Delhi, 12 April 2011.

30. Sarda, resident of Govindpuri, interview by author, New Delhi, 10 March 2011.

31. This formulation is heavily influenced by the comments received from a discussant's reading of a paper I presented in a workshop in Singapore. I express my thanks to Tarini Bedi.

32. Delhi Urban Shelter Improvement Board (DUSIB) official, interview by author, New Delhi, 20 March 2011.

33. Suresh, resident of Govindpuri, interview by author, New Delhi, 1 April 2011.

34. I was asked by a sociologist whether the card is a commodity. Given its free circulation within the slum as a counterfeit, as a bail resource, as an ID document, the card can be argued to have an exchange value. However, I am more interested in the card's contingent properties similar to the commodity's properties in the narratives of Das (2012) and McFarlane (2011), and less interested in the commodity form of the card.

35. Bharati, resident of Govindpuri, interview by author, New Delhi, 16 May 2011.

36. Raj Gandhi did not use the word naqli or fake ration card. Cluster residents used different words to refer to the practice of making V.P. Singh Cards: naqli but also *farzi* and jaali.

37. Raj Gandhi, interview by author, New Delhi, 4 April 2013.

38. Raj Gandhi, interview by author, New Delhi, 4 April 2013.

39. A few other residents had filed RTIs addressed to the MCD to secure information about the money spent on toilets built in the slum. One must also record here the collective struggles of Govindpuri's anganwadi workers to fight court cases to secure a huge backlog of salary payments.

40. Babita, resident of Govindpuri, interview by author, New Delhi, 20 March 2011.

41. Babita indicated that she could produce a photocopy of her original V.P. Singh Card, but were not copies meant to accentuate the existence of the original, she asked.

42. I am grateful to Mekhala Krishnamurty for her formulation of the term, 'codified discretion'.

43. Vidya, resident of Govindpuri, interview by author, New Delhi, 18 June 2011.

44. Retired food official, interview by author, 6 September 2013.

45. F.23 (2)/78-81-F&S (P&C), Delhi Specified Articles (Regulation of Distribution) Order, 1981, *Delhi Gazette, Extraordinary*, Part IV; emphasis added.

46. In describing places such as boarding houses, hotels, orphanages, and ashrams, censuses, and this one in particular, deploy the term 'institutional households'.

47. The 2001 census, for instance, speaks of how especially in rural areas, it was very plausible for households to occupy different huts to sleep, cook, and for use as a bathroom—but they are all to be counted as a single 'census house'. In urban areas too, this logic was to be extended. See *Census of India 2001*, District Census Handbook: All the Nine Districts, Series 8, Delhi: Directorate of Census Operations (2006: 17).

48. Until this Act was passed, no matter what the size of the family is, the food entitlement was kept uniform. However, with this Act, which provides for expanded coverage (up to two-thirds of the entire population) within the Targeted Public Distribution System, each beneficiary is now eligible to receive 5 kg of foodgrains every month at subsidized prices. Under the Food Security Act, 2013, each person is entitled every month to receive 5 kg of rice, wheat, and coarse grains for Rs 3, Rs 2, and Rs 1 per kg, respectively. The Food Security Act makes an exception to this rule of targeting individuals rather than families for purposes of issuing foodgrains every month in one instance: each Antyodaya Anna Yojana (AAY) family is alone entitled to receive 35 kg of foodgrains every month. See http://dfpd.nic.in/nfsa-act.htm, accessed on 24 May 2017.

49. V.P. Singh 'was totally aghast' at this fact presented to him by Madan Lal Khurana; Wig, 'Ration Cards for Slum-Dwellers: Norms Need to Be Drawn Up'.

50. 'Inhabited Jhuggis won't be Razed', *HT*, New Delhi, 19 January 1990.

51. Press note, cited in 'Inhabited Jhuggis won't be Razed'.

52. 'Slums Mushroom at a Fast Pace', *HT*, 16 January 1990; Harsha Vardhan, '"Grow More Slums Movement" in Delhi', *The Statesman*, New Delhi, 20 January 1990. *The Statesman* cited 'a mad rush for building new slums' owing to the policy of allocating 25 sq. m plots to residents whose jhuggis had been demolished.

53. 'Ration Cards issued to Jhuggi Dwellers'.

54. 'Unending Exodus threatens Delhi', *The Statesman*, New Delhi, 7 February 1990.

55. 'Unending Exodus threatens Delhi'.

56. Title unknown, *The Statesman*, 24 January 1990.

57. Gopal Sharma, 'The Politics of Slums', *The Statesman*, New Delhi, 20 February 1990.

58. One reader, O.P. Ratra, wrote a letter to the editor expressing praise for the drive as being a step in the right direction to 'monitor the growth of jhuggis'. Letter to the Editor, *HT*, New Delhi, 24 February 1990.

59. See A.R. Wig, 'Lessons from Fire Tragedy', *HT*, 21 January 1990; 'Fires of Greed', *HT*, New Delhi, 2 May 1990.

60. A letter sent to *HT* contains a petition made by 24 residents of the middle-class apartments in Pocket 4, Kalkaji Extension, New Delhi, to this effect; 'Tenements Sprout in DDA Park', *HT*, New Delhi, 22 March 1990.

61. Jai Bhagwan Jatav, co-founder of Jan Chetna Manch, interview by author, New Delhi, 25 January 2011.

62. See 'Don't Bulldoze Slum-Dwellers: V.P. Singh', *The Hindu*, 22 May 2000; 'Policemen Face V.P. Singh's Ire over Demolition of Slums', *The Times of India*, 30 May 2001; 'V.P. Singh Extends Help to Slum-Dwellers', *The Hindu*, 22 July 2006.

5

THE DOCUMENT IN THE DIGITAL

All IDs that are paper IDs are essentially non-IDs. They are simply tokens for service. But in the absence of a proper ID framework we are using ration card as an ID, or a driving licence as an ID, or a passport as an ID, whereas it's not a primary ID. Indians have never had a primary ID issued by the government before Aadhaar.[1]

A number-wallah coolie cannot be a thief.[2]

Sometimes, I have to think like an official.[3]

In more senses than one, the novelty of biometric systems is undeniable. The claims of those who engineered and brought forth the Aadhaar, that this is not a paper-based card or 'a piece of plastic', have a resonant ring of truth to them. It is argued, justifiably, that where biometric technologies underpin the card or the physical manifestation of the recorded identity, the card itself is only a part of a larger 'administrative and technological regime' that harbours 'complex and latent systems of identification' (Bennett and Lyon 2008: 3). The implications of a biometric and cloud-based technology like Aadhaar—which promises to modify the terms of citizenship as a discourse and language such that it addresses newer anxieties of recognizing and identifying the welfare beneficiary—are immense. The needs of the technology have ordered the very parameters for defining citizenship. The business of managing identities (Muller 2004) and rendering welfare legitimate through the production of machine-readable identities is something that has necessitated a 'card cartel' consisting of biometric service providers (Amoore 2008: 22; Bennett and Lyon 2008: 12). The unfolding of this multiple manned gatekeeping system has implied the impoverishment of the political capacities of citizenship such that the bodies of people take the place of their loyalties, nationalities, and ethnicities (Maringanti 2009; Muller 2004; Shukla 2010). It is through their bodies that people are able to clinch state resources, and markets have a role to play in carving sovereign state power. While it does partially draw on these significant premises, this chapter 'goes beyond' to argue that the material production of the Aadhaar has necessitated miming existing bureaucratic habits of inscription and mobilizing the rhetoric, ritualism, and the tangibility common to processes of issuing and verifying ID documents.

We will see how, far from being an electronic identifier that is insulated from the host of administratively restrictive genres of ID documents like ration cards and job cards, the Aadhaar is parasitic on their continued relevance. The creation and legitimization of Aadhaar as a mobile ID has rendered it nearly impossible to fashion a welfare claim without the unique number. The universal acceptance of a mobile identifier as the only secure address paradoxically 'forecloses' the welfare subject's abilities of moving within the welfare ecology, especially if she does not belong to this number-based collective (Amoore 2008; Franke 2009). The slow accretion of Aadhaar as the only technological alibi against anonymity has entailed projecting onto paper fearful fantasies of the impostor that Aadhaar itself is seen to be exempt from. But I will demonstrate through the narrative accounts of a rural migrant community that the category of address, however electronically mobile, is one that is implicated in a paper-mediated matrix of various things. These can be characterized as evolving caste formations, the politics of identity in welfare-claiming, elite norms of residence proof, forms of bureaucratic knowledge, and urban spatiality of power brokerage. Buffeted by the power of all these variables which it neither changes nor aspires to change, the Aadhaar, as a 'technological outpacing' (Sekula 1986: 4) of other modalities, can only reflect and deepen socially embedded bureaucratic truths.

In this scenario, marginalized subjects like the porters of this chapter can hope to stake out welfare claims not so much through possession of the Aadhaar but through acts of getting different sets of cards, some official and others of their own making, some legal, others quasi-legal. In order to get a sense of all this, we will proceed slowly, and try not to be ethnographically disheartened by the political and judicial affirmations, negations, contestations, statutory absences and victories, information overlaps and distinctions that have ensnared the Aadhaar in its now-necessary, now-voluntary checkered existence. This chapter relies on fieldwork in three different sites, namely, the bus terminal and by extension, the porter's union, Aadhaar enrolment centres in north Delhi, and the Department of Food and Supplies, Delhi, undertaken over 8–10 months in the year 2014. I was also able to speak and correspond with a few representatives of the UIDAI headquarters in Delhi. Conversations with an NGO were also helpful in writing up this ethnography of rural migrant encounters with the Aadhaar. The chapter also consults several original documents compiled and uploaded by the UIDAI on their website and disparate newspaper archives.

Contemporary Biometric Systems

The origins of fingerprinting in India have been traced to civil and not criminal ID. It was another matter that fingerprinting was popularized when it was used by police departments and prisons. The Chief Magistrate of the Hooghly district in Bengal, William Herschel, proposed the use of handprints and later fingerprints on deeds, contracts, and jail warrants (Cole 2001; Sengoopta 2004; Singha 2000). It was initially the enforcement of the civil obligations of contractors, indigo ryots, coolies, planters, and pensioners, and the dilemmas thrown up by perceived crises of fraud, impersonation, and forgery that drew Herschel closer to a technology with claims to infallible accuracy in matters of discriminating the identities of Indian subjects. Eventually, however, the temptation to use fingerprinting to police deviant criminal tribes was too overwhelming and fingerprinting was purposed—not unlike photography and anthropology—into the social categorization of individuals belonging to such communities (Anderson 2004). The functions which counted as welfare and development in the nineteenth century, namely, the disbursement of pensions and the payment of wages to coolies and ryots, were undergirded by an early biometric system; and in this sense, the Aadhaar is hardly new. The turn to automation in technologies of ID, which can be uniquely traced to the late twentieth century, was however inspired by a very distinctive set of concerns presented by the anonymity of individuals rather than the threat posed by a social collectivity like the criminal tribes.[4]

A biometric system has been defined as 'any automatically measurable, robust and distinctive physical characteristic or personal trait that can be used to identify an individual or verify the claimed identity of an individual' (Woodward, Orlans, and Higgins, cited in Gelb and Clark 2013: 8). In contemporary times, the turn to biometric identity systems has been accompanied by a disdainful disavowal by governments and international monetary institutions, such as the World Bank of the efficacy of paper-based systems. Paper regimes of authenticating persons have been dubbed undependable, corrupt, leaky, and vulnerable to manipulation. It has been argued that artificial labels and tags of recognition, such as serial numbers inscribed on documents, holograms that distinguish a document, and passwords issued to individuals, pale before more naturalistic abstractions of identity (Gelb and Clark 2013; Mordini and Rebera 2013). The erstwhile Chairman, Nandan Nilekani, and other officials of the UIDAI—the agency that has steered the process of issuing numbers or Aadhaars to every Indian resident—have repeatedly asserted that paper-based systems are primitive and that smart card-based technologies are inadequate compared to cloud-based systems of ID. Unlike smart card systems that are still reliant on integrated circuits and a chip which has a certain amount of data that can be read only within a region, cloud-based systems are not geographically constrained. 'Suppose that information is on the cloud and suppose I can authenticate your ID anywhere then I can suddenly make it a multi-shop solution' where people can go to any shop to get rice, said Nilekani once while extolling the virtues of biometric cloud-based authentication ('India and the Third Industrial Revolution', 2013). The use of fingerprints and photographs has been the most preferred biometric combination of authenticating individual identities, though some countries like America, Canada, the United Arab Emirates (UAE), and India have complemented this with the verification of irises.

These biometric technologies that pivot on a unique number identifier have been the key to welfare payments, e-passports, immigration control documents, and national identity cards, and the governmental sponsors of these schemes have tried to steadily destabilize and supplant 'unsecured' paper-based systems with the new and shiny models. Scholars following biometric ID systems have documented, alternatingly with a critical gaze and jaw-dropping fascination, the common and uncommon modes of authentication within this paradigm (Bennett and Lyon 2008; Breckenridge 2014; Gelb and Clark 2013; Maguire 2009; Mordini and Rebera 2013). The body can be scanned, smelled, measured, tracked in movement, genetically mapped, its blood circulation sensed, its imprints recorded, and images captured through the corresponding biometrics of fingerprints, odour, hand geometry, gait recognition, DNA analysis, vascular patterns, handwriting, lip movement, voice and iris recognition, and photography. What perhaps warrants emphasis here is that the Aadhaar is a 'reconstructive' (Mordini and Rebera 2013: 20) rather than a reflective form of identity documentation: it consists of biometric images that are 'data representations' (Alterman 2003) and 'abstractions from the social' (Mordini and Rebera 2013: 106). When these images are retrieved from the human body but computed (as a 60 per cent fingerprint match, for instance) and plotted in an electronic imaginary of the subject along with other demographic details, there is nothing that is naturalistic about them. They render 'the body into a fetish object' (Mordini and Rebera 2013: 102). The rhetoric, backing the Aadhaar and all biometric systems, of their superior claim of accessing the body and the person conceals the mimetic aspect of the technology. It is here that Taussig's observations in *Mimesis and Alterity* (1993) are most pertinent. Taussig writes that ethnographers and shamans attempt to convince their readers and believers that the embodied textual and spiritual models they create are imbued with the same spirit, power, and personality of the original (which itself is shown to be chimerical) and that the copy resembles a magical reproduction which takes on 'a sensuous sense of the real' (Taussig 1993: 16). It is not incongruous to trace a similar effect produced by the biometric system, which too drifts between 'photographic fidelity and fantasy, between iconicity and arbitrariness, wholeness and fragmentation' (Taussig 1993: 17).

Struggles to incorporate biometric card and number systems have taken shape not only within rarefied sovereign territorial realms but also within an extended space featuring private firms, banks, autonomous or semi-autonomous government-backed agencies, and international organizations. These actors have set the terms, heavily influenced the government, while often being influenced by the government, or replaced governmental agencies in creating the modalities

for such systems. Biometric initiatives, such as the Aadhaar occupy
the domain of e-government where 'a corporate managerial vision'
cannot be separated from the governmental and 'political language of
transparence' (Mazzarella 2006: 476). If, in India, an office that enjoys
executive authority called the UIDAI issues biometric numbers to
Indians, an autonomous technical agency called National Database and
Registration Authority (NADRA), supported by an ordinance passed
by the Government of Pakistan, has issued national identity cards called
Watan cards. The NADRA has simultaneously put in place a centralized
database that underpins a dazzling profusion of biometric applications.
The former Chairman and NADRA's founding figure, Tariq Malik's
warm and personal touch in describing the inroads the Authority
has made in the various walks of everyday life—resident transactions
with the state and the thoughtful methods of registering communities
living in remote regions, women, transgenders, and refugees—can be
very disarming, especially for a reader unfamiliar with Pakistan's info-
landscapes. The NADRA experiment has been pioneering and unique
in many ways as it has integrated biometric features into its passport
(being one of the first countries to do so), electoral rolls, welfare payments or pensions for old women under the Benazir Income Support
Programme (BISP), flood relief, and compensation for those living in
areas where counter-insurgency strikes were launched (Malik 2014).
Pakistan's diverse encounter with biometric card applications across
the spectrums of civilian life and military engagement has demolished
the boring binaries of welfare and security as the respective fulcrums of
these technologies in the developed and developing countries. Unlike
the UIDAI, whose mandate includes issuing numbers, collaborating
with institutional partners to set up an 'infrastructure' of creating and
updating 'digital identities', creating platforms for public and private
agencies to use Aadhaar, and 'develop Aadhaar-linked applications',
NADRA has more wide-ranging powers to influence the very process
of selecting welfare beneficiaries in the first place.[5]

The South African state repeatedly tried to enforce, first colony-
wide and later countrywide, biometric IDs and databases but did not
always succeed. Where a 'superpanopticon'[6] (Crush 1992: 833) drive
to routinize centralized databases and universal biometric ID through
the offices of the government failed, privatized models of welfare payments (unconnected with state-driven centralized database functions)

were incredibly popular. The latter was conceptualized through an agglomeration of information technology (IT) firms and banks. Keith Breckenridge, in his impressive genealogy of fingerprinting in South Africa, attributes the entry of private expertise into big data collection, biometric smart card production, and identity repository management to 'certain database and transactional services which are well beyond the capacities of even the most skilled officials' (Breckenridge 2014: 11). In Mexico, two ministries vied with each other to create biometric databases even as they debated questions, such as importing nationwide biometric standards into voter identity cards and the utility and the dangers implicit in recording geographic identity or georeferencing (Botello 2011: 762).[7] The tussle between the ministries over conflicting databases of fingerprinted identities in Mexico is reminiscent of India's own turf wars in biometric information collection. The Ministry of Information Technology and the MHA faced off when biometrics-gathering enrolment camps for both Aadhaar and the National Population Register (NPR, and allied to the NPR, the issuing of National Resident Cards [NRCs]) were set up. In the past, the MHA in India had argued that the NPR, which was consolidated by the Office of the Registrar General and Census Commissioner, is better placed than the UIDAI to collect biometric information as this authority has access to head of the household data which the latter does not gather.[8] A more recent legislation termed the Aadhaar (Targeted Delivery of Financial and Other Subsidies, Benefits and Services) Act, 2016 states that the UIDAI is authorized to deny access to biometrics to anybody, including the enrolled person herself, and under this new law, sharing biometrics with any governmental body, such as the MHA which manages the NPR is out of the question. Brazil implemented the 'Bolsa Familia' or the family allowance programme in which municipalities dispensed biometric cash benefits through an electronic card to ensure that these conditional cash transfers were tied to school attendance, immunization, and health check-ups for children and pregnant women ('Evaluating the Impact of Brazil's *Bolsa Familia*: Cash Transfer Programmes in Comparative Perspective', 2007).

International organizations have toyed with biometric standards for refugee registration and in so doing, have undercut the sovereign discourse of territorial governments and private firms working within national confines. In response to the war-related displacement of people from Kosovo, the United Nations High Commissioner for Refugees (UNHCR) in concert with Microsoft successfully created a software that was used to link biometric identity cards with centralized databases. These cards came to be used frequently in 'different field units' (Franke 2009: 357). This aside, the World Bank has pushed governments of Asia and Africa to embrace its philosophy made explicit in its impassioned call to modernize ID processes. Such a move to modernize is salient to the realization of sustainable development goals, such as financial inclusion, gender inclusion, and access to health services. Called Identification for Development (ID4D), this exhortation for biometric government is not removed from the paternalism of international monetary institutions that come bearing neo-liberal gifts in fixed welfare templates for the developing world.[9] It is against this backdrop of an overwhelming consensus, both in India and globally, of biometric systems' superior claims to modernity and India's desperate quest to showcase its leadership in the world of biometric technology that I frame my ethnography of contemporary forms of urban welfare claim-making.

The Aadhaar and India's biometric project have been framed in a global discourse marked by hyperbole and wide-eyed fascination. Not shockingly, these narratives can be traced to actors as diverse as the World Bank, which cites the project as a prototype of the ID revolution it would like to see in developing countries, *The Economist* (which called the Aadhaar the magic number), *The New York Times* (which referred to the project as a 'quiet revolution of social welfare policy'), and Hollywood. A film called *I Origins* juxtaposes poverty and biometrics in its representation of India as a country that struggles against all odds to provide for its impoverished masses through its impressive UID project. The common belief tying all these narratives is that the Indian government has taken the right approach by recognizing that which lies at the heart of inefficient welfare schemes and poverty alleviation programmes, namely, the crisis of poorly conceived ID technologies.[10]

Simultaneously, critics of the UID project have been numerous, comprising civil libertarians, lawyers, journalists, and activists who have justly dwelled on a rainbow assortment of questions. These range from privacy, cost-efficiency, the possibilities of information creep, ownership of user information, untested technology of biometrics, biometric claims to transparency, a panacea to corrupt governance, to the initiative's underlying narrative of ideological neutrality. I do not wish to be lured into a discussion about the superiority of paper-based or biometric systems even if I am to a great extent inclined to support the voices of reason that have critiqued the Aadhaar project. These figures have rightly challenged the Aadhaar in its various phases of inception and proliferation and challenged the aura of the indispensable that biometric governance has gathered around itself in India today. However, this chapter will concern itself with how insulated, how aloof, and how removed the Aadhaar project can afford to be from paper-based forms of ID. Continuous with this book's thrust of probing the urban poor's encounters with ID documents, this chapter will demonstrate how the welfare dispensation remains rooted in intricate administrative definitions of address and how claim-making, considered in all its diversity of caste and regional spaces, may belie the virtues of purely electronic representations of marginal communities. I trace, in particular, the implications of Aadhaar enrolment and its linkages with existing ID documents for a rural migrant community in Delhi composed of bus porters whose presence in the city is tenuous.

The Documentary Panics of the UIDAI

In an early document where the technological and normative basis for ID was spelt out clearly, the UIDAI laid special emphasis on the lack of a 'nationally accepted, verifiable and portable identity number' causing great distress to poor and undocumented persons.[11] This document clarifies the need to overcome the constraints of a full cycle of identity verification and suggests that if the creation of multiple identities and costs of different verification processes are to be avoided, then welfare delivery systems would stand to be revolutionized. For, attached to the older models of 'intermediation' is a great paraphernalia of form-filling, elaborate documentary checks, and cross-checking poorly updated databases. If the number were to be introduced, then government departments could be persuaded of the need for various classes of residents to 'prove identity *only once*' (emphasis added).[12] When Nilekani presented his plans for an Olympian system of ID, the then Congressled United Progressive Alliance (UPA) government was persuaded that this would deliver the Indian state from its disorderly chaos of multiple uncoordinated paper-based systems perceived to be so typical to the bureaucracies of developing countries.

Nilekani's lamentations are consistent with an age-old neo-liberal formulation crystallized in the writings of Hernando de Soto, particularly in his book called *The Mystery of Capital* (2000). It is not then pure coincidence that Nilekani's premises about modernization of ID documents as central to empowerment are heavily drawn from De Soto and not surprisingly, he cites De Soto in his book, *Imagining India* (2008). De Soto's own work researches poverty in developing countries in Asia, Africa, West Asia, and Latin America and conflates the global question of poverty with the structural failure of the poor to translate their assets into live capital that can be mobilized. He imputes this failure to the inability of developing countries to ease or integrate their excessively bureaucratized and over-regulated legal systems of registration and representation (De Soto 2000).

It is time to critically address an ideological conviction about biometric systems of governance and the Aadhaar in particular. This has to do with the view that biometric systems are efficient and superior precisely because they have no residues of writing as they keep no truck with paper-based systems of ID. A certain troubling dichotomy of paper-based and biometric systems can be detected in some of this writing (Gelb and Clark 2013). While it may be partly true that numbers do not necessitate the same kind of documentary indexing, retrieval, and storage, the chapter will inquire into the labours, ordeals, and inescapable factories of writing, applying, reapplying, and reading breeder documents. For the dispersed establishment issuing the Aadhaar, the process has entailed scouring ID documents for their legitimacy and evidentiary signs of law. For those applying, its production and usage have involved securing the mediation of writers, rendering translations of rural documents into urban ones, and navigating the banking labyrinths of electronic payments through endless paper pilgrimages. Fortifying the portals of Aadhaar from corruption and corruptibility has entailed not just an endless paper trail but also putting into motion an all-encompassing documentary edifice that solicits, as willing and unwilling accomplices, computer operators, company heads, bank officials, local state officials, NGOs, and the enumerated themselves. But in making this argument, I will try to partially rescue documents and writing from their aporias of vile, inaccurate, leaky, corrupt, red tape-dominated, discriminatory modes of dispensing welfare allocation. Such an argument is enabled by tracing the rigours of enrolling poor people, and the socio-spatial politics of claim-making narrated by a tightly-knit community of rural migrants vis-à-vis the expansive infrastructure of Aadhaar.

The Many Lives of Aadhaar

The UIDAI was set up through an executive order in the year 2009 as a central government office attached to the Planning Commission and, until very recently, it lacked statutory basis. Though the National Identification Authority of India Bill was presented early on to the Parliament, its passage was thwarted by the Standing Committee on Finance on various grounds covering privacy and security of information stored, cost benefit analysis, the inaccuracy risks implicit in biometrics, observed trends of irregularity, and the lack of statistics related to the marginalized sections in society (Standing Committee on Finance [2011–12] 2011).[13] In its present form, the Aadhaar can now claim statutory basis, a feat that was accomplished through dubious means when it was passed as a Money Bill in Lok Sabha (and bypassed in Rajya Sabha). The Aadhaar (Targeted Delivery of Financial and Other Subsidies, Benefits and Services) Act, 2016 has normalized the issuing of the biometric numbers and the byzantine project is now well-poised for a smoother integration with welfare schemes. This Act has not, in a substantive sense, addressed the many critical comments of the various civil society figures who the Standing Committee heard.

The Aadhaar represents a major spatial shift in projects of ID: if earlier, such initiatives were authored by state governments and their allied agencies, the UID marks a national investment in the question of ID.[14] It all started when the former CEO of Infosys, Nandan Nilekani, wrote his primer, *Imagining India*, in which he expansively fleshed out a vision for automating Indian welfare systems through an IT-enabled national ID system, which then would emancipate the people of this country from 'the moral scruples of our bureaucrats' (Nilekani 2008: 373). As it turned out, he found takers for this vision at the highest echelons of government. Contained in this primer was a single-narrative and single-template 'solution' to just about every imaginable *sarkari* (governmental) dysfunctionality writ large in the welfare system, be it the venality of bureaucracy, the leaky benefit transfers exemplified by the PDS, the migrant-unfriendly nature of subsidies offered, non-transparent land tenure and property rights mechanisms, fragmented penal systems, or technology-deficient urban mapping. The UID project that Nilekani helped pioneer was designed as much more than a single window to all of India's welfare conundrums. It was conceptualized as a move that lauded and consolidated geographically disparate IT revolutions and their authors everywhere in the fields of telecom (Sam Pitroda), computerization of land records (Rajeev Chawla), the municipal use of geographic information system (GIS) technologies in land and revenue mapping, and electronic transformation of the erstwhile paper-based securities market (C.B. Bhave) (Nilekani 2008). The key transition in most of these IT revolutions was the overcoming of the materiality of paper-based reform in the form of 'hand-drawn (map) sketches', old-fashioned records classifying land titles, and eminently forgeable ID documents unsecured by any foolproof technology (Nilekani 2008: 378). When I met her in the year 2014, the-then Deputy Director General of UIDAI, Sujata Chaturvedi, termed the Aadhaar an 'Online Digital Paperless ID'; and referring to all previous paper forms of ID, she declared:

> All IDs that are paper IDs are essentially non-IDs. They are simply tokens for service. But in the absence of a proper ID framework we are using ration card as an ID, or a driving licence as an ID, or a passport as an ID, whereas it's not a primary ID. Indians have never had a primary ID issued by the government before Aadhaar.[15]

It is this twin belief that the documentary residues of ID can, in a practical sense, be purged and that once purged, the dematerialized number identifier can produce a well-oiled machine of welfare governance that this chapter will try to interrogate.

The UID project, as it was originally designated, has been crafted to provide certain key nodes of reform in the existing dispensations of welfare distribution and development-oriented programmes. In later years, this project has colloquially gone by the name Aadhaar, which can ostensibly be translated to mean 'foundation' in 14 languages, and is accompanied by the logo of a rising sun contrived visually through the use of 'easily replicable' and 'auspicious good colours'[16] of red and yellow. The image of the rising sun was chosen, the-then Deputy Director General told me, for its rich symbolic potential in that it simultaneously resembled one of the biometrics used (the ridges of a finger or a fingerprint) and captured the idea of India as a big developed nation that uses technology on an unprecedented scale to embrace tens of millions of people through the Aadhaar.[17] This project has calibrated the technological incorporation of a 12-digit electronic number into public transactions, subsidy provision, visions of financial inclusion, departmental linkage, and more broadly speaking, banking and welfare reform. The Aadhaar is regarded by the UIDAI as delivering services of eKYC, or the electronic Know Your Customer, that banks, telecom, and other financial service actors, whose functions are regulatory in nature, now deem 'equivalent to paper documents'.[18] The authors of this project have sought its legitimacy from 'the creation of a strong identity for the transformation of delivery of social welfare programs by making them more inclusive of communities, now marginalized, from such benefits due to lack of identity'.[19]

Its claims of being superior to paper—partly because they are backed by an international complex of database service buyers and sellers—have enhanced the image of Aadhaar as a non-negotiable entity. Even in the years when it lacked statutory basis, the Aadhaar secured 'the force of law' even if it lacked its 'value' (Agamben, cited in Amoore 2008: 22), and this is the result of the dubious 'blurring of categories of law, policy, rule and obligation' and international consensus (Amoore 2008: 22). If enrolment for the Aadhaar was always benignly framed to be 'voluntary', its de facto linkages with welfare entitlements through schemes and programmes like the PDS, the LPG gas subsidy scheme, the Mahatma Gandhi National Rural Employment Guarantee Scheme, and other erstwhile local schemes, such as Annashree Yojana and the free gas connection scheme, have justly aroused suspicions of its furtively coercive elements. The voluntary–mandatory confusion of the Aadhaar has not waned after multiple ambiguous court judgements on the right to privacy as an extension of the right to life and the right to unimpeded access to entitlements compromised by digital exclusion from social welfare schemes.[20] The new Aadhaar Act, 2016 does not address these questions per se; and if anything, it has pre-empted the Supreme Court which was hearing various petitions at the time this legislation was passed, by making the Aadhaar a pre-requisite for claiming subsidies, benefits, and services for which expenditure is incurred from the Consolidated Fund of India. Not surprisingly, the new Act has re-stirred the already raging hornet's

nest built across various legal, political, and activist quarters and reset
the clock and agenda of resistance: issues now include the implications
of a conveniently broad-based category of national security; fears of
disclosure of personal data especially to law-enforcing agencies; the
unreliability or the dysfunctionality of existing legal channels for
redressing breaches of information; and persecuting guilty private or
governmental bodies.[21] This legislation and other related governmental
moves meant that residents were left to infer that haste makes waste,
for the more they delayed getting the Aadhaar, the closer they came to
being edged out of inalienable rights to register their marriage, secure
a PAN card, get an LPG connection, or even exercise their freedom of
franchise simply because they lack the number. The Aadhaar has, for all
these reasons, been aptly dubbed 'voluntarily compulsory'.[22]

The multipronged agenda of Aadhaar implementation was to be
carried out through biometric collection and authentication at various
points of identity verification, de-duplication, and number portability. From the year 2010, the UIDAI sought to issue 12-digit unique
numbers to enrollees. The early Aadhaar enrolment form solicited
information from every such applicant which was classified into biometric (photograph, irises, and fingerprints), demographic (name, date
of birth, sex, family details, and residential address), and additional data
(which included financial information that could be tendered if the
applicant so desired, phone number, and email id). The Aadhaar enrolment form underwent several changes in the better part of a decade
since its inception, and the later forms came to be labelled 'Aadhaar
Enrolment/Correction Form'—I will examine the aspects and material connotations of such modifications later. This information, once
electronically transmitted, was sent to a centralized repository termed
the Central Identities Data Repository (CIDR). The exercise of biometric enrolment and creation of numbers was to entail two stages of
de-duplication: first, in a specified bounded area (comprising locality,
district, and state); and second, against the entire database. The CIDR
was to perform the critical task of de-duplicating the demographic and
biometric set of data of each enrollee against the entire existing database. In enrolling Indians for Aadhaar, the idea was to move towards 'a
critical mass' of Aadhaar holders and until this was done, the UIDAI
was to focus on 'generating demand through both Registrars and residents'.[23] Intriguingly, the biometric technology interface did not always

permit an effortless capture of fingerprints owing to several issues, such as finger moisture, scratches on device, insufficient or excessive pressure applied, and fingers that were less than ideal owing to calluses and deformities. Where they could not succeed in capturing fingerprints with the allowed number of tries, the operators had to rely on what the UIDAI website terms the enrolment software's option of 'forced capture' of these biometrics.[24]

When enrolment for the Aadhaar began, the figures aspired to new extraordinary narrative pinnacles of coverage: in 2014, the overall figures of Aadhaar enrolment in the country exceeded 60 million (63,13,24,517) and 1 million (1,70,00,926) for Delhi alone.[25] A more recent figure reached on 4 April 2016 raised the tally to 1 billion or 100 crore for all of India.[26] The Cabinet Committee on the UID initially sanctioned the Aadhaar for 18 states, but this number later increased to 24 states and union territories. At the time of applying, a number of critical ID documents satisfying the heads of 'Proof of Identity' (PoI) and 'Proof of Address' (PoA) were to be tendered as well. The Aadhaar form, in fact, is striking in its impressive list of 18 PoI documents and 33 PoA documents that an applicant can pick from. If this chapter intends to critique this numerical narrative of documentary plenitude, it also seeks to challenge the imagination of *Aadhaar* as an infrastructure friendly to illiterate and quasi-literate persons.

The biometric standards were to be uniform across different users and operators to ensure interoperability—this meant that the various agencies authenticating UID numbers would have to rely on a similar interface in the form of biometric scanners or other 'capture devices, capture software and UID service delivery'.[27] A certain fusion of biometric standards consisting of 2 irises, 10 fingerprints, and a photograph was seen to be felicitous for achieving an 'overall de-duplication accuracy'.[28] Reliance on any single biometric in a country which was home to thousands of Indian labouring classes with a poor quality of fingerprints was regarded counterproductive. Demographic data of the kind which captured name, family, sex, and age was seen to be a useful addition in that it contextualized and rendered simple manual recognition after an electronic search had narrowed down the list to a few fingerprint matches. The UIDAI has repeatedly insisted that rights of privacy do not stand to be breached by the collection and the possible sharing of biometrics. They point out the principled abstinence of the Authority from sharing biometrics and demographic data—exceptions may be made only in the interests of national security, or alternately at the time of securing eKYC where consent is procured from the individual when he/she agrees to his/her biometric authentication.

A stark biopolitics riddled the Aadhaar as those who turned up for enrolment were treated in distinct ways depending on which demographic and biological category of people in need of assistance they fell into. Able-bodied men and women needed no more than the firm guiding hand of the computer operator pressing thumbs and fingertips on to the machine with a calibrated pressure. In addition to capturing their photograph, the computer operator also recorded their irises and all 10 fingerprints such that the total tallied up to 13 biometrics. While the biometrics of children could be captured, given the infancy of their biometrics, the fingerprints of their parents had to be recorded in addition, and they were required to resubmit their biometrics five years after they originally enrolled themselves. Disabled persons were required to comply with what was termed an 'exception management system' that allowed for all existing biometrics to be captured—the exception could be recorded as such by capturing the disabled applicant holding up her hand with the missing or deformed finger (for instance) when the photograph was taken (see Figure 5.1).[29] While several special disabled camps were held in Delhi—18 such camps were counted in 2014—the average disabled person going to a routine enrolment centre faced a grim challenge.[30] The bureaucratic emphasis on the presence of the supervisor as the only figure who could authenticate a disabled person and his erratic presence mocked the disabled-friendly enrolment centre image. The enrolment centres that I went to, as part of my fieldwork, did not have a supervisor who attended and the operator had to turn away disabled persons or direct them to other centres where this figure could be found. Even for those who were not disabled in the conventional sense, this technology proved to be challenging. Usha Ramanathan cites the research of the National Institute of Standards and Technology in the US which stipulates that 'the accuracy of biometric matching is extremely dependent on demographics and environmental conditions'.[31] Subsequently, activists like Jean Drèze, Reetika Khera, and others have wondered about the havoc that such a technological architecture can wreak on MGNREGS (a

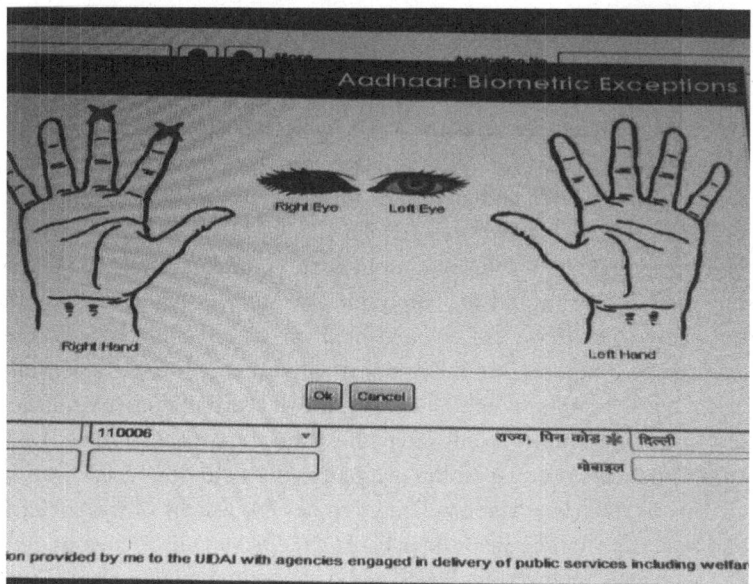

Figure 5.1   A Screenshot of the Aadhaar Biometric Capture Software
Source: Author.

rural employment programme) workers, construction workers, or simply put, the universe of manual labourers.[32]

Homeless persons, residents of orphanages, leprosy homes, and other
social welfare institutions, and individuals on the margins of society
who could not prove their local addresses were to be eased into the
CIDR through what was termed the 'introducer' system. This system
was designed to allow anyone who had already been enrolled to serve
as introducer to those who lacked the necessary PoA and PoI documents needed to secure the Aadhaar. But this putative introducer (who
could be an employee of the Registrar, an elected local body member, a
member of a local administrative body, a postman, an influencer, such
as a teacher, health worker, doctor, anganwadi/accredited social health
activist [ASHA] worker, and representative of a local NGO[33]) would
have to be willing to tender her own fingerprints upon introducing
the undocumented person. In Delhi, the Sheila Dikshit government
warmed to the introducer system and facilitated its implementation
through the Mission Convergence programme. This was a flagship

programme to provide what was termed a single window to fragmented government schemes strewn across various government departments. Funded partly by the United Nations Development Programme (UNDP), Mission Convergence was to entail a 'comprehensive survey' of homeless persons in Delhi, followed by the provision of personal photo identity cards and assistance for UID enrolment (Government of National Capital Territory of Delhi [GNCTD]–UNDP 2011). One NGO representative who was an introducer told me that ironically, homeless persons could not apply for the Aadhaar when they could not show that they were covered in this survey. Ursula Rao, whose ethnography inquires into the Aadhaar enrolment of homeless persons, also records a similar potential exclusion. Her work stresses 'patronage' and 'prior recognition' as informing the distinct approach of the UIDAI to communities residing on the margins of the state (Rao 2013: 74).

This introducer scheme collapsed under the weight of the societal and legal expectations invested in banks, NGOs, and miscellaneous others, such as employers, landlords, and documented middle-class Good Samaritans, and the naiveté of the UIDAI. While a number was issued directly to the undocumented person, the introducer could become ensnared in the everyday affairs of the enrolled undocumented person. The introducer was to undertake several responsibilities like confirm the resident's identity and address, sign the enrolment form, and tender her biometric.[34] As the-then Deputy Director General of the UIDAI herself said to me, 'Introducer based enrolments have not been a great success because of the larger question of how the society deals with these issues.'[35] She added that responsibility and social accountability were two things that introducers could not be forced to undertake. In implementing this clause, the UIDAI was unable to do anything either on the front of social accountability or that of the legal implications that donning this hat entailed for introducers. The Authority did not intervene in a timely fashion to mitigate the very real fears that NGO figures experienced of criminal interrogation. There was one reported instance of an introducer from an NGO who was 'hauled up by the police' when a homeless person died while carrying the survey slip with his name.[36] Here, the police assumed that if an NGO representative had in the past introduced a homeless person, they must know her or him in some capacity. It is thus that such agency representatives were rendered fair game for interrogation. Not surprisingly, some

NGOs backed out of Mission Convergence and the UID introducer scheme altogether.

Apart from the reservations that NGOs expressed about the legal consequences of playing an enabling role, they also raised ethical and humane questions of citizens' agency. One such representative expressed his angst by saying, 'who are we to introduce the undocumented? Why must an undocumented person become more trustworthy just because an NGO or a middle-class employer vouches for her/him? Does (s)he not have her own identity, her own dignity?'[37] Such an ID bearing another's address denudes the bearer of any real sense of being documented. This particular NGO has, by its own efforts, tried to get voter identity cards and ration cards issued to the porters and other homeless persons in Delhi; and in doing so, it has sought painstakingly to ensure that these documents bear their own address even if such an address consists only of a street name.[38]

The number once issued was printed on a letter and ostensibly lacked the material appearance of a card, though it was common practice to neatly cut out the 'tearaway portion which has the UID number, name, photograph and a 2D barcode of the finger print minutiae digest'[39] and laminate it such that it could be slipped easily into the pouch of a wallet. The process of universalizing enrolment for the Aadhaar saw the UIDAI enlisting a profusion of agencies banally termed Registrars and Enrolling Agencies, who could range from central and state government agencies, such as the oil ministry and the Life Insurance Corporation (LIC), to authorities that handle national and regional welfare programmes, such as the PDS, Integrated Child Development Services (ICDS), MGNREGS, Jan Dhan Yojana (JDY), and Mission Convergence. Simultaneously, schools, microfinance institutions, orphanages, leprosy homes, institutions for disabled persons, agencies handling tribal welfare and women's development, and a whole range of 'information distribution networks,' such as gender resource centres and homeless resource centres run by NGOs were to be mobilized into arranging enrolment for Aadhaar applicants. In Delhi, these registrars included deputy commissioners (Revenue), Mission Convergence and the DUSIB, banks, and India Post.[40]

The infrastructure of the Aadhaar was built for universal acceptance. With every new instance of a public and private agency seeding its database and operations to the UID number, Aadhaar was expected to become stronger as the sole identifier in the authentication sector. It is intriguing that the same argument was alternately cause for celebration and alarm depending on the camp that was making it. As per one perspective, the UIDAI believes that it has created the conditions for dispelling the 'last mile problem' or the problem that 'intended beneficiaries do not receive what is meant for them mainly due to distortions in the system at the receiver's end' (Rajadhyaksha 2013: xvii). Though the UIDAI does not mandate per se the seeding of welfare programmes with its database, it is built for these purposes. Government departments and the income tax department in particular, private and government banks, insurance providers, telecom companies, all are gravitating towards Aadhaar as a technological platform largely owing to UIDAI's promise of enabling Know Your Customer (KYC) authentication of intended beneficiaries. At the other end of the deep blue sea, civil libertarians and activists like Usha Ramanathan, Jean Drèze, Reetika Khera, and Kalyani Menon-Sen have conjectured that this convergence amounts to nothing less than social control and creeping surveillance.[41] Usha Ramanathan, who has been the most redoubtable of these critics, has convincingly demonstrated that PDS has been roped into the Aadhaar only to ensure extensive enrolment and universal acceptance for the Aadhaar.[42] It is this impulse that drives the UIDAI whenever it seeks to convince agencies like the Ministry of Food, the Ministry of Rural Development, and the EC of India to fashion linkages between the ration card and the Aadhaar, the job card and the Aadhaar, the EPIC and the Aadhaar. When these cards are due to be updated, the corresponding details of Aadhaar too would have to be updated, and it is through these furtive and enduring linkages that the Aadhaar gains prominence.

This leads us to an observation that undergirds this chapter: the Aadhaar rides on the continued relevance of existing paper-based ID documents. The Aadhaar hopes to be indispensable but not by supplanting these ID documents—having positioned itself as a 'guarantor of identity though not citizenship'—as this infrastructure's claim to welfare reform hinges on the very need to make existing paper-based ID documents more trustworthy. So, even as Indians show their laminated Aadhaar cards at airports, banks, and registration offices, thus exempting themselves from any further documentary liability, the welfare edifice as such is predicated on thousands upon thousands of applications for various other ID documents, such as food security cards, job cards, caste certificates, income certificates, and birth certificates. Where the poor possess the Aadhaar but cannot procure these paper-based ID documents, the humungous network of welfare entitlements will fail them.

As a quick aside, it would be crucial to mention here that around the same time that biometrics were collected for ID under the Aadhaar project, a parallel information-gathering exercise was under way. Called the NPR and mandated by the Office of the Registrar General and Census Commissioner, this project sought to aggregate biometric data of residents but linked it to household information under the decennial census. The impulses of the Aadhaar and the NPR were similar as both projects addressed 'the phantoms' of identity fraud such that welfare delivery under government schemes can be rendered more foolproof. Unlike the Aadhaar, the NPR, which was steered by the MHA, was not propelled by the rhetoric of empowerment proffered by a technocrat and IT mascot like Nilekani. The NPR was designed to be a comprehensive database of citizen identities and in this sense, was intended to be mandatory. Usha Ramanathan points out that the Citizenship Act, 1955 was amended in the year 2004 to make it mandatory for residents to register—once amended, this Act was seen to hold more sway than the Census Act, 1948, which required all census-related information to be strictly confidential.[43] Identification cards or NPR cards were issued to those who were enrolled in the centres that were held for the decennial census exercise. Aadhaar's claims to reducing duplication in processes of identity authentication were seriously dented when fingerprints, often of the same person, could be collected for two disparate projects—newspapers had a field day in projecting the irony of such grandiose ambitions when basic nitty-gritties of overlapping ministry and project jurisdictions could not be smoothed out.[44] It all ended in tragedy for the ministry managing the NPR when a new law was passed in 2016 that barred the UIDAI from sharing its biometrics with any governmental or private body. As the MHA had come to rely excessively on the sharing of Aadhaar biometrics, the enactment of this law meant nothing short of an abrupt and undignified death for the NPR project on which an estimated 4,800 crore rupees had already been spent.[45]

Centralization of Databases through Privatization of Information Gathering

The discussion so far has been crafted into setting up the context for an intricate argument about not only the complementarity of electronic identifiers and paper-based documents but also the discursive salience of both to the socio-technical imaginary of the UID. How does centralization of government authority figure in all this? Intriguingly, tendencies of centralization have been possible through the concurrent growth of a privatized biometrics industry whose services have been indispensable for the expansion of state functions. To be sure, the evolution of biometrics has been the story, in part, of the search for a more unitary and controlling state. But, far from being extensions of the early twentieth century manifestation of the centralizing state, contemporary models of state control are distinctly different as they are mediated through regimes of information and commodification of information (Gates 2008: 223). This refers to processes of extracting information from wage labourers as well as a larger consumer public such that production, markets, and even state functions may be better streamlined and securitized. This has been termed by Nikolas Rose to embody what he calls 'securitization of identity' (Rose 1999: 240) and it has, among other things, entailed the recasting of citizenship such that the most routine practices, such as travelling, banking, voting, purchasing houses, and securing employment, tied to everyday freedoms can occur only through the scrutiny of a 'proof of legitimate identity' (Rose 1999: 240). Information processes, welfare processes, security processes, and ID processes are all interwoven with a thin and invisible gauze that can be traced only through a careful inquiry.

In keeping with Rose's line of conjecture, it would then be possible to argue that far from enabling a straightforward state–citizens interaction, the centralization of databases has enabled the emergence of private industries of data collation, management, and creation of virtual information. The turn to biometric governance has been attended not only by the centralization of information but also by 'an ideological attack on big government' (Agar 2003: 374). As Breckenridge has pointed out, these private entities have positioned themselves successfully as carrying a skill set of 'database and transactional services' that far supersedes anything that state actors can hope to acquire by themselves (Breckenridge 2014: 11). So, though it may seem like a paradox, the development of centralized databases on the one hand, and the emergence of a panoply of actively engaged corporate managers of information and the commodification of information on the other hand, are related. Here, binaries of developed and developing countries would fall flat as centralization, standardization, and formalization of official identities is something that the US, the UK, South Africa, and India have all been able to carry out through dispersed entities and private firms that specialize in biometrics production. A careful reading of the UID documents would suffice to get a sense of the corporate impulses of national biometric projects—in explaining why it was so important to use fingerprinting as a biometric, the UIDAI Committee on Biometrics notes that fingerprinting has the largest market share of all biometrics modalities globally.[46]

In the recent decades, countries like South Africa and India have especially shown an inclination to contract out the expertise of enumeration and welfare payments to private service providers. If the various private firms hired by the UIDAI have been taking on government-like functions of application and document verification, number creation, and identity verification, it is perhaps a matter of time before India embraces a South Africa-style system of welfare payments. An ideological bias of this project towards neo-liberal modes of welfare payment can be teased out from an early document of the UIDAI which lays down the technology architecture, the vision for social inclusion, and the enrolment process for the unique number. This document anticipates a certain overwhelming governmental and public consensus in favour of direct cash benefits through electronic transfer once the number attains universal credence.[47] Critics too have latched on to this resounding call to use Aadhaar for cash transfers and termed it 'an alibi for the state to leave the citizen unmarked in the market for social services'.[48]

The trajectory of Aadhaar has also been similar to that of the Real ID Act passed in the US in 2005, which too has engendered an overwhelming reliance on private actors to manage biometric government. The Real ID Act, 2005 has entailed the implementation of a policy for importing federal and uniform standards into disparately existing ID documents in the states of America, like drivers' licences and personal ID cards. The Act has provoked resistance on the grounds that this

forced compliance with federal standards is tantamount to the surreptitious smuggling into policy of a national ID. Interestingly, such a move
to insert federal standards into existing ID documents was carried out
through the outsourcing of functions of document verification and
number creation to private contractors. While describing America's
Real ID Act, which has undergirded the importing of national biometric standards into disparate ID documents, Kelly Gates writes that
Digimarc is a company that has contracts with Departments of Motor
Vehicles (DMV) in 37 states, 'to provide document issuance services
and technologies' required for the transformation (Gates 2008: 219).
The next section shows how the material production of the Aadhaar
has been possible only through its footmen, that is, computer operators,
technicians, and supervisors, all of whom were in the employ of private
agencies hired by the UIDAI.

The Material Production of the Aadhaar
in the Enrolment Centres

While researching the Aadhaar and its material production, the enrolment centres where people thronged to apply for this electronic
document suggested themselves as one plausible logical site for an
ethnography. It was here that I got a sense of how deeply and unhappily mired the Aadhaar project was in the heavily bureaucratized yet
permissive regimes of ID production. Contrary to the benign claims of
the UIDAI, the entitlement of every person who wished to enter the
system could not be presupposed. Several categories of applicants must
be documented here.

Some of the enrollees were privileged in that they were able to mobilize authoritative genres of ID documents and address proofs like PAN
cards, voter identity cards, ration cards, passports, driving licences, bank
ATM cards, credit cards, electricity, water, rent agreements, vehicle registration certificates, telephone landline bills, and property tax receipts
into applying for the Aadhaar. Government employees, miscellaneous
wealthy middle-class applicants, and the socio-economically less privileged were able to take the less common but nonetheless respectable
route of producing farmers' licences, income tax orders, photo credit
card statement, government photo ID and service cards issued by
public sector undertakings (PSUs), pensioners' cards, freedom fighter

cards, Central Government Health Scheme (CGHS)/Ex-servicemen Contributory Health Scheme (ECHS) photo cards, caste and domicile certificates, and address card issued by the Department of Posts. But the people manning the enrolment centres also recognized the subaltern of ID documents churned out by modest and quasi-formalized factories of paper, such as copies of certificates attested by gazetted officers, *tehsildars* (land revenue and tax official), MBBS doctors, MLAs, and MPs. But those who slipped through the cracks and failed after multiple attempts to enrol themselves included those who were able to summon up some version perhaps of at least one of all these documents. Alongside the ID documents whose facsimiles had to be recorded and their details captured for processing applications, the bodily imprints of identity were not so amenable to capture either. Disabled persons, labouring classes with hands that resembled *pathar* (stone) in the words of a computer operator, elderly persons, and perverse individuals who wished to trick the system had to be accounted for. It is perhaps ironic that the enrolment process for these individuals had to mirror an intensely bureaucratic system where 'supervisors' who were authorized to recognize the disability were to be present and inscribe their biometric signature.[49] The enrolment centre operators struggled to convey a shared (by the UIDAI, the Indian bureaucracy, and the private agency that hired them) understanding of administratively and legally acceptable forms of identity, address, and bodily veracity to those who felt that they deserved to be enrolled despite everything. Without ensuring that the enrolment centre operators first attempted this, the Authority would not be able to realize its dream of 'leapfrogging' to the dematerialized platform of a paperless identity.

I spent a good three weeks researching, searching for, and finally locating and interviewing some of the key figures who ran enrolment centres in Delhi. While I went to several such centres, I was able to engage in long and freewheeling interviews with the 'computer operators and data maintenance staff' and 'the technicians' of two such centres in north Delhi. In order to protect the anonymity of the people who shared sensitive information with startling ease and little fear of consequences, I have changed the names of the persons interviewed and withheld specific information of the locations where they functioned. The staff I interviewed at both the centres were drawn from a private agency called NVR and Associates, which described itself as

'a leading software development and web-based application development company in Jhandewalan' striving 'to achieve leadership position
by tapping the Indian IT sector boom through a combination of our
extensive branch network and proprietary IT backbone'.[50] Among
the projects that they proudly advertised on their website, NVR and
Associates counted the socio-economic caste census, the NPR, and the
Aadhaar. The operators I spoke with told me that this company had
successfully bagged the tender for these projects in various parts of the
country, such as Delhi, Uttar Pradesh, Bihar, and Haryana. It was not
necessary that NVR and Associates should send its own employees to
run the camp; it could also assume the role of a middle agency that
contracts out the actual 'back-end work' (having secured the tender)
to a smaller firm.

These operators, who claimed to be employees of NVR and
Associates, had experience in handling biometric transactions for NPR
as well as Aadhaar. Early on, they received a modicum of training in
the offices of their company, and possibly even from officials of the
UIDAI, in preparation for their roles in the centres. But such training,
which had to do with handling the software, syncing the data, fixing
biometric machines that were prone to hang, and verifying and recognizing valid documents, was at best minimal and tapered off after
initial spurts of enthusiasm in the first few years. These operators had
to learn on their feet, but yet gave the impression that they were clued
into the job description. The centres varied in the amount of time they
remained open for. When I visited these centres in 2014, I was told
that the company was going to wind up operations in Delhi soon, the
reason being that the crowds in these centres were drastically thin-
ning out in the city. An interesting irony was at work here. The UIDAI
was keen to contract out its work of enrolment to companies, such as
NVR and Associates (and not to government functionaries) because
the employees of these firms could be trusted to not fall into erratic
and irresistible bureaucratic patterns of functioning. 'We do not treat
this as a 9 to 5 job, we are there for as long as applicants keep coming
on any given day,' said Ranjeet, a technician at an enrolment centre.[51]
That said, the company was not incentivized to continue functioning
when the crowd turned into a trickle and there were only six to seven
persons coming on a day. So, unless the UIDAI issued explicit instructions to continue the centre, the private agency was bound to ask its

operators and technicians to pack up and resume operations elsewhere. *'Yeh* company *walleh beedh ke aur bhaagte hein'* (These companies go chasing the crowds), said Harish.[52] However, the private firms that secured the tender to open enrolment centres could not be indifferent to the mandated requirements of the UIDAI either. The Authority may have relied, though I cannot state this with any confidence, on 2011 census data and in particular, responses to the question, 'do you have an Aadhaar?', in deciding the duration or the number of enrolment centres in different states.

On the first day of my interviews with Harish, a computer operator in one of the centres I spent consecutive days visiting, I was witness to an intriguing conversation. Harish was explaining slowly to a harassed old man with worn feet, wearing frayed clothes, that his ration card would not suffice as ID proof for his son as it did not bear his photo. A ration card can be an ID proof only for the head of the family whose photograph it contained. 'But we have no other form of identification for our son,' said the father desperately, adding, 'we are very harassed, *beta*, just make our Aadhaar with what we have already.' Harish responded to this plea of inadequacy with equanimity by saying, 'Take a photo, go to an MBBS doctor, ask him to use his letter pad and write a certificate for you. The certificate should contain the boy's photograph and the doctor's seal against it, the boy's name, his age, your name [meaning the father's name] and the doctor's signature.' The old man then asked, 'where will we find such a doctor?' Harish directed the old man to visit their local doctor who tends to them when he or his son fell ill. 'Get this certificate, this can be ID proof and get your electricity bill, this can be your address for your son and his Aadhaar will be done.'[53]

Later, Harish explained to me that any doctor with a clinic sign and doctor on his nameplate would not suffice—he would have to be a degree-holding MBBS to have the authority to issue such a certificate. The certified MBBS doctor would also have to leave his stamp against the photograph and not on any other part of the document. And while they could accept the father's electricity bill in this case as address proof for the son, the kinship relation cannot be anything other than that of direct progeny. That is, an uncle cannot submit his electricity proof for his nephew or a grandmother for her grandson. Also, the electricity bill cannot be dated more than three months old. Harish painstakingly explained to me that he deliberately chooses to point applicants in the direction of doctors—a breed of gazetted officers that the poor have no trouble locating—and not a police commissioner or an assistant commissioner whose offices are inaccessible for all practical purposes. There is also no point using terms like gazetted officer, for a lot of poor Indians may be familiar with the concept but not the actual practice, he pointed out. It was with some amount of deliberation and the knack of 'official *ke tarah sochna*' or 'thinking like an official' that these private agency-hired computer operators approached the task of 'public dealing' or dealing with the public in Indian officialese. Both computer operators, Sahil and Harish, said they did experience job satisfaction in their line of work, tracing it to their belief that they were essentially doing government work. It did not matter that it was their company's contract with the UIDAI that brought them there, it still got them face to face with the enrolling public. And so, when the time called for it, it was important to also think like the *aam aadmi* (the common man) who was befuddled by official habits. Biometric systems in this sense are not immune to the bureaucratic aspirations of those manning them and it would be naïve to argue that they 'have no relation to the social' (Franke 2009: 357) or that they transcend older discretionary 'intermediation' models.

This was only one instance of the numerous examples of subtle distinctions that Harish and other operators plied me with. At first glance, it appeared that their work did not leave much room for exercising imagination or discretion. As one other enrolment centre operator, Sahil, told me, 'we are tightly bound by the Aadhaar software and the list of PoA and PoIs that have been encrypted in it. If it is not a document that the software recognizes, we have no choice but to reject it' (see Figure 5.2).[54] But Sahil conceded that while the software guided operators in determining the broad acceptability of an ID card, recognizing the telltale signs of a valid document was a job that was all theirs. And so, while they trusted the software to tell them to accept an MP or an MLA's certificate of address but not their certificate of identity, the tehsildar's certificate of identity but not address, they still had to train their gaze to discern signifiers of bureaucratic veracity or the foil of such veracity, signifiers of what the operator termed kalakari (a sarcastic term in this context for workmanship in counterfeiting). The operators quickly internalized the uniquely sarkari habit of asking applicants to produce original documents to mentally cross off all possibilities of

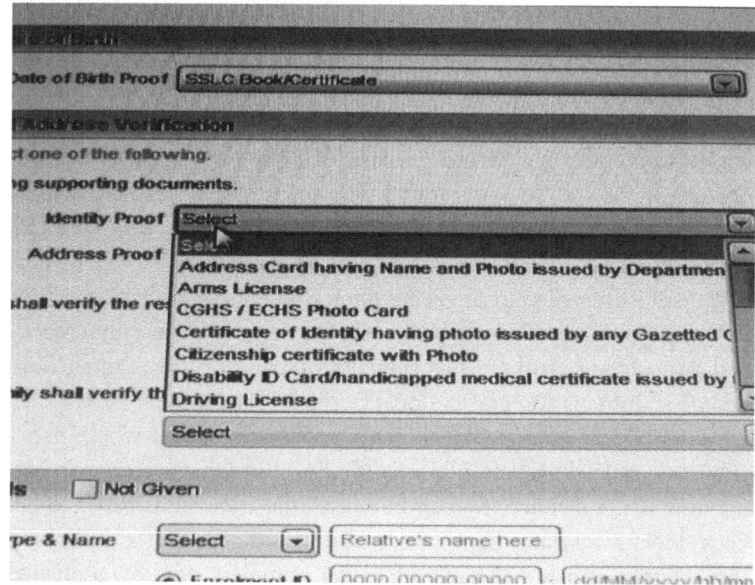

Figure 5.2   A Screenshot of the Operator's Data Entry Field Listing Genres of PoIs
Source: Author.

subversion. Flourishes of falsehood or *jaali kagaz* (counterfeit documents) could be traced to overwriting, fudging, inauthentic seals, cards with absent photographs, photographs with missing signatures, documents with uneven fonts, and blurred-looking ID photocopies. Driving licences and passports without expiry dates, voter identity cards without a hologram, insurance policies that had expired, and school certificates without the principal's letterhead were all too dangerously possible. The ration card was particularly amenable to manipulation—after all, a person can claim that he/she has been freshly added to the ration card. Operators claimed to have come across ration cards with names that were neatly penned into an otherwise fully computerized booklet. But these additions have an administrative process to them and 'computer *se dubara* correction *hota he*' (the corrections are again carried out through the computer) and 'we know that the ration card has been fully computerized for the last many years', said Sahil.[55]

A mere onus on the production of 'originals' was not all. The process of capturing demographic information was to be faithful to the breeder documents to the minutest detail. In recording the enrollee's name, age, nationality, gender, and address, operators had to ensure an exact correspondence with the counterparts of these entries in the breeder document. And so, an applicant's ability to enrol herself as a transgender—which was an option in the Aadhaar enrolment form—could be undercut by her voter identity card which may record her as a man. A progressive arrangement of gender choice in an ostensibly reformative ID project was thus tied to a pre-existing regime of socially embedded bureaucratic truths. When she talks of 'paper truths', Emma Tarlo describes dubious and part-fictional truths to gain authority when they are inscribed in a document which circulates in spaces where paper is bureaucratically valued (Tarlo 2003: 74). But what we are witnessing now is the inclination of an initiative that transcends paper to fall back, lock, stock, and barrel, on minute inscriptions of the slippery sort. Herein also lies the rub of easing homeless persons, orphaned children, and destitute women into the Aadhaar. It was all too common for rural migrants to come bearing breeder documents with addresses that could at best be described as ambiguous. These documents mentioned only the village name and the pin code; and while the operators could reflect this minimal information in the software, they could not supplement it with additional information, however relevant it may be. Ironically enough, this electronically transcribed fidelity to the breeder document occasionally allowed a few slips![56] Sahil told me that that he managed to enrol a man rendered homeless by a domestic squabble with his brother and sister-in-law. Even though he now had no roof he could claim his own, he still managed to keep a few vital ID documents with him. He requested the operator to enrol him by using his erstwhile stable residential address in the confidence that he would be able to 'download' the Aadhaar even if he could not collect it when it was dispatched.

This brings us to the vital question of the 'introducer'. In the initial concept and early implementation stages of the UID, it was felt that certain critical alternative modalities of enrolment were to be allowed if the UIDAI wished to see its promises about the inclusion of the undocumented fulfilled. As seen earlier, NGO representatives, domestic employers, and so on were given the option of standing surety for an undocumented person who lacked PoA and PoI. The computer operators too seemed to think this was a bad idea as the introducers could become glorified middlemen who used this facility for extorting money from poor and gullible persons. We should not be encouraging people to say, '*Mein tera* Aadhaar card *banwa doonga, tu mujhe itna de dena*' (I will make your Aadhaar card, just give me this much), said Harish.[57] He added that at any rate, the introducer route was no longer used in the enrolment centres and that even if he were to try and force the system to accept the enrolment of a person via the introducer, their application would later be rejected. Given that the introducer option was not feasible or even desirable, Harish preferred to ask the undocumented person to go to an MBBS doctor for ID proof and an MLA for address proof.

Interestingly, it is not only the verification process that features the trope of the original. Even though the process of the rollout is supposed to result in the production of a downloadable electronic number, the acknowledgement slip containing the enrolment number or the enrolment ID (EID) is one that is critical to retain. As the computer operators record, far too many people lose this number and when, even after three months, they do not receive their Aadhaar card, they end up returning to the enrolment centres and submitting their biometrics multiple times. But obviously, they are stymied by the CIDR which has strong in-built safeguards against breaking in. These people try to submit slips containing the EID of their second or third attempts, but these are not 'the original slips' which are generated upon the first genuine entry into the system. Also, nomenclatures like the original Aadhaar and e-Aadhaars in lieu of the original Aadhaar (which is dispatched to your house) are now in circulation, even if it is the case that there is no difference between the original Aadhaar and the e-Aadhaar.[58]

The retrieval of the lost Aadhaar number or even updating one's details once the Aadhaar has been registered entails a process that can be termed nothing if not quintessentially bureaucratic, albeit in a more contemporary sense of the term. The date and exact time of enrolment (quaintly termed 'timestamp') and the enrolment number were to be retrieved by calling a toll-free number. The applicants were to then carry their 'original slips', details of the date and time of enrolment (where they wished to update their Aadhaars), and breeder documents, in cases where applicants had lost their original acknowledgement slips, to Pragati Maidan in central Delhi where the regional office of the UIDAI was located (see Figure 5.3). Their physical presence was mandated and this embodied form of self-authentication could not be wished away in the instance of Aadhaar or 'original slip' loss and Aadhaar updation. Like so many things central to the life of the Aadhaar, this routine has undergone change and today, there are more flexible modalities of retrieving the number. But the image displayed outside one of the enrolment centres in north Delhi illustrated that this was the most acceptable way to modify one's Aadhaar in the year 2014 (see Figure 5.3).[59] Today, Aadhaar enrollees can use their registered phone numbers to generate one-time passwords (OTPs) that will act as an electronic trail of crumbs to their lost Aadhaars.

If the Aadhaar came with its package deal of the electronic bureaucracy and virtual identity trails, its paper avatar or 'the physical Aadhaar letter'—that was to be delivered home within 45 days of the acknowledgement slip being printed—was much less reliable. Very intriguingly,

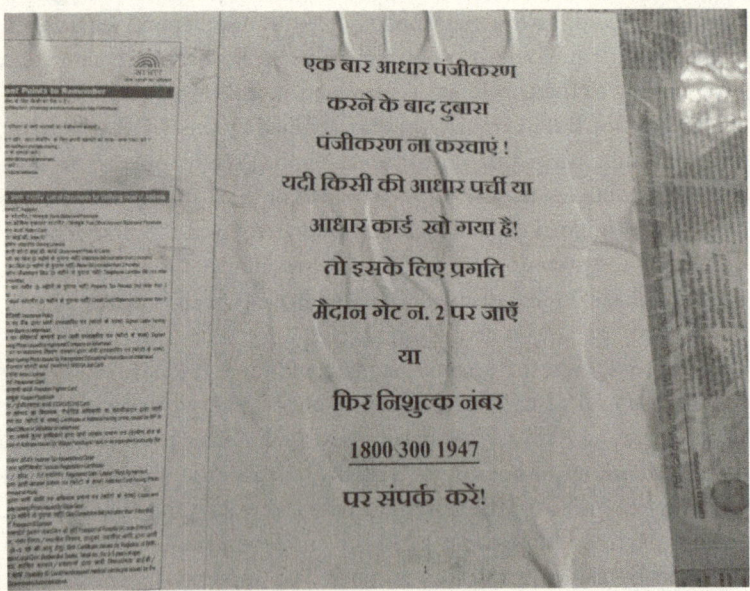

Figure 5.3   A Notice Outside an Enrolment Centre in Delhi Guiding People about the Process for Retrieving Lost Aadhaars
Source: Author.

the UIDAI has discursively acknowledged the value of paper-based proof of the Aadhaar—it has published a 32-page long document, titled 'The Process for Aadhaar Letters Returned by Post', that details the process that should be followed to recover the 'physical Aadhaar letter' in the event of various contingencies, such as death, insufficient address, change in address, the recipient's refusal to accept the letter, the disappearance of the addressee, or failure to claim the letter.[60] I have lost count of the bus porters I interviewed as well as the Govindpuri residents of the previous chapter who resented the fact that their Aadhaars never made it home by post. Even as I stood listening to people returning to the enrolment centres, a refrain I could not miss went something like this: *'sirf meri ladki ka aadhaar kyon nahin aaya'* (why didn't just my daughter's Aadhaar get delivered) or *'sirf meri wife ka aadhaar kyon nahin bana'* (why didn't my wife's Aadhaar alone get made)?

The operators had several hypotheses to proffer. They said that the postmen often carried the original Aadhaars in *boris* (sacks) which they unloaded in the house of a pradhan or a local political leader in a slum or resettlement colony. After all, such leaders were power brokers who had a stake in ensuring that everyone in their vicinity collected their Aadhaar. Besides, the operators were duty-bound to reflect the addresses, however inadequate they may be, of the breeder documents in the Aadhaar software. Where these addresses were incomplete, postmen too could not be faulted for failing to deliver the Aadhaars to their homes. Alternately, as Sahil and Prakash, both computer operators, told me, something wrong may have been detected with the biometrics or the documents belonging to these persons who did not get their Aadhaars. These people would have trouble printing out even their e-Aadhaars, they said. One last explanation they gave was that these people may have applied for the NPR, which too required them to furnish their biometrics. This may have led them to mistakenly harbour the belief that they had applied for Aadhaar. The operators were not always able to coherently convey that the capture of biometrics does not necessarily result in the creation of the Aadhaar, much less the postal delivery of the number document.

If one were to consider the process of Aadhaar enrolment holistically, biometrics is a feature that is not merely linked to the collection of applicants' fingerprints. The computer operator was required to lock and seal every applicant's entry using his own thumb impression as a biometric identifier and the supervisor was to endorse every applicant's entry similarly with his fingerprints. If heads of families or introducers were at all involved, then, theoretically, their biometrics too were collected; and the whole process resembled any old-fashioned college or university application process which entailed the collection of accumulating attestations (by gazetted officials) and breeder documents. The signatures for a single individual's application in this case, however, were limited to those of the operator and the supervisor. All the collated data of demographic and biometric information then travelled to the firm or the employer of these quasi-official operators. Here, each individual's case was thoroughly examined and the documents sealed before they were processed and sent upward to the UIDAI. The familiar ritualistic process entailing bureaucratic 'diffusion of responsibility' and the erasure of personal agency through the accumulation of multiple signatures (Hull 2012a: 115, 139–40) was re-enacted here too. Unlike the government files that were circulated across the rank and file of departments in which numerical jottings, comments, and notes jostled for space with individual signatures, the bureaucratic acts were confined to biometric attestation rather than anything else. This said, operators are definitely a subaltern class of employees who form the company's line of defence against the UIDAI's ire when it comes to mistakes. They sometimes fail to get their salaries on time, risk being blacklisted, and are often made to pay heavy penalties if mistakes in the capture of demographic and biometric information come to light.

Applying for the Aadhaar: The Case of a Rural Migrant Community

This section takes a look at the applications, petitions, transactions, and Aadhaar-related struggles of a poor community of rural migrants in north Delhi to inquire into the UID project's underlying claims of electronic emancipation for migrants. Given that the Aadhaar claims to emancipate the migrant worker from encumbrances of being verified afresh for claiming city-based entitlements, this seemed like a valid line of inquiry. I will do this by regarding the claims of a community which dwells in shifting residential spaces that straddle the urban and the rural. Also, given that the Aadhaar—by being a portable number identifier—promises to render obsolete the anchoring of existing documents like the ration card and the voter identity card to the administrative norm of residence within a state, a district, a village, and a constituency, a rural migrant community suggested itself as a strong field site. The search within the intricately knit community of bus porters in north Delhi for a malleable and obliging form of proof that can accommodate their double identities or their split urban–rural lives is what I offer here as an ethnography.

A few caveats and general remarks about the relevance of this case study to this chapter are in order here. I do not attempt this ethnography to argue the inadequacy of the Aadhaar, as an ID drive, and its affiliated welfare schemes to meet the anguished aspirations of poor subjects in India. Nor am I putting Aadhaar in the dock for the porters' immense disappointments with this ID document which did not absolve them from the burden of making endless representations of their localized identities. Instead, this ethnography is intended to help illustrate the discontents and the discursive complexities of documenting identity and address within the Aadhaar per se. How does an electronic scheme of ID that claims to transcend paper as a genre of knowing poor welfare subjects cope with vital crises of proof-making in practice? What can we make of a dream that paper can be morphed into a sediment of the electronic record and cajoled into vanishing its own traces? Or for that matter, how do we make sense of a dream that identity can now be verified without 'reading' the document as a means of 'seeing' the person? Do the lives of the urban poor allow or even mandate such a vanishing of paper and presence? To get a sense of all this, I spent 8–9 months in the year of 2014 in a busy and crowded bus terminal that was home to 168 coolies or porters. All interviews with the porters were held in the offices of the porters' union whose pradhans (leaders) were extremely gracious in working out the logistics of spending precious time away from their posts in the terminal simply to talk to me about their documentary and Aadhaar-related experiences. To ensure that they do not risk exposure, I have changed the names of all the porters cited in this chapter. Given that there are several porters from any specified state, I have taken care to not divulge details about any single porter beyond mentioning the state of his origin.

The Maharana Pratap Inter State Bus Terminal (ISBT) in north Delhi, colloquially called the bus *adda*, was created in the year 1976, and today runs services between Delhi and seven other states, namely,

Haryana, J&K, Uttar Pradesh, Punjab, Himachal Pradesh, Rajasthan, and Uttarakhand. Prior to this, a makeshift bus terminal was operational, first, in New Delhi and then, in Old Delhi. However, a high-end, spacious terminal that could accommodate the burgeoning numbers of inter-state passengers, with its own government-based regulatory authorities, was desired. While the DDA initially took over the operation and maintenance of the terminal, the Delhi Transport Department became the governing authority in 1993. Around the same time, two other bus terminals, at Anand Vihar and Sarai Kale Khan, also became functional. Over the years, this move saw the diversion of many crucial inter-state bus services to the new terminals, resulting in the steady decline of work for the porters at Kashmere Gate. In the last few years, the porters were affected by the declining commerce in their terminal which was inversely proportionate to the increasing popularity of the other two bus terminals in the city. This prompted some of the porters to seek transfers to the new terminals, and some even managed to get them only to find that they could not secure work at these two new terminals owing to political and administrative tussles.

Ever since 2010, the transport department has authorized a fully government-owned corporation called the Delhi Transport Infrastructure Development Corporation Limited (DTIDCL) to operate and manage all functional and non-functional ISBTs (there are two non-functional terminals at Dwarka and Narela). With this move, the porters too have automatically become the charges of the new corporation. I use the word 'charges' here with some reservations because though the corporation was to issue these porters new ID cards (where earlier, they were issued these by the transport department), it has not considered them its responsibility in any paternalistic welfare sense. The department, and now the corporation, has deliberately avoided treating these porters like government employees for that would entitle them to salary, pension, leave, and insurance, all of which have eluded them (even though the union has repeatedly petitioned several Delhi government authorities for these privileges).[61] An official of the DTIDCL that I spoke with (who did not wish to be quoted) reiterated that these porters could hardly demand any entitlement to pensions for they do not exist on the payrolls of the government. In an interview with me, he said, 'The porters are not regular employees. They only work on the basis of a licence. We are only allowing them to work here. We don't keep any record of their attendance, so don't expect us to give them concessions like salaries, pensions and holidays either.'[62] Also, owing to their unionized status, the porters do not fit the bill of unorganized workers who are now covered by a piece of legislation, the Unorganized Workers' Social Security Act, 2015, that extends an entitlement to a smart card bearing the unique ID number and access to social security schemes and assorted benefits.

The porters at ISBT, originally inhabitants of different states in north, north-west, and south India like Uttar Pradesh, Rajasthan, Haryana, Andhra Pradesh, and Tamil Nadu. Most of them are Dalit or Muslim seasonal farmers who divide their time between working at ISBT and their fields back home because they wish to supplement their meagre agricultural incomes with some steady job in the city. The ISBT porters' union acts as a strong nodal point of the porters' negotiation with disparate authorities like the DDA, the transport department, and the social welfare department, among others. The union steps in to take care of various pressing everyday matters like applying for porters' licences, renewing such ID documents, resolving questions of inheritance therein, and fixing the shift system (where porters share the workload in an equitable arrangement in which they are assigned spots on rotation). While the existence of the union has greatly sheltered individual porters on several matters like securing a post for a relative, getting a medical fitness certificate issued, getting licences renewed, and providing accommodation, the union has occasionally wielded its formidable influence and brought to bear its authority on the workers' fates. The union has always believed that it is important to deny entry to those outside the existing kinship network. In fact, one of the union members told me that if they opened the gates to all job seekers, then their daily wages, already compromised by the two new terminals, would shrink even further.

Porter licences or ID cards can be 'inherited' or passed on from father to son, brother to brother, father-in-law to son-in-law, grandfather to grandson (both son's son and daughter's son), and uncle to nephew (both sister's son and brother's son). Some of these relationships have been recently recognized as legitimate for purposes of inheritance as a result of the sustained pressure that the union brought to bear on successive transport department ministers to recognize indirect and non-blood-based kinship ties, like the one between the

father-in-law and the son-in-law. Where earlier these licences bore the
words 'Transport Department Government of NCT Delhi', they now
read, 'Delhi Transport Infrastructure Development Corporation Ltd (an
enterprise of Government of NCT of Delhi)'. The ID card or licence
has led to an intense insecurity as their fragile jobs now seem even
more tenuous. This is because the 'Limited' part of the DTIDCL gives
the authority the aura of a company. While the porters have always
wanted their jobs to be more secure—they have, for instance, craved
salaried payment and pensions—they never had to regard themselves
as contractual employees until now. The porters cannot shake off the
conviction that they have now been rendered ad hoc employees of a
'limited-wallah *adhikari*' (the authorities of a corporate establishment
implicit in the word 'limited').[63] But there is also a pun concealed in
such a construction as the new establishment has only further 'limited'
the governmental protections of these porters.

The new regime also made periodic medical tests compulsory, tying
the renewal of licences to the production of fitness certificates issued
by MBBS-qualified doctors. In one stroke, this rendered ageing, injured,
unwell, and convalescing porters vulnerable to the loss of their licences.
The porters' union has dealt with the deep insecurities caused by their
corporatized identities by making their own identity cards bearing the
insignia of the union (see Figure 5.4). Alternately, individual porters
have retained a laminated photocopy of their old ID cards carrying the
seal of the Delhi Transport Department. Though both versions of these
cards are useless when they negotiate with the transport department or
apply for the Aadhaar, it has helped them certify themselves as workers attached to a governmental organization when they approach the
social welfare department for pensions, when they are implicated in
criminal cases, and when they travel in the city and claim concessions.

The porters' union was a beehive of always ongoing paperwork.
Apart from handling new applications, a record was meticulously
maintained by the office-bearers, with each page serving as a paper
trail of the porter's ID history. While the first part of the page contained the porter's family predecessor (who he inherited his ID from),
the latter part contained details of the present incumbent. The details
for both the previous and the incumbent porter were the same: the
photo, name, father's name, temporary address, permanent address
and age, and signature or thumb print. The union stuck to strict rules,

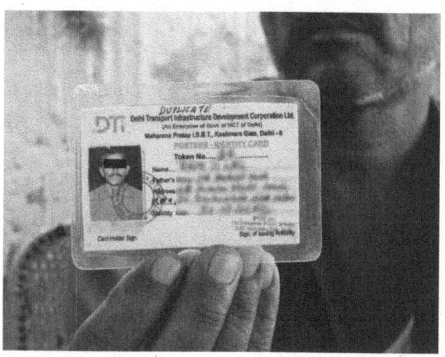

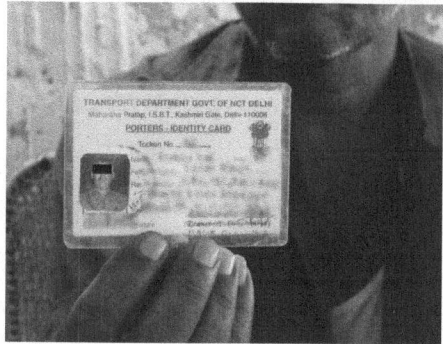

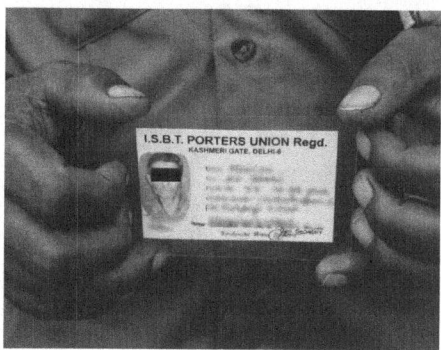

Figure 5.4 Three Different Types of the ISBT Porter Licence Issued by
Disparate Authorities
Source: Author.

such as the porter had to leave his badge (a metallic token bearing a number) behind along with a leave letter that the union issued when he goes back to his village (Figure 5.5). These various documents carried immense evidentiary value: the leave letter supported by the register and the badge recorded the days of his absence, thus helping many a porter fend off criminal charges on being falsely accused of some crime back in his village. The pradhans of this democratically and annually elected union body also pointed out to me that if any government department wished to know the urban status of the porter or verify his residential history, it needed only to consult its meticulously preserved records where each page sufficed as an employment and residential history of a single porter. But even as the Aadhaar enrolment machinery mobilizes the rich material culture of 'collateral evidence' in the form of MBBS-certified ID proof and tehsildar-issued address proof, it has, until very recently, not privileged these alternate document forms.

Figure 5.5 Porter's Metallic Token and the Union Leave Letter
Source: Author.

The Imagination of Caste in Electronic Claim-making

In imagining the urban poor canvas in which Aadhaar-related complexities converge, it has been common to invoke schemes like the JDY, PDS benefits, cash transfers, and even old-age pensions. The caste certificate hardly features in these scholarly and policy discussions about the Aadhaar; and this only reinforces the truth of an observation made by, among others, M.S.S. Pandian about postcolonial formulations of modernity that caste must always belong 'somewhere else'. He writes that through acts of 'transcoding caste and caste relations' into things that belong in 'the pre-modern realm', upper-caste autobiographies tend to cleverly acknowledge caste while simultaneously disavowing it (Pandian 2014: 393). As the discussions around Aadhaar and the alienness of caste to them clearly demonstrate, the transformation of caste within a technology-driven modernity is perhaps not relevant because the lower castes have always resided on the margins of a secular–modern, universal public sphere. If one is to contest the continued perpetuation of caste as 'the other of the modern' (Pandian 2014: 397) and uncover the operation of caste in 'spatially ambiguous contexts' (Guru 2014: 416), one must seek out its opacities in disembodied and dematerialized technological spaces and question its transparency in political spaces that appear immune to technology. And so, this project insinuates itself not only into upper-caste politics of denouncing reservations but also into universal legal and technological architectures of welfare. When certain technologies of ID produce aggravated, as against merely unmitigated, effects of discrimination, the challenge may be to inquire into the residues and even the aspirations of caste-based and paper-driven structures in electronic regimes.

The majority of the 168 porters in ISBT were Dalit. In all, porters self-identified their castes to be SC (90), other backward class (OBC, 20), and upper caste (32). Apart from this, there were 21 Muslims and 2 porters who migrated to ISBT from Nepal. While a good number of porters belonging to the lower castes were members of the *Chamar* community residing in Muzaffarnagar in Uttar Pradesh, several others came from the *Khatik, Kumhar, Prajapati, Jatav, Chauhan, Nai, Mali, Chuhra,* or *Balmiki* communities from Uttar Pradesh, Rajasthan, Haryana, and Delhi. It is necessary to note this diversity within Dalit and backward caste porters in order to characterize the bureaucratic aspects and the regional politics of claim-making around the caste certificate. Along with applying for other documents like income certificate, the porter's licence, BPL ration cards, and voter identity cards, it was paramount for them to factor the caste certificate into their welfare-claiming itineraries. Many of the Dalit and OBC porters I interviewed stated that they had got their caste certificates made in their villages. The porters experienced the duality of their rural–urban existences very keenly in their caste-specific struggles of claim-making in the city. One such Dalit porter from Uttar Pradesh, Rajesh Kumar, astutely pointed out that the Aadhaar was akin to the caste certificate in that both forms of ID (one documentary and the other electronic) constituted an interface through which multiple welfare claims were recognized and concessions granted.[64] Mere possession of either the caste certificate or the Aadhaar did not suffice; it was important to demonstrate other things like one's marks, one's income, and one's BPL status for an educational scholarship, eligibility for a concessional bank loan, or PDS rations. Within the lifeworlds of a poor Dalit in India, the caste certificate was synonymous with his/her existence as a welfare subject. While there is a deeply fraught history to the certification and the codification of castes in India—ranging from the battle over separate electorates, caste censuses, and the claims of certain castes to reservation—the place of the caste certificate has been under-theorized in Indian social science scholarship. As Bhanu, a Dalit porter from Uttar Pradesh, put it: the upper castes are suddenly upset that the Aadhaar is indispensable for their everyday relationship with the state, but a single document being a ticket to survival was nothing new to the Dalits of India. He said, '*Rozgaar ho ya padhai ho, har chees ki* ticket caste certificate *he*' (to get a job, to study or to secure anything, the caste certificate is our ticket).[65]

If, for the upper-caste rural migrant, the Aadhaar was necessary to smoothen out the tangles of urban–rural spatial specificities of claim-making, for the Dalit and backward caste porter, much more than this was needed. I gathered that while the process of applying for a caste certificate was many-layered, the end in sight was not elusive in rural tehsildar offices (where traditionally one applied for these certificates) where residents often either intimately knew the sarpanch (village head) or someone related to him. When one applied for the caste certificate in rural offices, the process was tedious, involving multiple stops, but not one that was frustrating and elusive as it often was when they applied in the city. 'Besides, the SDM's office in the city demands a lot of dalali, you have to deal with half a dozen petty middlemen before you can get to the SDM's counter,' said Pradeep, a porter who belonged to an OBC caste and whose home was in Uttar Pradesh.[66] Besides, the modalities of recognition are painfully formal: the Delhi government's revenue department rules state that where a lower-caste individual was not able to submit a caste certificate of a relative from the paternal side, she/he was supposed to secure certificates from two government servants to this effect. In comparison, he found the process of applying for a certificate in his village somewhat smooth:

> When I applied in my village, there was no *rukavat*. The neighbour's testimony, a letter from the Sarpanch, evidence from the patwari and an affidavit for which I went to an advocate [read notary public] was all I needed. It does not even matter if you can't produce an SC certificate of one of your relatives from the paternal side—the tehsildar's office in our village finds a way around the problem.[67]

Even for someone like Sundar, who belonged to an OBC community, the fact that he had spent his whole life in Delhi and that his brother and father were both certified OBC did not exempt him from the three-year wait for the caste certificate. The proposed integration of the caste certificate with the Aadhaar would only threaten to perform certain de-duplications that collapses urban and rural data of caste certificate holders into permanent categories. Through this integration, the Aadhaar may well render the act of applying for a caste certificate into one where a lower-caste person is assigned a specific reserved caste status in perpetuity. But in a polity where caste itself is always on the cusp of transformation within a matrix of region, religion, and electoral and administrative politics, how just can this be? When he suggests the operation of certain discourses central to the reproduction of caste, Gopal Guru (2014: 415) advises scholars to undertake the keen study of artifacts and quantitative data in order to retrieve these discourses. To this can be added the use of a certain language, in this instance, of welfare reform where administrative anxiety of abounding fraud and inaccuracy can perform a discursive act of negating fluid choices of declaring one's caste. So, very recently, when the centre issued orders to link caste and domicile certificates for students in Class 5 or Class 8, it did so in the belief that there will be 'no frauds at the stage of seeking admissions on the basis of quota in higher educational institutions or joining government jobs'.[68]

In India, the various articles of the Indian Constitution (such as Articles 15, 46, 330, 332, 334, 335, and 338, to cite merely a few provisions) and the Scheduled Castes and Scheduled Tribes (Prevention of Atrocities) Act, 1989 provide the basis for securing welfare benefits and reservations for the SCs and STs of India. However, the list of SCs and STs is not uniform across all the states and the various administrative units of India have prepared their own inventories. The OBCs are also variable across Indian states and some of the agitations, such as those spearheaded by the Gujjars and the Jats, centre on the specific demand of caste recognition within a state like Rajasthan or Haryana. A community that is certified OBC or SC in one state may not find the same recognition in another state. Even if a porter finds that he is certified OBC in both the states (for example, Uttar Pradesh and Delhi), he still may not be able to leverage his village-issued caste certificate to apply for urban benefits. Thus, when these rural lower-caste migrant porters applied for a caste certificate in Delhi, they invariably faced insurmountable obstacles in persuading the counterpart of the rural tehsildar in Delhi's sub-divisional magistrate's (SDM's) offices that they resided in the city or that they had relatives living in the city. There is also no counterpart of the sarpanch as a familiar point of reference in the city. In fact, some of the questions that were repeated in their conversations at the union office by the OBC and SC porters were as follows. Can the Aadhaar break this debilitating linkage between my caste and my village? If I get an Aadhaar, will I be able to get a caste certificate made from the city? If I get my Aadhaar, will my caste certificate transcend differences of city and village? Will the Aadhaar ensure that I never have to step inside an SDM's office? Can the Aadhaar do away with the *rishwat pratha* associated with the caste certificate in the SDM's office?

In the year 1988, the National Housing Bank was set up as an autonomous long-term housing finance institution that was fully owned by the Reserve Bank of India. This institution's mandate, after much reflection, was to ensure the financial viability of all households, but particularly those from weaker income and backward castes that sought affordable housing. It sought, in particular, to 'integrate the housing finance system with the overall financial system' and lay down the guidelines for identifying and privileging lower-income SC and ST communities for concessional bank loans.[69] However, where bank loan application procedures were strongly wedded to caste certificates and where the regional politics of designating certain castes SC was itself undergoing fast transition, claim-making was murky. In 2005, the Uttar Pradesh government counted the *Kumhar* (alternately termed *Prajapati*) or the earthen pot-maker community as one of the 16 castes that was to be added to the list of SCs in the state.[70] It was after getting the SC certificate made from Uttar Pradesh that Ramnath, a porter who belonged to this community (which is certified OBC in Delhi), sought the assistance of a Punjab National Bank branch in Delhi for a concessional housing loan.

> When I approached the bank, they refused to accept the caste certificate that I had gotten made from my village and they demanded that I produce a document showing that I fulfilled the caste certification norms in Delhi. But how can I make an SC certificate from Delhi when this state explicitly counts us as OBCs? I now have the Aadhaar as well as a caste certificate from the village simply because I am tired of being excluded from government schemes on the grounds that I am an SC back in my village and not in Delhi. The Aadhaar will possibly resolve this, we will have one identity nation-wide.[71]

Even if one were to leave state-specific caste quotas aside, the UIDAI explicitly does not collect information of the caste of the applicant and de-duplication can only confirm the identity of an individual whose caste records are the separate domain of the state government. If the Aadhaar cannot possibly address these irreducibly complex intra-state and inter-state caste politics of inclusion, its integration with the caste certificate threatens only to mire people from lower castes into more nested conundrums.

Many administrative offices, in fact, tended to render the submission of Aadhaar compulsory in processing applications for caste certificates even after the Supreme Court judgement that sought to decouple welfare benefits from the Aadhaar.[72] The SDM branches in Delhi too asked for its production in applications for caste certificates and were inclined to turn away applicants who did not possess the Aadhaar on grounds that the computer software rejects the application unless it contained the unique number. It was only after the intervention of the chief information commissioner (an authority who regulates the enforcement of the RTI legislation), who pointed out that such furtively mandatory rules violated the right to transparent information, that SDMs refrained from demanding Aadhaar.[73] These kinds of incidents electronically re-enacted histories of marginalization of Dalits such that overlapping discriminatory protocols only served to preclude these communities from critical welfare networks. It is imperative for researchers to mobilize the immensely rich philosophical resources of writings by Dalits to demonstrate how modernized processes of enrolment and registration work in social spheres. These processes simultaneously obliterate the enabling self-identification of Dalits and expunge the coercive roles of conventional actors, such as upper-caste officials, political leaders, bureaucrats, and other influential men in perpetuating marginal statuses.

Brick-and-Mortar Materiality and the Unabated 'Factum of Residence'

Let us return for a moment to the application process for this portable, cloud-based electronic number. The porters have noted that it is painfully conventional not only in its intractable insistence on the production of PoA and PoI but also, according to one porter, in its inherent 'camp culture'. Applying for a ration card or a voter identity card is now fully automated such that the claimant no longer needs at any point to visit the circle office or the voter registration centre unless his/her ID document requires modification. But evidently the Aadhaar enrolment process cannot be automated because it paradoxically requires the physical presence of the applicant for capturing the biometrics that are needed to render identities unique and portable. The brick-and-mortar materiality of the enrolment centre is something that these porters have had to grapple with. A common complaint took this form, '*Jab hum gaon me the tab yahan* camp *laga tha aur jab yahan* camp *laga tha tab humare* document *saare ke saare gaon me rehgaye*' (when we were in the village, that was when the enrolment camp was held here and when the camp was set up here, we realized we had left our documents back home).[74] This problem could have been easily addressed if the porters were given a month's notice to gather their documents but this never materialized.

In mid-2014, an enrolment camp was, without sufficient notice, held on the premises of the bus terminal. However, this centre ran into all sorts of technical problems and did not even result in the production of proper acknowledgement slips containing the enrolment number. The biometric systems failed to function properly owing to a fluctuating power connection—several porters turned up for enrolment and even had their biometrics captured but could not be issued slips. Repeated requests to the UIDAI (made by the union to the men who ran the enrolment centre, by an NGO to the UIDAI, and this researcher to the Authority to follow up on enrolment of the porters) as well as to the persons who held the enrolment camp to finish what they had started seemed to yield few results; and as the enrolment centres started to wind up their operations in Delhi, those porters who had not managed to enrol often waited for camps to be held in their home states where they could apply. In these circumstances, it was important for the pradhans to hold on to the acknowledgement slips so that the union could demonstrate to either the enrolment centre or the UIDAI that only the bearers of these slips had successfully applied for the Aadhaar. The pradhans allowed an enrolled porter to take copies but he had to deposit the original acknowledgement slip in the union office for safekeeping and further processing. Finally, in the year 2016, nearly two years after the union began its entreaties to computer operators and the UIDAI, all the porters of ISBT received their Aadhaars. While all the porters did finally secure their Aadhaars, the pradhans were unsure if this was because the operators now recognized their licenses.

As a concession to the porters who continue to render an undeniable service to commuters, the Delhi government enabled these workers to reside in the premises of the terminal. The porters used to stay at a decrepit *vishram griha* or a dorm-like single restroom with battered lockers and poorly functional toilets (see Figure 5.6). A plan to create an expanded and refurbished restroom, pursued by the porters, materialized finally after several years of ceaseless talks initiated by an NGO and the union with successive governments. But the restroom was significant not merely as a material comfort in that it buffered the porters from the extremities of the infamous Delhi weather. It was also mobilized into a residential address: the porter's licence stipulated the vishram griha to be the place of residence for all those porters who did not have any stable dwelling in the city. If one were to leave out the few

Figure 5.6 The Erstwhile Restroom in the Bus Terminal
Source: Author.

Delhi-based residents, this licence served as the only PoA in Delhi for most other migrant porters.

Of the 70 porters I interviewed, only 16 porters were in possession of coherent Delhi-based address proof. One porter residing in a mosque in Old Delhi had somehow managed to get a voter identity card and ration card issued in his name that recognized this address. For this Muslim porter, his lack of a stable residential address did not matter that much because he possessed breeder documents which testified to his presence in Delhi. But no other rural migrant porter was lucky enough to have his liminal state of urban dwelling rendered into a fungible form of address proof that was discrete from his residence back home. Such porters, if they possessed voter identity cards and ration cards at all, could only claim to have such ID documents issued by authorities in their home states. The union, through the admirable help of an NGO, sought repeatedly to get voter identity cards and ration cards issued to some migrant porters on the strength of their bus adda restroom address. Briefly, the Department of Food and Supplies, Delhi and the voters' registration centre obliged them; but soon after the cards were issued, they were rapidly cancelled owing to political interference from a few MLAs. In what turned out to be a narrative of diminishing electoral returns, these MLAs—because they felt shortchanged by the porters' dependence on other facilitators like NGOs and district resource centres—objected to the issuing of ration cards and voter identity cards citing that these people lacked legitimate Delhi-based ID proof.[75] These are important things to note because the Delhi bus porters constitute, in every sense, the poorly documented constituency of rural migrants whose generic welfare status the UIDAI has pledged to transform through Aadhaar enrolment. This case history is also critical to establish that the migrant porter's application for an Aadhaar was an unmitigated and intensified quest for a spatially enabling address proof.

Let us now consider the application process for the Aadhaar and how porters sought to enter the portals of biometric ID. The union members pointed out to me unhappily that the Aadhaar enrolment centres, for a very long time, refused to issue an Aadhaar on the strength of the porter's licence taken either as a PoA or PoI. Back when operators refused to accept the licence, one union leader proclaimed, 'Aadhaar *ke sambandh me, humare* licence *ka koi manyata nahin raha hai*' (as far as the Aadhaar goes, our licences have had no validity).[76] In the initial days, when the porters tried to show their licences that underlined their place of residence in the terminal, they were told by the operators manning the enrolment centres that this would not do. When an enrolment centre was held in the premises of the union office, union members tried to explain to the Aadhaar operators that the porter's licence was a legitimate ID document bearing the seal and signature of a government department under the National Capital Territory of Delhi (NCTD). The porter's licence, not unlike the railway porter's licence, is issued through an elaborate verification process that has required all manner of representations, statements, and affidavits. Porters have had to satisfy various litmus tests of PoI, PoA, and medical fitness; thus, on their path to registration, they were not spared any documentary burdens either of the formal legal or of the administratively pertinent variety. It was only after furnishing police verification certificates, medical certificates, no objection certificates from competing sons and even daughters, and ration cards or voter identity cards that they were issued licences. Why did these cards then fail to be a pukka address or ID proof for the longest time and why was the enrolment centre loath to recognize it until recently?

The official line on this is multifold but I will construe it in two significant senses: (a) as the bus adda is a government undertaking, the restroom is not a private residential space and therefore, such an address would lack legitimacy; and (b) the porters are not government employees, hence this cannot be a proof of ID either in the strict sense of the term. Just as they are not entitled to salaries and pensions, they lack any prima facie claim to a government-issued ID document. This has left the porters desperate for an ID document outside their porter network in the city, and the Aadhaar has eluded them for the same reasons that they have desired it. It was important to secure an Aadhaar because it was valid across different states, and the whole point of issuing this number was to ensure that certain governmental benefits were not held back by immutable notions of address. But the porters' papers were not good enough to constitute an Aadhaar. Here, the reader may ask: why fuss so much about the porter's licence not being admissible as proof where so many other identities could be mobilized into Aadhaar's PoI and PoA? The answer to this question lies in the Aadhaar's selective quest to make certain governmental ID documents portable while disregarding others as microscopic and rudimentary fragments of local identity. If the food security card (or the ration card), the MGNREGS job card, and even the EPIC were deemed worthy in Aadhaar's enterprise to make documents technologically compatible with its architecture, others like the porter's licence, the union's porter records, vendor's permit, and the rickshaw puller's licence were not ready reckoners. From my interview with the DTIDCL official, I gathered that the government would not be interested in integrating the porter licence with the Aadhaar number. 'This is a licence, not really a government ID even if the porters pretend that it is—there is no question of making it more pukka,' this official indicated.[77] Miraculously, however, the searing negativity of the DTIDCL and the early reluctance of the enrolment centre notwithstanding, an operator came back to the bus adda and arranged for all the remaining porters to be issued Aadhaars on the strength of their licences.

Without an Aadhaar, the porters would not have been eligible to apply for the food security cards either. Interestingly, when I reported the porters' difficulty in getting Aadhaars made, officials in the food and supplies department helped me map out the contrasting points of entry of a homeless person into the PDS. Delhi's slum-related housing agency, the DUSIB, which manages the *ren baseras* (night shelters) of Delhi, can certify that homeless persons are residing in these shelters—in fact, DUSIB can get forms of such homeless persons from the department, fill them out, and send them back. The department has to merely approve these forms. 'If needed, we can help these persons secure Aadhaars. Otherwise, they can apply online or the old-fashioned way by going to the circle office and submitting an application and nothing prevents our officials from doing field verification of their (informal) residence and documents.'[78] In the past, the department has taken the help of NGOs to identify homeless persons but considering the scale and the diversity of homelessness in Delhi induced by slum displacement, migration, and short-term construction labour, there were always people who fell through the cracks. And the porters being neither here nor there, neither qualifying as unorganized workers nor as contractual wage labour, neither being homeless nor making the cut as urban dwellers, could not rely on governmental channels to help them out. Indeed, the porters owe their newly acquired Aadhaars to the creditable perseverance of the union that took on every other such issue with an equal ferocity. The union was successful in its negotiations with governmental and bureaucratic authorities on two particular fronts: petitioning the Delhi government to provide them with a new and cool restroom facility with lockers for every porter; and petitioning the various actors responsible for issuing new Aadhaars.[79]

Mobilizing Aadhaar for Rations and Other Welfare Programmes

I would now like to make a few brief comments on the largest and the most hoary government scheme within postcolonial paper-based welfare memory, namely, the distribution of food rations. My ethnographic reflections for this section are deliberately brief because the Aadhaar applications for the Food Security Act, 2013 are still rapidly evolving. The biometric and policy-based remodelling of ration cards in Delhi has been mercurial when seen in terms of the categories of PDS entitlement and the broad technological approach deployed. Earlier,

the Delhi-based model recognized several classes of a diversely defined
urban poor population, such as the Jhuggi Ration Card (JRC) and
the Resettlement Colony Ration Card (RCRC). All such cardholders
fell within the genre of those who were issued 'stamped' ration cards
which were reserved for those whose family incomes were less than
a lakh per year. In recent times, the food and supplies department in
Delhi replaced this model with a new and sparser one in deference
to the provisions of the Food Security Act, 2013. This Act assured 50
per cent coverage for India's urban population and 75 per cent for the
rural population.

After the Act was passed, the classes of ration cardholders in Delhi
were watered down to three categories: priority; priority sugar; and
the older Antyodaya Anna Yojana (AAY). These new categories did not
allow urban poor residents to leverage their built urban environment
to apply for rations.[80] However, for the implementation of 'exclusion
criteria', the food and supplies department relied on the agency of the
MCD to classify house owners or tenants in order to render certain
classes ineligible to receive rations. The food and supplies department
in Delhi, not unlike its counterparts in other states, believed that the
intersection of the Food Security Act and the Aadhaar supplied the
opportune moment to address the eternal anxiety around fake ration
cards, PDS fraud, and the drain on the public exchequer.[81] Though
the department was chastised when it sought to make ration cards
incumbent on the possession of the Aadhaar,[82] it has gone way beyond
merely linking ration cardholders to Aadhaar in the years following the
passage of the Food Security Act. Food officials in this department were
critical of petitions filed in the Supreme Court demanding that government benefits should not be tied to Aadhaar. 'The petitioners behind
such cases are always people who don't want to apply for the Aadhaar
because they have bogus cards and they wish to break the system,' said
another food official who did not wish to be named.[83]

An unshakeable conviction and love for electronic systems of ID
cannot be separated from the state's dogged suspicion of those who
do not wish to be tricked into conforming to such systems. The uni-
versalization of practices of ID within legal and administrative modernity—where earlier they may have been selectively deployed against
criminal tribes, indigo ryots, indentured labour, impoverished pilgrims,
seditious elements (Naidu and Lal 1995; Sengoopta 2004; Singha

2000)—has now taken an unmistakable turn. In *The Princely Impostor* or the nineteenth century fascinating tale of a prince-turned-sanyasi welfare claimant in colonial India, Partha Chatterjee aptly writes that the benign dictum of penal regimes to presume an individual innocent until proven guilty found its parallel in welfare regimes that presumed individuals to be impostors until found genuine. He adds that both dictums, far from being contradictory, are 'entirely consistent within the domain of modern governance' (Chatterjee 2002: 366). But present-day welfare consciousness has not remained stable: it has willed certain technologies of ID to extend their legitimacy such that the new dictum would soon read 'impostor until electronically enrolled'. The food official is not alone in his fearful biases against paper-based claimants, his suspicions are resonant with those of international financial institutions, welfare establishments in countries like South Africa and Pakistan and others which seek to justify ambitious government schemes to their national publics.

In what would make Aadhaar's vociferous libertarian critics cringe, the Delhi government guidelines even make room for requesting the UIDAI to download the photographs of the head of the family. The linkage of a biometrically defined ID to food security cards—which has been ongoing since September 2013—has entailed remodelling the dispensation of distributing rations to enable biometrically responsive point of sale (PoS) machines. The old system of comprehensively documenting PDS transactions, recording ration cardholders' details and ration allotments, recording the remaining stock balance, and issuing cash memos using master register, sale register, and stock register typical to FPSs is now gradually being phased out. The same food official told me that the FPS owner will now feed the card number into the PoS machine, scan the thumb impression or the iris of the cardholder for authentication, and then issue rations. During this interview that took place in June 2016, the official also revealed to me that as of now, only 42 FPSs are using the PoS devices out of a total of 2,534 FPSs and 2,300 functional FPSs in Delhi's 70 circles—tenders had been refused four times and the department was happy only with one bidder's PoS technological interface. The popular reception of these machines where they have been installed in other parts of the country like Rajasthan, Jharkhand, and Andhra Pradesh has been stingingly critical; and the rejection of the fingerprints of the elderly and the labouring classes have unconscionably compromised food security rations and pensions over an extended period. But, more interestingly, in a rabid move aimed at weening intermediary government-approved vendors off the paper-based PDS, Rajasthan's dealers were not allowed access to lists of eligible households from 'the manual system'.[84]

Jean Drèze writes that dependence on both the manual and PoS systems has persisted. This is a practice that he deems dangerous as only PDS dealers can decide when to use the register system. At the same time, exclusive dependence on the PoS machine can only engender myriad interlocking risks. He writes, 'the system requires multiple fragile technologies to work at the same time: the PoS machine, the biometrics, the Internet connection, remote servers and often other elements such as the local mobile network' and correct seeding of Aadhaar number into the PDS database.[85] There is another danger quite apart from those that Drèze fearfully catalogues. The transition of the remaining majority paper-based FPSs into PoS-based FPSs is a process that can only be riddled with terrible complexity as it will, in all likelihood, be accompanied by an intense policing and selective acceptance of old registers. Where older documentary practices of welfare distribution have persisted even after the introduction of the two pieces of legislation, namely, the Food Security Act and the Aadhaar Act, their slow disappearance is possible only through discriminating acts of interrogating the materiality and the authenticity of dates, official signatures, photographs, and serial numbers in ration cards, FPS inscriptions of allocations, and stock balances in registers. Whether it is the Aadhaar enrolment centres or the food and supplies department that engages in these material acts of rendering paper-based IDs into electronic artifacts, such processes engender invisible forms of discretion, that is, partial rejection of documents on the one hand, and ritualistic habits of privileging 'the signs' of truth within the document on the other.

The JDY, a flagship programme introduced by the Modi government, holds out grand promises of accident and life insurance cover and is aimed at nurturing habits of thrift and savings among the poor. This programme, which hinged on the possibility of a zero-balance account that can be opened 'anywhere', has served to inflate the desirability of Aadhaar. The Aadhaar, though not compulsory, is almost ubiquitously accepted as a gateway into this acclaimed portal of financial inclusion.

Almost every porter I interviewed had heard of the Aadhaar and several of them had an interest in securing the Aadhaar purely owing to their interest in this scheme. If they could not get such accounts opened in their own name because they already had active accounts, they tried to get their wives to open such accounts. Though the government has offered laudatory figures of the number of JDY accounts opened,[86] conversations with officials of two State Bank of India (SBI) branches in north Delhi yielded sobering insights of how very few of these 'low-cadre, low-profile' (in one official's description), small account holders were actually able to fulfil the demanding conditions (where account holders were to demonstrate regular transactions for six months). Where these conditions were not met, a successful claim to the insurance benefits could not be clinched. Where account holders did not possess an Aadhaar, they could not avail the overdraft entitlement either.[87] Ursula Rao, in her article provocatively termed 'Biometric Marginality', suggests that these banks implicitly assume identity to encompass not simply the physical trace of the individual but also social standing and trust (Rao 2013: 72). I secured a corroboration of this in a personal interview with a representative of the UIDAI, 'Banks don't want so much of a burden, you know, the social inclusion in business has had a limited success. So somebody will have to go after the banks with a big hammer and say, "you get it done", and only then they will do it.'[88] A few porters also testified to their inability to get zero-balance accounts opened owing to an intractable insistence on local residence proof in Delhi's banks even if they were able to produce the Aadhaar. Owing to the negligible numbers of JDY account applications that some branches receive and the attendant fuzzy understandings of bank officials of the finer aspects of this programme, as well as the poor channels of communication between life insurance providers and the general bank branches, the JDY's successes in 'papering over' residence norms may be overestimated.

*

Instead of asking whether or not the Aadhaar should be dismantled, this chapter sought to debate the very implications of the material acts that the production of the Aadhaar has entailed. The transition to an electronic era of welfare dispensation in the case of Aadhaar was possible only through intimate and ritualistic moves of reading and indexing breeder documents. Such acts of reading were designed to privilege signs of authenticity, tangibility, fakeness, and correspondences with the applicant's self. Socially embedded bureaucratic truths were, in this sense, privileged over progressive notions of identifying the undocumented or the documentarily disabled. The UID enrolment software demonstrated a strangely obsessive fidelity to the scattered postcolonial forms and signs of the ID document. It had to reflect addresses (however incomplete), ID card-inscribed genders (however dissatisfactory to the cardholder), and date of birth (which, if 'verified', had to correspond with the document produced), giving little leeway to claimants who sought to fashion 'a demographic field of their own choice' (Cohen 2014). Acts of discretion on the part of the computer operator to enrol or pass over a person in haste were not uncommon owing to official affects attached to the sarkari adhikari and aam aadmi in verifying documents. While operators exercised discretion, it had to be justified within certain electronically available categories. Paper-based ID documents did not disappear after their information was transcribed for generating the unique number. If anything, the process of document verification intensified as applicants queued up to testify that they were Aadhaar-enabled claimants to food rations, pensions, scholarships, and bank benefits. While the Aadhaar manifested a symbiotic dependence on existing ID documents, it simultaneously fashioned itself as indispensable to document-bearing welfare claimants. In producing a virtual community of number-bearing claimants, the UIDAI may be seeking to create a de-spatialized existence or a space 'without a corresponding referent on the ground' (Franke 2009: 358; Giese 1998). But this project may have simply 'foreclosed' possibilities of 'moving freely' within the welfare ecology as people can no longer be 'unlocatable' (Franke 2009: 358) within the CIDR or the Aadhaar database.

So even if the UIDAI claims to be able to liberate documented identities from administrative vestiges of urban or rural address, this may not be possible simply on the strength of its biometrically fashioned unique number. The rich narratives of a tiny universe of migrant welfare claimants have helped establish the negligible benefits of number portability in any considered aspect of urban life. The linking of caste certificates to Aadhaar represents, for instance, the inherent dangers of freezing a social category that is constantly on the cusp of transformation. The convergence of Aadhaar with any ID document may be fraught with disaster if it does not attend to the dynamics of paper-based forms of ID and associated practices of brokerage, bureaucratic knowledge, and the politics of identity. Both the enrolment for Aadhaar and its link-age to welfare schemes have tended to draw on debilitating legacies and norms of residence that penalize the inhabitants of in-between modes of dwelling. The porters can neither be ideal urban residents nor homeless subjects because they cannot demonstrate permanent resi-dence and because they dwell in their place of work. Perhaps because Aadhaar's claim to strengthening their welfare statuses was so fragile, and because they were so used to being policed, the porters of ISBT were convinced that the Aadhaar existed merely to render them less suspicious from a purely criminal gaze of the state. When a porter said to me in an unmistakable Govinda-like voice from the Bollywood film *Coolie No. 1*, 'Number-wallah coolie *kabhi chor nahin ho sakta*' (the number-bearing coolie can never be a thief), he was referring simulta-neously to the metallic plate that legitimized his presence in the ter-minal and the Aadhaar that contained his fingerprints.[89] The Aadhaar was also selective in the categories of collateral evidence it considered, privileging certain informal-material genres of paper, rejecting others, wearily accepting a few others, even as it failed to consider its own introducer scheme carefully. For any new-age ID scheme to work, its architects should consider allowing welfare subjects to script and inscribe their own electronic identities, and determine the nature and range of ID documents that can desirably be linked to a unique number with full knowledge of the liabilities in doing so. Having said that, one would still have to wonder whether we need a legal-normative field of superimposing identifiers and a centralized database just to assuage the litany of evidentiary fears that the welfare edifice harbours.

Notes

1. Interview with the-then deputy director general of UIDAI, Sujata Chaturvedi, UIDAI Head Office, New Delhi, 21 May 2014.
2. Interview with a bus porter, Inter State Bus Terminal (ISBT) Porters' Union Office, north Delhi, 16 September 2014.
3. Interview with a computer operator, UID enrolment centre, Delhi, 24 May 2014.

4. This chapter is absolutely indebted to Usha Ramanathan's razor-sharp observations and her close reading. With regard to the point on verification of identities, this is not to say that all classes of citizens and non-citizens are equally suspect in the eyes of the present-day Indian state. Some cases of claimants like the Bangladeshi migrants are viewed with more suspicion than others. A project that predated Aadhaar but was more akin to the National Population Register (NPR) was the Multipurpose National Identity Card (MNIC) which tried to sort residents into citizens and illegal immigrants.

5. See UIDAI's vision and mission, available at https://uidai.gov.in/about-uidai/about-uidai/vision-mission.html, accessed on 26 June 2017.

6. Jonathan Crush brilliantly conjures the superpanopticon in the African gold mines where workers are subjected to a tight regime of control over their mobility through electronic ID cards, whose functions eerily imitate the architectural ingenuities of the prison-like industrial complexes of colonial modernity. Crush's point is to show how computerized ID-based spatial surveillance that allows for interception of the worker's location and the allied tactical management of the worker population carries techno-utopias of panopticon beyond the conventional imagination (Crush 1992).

7. It was feared that if geographical identities or address details were included in the computerized identity cards that Mexicans received, then it would compromisingly reveal the electoral wards in which these voters stayed, rendering them susceptible to intimidation and coercion by political leaders (Botello 2011: 763).

8. Bharti Jain and Sidhartha, 'Battle over Turf Muddies Water', *The Times of India*, 17 February 2013.

9. The World Bank seeks to provide 'technical assistance, financial support and global expertise' for countries that wish to modernize their ID systems—in their narratives on various blogs supported by the ID4D website, authors gesture that the countries of sub-Saharan Africa and Asia have wrongfully overlooked the enforcement of what constitutes a basic and universal human right of birth registration of their citizens. The jargon and the anxieties that drive the World Bank in its advocacy of biometric registration are not too different from their counterparts in a country like India: fragmented identity management systems, integrating disparate, costly-to-maintain individual databases, and rendering visible the missing billions.

10. See http://blogs.worldbank.org/ic4d/making-invisible-billion-more-visible-power-digital-identification, accessed on 24 March 2016; 'India's Identity Scheme: The Magic Number', *The Economist*, 14 January 2012; Siddharth George and Arvind Subramanian, 'Transforming the Fight against Poverty in India', *The New York Times*, 22 July 2015.

11. UIDAI Strategy Overview: Creating a Unique Identity Number for Every Resident in India', Unique Identification Authority of India (unclassified) (n.d.), p. 5.
12. UIDAI Strategy Overview (unclassified) (n.d.), p. 5.
13. See also 'Aadhaar Bill Fails to Incorporate Suggestions by the Standing Committee', *The Wire*, 10 March 2016. It has been argued that these pressing concerns of the Standing Committee headed by Yashwant Sinha, which heard the statements of the National Human Rights Commission, Confederation of Indian Industries, legal activist Usha Ramanathan, economist Reetika Khera, and academic Ramakumar, among others, were not addressed in the new avatar of the bill, namely, the Aadhaar (Targeted Delivery of Financial and Other Subsidies, Benefits and Services) Bill, 2016.
14. States have, in the past, experimented with smart card and biometric technologies. Bihar government's e-Shakti experiment under Nitish Kumar to issue electronic job cards and muster rolls which incorporated iris and fingerprint ID is one example. 'Backward Bihar goes for the Smartest Cards', available at http://swaminomics.org/?p=1708, accessed on 8 September 2009. In Gujarat, smart card technology was utilized while issuing driving licences in 1999. In the last decade, smart card technology was harnessed in Andhra Pradesh, Rajasthan, Haryana, and Chandigarh for payment of old-age pensions, rural employment guarantee scheme, wages, health insurance, and PDS transactions (P.T. Sebastian, 'The Card Trick', *Outlook Business*, 3 May 2008; Sriraman 2013b). In 2007, a national health insurance scheme called Rashtriya Swasthya Bima Yojana was widely implemented across the country which issued cards carrying biometric features.
15. Interview with Sujata Chaturvedi, 21 May 2014.
16. Interview with Sujata Chaturvedi, 21 May 2014. The-then deputy director general hastened to add that these colours were common to Indian tradition taken as a composite whole and did not denote their religious specificity in any single faith.
17. Interview with Sujata Chaturvedi, 21 May 2014.
18. Available at https://uidai.gov.in/images/commdoc/FAQs-EKYC.pdf, accessed on 7 July 2016.
19. 'UIDAI Strategy Overview: Creating a Unique Identity Number for Every Resident in India', Unique Identification Authority of India (unclassified), p. 2.
20. Eben Moglen and Mishi Choudhary, 'Aadhaar and the Right to Privacy', *The Hindu*, 20 October 2015.
21. 'The Government Has Introduced a Bill on Aadhaar and It Is Not Good News', *Scroll.in*, 26 June 2017. This article cites Jean Drèze as gesturing to

the very stark attempt by the ruling central government to pre-empt any more debate via the courtrooms of the Supreme Court on the voluntariness of Aadhaar. He is quoted as saying, 'The government has reappropriated that power under the Aadhaar Bill, ending the pretence that Aadhaar is voluntary.'

22. 'Voluntarily Mandatory', *The Hindu*, 30 September 2013; see also Surabhi Shukla and Upasana Garnaik, 'Is the Aadhaar Voluntary? It's Not yet Clear?', *The Wire*, 16 September 2015, for a cutting analysis of how these judgements have undercut the very notion of clarity by stating incongruously that the Aadhaar cannot be rendered a condition for obtaining benefits and that the Aadhaar can be used selectively for the distribution of foodgrains and cooking oil and the LPG scheme.

23. 'UIDAI Strategy Overview, 2010.

24. Available at https://www.uidai.gov.in/component/fsf/?view=faq&catid= 0&tmpl=component&faqid=215, accessed on 26 June 2017. I am very grateful to Usha Ramanathan for directing my attention to this aspect.

25. I got this figure from an email correspondence on 23 May 2014 with the deputy director, UIDAI, consisting of responses to a questionnaire I had prepared.

26. See http://pib.nic.in/newsite/PrintRelease.aspx?relid=138555, accessed on 10 January 2017.

27. Biometrics Design Standards for UID applications, Version 1.0 prepared by UIDAI Committee on Biometrics, December 2009.

28. Biometrics Design Standards for UID applications, Version 1.0 prepared by UIDAI Committee on Biometrics, December 2009.

29. Interview with computer operator Harish, UID enrolment centre in north Delhi, 24 May 2014.

30. Email correspondence with the deputy director, UIDAI, 23 May 2014; 'Special Drive to Enroll People with Disabilities for Aadhaar', *The Hindu*, 22 November 2011. This kind of negligence runs contrary to the promises of the UID document on 'Social Inclusion and Aadhaar', which advises special enrolment camps for persons with disabilities and sensitive arrangements like extra volunteers and machines, assistance with form-filling, placing fingers on scanners, and even physiotherapeutic exercise; UIDAI (2012).

31. 'Threat to Citizen Rights', Interview with Usha Ramanathan by V. Sridhar, *Frontline*, 15 April 2016. Ramanathan cites the findings of this institute from a UIDAI notice 'inviting applications for hiring of a biometric consultant' to help in 'proof of concept of biometric solutions for UIDAI project'. Also, see her article in *The Statesman*, available at http://www.thestatesman.com/the/aadhaar-unmasked-biometrics-the-story-so-far-6th-july-2013-5246.

html. Usha Ramanathan also very kindly shared this link with me, https://uidai.gov.in/images/uid_download/Hiring_of_experienced_individual_Biometric_consultant_for_PoC_study.pdf.

32. Bharat Bhatti, Jean Drèze, and Reetika Khera, 'Experiments with Aadhaar', *The Hindu*, 28 June 2012.

33. Available at https://uidai.gov.in/faq.html?catid=36, accessed on 27 March 2016.

34. The introducer system also allowed the same NGO representative to serve as introducer for multiple residents. Procedural checks were to be followed in order to ensure the bona fide status of the introducer who could only vouch for residents within the Registrar's jurisdiction; GNCTD–UNDP (2011).

35. Interview with the Deputy Director of UIDAI, 21 May 2014.

36. Nitin Sethi, 'NGO's Shelters Shut after it Pointed out UID Flaws', *The Times of India*, 4 July 2011.

37. Interview with NGO representative, New Delhi, 24 May 2014.

38. Tarangini Sriraman, 'Bus Porters' Petition for Aadhaar: A Political Analysis', 22 February 2015.

39. UIDAI Strategy Overview, 2010, p. 15.

40. Email correspondence with the Deputy Director, UIDAI, 23 May 2014; and UIDAI (2012).

41. For a sample of these activists' critical lines on social control, the surreptitious aspects of coercion, and the erroneous assumptions of UIDAI about the causes for welfare misappropriation, see Khera (2011); Jean Drèze, 'A Unique Identity Dilemma', *The Indian Express*, 19 March 2015; Menon-Sen (2015); and R. Ramakumar, 'What the UID Conceals', *The Hindu*, 22 October 2010.

42. Read, in particular, Ramanathan (2010: 10–11). Ramanathan has made several nuanced interventions, all extremely critical to shaping the public debate. She has asked allied questions about privacy, the security, and ownership of information vested in the CIDR; the dubious history of surveillance attached to the companies that the UIDAI is currently doing business with; and exploitation of the population database for 'business opportunities'. To get a sense of the scale of criticism that Ramanathan alone has levelled, see Usha Ramanathan, 'Aadhaar: Private Ownership of UID Data—Part I', 20 April 2013, available at http://www.moneylife.in/article/aadhaar-private-ownership-of-uid-data--part-i/32430.html, accessed on 30 March 2016; 'Aadhaar: Who Owns the UID Database?—Part II', 30 April 2013, available at http://www.moneylife.in/article/aadhaar-who-owns-the-uid-database-ndashpart-ii/32440.html, accessed on 30 March 2016; and 'The Future is Here: A Private Company Claims It Can Use

Aadhaar to Profile People', *Scroll.in*, 16 March 2016, available at http://scroll.in/article/805201/the-future-is-here-a-private-company-claims-to-have-access-to-your-aadhaar-data, accessed on 30 March 2016.

43. Usha Ramanathan lays bare the loaded implications of implementing the NPR under the framework of the Citizenship Act rather the Census Act. The Census Act contains an explicit provision against making information available to the public through its confidentiality clause. This clause that secured census information from inspection and submission into evidence made it inconvenient for the MHA to invoke the Census Act, she argues. See Usha Ramanathan, 'Implications of Registering, Tracking, Following', *The Hindu*, 5 April 2010.

44. Chetan Chauhan, 'Have Aadhaar: You still have to Enroll for NPR', *HT*, 28 January 2012; Aloke Tikku, 'Aadhaar–NPR Duplication—A Pain and Expensive too', *HT*, New Delhi, 30 November 2012; 'Government Favours Aadhaar–NPR Synergy', *The Hindu*, 4 July 2014.

45. Aloke Tikku, 'National Population Register now a Rs 4800-crore Sinkhole', *HT*, 8 August 2016.

46. 'Biometrics Design Standards for UID Applications', Version 1.0, December 2009.

47. UIDAI Strategy Overview, 2010.

48. R. Ramakumar, 'Freedom in Peril', *Frontline*, 15 April 2016.

49. There have been reported 'discrepancies' where Delhi's enrolment centres chose to simply record people as falling under biometric exception even when they were not, strictly speaking, disabled simply 'to hasten the process'; 'Second Round of UID Enrolment to begin', *HT*, 14 August 2012.

50. Available at http://www.nvrltd.com/NVRTechnology.aspx, accessed on 24 June 2016.

51. Interview with Ranjeet, UID enrolment centre in north Delhi, 22 May 2014.

52. Interview with Harish, UID enrolment centre in north Delhi, 22 May 2014.

53. Interview with Harish, UID enrolment centre in north Delhi, 26 May 2014.

54. Interview with Sahil, UID enrolment centre in north Delhi, 30 May 2014.

55. While the UIDAI required full conformity of people's testimonies of their addresses to the documents they produced, ironically, there were multiple complaints that the Aadhaar enrolment process did not allow people to choose the addresses which they felt corresponded to their places of residence. This was because the software only allowed the enumerator to choose the addresses that were compatible with an area's prerecorded pin codes. Interview with Sahil, UID enrolment centre in north Delhi, 30 May 2014.

56. The software could also be manipulated to transcribe a Hindi spelling such that it corresponded more closely to the English equivalent of an enrollee's name. While the software transcribed Mohammad-e-Azam to read Mohammadey Azam in Hindi, the operator had the liberty to force the software to accept a different transcription.

57. Interview with Harish, UID enrolment centre in north Delhi, 27 May 2014.

58. Neelam Pandey, 'No UID Card? Now get an eAadhaar Card', *HT*, New Delhi, 1 February 2013.

59. In his email correspondence, an official explained to me that demographic and biometric cases can be updated by visiting permanent enrolment centres. Where only demographic corrections needed to be carried out, they could also be done online or by post. Email correspondence with the deputy director, UIDAI, 23 May 2014. One UIDAI strategy overview document specifies that demographic updates can be carried out through three channels: permanent enrolment centres; self-service updates; and requests by post. The UIDAI Strategy Overview, UIDAI, unclassified document. In the year 2014, the computer operators of the two enrolment centres I interviewed insisted that all such corrections would have to be undertaken in the UIDAI regional office at Pragati Maidan.

60. 'Process for Aadhaar Letters Returned by Department of Posts', Version 1.3.2, Delhi: Unique Identification Authority of India (n.d.).

61. Relatively speaking, the bus porters feel that the railway porters are better placed: they have one sanctioned holiday for the family per year, two uniforms for which they bear no cost, medical facilities at a railway hospital, and concessions related to admission of children in railway schools subject to availability of seats. Porters pointed out that, in recent times, railway employees have even been given permanent sweeper jobs.

62. Interview with official of DTIDCL at ISBT, north Delhi, 3 November 2014.

63. Interview with Sanjay, ISBT Porters' Union, north Delhi, 9 June 2014.

64. Interview with Rajesh Kumar, ISBT Porters' Union, north Delhi, 4 July 2014.

65. Interview with Bhanu, ISBT Porters' Union, north Delhi, 11 August 2014.

66. Interview with Pradeep, ISBT Porters' Union, north Delhi, 10 July 2014.

67. Interview with Pradeep, ISBT Porters' Union, north Delhi, 10 July 2014.

68. The centre has already moved to integrate the Aadhaar with caste and domicile certificates for children; see Aman Sharma, 'Link SC/ST certificates with Aadhaar, says Centre', *HT*, 16 June 2016.

69. Available at http://www.nhb.org.in/AboutUs/about_us.php#Genesis, accessed on 15 June 2016.

70. 'UP Government gives SC, ST Status to 16 More Castes', *The Hindu*, 6 October 2005.

71. Interview with Ramnath, ISBT Porters' Union, north Delhi, 10 September 2014.

72. 'Don't deny Benefits to those without Aadhaar', *The Economic Times*, 24 September 2013; Dhananjay Mahapatra, 'Aadhaar's Purpose in Doubt as SC says it is Not Mandatory', *The Times of India*, 24 September 2013.

73. 'Not Issuing Caste Certificate without Aadhaar Unlawful: Central Information Commissioner', *The Economic Times*, 9 December 2014.

74. Interview with Srikant, ISBT Porters' Union, north Delhi, 11 August 2014.

75. Interview with NGO representative, New Delhi, 1 October 2014.

76. Interview with Pradhan Masar, ISBT Porters' Union, north Delhi, 3 July 2014.

77. Interview with DTIDCL official, ISBT, north Delhi, 3 November 2014.

78. Interview with food official, Department of Food and Supplies, New Delhi, 14 June 2016.

79. When after repeated entreaties, their request for a new restroom was not heeded, the union filed a complaint with the Delhi government's Public Grievance Monitoring System (PGMS). Swati Maliwal, who enjoyed a post as advisor to Arvind Kejriwal's government in Delhi, inspected their grievance and assisted the union in getting a new restroom built. Sunil Kumar Aledia, the NGO head of Centre for Holistic Development, also persistently lobbied the Delhi government, met Kejriwal, and undertook media advocacy on behalf of the union. These collective efforts culminated in a new vishram griha, the construction work for which was finally completed in December 2015.

80. Only those households earning less than one lakh rupees were to be eligible to be counted as priority or AAY under the Food Security Act and considered for sanctioning ration cards which were now to be deemed food cards. The holders of JRC and RCRD would now either be considered for priority or AAY rations.

81. Food officials in this department strike a self-congratulatory note when they record their success in filtering out 4.43 lakh UIDs and 8.5 lakh EID numbers out of 65.22 lakh families that had submitted their applications along with their UID or EID numbers. Vishal Kant, 'Aadhaar Helps to Weed Out Fake Ration Cards', *The Hindu*, 10 September 2014.

82. Aneesha Mathur, 'HC Notice to Government over Plea on Food Security Card Data', *The Indian Express*, 4 June 2014.

83. Interview with food official, Department of Food and Supplies, New Delhi, 14 June 2016.

84. Rosamma Thomas, 'Machine Fails to Read Fingerprints, 1.4 cr Rajasthanis Go without Rations', *The Times of India*, 28 June 2016.

85. Jean Drèze, 'Dark Clouds over the PDS', *The Hindu*, 10 September 2016. Drèze writes of travelling to PDS shops in Ranchi where people could not draw their rations because they had no number or because their number could not be matched properly. Also, the machine often failed to recognize ration cardholders' biometrics.

86. Subodh Varma, 'Jan Dhan Scorecard: 22 Crore Bank Accounts Opened, Average Balance of Rs. 1725 in Each', *The Times of India*, 26 May 2016. This article is sceptical of the government's self-congratulatory aggregate of JDY account holders on the grounds that many of these were second accounts. The belief that government benefits would flow only into these accounts may have induced people to open a JDY account even if they were in possession of a bank account already, this article suggests.

87. Interview with official of an SBI branch, north Delhi, 9 December 2014; and interview with official of an SBI branch, north Delhi, 17 June 2016.

88. Interview with the Deputy Director General of UIDAI, New Delhi, 21 May 2014.

89. Interview with Manno, ISBT Porters' Union, north Delhi, 16 September 2014.

CONCLUSION

A common sight in Govindpuri, one of the field sites of this book, was men, but more often women, walking briskly, clutching some *pehchan patra* or the other, to either the ration office, the SDM's office, the MCD office, a school, dispensary, hospital, or, sometimes, simply to a neighbour's house. As they bustled to these 'paper shrines' (Hull 2012a: 113), they would stop once in a while to exchange stories of denial, victory, and perseverance in securing or renewing a document. Every such trip to a government office required homework, elaborate consultations with neighbours and the local pradhan, some money in hand, and wherever possible, a recommendation letter from a political leader or an MCD councillor. On one agonizingly hot day in the summer of 2013, Rakhi, a resident of Govindpuri, was sitting in her house with two other balwadi teachers filing entries in a record of the classes they were taking every week. A few other women sauntered into her house to talk about the ration cards they had failed to renew. They began to compare notes on their experiences in the ration office, acquiring a caste certificate at the SDM's office, and claiming the widows' pension at the social welfare department in Delhi. My ongoing conversation with Rakhi about her ration card journeys in Govindpuri were enough to incite the visitors to launch into an energetic exchange of how to mitigate the chaos of their *kaghazi zindagi*. I spoke at length with a woman who claimed that her BPL ration card was designated 'a duplicated card' because it featured all her demographic details but the wrong photograph owing to which she was cut off from rations for the last two years (see Figure C.1). Interestingly, this terminology

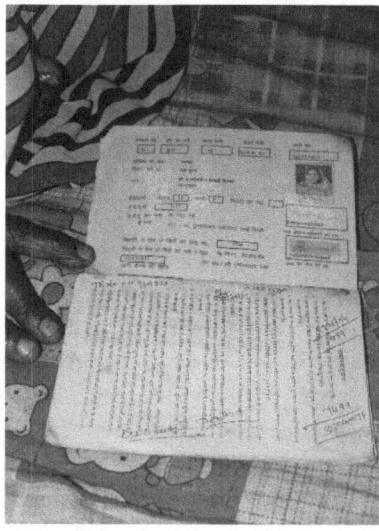

Figure C.1   A BPL Card which Was Designated a 'Duplicated Card'
Source: Author.

did not mark her out as a counterfeiter or a fraudulent person; it just plotted her as a person who was the victim of twisted circumstance, and perhaps also official negligence. Nonetheless, this did not exempt her from being denuded of governmental welfare support.

Her friend consoled her by narrating her own family's fiasco with the errant ration card, which, in her case, translated into an inability to access kerosene oil owing to a mix-up in the kerosene oil depot she was assigned. These women told me how they had, in the 1990s and the 2000s, employed different strategies to get their cards changed, faced delays in getting cards made, confronted FPS dealers (government-approved shopkeepers) to issue rations on time, and tracked down shifting ration card offices. In the face of these predicaments, it was important to educate each other about how to fill in application forms, how to present applications by invoking law and its many iterations in the slum, how to cite political affiliation, how to summon influence, and how to exact responses in official and unofficial spaces. Years of presence in the slum as a low-level government worker constituted an important entry point into Rakhi's bureaucratic struggles (Sriraman 2013b). She talks of filling out ration and voter identity card forms

in Hindi for countless neighbours, as well as accompanying women
to ration offices to make a show of numbers and thus intimidate the
dealer into weighing rations properly.

A study of ID documents is the study of a material form taken
by immaterial and intangible processes, often initiated by the state,
through which people from well-marked and not so properly marked
territorial spaces become citizens.[1] But though initiated by the state,
IDs are creatures of the everyday sociality that marks the processes
of claiming welfare governance in India. The queue outside the ration
shop is one such site where women and men advised each other on
schemes of citing authority and its lapses, summoning law, capturing its
liabilities, and devising alternatives to achieve the results they desired.
It is for these reasons that Figure C.2 suggested itself as an inspiration
for the cover illustration of this book.

These alternatives came in different forms, that is, legal and illegal,
paralegal and quasi-legal, for the protagonists of this book. One woman
in Govindpuri asked me fiercely, 'If people don't get cards on time,
will they not feel the need to go to dalals? There were dalals at all
times, but the confusions of the last few years with the shifting of the
offices have made the dalal business lucrative.' So, while some families
counterfeited ID documents, others grudgingly approached dalals or

Figure C.2   A Queue Outside the Ration Office in Govindpuri
Source: Author.

middlemen who had an 'arrangement' with the FSO to secure BPL ration cards. As Veena Das (2012) has documented in her work with the urban poor of Noida, there have been other instances where ration cards have been tentatively issued to enable their holders to draw rations beyond their expiry date. This book does not, however, want to overstate the claim-making possibilities that ID document regimes allow. The written world of banal procedures perpetuates deep social inequalities and disadvantages even when it is located in the popular realm of makeshift and alternative practices of ID.

As Chapter 3 goes to show, male refugees were more persuasive than their female counterparts when they made housing claims to the Ministry of Rehabilitation. In concept and practice, this ministry refused to concede, especially in housing compensation applications, that women could be the bearers of 'collateral evidence'. When female 'refugee squatters' submitted their ration cards, they were rebuffed on the grounds that these ID documents were not issued in the names of their husbands. Even within the subaltern spaces of the slum, the fashioning of unconventional, quasi-legal, and illegal genres of ID documents was not friendly to women. In Govindpuri, several men laughed disbelievingly when asked whether women in the household have ever secured an ID document through a dalal. When asked why he thought dalali and its spaces were not appropriate for women, one man said that he endured hardship and humiliation in acquiring certain documents—he had to pay a bribe of Rs 5,000 to a dalal to procure an income and a caste certificate through official channels—and asked, 'Do you think I will trust my daughter-in-law who is nursing a one-year old to these predators (read middlemen)?' (Sriraman 2013b). Several women in Govindpuri willed themselves to transgress these presumptive urban norms of political morality that informed their access to alternative ID mechanisms. Chapter 4 narrates the stories of a few women who, out of the tremendous anxiety they experienced either for their own prospects or for their children's prospects, counterfeited a treasured housing document called the V.P. Singh Card that was issued exclusively to Delhi's slum residents.

The Historical Dissonances of ID Document Regimes

This book has devoted itself mainly to narrating, in a geographically circumscribed sense, an urban story of how states are able to administer (poor) subjects and provide welfare benefits to them through popular knowledge forms. State conventions of issuing ID documents and governing the poor by absorbing popular knowledge practices did not manifest themselves abruptly or evenly. The very terms and connotations of people demanding certain genres, that is, making and remaking ID documents, cannot be read independently of the historical and socio-spatial contexts in which relations between the state and its subjects unfolded. Colonial authorities during the Second World War were primarily interested in introducing the ration card for handling wartime scarcity and managing political dissent. However, they found that they could not accomplish this without also formalizing the genre(s) of the ration card, shaping norms of residential address and household, and documenting home and homeless subjects. Chapter 1 shows how the wealth and the specific genres of the rationing documents produced between 1940 and 1945 were byproducts of the popular mobilizations and demands made by certain collectives.

In particular, this chapter has documented the enormous pressure exerted in Delhi by textile workers' unions, railway unions, washermen's groups, and religious communities on colonial authorities to issue special or supplementary ration cards. The ration card for the heavy manual worker could not possibly have been issued had it not been for the threatening entreaties of these popular forces. While counterfeiting and other subversions of rationing documents were attempted during this phase, the book does not class these wartime manipulations as instances of the popular making or remaking of the ID document. The colonial regime of rationing documents opened the floodgates to a deluge of genres which varied on the basis of province, state, and region. In Delhi, where rationing took on a frenzied urgency owing to its status as a wartime supply base and diplomatic hub, individual ration cards, over-printed food permits, cloth permits and allied coupons, temporary cards for visitors, and motor spirit coupons were created along with their disparate issuing authorities. Given the overwhelming force of suspicion that all such genres were subjected to, colonial rationing authorities often ended up changing features of the application form and the ration card, with the result that stray counterfeiting attempts were many a time confounded.

When compared to this wartime phase dogged by colonial fears of the eclipse of the empire, the post-Partition era of welfare governance made possible a popular politics of remaking ID documents within a historical context of inescapable normative commitments to the refu-gee. It was the twin conundrum born out of the necessity to compen-sate the riot-ravaged Hindu and Sikh refugees and the inability to do so owing to a crisis in the very norms of stipulating identity that pushed authorities to accept popular forms of self-identification. Subsequently, though the nascent Indian state came up with categories like the bona fide and the mala fide refugees, they were helpless in their efforts to enforce them with any rigour in the absence of a viable infrastructure of evidence. The period that spanned the years between the Partition and 1960 was marked by a pronounced de-fetishization of proof for certain classes of refugee 'squatters' in Delhi. In response to a barrage of memorandums, depositions, and declarations that refugees and refu-gee associations unleashed upon the Ministry of Home Affairs and the Ministry of Rehabilitation, the RC came to be under-emphasized for certain classes of urban poor. While this latitude slowly disintegrated over time, especially with the monopoly that the DDA gradually came to exercise over housing plans in Delhi from the late 1950s onwards, the interim period before its formation was one where refugee associa-tions enjoyed moral and legal clout. The ingenuity shown by these asso-ciations was impressive as they undertook censuses, guided censuses, issued their own identity cards, and rendered their personal archives into pathways of evidence gathering. Refugee associations were able to string together life stories, mundane and tragic occurrences into a body of evidence. Where refugees presented ID documents in their posses-sion, such as declarations of age, employment letters, ration cards, shop-keeper bills, and affidavits of slum occupation, they were successful in narrativizing and fashioning their identity. I use the term 'narrativizing' here to signify an act of using any existing material forms of identity and moulding them into officially recognized genres of ID.

Seen in comparison, the market of counterfeiting that emerged in the scramble for housing resettlement after the year 1990 marked a very distinctive moment—not so much of popular narrativization as of popular reproduction of a temporally significant ID document which went by the name of the V.P. Singh Card. Urban authorities in the 1990s did not have to grapple with the same bewildering void of ID norms, even though certain forms of proof were waived for the pur-poses of this initiative. In the housing surveys that came to be under-taken after 1990, slum residents did not really enjoy the same kind of evidentiary latitude that refugees in the 1950s benefited from. Housing policy hardened with the end of the 1960s owing to various town and city planning schemes that demarcated zones and land use for the foreseeable urban future. Though the V.P. Singh administration made sure that all slum residents in Delhi received ration cards, urban authorities after this historic initiative did not bother to loosen the proof regimes of housing resettlement. Given all this, counterfeiting was a no-holds-barred measure, not always universally supported even within the slum, to ensure that one was not left behind or tricked out of resettlement (Srivastava 2012). However, the V.P. Singh Card, counterfeit or not, was equally indispensable to the Delhi administration which wished to retain at least an illusion of even-handedness in allotting housing to the poor through its dateline-enabled classifications.

This book has consciously selected moments in the history of ID documents that have been described, or at the very least, acknowledged implicitly, as constituting munificent moves of 'documenting' the poor and not just in the grand theatre of the nation. The historical ethnography around each of these moments, however, testifies to something else. If the sovereignty of the new nation was predicated on liberally recognizing the Hindu and Sikh refugees, though not the Muslim refugees, this was worked out to institute safeguards for the urban poor subject in Delhi as well. However, this story of the immense power wielded by refugee associations, even when they were made up of poor 'squatters', came up short especially when juxtaposed with the empty claims of the Muslim refugees inside India. The intense onus placed on the Dalit refugee to demonstrate his/her caste-ness to the Displaced Harijans Rehabilitation Board and the HSS is also very telling. From rural compensation to urban allotments, Dalit refugee claim-making was burdened by the decree to prove caste in addition to satisfying other markers, such as nationality and urban presence. The enumeration and ID initiative of 1990 had at its helm a prime minister who lowered his sights to the micro-spaces of the slum in Delhi and extended to their residents the largesse of his administration. The housing policy that emerged in the aftermath of this initiative only put in place an architecture for enveloping the slum resident more comprehensively within the ambit of the Delhi Master Plan. The very conditions for applying popular touches of kalakari to ID documents can be traced to the emotional datelines of the survey. Had slum residents not experienced emotional upheavals caused by the very real prospects of being denied a plot or a house on grounds of non-possession of the 1990 V.P. Singh Card, the temptation to counterfeit would have been moot.

Marking the Transition: ID Documents in the New Welfare Dispensation

Given that consecutive administrations after V.P. Singh had no real means of verifying the veracity of a card for want of an electronic record, counterfeiting was also the byproduct of urban existence in a conventional 'documentary state' (Breckenridge 2014: 8). The turn of the century was heralded by information panics, scares of welfare fraud, bureaucratic mismanagement of identity, and a call for more transparency in the ID of beneficiaries and provisioning of subjects. An alarmist rhetoric about 'vulnerable documents' can perhaps be dated to late colonial rule when rationing was introduced for the first time, and this has only persisted ever since the channelling of food benefits through the PDS.[2] Since the dawn of the new century that has seen legislations, such as the RTI Act and initiatives such as the UID project, this rhetoric has been reconfigured to distastefully mark the obsolescence of paper where cloud-based biometric authentication is possible.

In recent times, there has been an efflorescence of writing on the change in the terms and language of citizenship discourse such that it has become inextricable from the electronic management and the securitization of identities (Amoore 2008; Muller 2004; Rose 1999). There has been a quiet shift in bureaucratic vocabularies of welfare payment from document verification to identity authentication—the overarching roles of the UIDAI and the very ontological aspect of biometric reader machines have in no small way contributed to this shift. Chapter 5 discusses how, even though their reliability has been greatly disputed, biometric machines enjoy a certain aura of infallibility owing to their perceived fidelity to the bodily and unmanipulable imprints of the individual. It has been argued that the Aadhaar as a biometric and cloud-based ID is nothing short of a primary ID document. However, the people who endorse binaries such as primary ID documents (read electronic and biometric ID documents) and paper ID documents, number identifiers, and cloud-based authentication exist not only among the bureaucratic circles of the UIDAI but can also be found in a veritable complex of private firms, banks, government agencies, and international organizations. Part of the story of the gathering relevance of this complex is bound up with the shaming of welfare bureaucracies which have been so slow to modernize and jettison paper in their functioning. The other part has to do with exhorting people into believing that their drawn-out crises of welfare claim-making are the outcomes of their undocumented statuses or a vicious cycle of identity verification.

The most cathartic tale of the wilful inefficiency of welfare dispensations has been the fake ration card racket typical to almost all the PDS states of the country.[3] Yet another site for loud lament has been the absence of a regulatory welfare framework owing to which governments have to endure the loss of crores of wasteful expense. Such expenses are incurred when middle-class consumers purchase over and above the optimum LPG gas connections; it is noteworthy here that, historically, a sizeable subsidy has been attached to the purchase of these gas connections. However, above all, biometrics companies, government banks, the Reserve Bank of India, credit rating agencies, the World Bank, the Confederation of Indian Industries, and Narendra Modi have all supported the turn to electronic applications to transform the ways in which people go about managing their finances and banking transactions. This has had peculiar implications for those poor subjects to whom government authorities have effectively conveyed that their fiscal survival depends on the possession of Aadhaar and Aadhaar-linked bank accounts (for example, Jan Dhan accounts). With confusing information about cut-off dates for creating these accounts, where the poor have not been able to create these accounts for want of KYC verification, where the spread of banks and bank correspondents has been patchy causing delay in opening accounts, where applicants have had to link their Aadhaar to these accounts, their abilities to access welfare schemes have been stunted.[4] State-of-the-art Aadhaar 'intermediation' armed with exemplary features, such as number portability and de-duplication, has presented itself as the messianic need of the hour for welfare overhaul and the precise delivery of citizen entitlement. If it is difficult to answer the question, who started the Aadhaar fire, it is even more pointless to ask, who stoked the Aadhaar fire, as the applications for this infrastructure are multiplying at the rate of a breathless news-story per day. In addition to direct benefit transfers,

Aadhaar is now vaunted and wanted for performing identity authentication relevant to payment systems driven by the Unified Payments Interface (UPI) launched by National Payments Corporation of India, government and privately run mobile wallets, and bank interoperability. The newest of these adventures has been the Aadhaar-enabled payment system which will possibly allow people to make purchases through fingerprint readers installed on Android smartphones.[5]

In short, Aadhaar has been rendered indispensable to welfare governance within its technological, epistemological, and political realms. Technologically, it is now difficult for beneficiaries to survive in the welfare ecology without possessing the number identifier as we are witnessing a remarkable convergence of schemes and financial benefits around the Aadhaar. Epistemologically, the very construction of the poor subject is beginning to be predicated on the knowability and the credibility of the person making a welfare claim. Given the ever-present, but never more hated as the here and now, bête noires of ghost beneficiaries, the very personhood of the ration card beneficiary rides on his/her credentials as established through the Aadhaar. Though it is not really a talking point now, the Aadhaar has a claim to the indispensable also owing to the political endeavours that make it so. In this sense, the transition of ID document regimes is perhaps more bound up with power than ever before. Perhaps, the most compelling explanation of this can be traced to exercises as disparate as the JDY across India and the National Register of Citizens in Assam. The JDY was engineered as a political move by the present establishment led by Prime Minister Narendra Modi to pile populist benefits, such as insurance schemes onto a technological platform provided by bank accounts supported by the Aadhaar. The second initiative is unique to the state of Assam which is no stranger to a vitiated linguistic and regional politics of parochialism. This initiative seeks, above all else, to satisfy itself on the point of who is a bona fide resident, and hence a legitimate citizen in Assam, and is oriented towards an unspecified future of deportations of the state's non-Assamese residents. It is feared that such an initiative may well privilege 'the ethno-religious assertion' of being an Assamese person (Roy 2016: 143). Here, the 'benefits' of the UID project—that provides only authentications of identity and residence and not citizenship—have been coupled with a National Register of Citizens which dates back to 1951. The Aadhaar has here been purposed with injecting legitimacy into a project that will carry out inquiries into Assamese regional and cultural identity of a heterogeneous people, many of whom are Muslim and persecuted tribal groups.[6]

As far as the welfare dimensions of Aadhaar or other ID documents go, this book has concerned itself mainly with the prospects of the urban poor. Even as the future of (poor) Indians' economic existence is plotted in terms of Aadhaar and its kaleidoscopic schemes and applications, we would do well to catch our breath by taking stock of the welfare domains in which they have unfolded. Have electronic regimes done away with the burdens of document verification, such as discretionary selection and errors of inclusion and exclusion, and exorcised existing welfare dispensations of their notorious paper phantoms of fraud and ghost beneficiaries? If one were to take two relevant sites for answering this portentous question, namely, LPG reform and PDS reform, there is sufficient evidence to the contrary. A relatively recent report of the Comptroller and Auditor General (CAG) on the implementation of Pratyaksh Hastantrit Labh Yojana (PAHAL), the direct benefit transfer of LPG (DBTL) scheme, is damning of Aadhaar-enabled authentication of welfare beneficiaries on several counts. This scheme was introduced to enable transfers of subsidies directly to consumers who had set up linkages between their Aadhaar, bank account, and their LPG consumer ID. The CAG audit report showed, among many things, that many people holding multiple gas connections were not blocked and that people could not be stopped from securing more than the permitted number of cylinders. Furthermore, it was observed that multiple LPG connections were found with the same Aadhaar number or the same bank account number; same name, same address; same name, same date of birth; and same registered mobile number in the consumer database of the oil and marketing companies (OMCs).[7]

In the last chapter, I cited Jean Drèze who writes that the National Food Security Act (NFSA) has been deterred by the implementation of Aadhaar-based biometric authentication through the PoS machines in states like Rajasthan and Jharkhand. My own interviews with Delhi's food and supplies department officials reinforced Drèze's findings that the old master register system of keeping FPS accounts could not be phased out in this city as well. In these states, only a certain percentage of rations found their way through the PoS system (63 per cent recorded in July 2016 in Rajasthan) even as FPSs ended up having to rely on the 'old register' system. Drèze indicates that both options of relying exclusively on PoS systems or relying haphazardly on both systems are replete with potent dangers. Using the PoS system exclusively would mean the normalization of a situation where biometric machines, for various reasons, do not recognize the NFSA beneficiaries.[8] And finally, in Chhattisgarh, which was vastly celebrated as a shining model of food security success, the introduction of a pilot project for Aadhaar-enabled cash transfers has been shown to be nothing short of an unmitigated disaster. A study of 103 households conducted in the four-month pilot project period shows how the replacement of food rations with cash transfers through Aadhaar-enabled bank accounts resulted in 20 per cent not getting money; 70 per cent getting the money but only after significant delays and repeated trips to the bank; and a 56 per cent reporting that they were not able to secure rations in one specified month. These results compared unfavourably with statistics of these households reporting 96 per cent success in withdrawing rations before and 91 per cent success after the pilot period.[9] The turn to biometric authentication and the use of PoS machines in food allocation under the PDS have especially yielded such sobering results that activists have taken to writing strongly worded petitions to chief ministers not to repeat the experiment elsewhere. Economists and activists like Jean Drèze, Reetika Khera, Kamayani Swami, and Ashish Ranjan have wished states to instead stick with 'timely door-step delivery of grain, putting ration lists and other PDS data online and ensuring a fixed schedule for delivery of grain'.[10] In effect, these activists have, in a chorus, asked for the reinstitution of the ration card system as it functioned prior to the flutter caused by Aadhaar linkages to bank accounts, welfare schemes, and PoS machines.

*

This book, especially, in its last chapter, argues that nesting welfare claim-making within a technological ecosystem, such as the Aadhaar and Aadhaar-enabled infrastructures can be quite regressive for urban poor subjects. This is especially so because such an ecosystem does not simply reflect the bureaucratic truths of these ID documents, it deepens them. Aadhaar does not innocently map on to paper-based ID documents. It throws in a combustible concoction into the dynamic social contexts within which artifacts like ration cards, caste certificates, and income certificates operate. Such a concoction is made up of technological immutability, an emphasis on bodily identification of the individual, and compatibility of all interfaces with the UID architecture. Where the politics of welfare claiming have benefited from spatial knowledges of power brokerage, narrativizations of identity, and popularly rendered administrative practices in a historical sense, a technology like the Aadhaar can 'foreclose' the abilities of the welfare subject to move freely (Franke 2009). Where the Indian state has been able to administer its poor subjects through popular innovations and contrivances, the Aadhaar threatens to undo these reciprocities and dynamics of welfare governance. We may then be in clamorous need of paper-based infrastructures and potentialities of engendering evidentiary knowledge of the welfare subject where they allow for such innovations.

To conclude, while this book hopes to have traversed the historical terrain of ID document production within the urban domains of welfare governance in this country, I am only too painfully aware that such an endeavour diminishes and obscures many potential 'other' histories. The use of the article 'a' preceding the subtitle of this book as in 'a history of identification documents' is deliberate in that it stages my humble disavowal of any claim to comprehensiveness of such a project. I would like to inventory a few omissions that this book may be guilty of. Readers may be mystified by the non-appearance of ID documents, such as the birth certificate and the life certificate, both of which are oft-narrated subjects of an existential bureaucratic comedy of errors in India. For a fascinating foray into the history of the life certificate and the world of civilian and military pensions it populates, one must read Poorva Rajaram's (2016) remarkable MPhil thesis titled, 'Get a Life: Pensions in 19th Century Colonial India'.[11] The birth certificate remains a mystery to me, and it occurs to me that its valence is marked only in circumscribed and relatively recent postcolonial spaces and my frantic historical quests for this ID document have proved in vain. I must add that these ID documents are missing in this book also because they were not central or even of secondary importance to urban claim-making in food and housing entitlements even if they featured in other welfare domains. Since these have been more or less the empirical pursuits of this book, I have not thought fit to touch upon them. Another ID document egregiously absent is the voter identity card. I know that an expansion of my research fields to configure the

EPIC as an ID document that supports welfare frameworks would have enriched this study. Here, I can only plead a certain paucity of resources of time and financial support when it mattered.

In addition, though the book has touched on Hindu and Sikh refugees in India in post-Partition Delhi, I have not really touched comprehensively on refugee regimes of proof—as, for instance, in West Bengal—that may run contrary to the urban story in this book. Nor have I dwelled on three other conspicuous refugee cases of 'the pursuit of proof': the Sri Lankan Tamils, the Tibetans, and the Chakmas in India. I have also paid little if no heed to the Bangladeshi refugees who crossed borders to inhabit and make welfare claims in not only parts of West Bengal but also a city like Delhi whose slums are peopled by many such subjects. I have not touched on the claims of internally displaced persons under the heads of river erosion, riots, or earthquakes, to cite a few drivers of this phenomenon. I can only say that any such research commitments would require immersion into any given region's political, administrative, and cultural particularities, which is beyond the scope of this book. Finally, though this project has meant unearthing urban specificities, I am aware that some of the most interesting contemporary enactments of welfare governance have occurred in rural domains of participatory democracy. The Forest Rights Act, 2006 has been one remarkably fascinating terrain of legislation that allows forest-dwelling tribal communities to stake out their individual and community rights of cultural and economic existence on the strength of (technological and discursive) claims of location, and proof of their subject statuses as rights-bearing individuals. While being cognizant of all these omissions, I would like to venture with bright-eyed hope that this book may infuse other researchers with the ambition to embark on similar foolhardy expeditions. Where they already find themselves muddling through rich, confusing, disquieting, and disagreeable pastures of knowledge production about ID documents, researchers should revel in these ambivalences because such research subjects gather their loveliness from defying a singular frame of analysis.

Notes

1. I thank Sanjay Palshikar for helping me work out an early version of this formulation.

2. 1000 (15), Food, Rationing, 1944, NAI. In the NAI files on wartime food rationing, there is a recurring use of the term 'vulnerable documents' invoked in a manner that places ID documents at the centre of colonial engagement with fraud. The colonial government at the centre would ask provinces and states to file reports that enumerated the instances of fraud involving vulnerable documents and specified the countermeasures implemented in their jurisdiction. Where ID documents were armed with security features, they were regarded battle-ready; and when lacking these features, they were 'vulnerable' or liable to be imitated and appropriated. ID documents, whether vulnerable or secured, remained a central point of reference to discussions on rationing fraud.

3. See, for example, Vishal Kant, 'Aadhaar Helps to Weed out Fake Ration Cards', *The Hindu*, 10 September 2014; and Dipak K. Dashi, 'Digitization Helps Government Weed out Fake Ration Cards', *The Times of India*, 15 May 2016. It is perhaps curious that there have been news reports lately of Aadhaar-linked fake ration cards as well! 'Fake Aadhaar-linked Ration Cards issued, Government orders Inquiry', *DNA*, 15 May 2016, available at http://www.dnaindia.com/india/report-fake-aadhar-linked-ration-cards-issued-government-orders-inquiry-2277037, accessed on 4 January 2016.

4. M. Saraswathy, M. and Abhijit Lele, 'Universal Financial Access Faces Multiple Challenges', *Business Standard*, 29 August 2014.

5. Gopal Sathe, 'Aadhaar Payments: What Are They and How You Can Use Them?', 26 December 2016, available at http://gadgets.ndtv.com/apps/features/aadhaar-payments-what-are-they-how-can-you-use-them-1641916?site=classic, accessed on 3 January 2017.

6. Preparation for the National Register of Citizens is under way. While they use information from the National Register of Citizens of 1951, authorities will also update this information through consultation of electoral rolls from 1966 and 1971.

7. Consider the following passage from the report, 'While 4.48 crore multiple connections were identified by OMCs from June 2012 to 30 October 2015, only 0.98 crore connections remained blocked with 2.01 crore connections having been regularised after submission of KYC forms by the consumers. Only limited number of connections, *i.e.*, only 2.50 lakh, (till October 2015) have actually been terminated on this account. The majority of the connections which had been blocked due to suspected multiple connections have, thus, been subsequently un-blocked.' In addition, this audit found that 74,180 customers were linked to 37,009 Aadhaar numbers. This clearly indicated that people purchased multiple connections. Other bloopers included wrong captures of date of birth: 73.50 lakh consumers were recorded as being born between January and December 1900, while

another 2,100 consumers were born in the future. I would not have come across this report had it not been for Himanshu Upadhyaya's helpful intercession. He thoughtfully sent me the report as well as his own useful quick summary of a 62-page technical document. See *Report of the Comptroller and Auditor General on Implementation of PAHAL (DTBL) Scheme (for the period ended 31 March 2016)* (2016), p. 26.

8. This was what was shown to have taken place in Ranchi district where less than half the beneficiaries received food rations under the NFSA legislation owing largely to the failures of the PoS machines in reading biometrics. The study in question was undertaken by Jean Drèze and Sneha Menon: these economists approached individuals listed as NFSA beneficiaries on the official website to find out if each of them received rations through the PoS system in a specified period. Gaurav Vivek Bhatnagar, 'Aadhaar-based PDS Means Denial of Rations for Many, Jharkhand Study Shows', *The Wire*, 8 August 2016. Also see Jean Drèze, 'Dark Clouds over the PDS', *The Hindu*, 10 September 2016.

9. 'Chhattisgarh's Experiments with Cash Transfers for Food Rations Has Been a Disaster', *Scroll.in*, 7 September 2015.

10. Gaurav Vivek Bhatnagar, 'Don't Fall for Aadhaar and Biometric-based PDS-based Reforms, Academics Tell Nitish Kumar', *The Wire*, 13 August 2016.

11. The life certificate owes its origins to nineteenth century colonial legislations on pension fraud as officials found the document useful to discern if pensions were being disbursed to dead or made-up beneficiaries. She writes that the certificate was also a much-needed countering device to mitigate the panics spurred by the shocking revelations of the mid-nineteenth century surrounding pension fraud which involved several accomplices, official and non-official, and spanning several decades and costing many substantial rupees of the colonial exchequer. However, the concept and practice of the life certificate has been resonant of the comic relief that the Indian bureaucracy provides to its critics. Where a pensioner is alive, her necessity to produce the life certificate in person to avail of financial benefits can only be an irony unto itself.

GLOSSARY

aam aadmi	the common man
adda	terminal
adhikari	official
anganwadi/balwadi	pre-school government programmes
anna	one-sixteenth of a rupee
annadata	food giver or provider of food
bahu	daughter-in-law
balti	bucket
barats	wedding processions
beta	son
bori	sack
chakki	flour mill
challan	bank receipt
chapati	traditional Indian bread
charpoy	bed
chulha	stove
coolie	porter
dalal	middleman
dalali	brokering
dawakhanas	indigenous dispensaries
diwan	council held by certain Sikh members
farzi	forged
gadda	mattress
ghats	cremation grounds

hafta	weekly fine
halwai	sweet shop
ilaqa	area
jaali	counterfeit
jaali kagaz	counterfeit documents
jamabandi	record of land rights
jhuggi, *jhopdi, jhopadpatti*	slum
kabooliyat	acceptance
kabza	occupied
kachchi zamanat	loose bail
kaghazi zindagi	paper-driven existence
kalakari	craftsmanship of an artist
katra	enclosed residential-cum-trading area
khandsari	unrefined white cane sugar
kisan	farmer
lal parda	red colour background for photographs
langar	charitable community meal prepared at the Gurudwara
mahila mandal	women's council
masala	a mixture of ground spices used in Indian cooking
mohalla sabhas	neighbourhood councils
mohur	stamp
naqli	fake
nazul	local territories in Mughal emperor's possession
pakka rakka	legitimate beyond a doubt
pathar	stone
patwari	land records official
pehchan patra	identification document
pradhan	local leader or unelected leader in a slum
pradhikaran patra	identification that extends a right
pukke makan	concrete houses
pukki zamanat	concrete bail
purdah	veil
rasoi	kitchen
ren basera	night shelter
rishwat pratha	bribing tradition

rukavat	obstacles
saas	mother-in-law
samitis	a committee, society, or association
sangats	religious body of Sikhs
sanyasi	mendicant sage
sarkari	governmental/state
sarpanch	village head
seer	unit of measuring rice with vast local variations
shamlat deh	common grazing grounds
swarajya	self-rule/self-government
tariqa	process
tehbazari	hawking
tehsildar	land revenue and tax official
thana	police station
Veddera	a backward caste
vishram griha	restroom

BIBLIOGRAPHY

Contemporary Works

Edwardes, S.M. 1923. *The Bombay City Police: A Historical Sketch, 1672–1916*. London, Bombay, and Madras: Oxford University Press. Available at http://archive.org/stream/bombaycitypolice030564mbp/bombaycitypolice030564mbp_djvu.txt, accessed on 31 July 2015.

Herschel, William James. 1916. *The Origin of Finger-printing*. Oxford: Oxford University Press.

Knight, Henry. 1954. *Food Administration in India, 1939–1947*. California: Stanford University Press.

Rao, Bhaskar. 1967. *The Story of Rehabilitation*. Delhi: Department of Rehabilitation, Ministry of Labour, Employment and Rehabilitation, Government of India.

Rao, V.K.R.V. and P.B. Desai. 1965. *Greater Delhi: A Study in Urbanisation, 1940–1957*. Bombay: Asia Publishing House.

Memoirs, Letters, Speeches, and Writings

Gandhi, Indira. 1971. *Selected Speeches of Indira Gandhi (January 1966 to August 1969)*. New Delhi: Ministry of Information and Broadcasting, Government of India.

Grover, Verinder and Ranjana Arora. 1998. *Rajkumari Amrit Kaur: A Biography of Her Vision and Ideas*. New Delhi: Deep and Deep Publications.

Jain, Ajit Prasad. 1965. *Rafi Ahmad Kidwai: A Memoir of His Life and Times*. Bombay: Asia Publishing House.

Nehru, Jawaharlal. 1954. *Jawaharlal Nehru's Speeches, 1949–1953*, Vol. 2. New Delhi: Ministry of Information and Broadcasting, Government of India.

Sarvepalli Gopal (ed.). 1997. *Selected Works of Jawaharlal Nehru (SWJN)* (vari-
ous vols). New Delhi: Orient Longman.
Shastri, Lal Bahadur. 1974. *Selected Speeches of Lal Bahadur Shastri (June
11, 1964 to January 10, 1966)*. New Delhi: Ministry of Information and
Broadcasting, Government of India.
Singh, V.P. 1993. *V.P. Singh: Selected Speeches and Writings 1989–90*. New Delhi:
Ministry of Information and Broadcasting, Government of India.

Records, Reports, Manuals, and Gazetteers

Census of India, 1961. 1966. Delhi: Manager of Publications.
Census of India, 1981: Delhi, a Portrait of a Population, Series 28. 1989. Delhi:
Directorate of Census Operations.
Census of India 2001. 2006. 'District Census Handbook: All the Nine Districts',
Series 8, Delhi: Directorate of Census Operations.
Delhi Development Authority (DDA). 2010. *Modified Master Plan for Delhi 2021*
(as amended up to 15th October 2009). Delhi: V.K. Puri and JBA Publishers.
Delhi Gazette, Extraordinary, Part IV. 1941–90.
'Evaluating the Impact of Brazil's *Bolsa Familia*: Cash Transfer Programmes in
Comparative Perspective'. 2007. Evaluation Note No. 1, Published by the Inter-
national Poverty Centre, United Nations Development Programme (UNDP).
Government of National Capital Territory of Delhi (GNCTD)–UNDP. 2011.
Homeless Survey 2010 (Draft). Delhi: Project Management Unit, GNCTD–
UNDP Project, Administrative Reforms Department, Government of Delhi.
Manual of Instructions. n.d. Delhi: Department of Food, Supplies and Consumer
Affairs.
Ministry of Health, Government of India. 1956 [?]. *Interim General Plan for
Greater Delhi*. Prepared by the Town Planning Organisation, Delhi.
Planning Commission, Government of India. 2005. *Performance Evaluation of
Targeted Public Distribution*. New Delhi: Programme Evaluation Organisation.
Rationing of Consumer Goods. 1942. *Columbia Law Review*, 42(7): 1170–81.
*Report of the Comptroller and Auditor General on Implementation of PAHAL
(DTBL) Scheme (for the period ended 31 March 2016)*. 2016. Report No. 25
(Compliance Audit). New Delhi: Ministry of Petroleum and Natural Gas,
Union Government (Commercial), p. 26.
Report of the Foodgrains Investigation Committee (1950). 1949. Ministry of Food,
Government of India. Delhi Manager of Publications.
Report of the Foodgrains Policy Committee (1944). 1943. Government of India.
Delhi Manager of Publications.
*Report of the High Level Committee on Reorienting the Role and Restructuring of
Food Corporation of India*. 2015. New Delhi: Ministry of Consumer Affairs,
Food and Public Distribution, Government of India.

Standing Committee on Finance (2011–12). 2011. *National Identification Authority of India Bill 2010: Forty Second Report*. New Delhi: Ministry of Planning, Lok Sabha Secretariat.

Tata Institute of Social Sciences (TISS). 2005. *The State and Civil Society in Disaster Response: An Analysis of the Tamil Nadu Tsunami Experience*. TISS Publications.

The Gazette of India, Extraordinary. 2001. Part IV. 1941–55.

Unique Identification Authority of India (UIDAI). 2009. 'Biometrics Design Standards for UID Applications, Version 1.0', Prepared by UIDAI Committee on Biometrics, December.

Unique Identification Authority of India (n.d.). Process for Aadhaar Letters Returned by Department of Posts', Version 1.3.2, Delhi.

———. 2010. 'UIDAI Strategy Overview: Creating a Unique Identity Number for Every Resident in India', Planning Commission, New Delhi.

———. 2012. 'Social Inclusion and Aadhaar: Introduction and Concept Paper', Planning Commission, New Delhi, 30 April.

National Archives of India (NAI)

Food Files, Policy Branch.

Food Files, Rationing Branch.

Home Files, Appointments Branch.

Home Files, Establishments Branch.

Home Files, NGS Section Branch.

Home Files, Public Branch.

Ministry of Health, LSG Section Branch.

Ministry of Home Affairs Files, Rehabilitation Division Branch (Housing Section I, RHA Section, RHB Section).

Ministry of Rehabilitation Files, RHA Branch.

Ministry of States Files, G (R) Branch.

Ministry of States Files, Kashmir Branch.

Mysore Residency Files, Bangalore Branch.

Office of the Regional Commissioner, Abu Files, Regional Branch.

Office of the Regional Commissioner, Abu Files, Rajputana Agency Branch.

Delhi State Archives (DSA)

Chief Commissioner's Office Files, Civil Supplies Branch.

Chief Commissioner's Office Files, Confidential Branch.

Chief Commissioner's Office Files, Special Press Advisor Branch.

Chief Commissioner's Office Files, War and Civil Supply Branch.

Maharashtra State Archives (MSA)

Political Services Files, 'D' Branch.
Political Services Files, 'H' Branch.

Private Papers, Nehru Memorial and Museum Library (NMML)

Ajit Prasad Jain Papers, Manuscripts Section, NMML.
Mohanlal Saksena Papers, Manuscripts Section, NMML.
Rameshwari Nehru Papers, Manuscripts Section, NMML.
Sukumar Sen Papers, Manuscripts Section, NMML.

Newspapers in NMML Archives

Hindustan Times. 1941–7.

Newspapers (Current)

Business Standard. 2014.
Frontline. 2016.
Hindustan Times. 2012, 2013, 2016.
India Today. 2011.
Outlook Business. 2008.
The Economic Times. 2013–14, 2017.
The Economist. 2012.
The Hindu. 2005, 2010–16.
The Indian Express. 2011–17.
The New York Times. 2015.
The Statesman. 2013.
The Times of India. 2012, 2013, 2016.
The Wire. 2015, 2016.

Lectures, Working Papers, Unpublished Dissertations, Articles, and Conference Papers

Bakewell, Oliver. 2007. 'The Meaning and Use of Identity Papers: Handheld and Heartfelt Nationality in the Borderlands of North-West Zambia', working paper, International Migration Institute, Oxford.
Basu, Somnath. 2014. 'Land Use and Land Prices in Semicontrolled Land Market: A Case Study of Delhi', unpublished PhD dissertation submitted to Jawaharlal Nehru University (JNU).

Chakravarty, Pallavi. 2014. 'Post Partition Refugee Rehabilitation in India with Special Reference to Bengal 1947–71', unpublished PhD dissertation submitted to University of Delhi.

Cohen, Lawrence. 2014. 'De-duplicating India: On the Promise of Immateriality', Paper presented at the international workshop on The Social and Cultural Life of Information, Centre for the Study of Developing Societies (CSDS), New Delhi, 14 November.

Das, Veena. 2012. 'Poverty and the Imagination of a Future: The Story of Urban Slums in Delhi, India', *Asia Colloquia Papers*, 1 (4). Lecture delivered at York University.

Gelb, Alan and Julia Clark. 2013. 'Identification for Development: The Biometrics Revolution', working paper no. 315, submitted to the Center for Global Development, Washington, DC. January.

'India and the Third Industrial Revolution'. 2013. Public Lecture by Nandan Nilekani, NMML, 10 October.

Marcus, G.E. 2005. 'Multi-sited Ethnography: Five or Six Things I know about it Now', Paper presented in 'Problems and Possibilities in Multi-sited Ethnography Workshop', University of Sussex, 27–8 June.

Rajaram, Poorva. 2016. 'Get a Life: Pensions in 19th Century Colonial India', unpublished MPhil dissertation submitted to JNU.

Popular Fiction (Translated, Hindi, and Indian English)

Chughtai, Ismat. 2009. 'The Survivor', *Lifting the Veil: Selected Writings*, pp. 117–28. New Delhi: Penguin Books.

Ghosh, Amitav. 1986. *The Circle of Reason*. Delhi: Ravi Dayal and Penguin.

Manto, Saadat Hasan. 1997. *Mottled Dawn: Fifty Sketches and Stories of Partition*. New Delhi and New York: Penguin Books.

———. 2001. 'The Dog of Tetwal', in Attia Hosain, Ravikant, and Tarun K. Saint (eds), *Translating Partition: Essays, Criticism*, pp. 94–103. New Delhi: Katha.

Mistry, Rohinton. 1996. *A Fine Balance*. London: Bloomsbury House.

Reza, Rahi Masoom. 1994. *Aadha Gaon*. London: Penguin Books.

Singh, Khushdeva. 1995. 'Love is Stronger than Hate', in Mushirul Hasan (ed.), *India Partitioned: The Other Face of Freedom*, pp. 146–53. New Delhi: Roli Books.

Yashpal. 2010. *This Is Not that Dawn*. New Delhi: Penguin.

Secondary Works

Agar, Jon. 2003. *Government Machine: A Revolutionary History of the Computer*. Cambridge, MA: MIT Press.

Albrow, Martin. 1997. *Do Organizations have Feelings?* London and New York: Routledge.

Alterman, Anton. 2003. 'A Piece of Yourself: Ethical Issues in Biometric Identification', *Ethics and Information Technology*, 5: 139–50.

Amoore, Louise. 2008. 'Governing by Identity', in Colin J. Bennett and David Lyon (eds), *Playing the Identity Card: Surveillance, Security and Identification in Global Perspective*, pp. 21–36. London: Routledge.

Anderson, Clare. 2004. *Legible Bodies: Race, Criminality and Colonialism in South Asia*. Oxford and New York: Berg.

Anjaria, Jonathan Shapiro. 2011. 'Ordinary States: Everyday Corruption and the Politics of Space in Mumbai', *American Ethnologist*, 38(1): 58–72.

Appadurai, Arjun. 1986. 'Introduction: Commodities and the Politics of Value', in Arjun Appadurai (ed.), *The Social Life of Things: Commodities in Cultural Perspective*, pp. 3–63. Cambridge: Cambridge University Press.

———. 1993. 'Number in the Colonial Imagination', in Carol A. Breckenridge and Peter van der Veer (eds), *Orientalism and the Postcolonial Predicament*, pp. 314–40. Philadelphia: University of Pennsylvania Press.

Arendt, Hannah. 1967. *The Origins of Totalitarianism*. San Diego, New York, and London: Harcourt Brace.

Bandyopadhyay, Ritajyoti. 2009. 'Hawkers' Movement in Kolkata 1975–2007', *Economic and Political Weekly*, 44(17): 116–19.

Banerjee, Mukulika. 2013. *Why India Votes*. New Delhi: Routledge.

Batra, Lalit and Diya Mehra. 2008. 'Slum Demolitions and the Production of Neo-liberal Space: Delhi', in Darshini Mahadevia (ed.), *Inside the Transforming Urban Asia: Processes, Policies and Public Actions*, pp. 319–414. New Delhi: Concept Publishing.

Baviskar, Amita and Raka Ray (eds). 2011. *Elite and Everyman: The Cultural Politics of the Indian Middle Classes*. New Delhi: Routledge.

Bennett, Colin J. and David Lyon. 2008. 'Playing the ID Card: Understanding the Significance of Identity Card Systems', in Colin J. Bennett and David Lyon (eds), *Playing the Identity Card: Surveillance, Security and Identification in Global Perspective*, pp. 3–20. London: Routledge.

Bhargava, Gopal. 1981. *Urban Problems and Perspectives*. New Delhi: Abhinav Publications.

Bhattacharya, Sanjoy. 2001. *Propaganda and Information in East India, 1939–1945: A Necessary Weapon of War*. Richmond: Curzon.

Black, Edwin. 2001. *IBM and the Holocaust: The Strategic Alliance between Nazi Germany and America's Most Powerful Corporation*. New York: Crown Publishers.

Botello, Nelson Arteaga. 2011. 'Biological and Political Identity: The Identification System in Mexico', *Current Sociology*, 59(6): 754–70.

Bowker, Geoffrey and Susan Leigh Star. 1999. *Sorting Things Out: Classification and Its Consequences*. Cambridge, MA: MIT Press.

Brass, Paul R. 2011. *An Indian Political Life: Charan Singh and Congress Politics*. Thousand Oaks: Sage.

Breckenridge, Keith. 2014. *The Biometric State*. Cambridge: Cambridge University Press.

Brenneis, Don. 2006. 'Reforming Promise', in Annelise Riles (ed.), *Documents: Artifacts of Modern Knowledge*, pp. 41–70. Ann Arbor: University of Michigan Press.

Brown, Cheryl L. 2008. 'China's Second-generation National Identity Card: Merging Culture, Industry and Technology', in Colin J. Bennett and David Lyon (eds), *Playing the Identity Card: Surveillance, Security and Identification in Global Perspective*, pp. 57–74. London: Routledge.

Butalia, Urvashi. 2000. *The Other Side of Silence: Voices from the Partition*. Durham, NC: Duke University Press.

Caplan, Jane. 2001. '"This or That Person": Protocols of Identification in Nineteenth-century Europe', in Jane Caplan and John Torpey (eds), *Documenting Individual Identity: The Development of State Practices in the Modern World*, pp. 49–66. Princeton and Oxford: Princeton University Press.

———. 2009. 'Illegibility, Reading and Insecurity in History, Law and Government', *History Workshop Journal*, 68: 99–121.

Caplan, Jane and John Torpey (eds). 2001. *Documenting Individual Identity: The Development of State Practices in the Modern World*. Princeton and Oxford: Princeton University Press.

Chakrabarty, Dipesh. 2008. *Provincializing Europe: Postcolonial Thought and Historical Differences*. Princeton, NJ: Princeton University Press.

Chaplin, Susan E. 1999. 'Cities, Sewers and Poverty: India's Politics of Sanitation', *Environment and Urbanization*, 11(1): 145–58.

Chatterjee, Partha. 2000. 'Development Planning and the Indian State', in Zoya Hasan (ed.), *Politics and the State in India*, pp. 120–5. New Delhi and Thousand Oaks, California: Sage.

———. 2002. *A Princely Impostor: The Kumar of Bhawal and the Secret History of Indian Nationalism*. New Delhi: Permanent Black.

———. 2004. *The Politics of the Governed*. Delhi: Permanent Black.

Chatterji, Joya. 2001. 'Rights or Charity? Government and Refugees: The Debate over Relief and Rehabilitation in West Bengal, 1947–1950', in Suvir Kaul (ed.), *Partitions of Memory*, pp. 74–110. Delhi: Permanent Black.

Chaudhri, Mohammed Ahsen. 1957. 'Evacuee Property in India and Pakistan', *Pakistan Horizon*, 10(2): 96–109.

Chibber, Vivek. 2003. *Locked in Place: State-Building and Late Industrialization in India*. Princeton: Princeton University Press.

Chitre, Dilip. 2011. 'Indira Gandhi: The Gatecrasher', in Laeeq Futehally, Achal Prabhala, and Arshia Sattar (eds), *The Best of Quest*, pp. 285–95. Chennai: Tranquebar Press.

Chowdhuri, Arka Roy and E. Somanathan. 2001. 'Impact of Biometric-based Transfers', *Economic and Political Weekly*, 46(21): 77–80.

Clanchy, Michael. 2013. *From Memory to Written Record, England 1066–1307*. Malden: Wiley Blackwell.

Clough, Patricia Ticineto. 2007. 'Introduction', in Patricia Ticineto Clough and Jean Halley (eds), *The Affective Turn: Theorizing the Social*, pp. 1–33. Durham and London: Duke University Press.

Cody, Francis. 2009. 'Inscribing Subjects to Citizenship: Petitions, Literacy Activism, and the Performativity of Signature in Rural Tamil Nadu', *Cultural Anthropology*, 24(3): 347–80.

———. 2013. *The Light of Knowledge: Literary Activism and the Politics of Writing in South India*. Delhi: Orient Blackswan.

Cohn, Bernard. 1987. 'The Census, Social Structure and Objectification in South Asia', *An Anthropologist among the Historians and Other Essays*, pp. 224–54. New Delhi and New York: Oxford University Press.

Cole, Simon. 2001. *Suspect Identities: A History of Fingerprinting and Criminal Identification*. Cambridge, MA: Harvard University Press.

Corbridge, Stuart, Glyn Williams, Manoj Srivastava, and Rene Veron (eds). 2005. *Seeing the State: Governance and Governmentality in India*. New York: Cambridge University Press.

Crais, Clifton. 2003. 'Chiefs and Bureaucrats in the Making of Empire: A Drama from the Transkei, South Africa, October 1880', *The American Historical Review*, 108(4): 1034–56.

Crush, Jonathan. 1992. 'Power and Surveillance on the South African Gold Mines', *Journal of South African Studies*, 18(4): 825–44.

Das, Samir Kumar. 2003. State Response to the Refugee Crisis, in Ranabir Samaddar (ed.), *Refugees and the State: Practices of Asylum and Care in India 1947–2000*, pp. 106–51. New Delhi: Sage.

Das, Veena. 1998. 'Wittgenstein and Anthropology', *Annual Review of Anthropology*, 27: 171–95.

———. 2006. *Life and Words: Violence and the Descent into the Ordinary*. Berkeley: University of California Press.

———. 2011. 'State, Citizenship and the Urban Poor', *Citizenship Studies*, 15(3–4): 319–33.

Das, Veena and Shalini Randeria. 2015. 'Politics of the Urban Poor: Aesthetics, Ethics, Volatility, Precarity', *Current Anthropology*, 56(11): S3–S14.

Datta, A. 1983. 'Delhi', *Cities*, 1(1): 3–9.

De, Rohit. 2014. '"Commodities Must Be Controlled": Economic Crimes and Market Discipline in India (1939–1955)', *International Journal of Law in Context*, 10(3): 277–94.

De Soto, Hernando. 2000. *The Mystery of Capital: Why Capitalism Triumphs in the West and Fails Everywhere Else*. London: Black Swan.

Deshpande, Satish. 2014. 'Caste and Castelessness: Towards a Biography of the General Category', in Satish Deshpande (ed.), *The Problem of Caste*, pp. 402–10. New Delhi: Orient Blackswan.

Dirks, Nicholas B. 2001. *Castes of Mind*. Princeton, NJ: Princeton University Press.

Dupont, Veronique. 2008. 'Slum Demolitions in India since the 1990s: An Appraisal', *Economic and Political Weekly*, 43(28): 79–87.

Dupont, Veronique and Damien Vaquier. 2013. 'Slum Demolition: Impact on the Affected Families, and Coping Strategies', in Marie-Caroline Saglio-Yatzimirsky and Frédéric Landy (eds), *Social Exclusion, Space and Urban Policies in Brazil and India: Urban Challenges*, Vol. 1, pp. 307–61. London: Imperial College Press.

Dutta, V.N. 2000. 'Punjabi Refugees and the Urban Development of Greater Delhi', in Mushirul Hasan (ed.), *Inventing Boundaries: Gender, Politics, and the Partition of India*, pp. 267–86. New Delhi and New York: Oxford University Press.

Eckert, Julia. 2004. 'From Subjects to Citizens: Legalism from Below and the Homogenisation of the Legal Sphere', *The Journal of Legal Pluralism and Unofficial Law*, 36(50): 29–60.

Emigh, Rebecca Jean. 2002. 'Numeracy or Enumeration? The Uses of Numbers by States and Societies', *Social Science History*, 26(4): 653–98.

Fawaz, Mona. 2009. 'The State and the Production of Illegal Housing: Public Practices in Hayy el Sellom, Beirut-Lebanon', in Kamran Asdar Ali (ed.), *Comparing Cities: The Middle East and South Asia*, pp. 197–220. Oxford: Oxford University Press.

Ferguson, James. 1994. *The Anti-Politics Machine: 'Development', Depoliticisation and Bureaucratic Power in Lesotho*. Cambridge: Cambridge University Press.

Foucault, Michel. 1984a. 'Right of Death and Power over Life', in Paul Rabinow (ed.), *The Foucault Reader*, pp. 258–72. New York: Pantheon Books.

———. 1984b. 'Docile Bodies', in Paul Rabinow (ed.), *The Foucault Reader*, pp. 179–87. New York: Pantheon Books.

———. 1984c. 'Nietzsche, Genealogy and History', in Paul Rabinow (ed.), *The Foucault Reader*, pp. 76–100. New York: Pantheon Books.

———. 1984d. 'Panopticism', in Paul Rabinow (ed.), *The Foucault Reader*. New York: Pantheon Books.

Foucault, Michel. 1988. 'The Political Technology of Individuals', in Luther H.
    Martin, Huck Gutman, and Patrick H. Hutton (eds), *Technologies of the Self:*
    A Seminar with Michel Foucault, pp. 145–62. Massachusetts: University of
    Massachusetts Press.

————. 1991. 'Governmentality', in Graham Burchell, Colin Gordon, and Peter
    Miller (eds), *The Foucault Effect: Studies in Governmentality*, pp. 87–104.
    London: Harvester Wheatsheaf.

Franke, Mark F.N. 2009. 'Refugee Registration as Foreclosure of the Freedom to
    Move: The Virtualisation of Refugees' Rights within Maps of International
    Protection', *Environment and Planning: Society and Space*, 27: 352–69.

Frykenberg, R.E (ed.). 1986. 'The Study of Delhi: An Historical Introduction',
    Delhi through the Ages, pp. 1–18. Delhi and New York: Oxford University
    Press.

Fuller, C.J. and John Harriss. 2001. 'For an Anthropology of the Modern Indian
    State', in C.J. Fuller and Veronique Benei (eds), *The Everyday State and*
    Society in Modern India, pp. 1–30. London: C. Hurst.

Gates, Kelly. 2008. 'The United States Real ID Act and the Securitization of
    Identity', in Colin J. Bennett and David Lyon (eds), *Playing the Identity Card:*
    Surveillance, Security and Identification in Global Perspective, pp. 218–32.
    London: Routledge.

Ghertner, David Asher. 2010. 'Rule by Aesthetics: World-class City Making
    in Delhi', in Ananya Roy and Aihwa Ong (eds), *Worlding Cities: Asian*
    Experiments and the Art of Being Global, pp. 279–306. Malden: Blackwell
    Publishing.

Ghosh, Durba. 2004. 'Decoding the Nameless: Gender, Subjectivity, and
    Historical Methodologies in Reading the Archives of Colonial India',
    in Kathleen Wilson (ed.), *A New Imperial History: Culture, Identity and*
    Modernity in Britain and the Empire, 1660–1840, pp. 297–316. Cambridge,
    UK: Cambridge University Press.

————. 2006. *Sex and the Family in Colonial India*. New York: Cambridge
    University Press.

Giddens, Anthony. 1982. *Profiles and Critiques in Social Theory*. Berkeley and
    Los Angeles: University of California Press.

Giese, Mark. 1998. 'Constructing a Virtual Geography: Narratives of Space in
    a Text-based Environment', *Journal of Communication Inquiry*, 22: 152–76.

Goody, Jack. 1986. *The Logic of Writing and the Organization of Society*.
    Cambridge, UK: Cambridge University Press.

Gordillo, Gaston. 2006. 'The Crucible of Citizenship: ID-paper Fetishism in the
    Argentinean Chaco', *American Ethnologist*, 33(2): 162–76.

Gould, William. 2010. *Bureaucracy, Community and Influence in India: Society*
    and the State, 1930s–60s, London: Routledge.

Graham, Mark. 2002. 'Emotional Bureaucracies: Emotions, Civil Servants and Immigrants in the Swedish Welfare State', *Ethos*, 30(3): 199–226.

Groebner, Valentin. 2001. 'Describing the Person, Reading the Signs in Late Medieval and Renaissance Europe: Identity Papers, Vested Figures, and the Limits of Identification, 1400–1600', in Jane Caplan and John Torpey (eds), *Documenting Individual Identity: The Development of State Practices in the Modern World*, pp. 15–27. Princeton: Princeton University Press.

———. 2007. *Who Are You? Identification, Deception and Surveillance in Early Modern Europe*. New York: Zone Books.

Gross, Daniel M. 2006. *The Secret History of Emotion: From Aristotle's Rhetoric to Modern Brain Science*. Chicago: University of Chicago Press.

Guha, Ramachandra. 2007. *India after Gandhi: The History of the World's Largest Democracy*. London: Pan Macmillan.

Guha, Ranajit. 1987. 'Chandra's Death', in Partha Chatterjee and Gyanendra Pandey (eds), *Subaltern Studies V: Writings on South Asian History and Society*, pp. 135–65. New Delhi: Oxford University Press.

———. 1999. *Elementary Aspects of Peasant Insurgency in Colonial India*. Durham and London: Duke University Press.

Guha, Sumit. 2003. 'The Politics of Identity and Enumeration in India, c. 1600–1990', *Comparative Studies in Society and History*, 45(1): 148–67.

Gulati, Leela. 1977. 'Rationing in a Peri-Urban Community: Case Study of a Squatter Habitat', *Economic and Political Weekly*, 12(2): 501–6.

Gupta, Akhil. 2012. *Red Tape: Bureaucracy, Structural Violence, and Poverty in India*, Durham: Duke University Press.

Gupta, D.N. 2008. *Communism and Nationalism in Colonial India 1939–45*. New Delhi: Sage.

Gupta, Narayani. 1986. 'Delhi and Its Hinterland: The Nineteenth and Early Twentieth Centuries', in R.E. Frykenberg (ed.), *Delhi through the Ages*, pp. 137–56. Delhi and New York: Oxford University Press.

———. 2000. 'Concern, Indifference, Controversy: Reflections on Fifty Years of Conservation in Delhi', in Veronique Dupont, Emma Tarlo and Dennis Vidal (eds), *Delhi: Urban Space and Human Destinies*, pp. 157–172. Delhi: Manohar.

———. 2002. 'Delhi between the Two Empires 1803–1931', in R.E. Frykenberg. Percival Spear and Narayani Gupta (eds), *The Delhi Omnibus*. New Delhi: Oxford University Press.

Guru, Gopal. 2014. 'The Archaeology of Untouchability', in Satish Deshpande (ed.), *The Problem of Caste*, pp. 411–19. New Delhi: Orient Blackswan and EPW.

Hacking, Ian. 1982. 'Biopower and the Avalanche of Printed Numbers', *Humanities in Society*, 5(3–4): 279–95.

Handelman, Don. 1981. 'Introduction: The Idea of Bureaucratic Organization', *Social Analysis*, 9: 5–23.

Hansen, Thomas Blom. 2001. *Wages of Violence: Naming and Identity in Postcolonial Bombay*. Princeton: Princeton University Press.

Harriss-White, Barbara. 2003. *India Working: Essays on Society and Economy*. Cambridge: Cambridge University Press.

Hasan, Mushirul. 1993. *India's Partition: Process, Strategy and Mobilization*. New Delhi: Oxford University Press.

———. 1995. *The Other Face of Freedom*. New Delhi: Roli Press.

———. 1997. *Legacy of a Divided Nation: India's Muslims since Independence*. Boulder, CO: Westview Press.

Heidegger, Martin. 1993. 'The Question Concerning Technology', in David Farrell Krell (ed.), *Martin Heidegger: Basic Writings*, pp. 308–41. San Francisco: Harper.

Higgs, Edward. 2004. *The Information State in England: The Central Collection of Information on Citizens since 1500*. Hampshire, England, and New York: Palgrave.

Hoag, Colin. 2011. 'Assembling Partial Perspectives: Thoughts on the Anthropology of Bureaucracy', *PoLAR: Political and Legal Anthropology Review*, 34(1): 81–94.

Holston, James. 2009. 'Insurgent Citizenship in an Era of Global Urban Peripheries', *City & Society*, 21(2): 245–67.

Hosagrahar, Jyoti. 2005. *Indigenous Modernities: Negotiating Architecture and Urbanism*. London and New York: Routledge.

Hossain, Attia, Ravikant, and Tarun K. Saint (eds). 2001. *Translating Partition*. New Delhi: Katha.

Hull, Matthew S. 2008. 'Ruled by Records: The Expropriation of Land and the Misappropriation of Lists in Islamabad', *American Ethnologist*, 35(4): 501–18.

———. 2012a. *The Government of Paper: The Materiality of Bureaucracy in Urban Pakistan*. Berkeley: University of California Press.

———. 2012b. 'Documents and Bureaucracy', *Annual Review of Anthropology*, 41: 251–67.

Jain, A.K. 1990. *The Making of a Metropolis: Planning and Growth of Delhi*. New Delhi: National Book Organization.

Jauregui, Beatrice. 2014. 'Police and Legal Patronage in Northern India', in Anastasia Piliavsky (ed.), *Patronage as Politics in South Asia*, pp. 237–58. Cambridge: Cambridge University.

Joseph, S. 2013. 'Identity Card', in K. Satyanarayana and Susie Tharu (eds), *The Exercise of Freedom: An Introduction to Dalit Writing*, pp. 178–9. New Delhi: Navayana Publishing.

Joseph, S.C. 1961. *Food Policy and Economic Development in India*. Bombay: Allied Publishers.

Kaluszynski, Martine. 2001. Republican Identity: Bertillonage as Government Technique', in Jane Caplan and John Torpey (eds), *Documenting Individual Identity: The Development of State Practices in the Modern World*, pp. 123–38. Princeton and Oxford: Princeton University Press.

Kamtekar, Indivar. 2002. 'A Different War Dance: State and Class in India 1939–1945', *Past and Present*, 176(1): 187–221.

Kaur, Ravinder. 2007 *Since 1947: Partition Narratives among Punjabi Migrants of Delhi*. New Delhi and New York: Oxford University Press.

———. 2009. 'Distinctive Citizenship: Refugees, Subjects and Post-colonial State in India's Partition', *Cultural and Social History*, 6(4): 429–46.

Kaviraj, Sudipta. 1999. 'The Imaginary Institution of India', in Partha Chatterjee and Gyanendra Pandey (eds), *Subaltern Studies VII*, pp. 1–39. New Delhi: Oxford University Press.

———. 2010. *The Imaginary Institution of India: Politics and Ideas*. New York: Columbia University Press.

Kelly, Tobias. 2006. 'Documented Lives: Fear and the Uncertainties of Law during the Second Palestinian Intifada', *Journal of the Royal Anthropological Institute*, 12(1): 89–107.

Khera, Reetika. 2011. 'The UID Project and Welfare Schemes', *Economic and Political Weekly*, 46(9): 38–44.

Kidwai, Anis. 2011. *In Freedom's Shade*. New Delhi: Penguin Books.

Kim, Jaeeun. 2011. 'Documents, Performance and Biometric Information in Immigration Proceedings', *Law and Social Inquiry*, 36(3): 760–86.

Kochanek, Stanley A. 1974. *Business and Politics in India*. Berkeley: University of California Press.

Kopytoff, Igor. 1986. 'The Cultural Biography of Things: Commoditization as Process', in Arjun Appadurai (ed.), *The Social Life of Things: Commodities in Cultural Perspective*, pp. 64–91. Cambridge: Cambridge University Press.

Koster, Martijn. 2013. 'Fear and Intimacy: Citizenship in a Recife Slum, Brazil', *Ethnos: Journal of Anthropology*, available at http://dx.doi.org/10.1080/0014 1844.2012.732955, accessed on 30 April 2016.

Kumari, Amita. 2013. 'Delhi as Refuge: Resettlement and Assimilation of Partition Refugees', *Economic and Political Weekly*, 48(44): 60–7.

Kundu, Amitabh. 2003. 'Politics and Economics of Land Policies: Delhi's New Master Plan', *Economic and Political Weekly*, 38(34): 3530–2.

———. 2004. 'Provision of Tenurial Security for the Urban Poor in Delhi: Recent Trends and Future Perspectives', *Habitat International*, 28: 259–74.

Lampland, Martha and Susan Leigh Star. 2009. *Standards and Their Stories: How Quantifying, Classifying, and Formalizing Practices Shape Everyday Life*. Ithaca: Cornell University Press.

Latour, Bruno. 2005. *Reassembling the Social: An Introduction to Actor-Network-Theory*. Oxford and New York: Oxford University Press.

Lau, Estelle. 2006. *Paper Families, Identities, Immigration Administration and Chinese Exclusion*. Durham: Duke University Press.

Legg, Stephen. 2007. *Spaces of Colonialism: Delhi's Urban Governmentalities*. Malden: Blackwell Publishing.

Lipsky, Michael. 2010. *Street-level Bureaucracy: Dilemmas of the Individual in Public Services*. New York: Russell Sage Foundation.

Longman, Timothy. 2001. 'Identity Cards, Ethnic Self-perception, and Genocide in Rwanda', in Jane Caplan and John Torpey (eds), *Documenting Individual Identity: The Development of State Practices in the Modern World*, pp. 345–58. Princeton and Oxford: Princeton University Press.

Loveman, Mara. 2007. 'Blinded like a State: The Revolt against Civil Registration in Nineteenth-century Brazil', *Comparative Studies in Society and History*, 49(1): 5–39.

Lutz, Catherine and Geoffrey M. White. 1986. 'The Anthropology of Emotions', *Annual Review of Anthropology*, 15: 405–36.

Lyon, David. 2001. 'Under my Skin: From Identification Papers to Body Surveillance', in Jane Caplan and John Torpey (eds), *Documenting Individual Identity: The Development of State Practices in the Modern World*, pp. 291–310. Princeton and Oxford: Princeton University Press.

Maguire, Mark. 2009. 'The Birth of Biometric Security', *Anthropology Today*, 25(2): 9–14.

Malik, Tariq. 2014. 'Technology in the Service of Development: The NADRA Story', available at http://www.cgdev.org/publication/ft/technology-service-development-nadra-story, accessed on 8 March 2016.

Malkki, Liisa. 1992. 'National Geographic: The Rooting of Peoples and the Territorialization of National Identity among Scholars and Refugees', *Cultural Anthropology*, 7(1): 24–44.

Mann, Michael. 2007. 'Collectors at Work: Data Gathering and Statistics in British-India, c. 1760–1860', *Journal of the Asiatic Society of Bangladesh*, 52(1): 57–84.

Maringanti, Anand. 2009. 'Sovereign State and Mobile Subjects: Politics of the UIDAI', *Economic and Political Weekly*, 44(46): 35–40.

Marshall, T.H. 1994. 'Citizenship and Social Class', in Bryan S. Turner and Peter Hamilton (eds), *Citizenship: Critical Concepts*, Vol. 2, pp. 5–44. London and New York: Routledge.

Marx, Karl and Friedrich Engels. 1891. *Civil War in France* (with an introduction in 1891 by Friedrich Engels on the 20th anniversary of the Paris Commune), available at https://www.marxists.org/archive/marx/works/1871/civil-war-france/intro.htm, accessed on 14 April 2016.

Mathur, Nayanika. 2012. 'Transparent-making Documents and the Crisis of Implementation', *PoLAR*, 35(2): 167–85.

———. 2016. *Paper Tiger: Law, Bureaucracy and the Developmental State in Himalayan India*. Cambridge: Cambridge University Press.

Mazzarella, William. 2006. 'Internet X-Ray: E-governance, Transparency and the Politics of Immediation in India', *Public Culture*, 18(3): 473–505.

McConnell, Fiona. 2013. 'Citizens and Refugees: Constructing and Negotiating Tibetan Identities in Exile', *Annals of the Association of American Geographers*, 103(4): 967–83.

McFarlane, Colin. 2011. 'Assemblage and Critical Urban Praxis: Part One', *City*, 15(2): 204–24.

Menon, Ritu and Kamla Bhasin. 1998. *Borders and Boundaries: Women in India's Partition*. New Brunswick, NJ: Rutgers University Press.

Menon-Sen, Kalyani. 2015. 'Aadhaar: Wrong Number or Big Brother Calling?', *The Socio-Legal Review*, 11(2): 85–108.

Menon-Sen, Kalyani and Gautam Bhan. 2008. *Swept off the Map: Surviving Eviction and Resettlement in India*. New Delhi: Yoda Press and Jagori.

Merton, Robert. 1940. 'Bureaucratic Structure and Personality', *Social Forces*, 18(4): 560–8.

Messick, Brinkley. 1993. *The Calligraphic State: Textual Domination and History in a Muslim Society*. Berkeley, Los Angeles, and London: University of California Press.

Mitchell, Timothy. 2006. 'Society, Economy and the State Effect', in Aradhana Sharma and Akhil Gupta (eds), *The Anthropology of the State: A Reader*, pp. 169–86. Malden, Oxford, and Victoria: Blackwell Publishing.

Mongia, Radhika. 1999. 'Race, Nationality, Mobility: A History of the Passport', *Public Culture*, 11(3): 527–55.

Mooij, Jos. 1999. *Food Policy and the Indian State: The Public Distribution System in South India*. Calcutta, Chennai, and Mumbai: Oxford University Press.

Mordini, Emilio and Andrew P. Rebera. 2013. 'The Biometric Fetish', in Ilsen About, James Brown, and Gayle Lonergan (eds), *Identification and Registration Practices in Transnational Perspective: People, Papers and Practices*, pp. 98–110. Oxford: Palgrave MacMillan and St. Anthony's College.

Muller, Benjamin J. 2004. '(Dis)qualified Bodies: Securitization, Citizenship and "Identity Management"', *Citizenship Studies*, 8(3): 279–94.

Nadai, Eva and Christoph Maeder. 2005. 'Fuzzy Fields: Multi-sited Ethnography in Sociological Research', *Open Journal, Forum: Qualitative Social Research*, 6(3), available at http://www.qualitative-research.net/index.php/fqs/article/view/22/47, accessed on 6 November 2016.

Naidu, Paupa Rao and Vinay Lal (eds). 1995. *The History of Railway Thieves with Illustrations and Hints on Detection*. Gurgaon: Vintage Books.

Nair, Janaki. 2005. *The Promise of the Metropolis*. New Delhi: Oxford University Press.

———. 2009. 'The Body Politic: Gender and the Practice of Power in the City', in Kamran Asdar Ali and Martina Rieker (eds), *Comparing Cities: the Middle East and South Asia*, New Delhi: Oxford University Press

Narayan, Badri. 2010. 'History Produces Politics: The Nara–Maveshi Movement in Uttar Pradesh', *Economic and Political Weekly*, 45(40): 111–9.

Navaro-Yashin. 2007. 'Make-believe Papers, Legal forms and the Counterfeit: Affective Interactions between Documents and People in Britain and Cyprus', *Anthropological Theory*, 7(1): 79–98.

Nilekani, Nandan. 2008. *Imagining India*. New Delhi: Allen Lane.

Niranjana, Seemanthini. 2001. *Gender and Space : Femininity, Sexualization and the Female Body*. New Delhi, Thousand Oaks: Sage Publications.

Noiriel, Gerard. 2001. 'The Identification of the Citizen: The Birth of Civil Republican Status in France', in Jane Caplan and John Torpey (eds), *Documenting Individual Identity: The Development of State Practices in the Modern World*, pp. 28–48. Princeton and Oxford: Princeton University Press.

Nussbaum, Martha. 2001. *Upheavals of Thought: The Intelligence of Emotions*. Cambridge: Cambridge University Press.

Ogasawara, Midori. 2008. 'A Tale of the Colonial Age, or the Banner of New Tyranny? National Identification Card Systems in Japan', in Colin J. Bennett and David Lyon (eds), *Playing the Identity Card: Surveillance, Security and Identification in Global Perspective*, pp. 93–111. London: Routledge.

Ogborn, Miles. 2007. *Indian Ink: Script and Print in the Making of the East India Company*. Chicago: University of Chicago Press.

Olsen, Wendy. 1989. 'Eat Now Pay Later: Impact of Rice Subsidy Scheme', *Economic and Political Weekly*, 24(28): 1597–611.

Palshikar, Sanjay. 2005. 'Understanding Humiliation', *Economic and Political Weekly*, 40(51): 5428–432.

Pandey, Gyanendra. 1997. 'Partition and Independence in Delhi: 1947–48', *Economic and Political Weekly*, 32 (36): 2261–72.

———. 2001. *Remembering Partition: Violence, Nationalism and History in India*. Cambridge, New York: Cambridge University Press.

Pandian, M.S.S. 2014. 'One Step Outside Modernity: Caste, Identity Politics and Public Sphere', in Satish Deshpande (ed.), *The Problem of Caste*, pp. 393–401. New Delhi: Orient Blackswan and EPW.

Parry, Jonathan. 2000. 'The "Crisis of Corruption" and "The Idea of India": A Worm's Eye View', in I. Pardo (ed.), *The Morals of Legitimacy*, pp. 27–55. New York and Oxford: Berghahn Books.

Pateman, Carole. 1988. *The Sexual Contract*. Stanford: Stanford University Press.

Peabody, Norbert. 2001. 'Cents, Sense, Census: Human Inventories in Late Precolonial and Early Colonial India', *Comparative Studies of Society and History*, 43(4): 819–50.

Piliavsky, Anastasia (ed.). 2014. 'Introduction', *Patronage, as Politics in South Asia*. Cambridge: Cambridge University.

Poole, Deborah. 2004. 'Between Threat and Guarantee: Justice and Community in the Margins of the Peruvian state', in Veena Das and Deborah Poole (eds), *Anthropology in the Margins of the State*. Santa Fe: SAR Publications; Delhi: Oxford University Press.

Poovey, Mary. 2010. *History of the Modern Fact*. Chicago: University of Chicago Press.

Portelli, Allesandro. 1998. 'What Makes Oral History Different', in Robert Perks and Alistair Thomson (eds), *The Oral History Reader*, pp. 63–74. London and New York: Routledge.

Rajadhyaksha, Ashis. 2013. 'Digital Delivery of Services: The Indian Landscape', in Ashish Rajadhyaksha (ed.), *In the Wake of Aadhaar: The Digital Ecosystem of Governance in India*, pp. xi–l. Bangalore: Centre for the Study of Culture and Society.

Raman, Bhavani. 2012. *Document Raj: Writing and Scribes in Early Colonial South India*. Chicago: University of Chicago Press.

Ramanathan, Usha. 2010. 'A Unique Identity Bill', *Economic and Political Weekly*, 40(30): 10–14.

Rao, Ursula. 2013. 'Biometric Marginality: UID and the Shaping of Homeless Identities in the City', *Economic and Political Weekly*, 48(13): 71–7.

Rao, V.K.R.V. 1952. 'India's Five-Year Plan: A Descriptive Analysis', *Pacific Affairs*, 25 (1), 3-23.

Rege, Sharmila. 2006. 'Introduction', *Writing Caste/Writing Gender: Narrating Dalit Women's Testimonies*, pp. 1–10. New Delhi: Zubaan.

Riles, Annelise. 2006. 'Introduction: In Response', in Annelise Riles (ed.), *Documents: Artifacts of Modern Knowledge*, pp. 1–38. Ann Arbor: University of Michigan Press.

Robertson, Craig. 2009. 'A Documentary Regime of Verification: The Emergence of the Passport and the Archival Problematization of Identity', *Cultural Studies*, 23(3): 329–54.

Rose, Nikolas. 1999. *Powers of Freedom: Reframing Political Thought*. Cambridge, MA: Cambridge University Press.

Rosenblatt, P.C., R.P. Walsh, and D.A. Jackson. 1976. *Grief and Mourning in Cross-cultural Perspective*. New Haven: HRAF Press.

Rosenwein, Barbara H. 2002. 'Worrying about Emotions in History', *The American Historical Review*, 107(3): 821–45.

Roy, Anupama. 2016. *Citizenship in India*. New Delhi: Oxford University Press.

Ruud, Arild Engelson. 2000. 'Corruption as Everyday Practice: The Public–Private Divide in Local Indian Society', *Forum for Development Studies*, 27(2): 271–94.

Salter, Mark B. 2003. *Rights of Passage: The Passport in International Relations*. Boulder and London: Lynne Rienner Publishers.

Schectman, Joseph B. 1951. 'Evacuee Property in India and Pakistan', *Pacific Affairs*, 24(4): 406–13.

Scherz, China. 2011. 'Protecting Children, Preserving Families: Moral Conflict and Actuarial Science in a Problem of Contemporary Governance', *PoLAR: Political and Legal Anthropology Review*, 34(1): 33–50.

Scott, James. 1985. *Weapons of the Weak: Everyday Forms of Peasant Resistance*. New Haven: Yale University Press.

———. 1998. *Seeing Like a State: How Certain Schemes to Improve the Human Condition have Failed*. New Haven and London: Yale University Press.

Sekula, Allan. 1986. 'The Body and the Archive', *October*, 39: 3–64.

Sen, Amartya. 1981. 'Ingredients of Famine Analysis: Availability and Entitlements', *The Quarterly Journal of Economics*, 96(3): 433–64.

Sengoopta, Chandak. 2004. *Imprint of the Raj: The Colonial Origins of Fingerprinting and Its Voyage to Britain*. London: Pan Books.

Sengupta, Ranjana. 2007. *Delhi Metropolitan: The Making of an Unlikely City*. New Delhi: Penguin.

Sharan, Awadhendra. 2014. *In the City, Out of Place: Nuisance, Pollution and Dwelling in Delhi c. 1850–2000*. New Delhi: Oxford University Press.

Shouse, Eric. 2005. 'Feeling, Emotion, Affect', *M/C Journal*, 8(6), available at http://journal.media-culture.org.au/0512/03-shouse.php, accessed on 3 April 2012.

Shukla, Ravi. 2010. 'Reimagining Citizenship: Debating India's Unique Identification Scheme', *Economic and Political Weekly*, 45(2): 31–6.

Simon, Jonathan. 1993. *Poor Discipline: Parole and the Social Control of the Underclass, 1890–1990*. Chicago: University of Chicago Press.

Simone, Abdoumaliq. 2004. 'People as Infrastructure: Intersecting Fragments in Johannesburg', *Public Culture*, 16(3): 407–29.

Singha, Radhika. 1998. *A Despotism of Law: Crime and Justice in Early Colonial India*. Oxford: Oxford University Press.

———. 2000. 'Settle, Mobilize, Verify: Identification Practices in Colonial India', *Studies in History*, 16(2): 151–98.

———. 2013. 'The Great War and a "Proper" Passport for the Colony: Border-crossing in British India, c. 1882–1922', *Indian Economic and Social History Review*, 50(3): 289–315.

Sivaramakrishnan, K. and Arun Agrawal (eds). 2003. *Regional Modernities: The Cultural Politics of Development in India*. Oxford and New York: Oxford University Press.

Smith, Richard Saumarez. 1985. 'Rule-by-Records and Rule-by-Reports: Complementary Aspects of the British Imperial Rule of Law', *Contributions to Indian Sociology*, 19(1): 153–76.

Spear, Percival. 2002. *Delhi: A Historical Sketch*, in Percival Spear, Narayani Gupta and R.E. Frykenberg (eds), in *The Delhi Omnibus*. New Delhi: Oxford University Press.

Srimanjari. 2009. *Through War and Famine Bengal 1939–45*. New Delhi: Orient Blackswan.

Sriraman, Tarangini. 2011. 'Revisiting Welfare: Ration Card Narratives in India', *Economic and Political Weekly*, 46(38): 52–9.

———. 2013a. 'Feeling the Rules: Documentary Practices of Rationing and the Signature of the Official', *Contributions to Indian Sociology*, 47(3): 335–61.

———. 2013b. 'Enumeration as Pedagogic Process: Gendered Encounters with Identity Documents in Delhi's Urban Poor Spaces', *South Asia Multidisciplinary Academic Journal* (SAMAJ) (Online), 8, 2013. Available at http://samaj.revues.org/3655, accessed on 14 November 2016.

———. 2013c. 'Assault and Assuage: Identification Documents, Colonial Rationalities and Epidemic Control in British India', in Nivedita Menon, Aditya Nigam, and Sanjay Palshikar (eds), *Critical Studies in Politics: Exploring Sites, Selves, Power*, pp. 271–318. Delhi: Orient Blackswan.

———. 2014. 'A Petition-like Application? Rhetoric and Rationing Documents in Wartime Delhi 1941–45', *Indian Economic and Social History Review*, 51(3): 353–82.

Srivastava, Sanjay. 2012. 'Duplicity, Intimacy, Community: An Ethnography of ID Cards, Permits and Other Fake Documents in Delhi', *Thesis Eleven*, 113(1): 78–93.

Stoler, Ann Laura. 2002. 'Colonial Archives and the Arts of Governance', *Archival Science*, 2: 87–109.

———. 2004. 'Affective States', in Nugent, David and Joan Vincent (eds), *A Companion to the Anthropology of Politics*, pp. 4–20. Malden, MA: Blackwell Publishers.

Strathern, Marilyn. 2006. 'Bullet-Proofing: A Tale from the United Kingdom', in Annelise Riles (ed.), *Documents: Artifacts of Modern Knowledge*, pp. 181–205. Ann Arbor: University of Michigan Press.

Sundaram, Ravi. 2010. *Pirate Modernity: Delhi's Media Urbanism*, p. 17. London, New York, and New Delhi: Routledge.

Tabassum, Azra and Shveta Sarda (eds). (2010) *Trickster City: Writings from the Belly of the Metropolis*. New Delhi: Penguin Viking.

Tarlo, Emma. 2003. *Unsettling Memories: Narratives of the 'Emergency'*. Delhi: Permanent Black.

Taussig, Michael. 1993. *Mimesis and Alterity: A Particular History of the Senses*. New York and London: Routledge.

———. 1997. *The Magic of the State*. New York: Routledge.

Teltumbde, Anand. 2016. 'Rohith Vemula's Dalitness', *Economic and Political Weekly*, 51(28): 10–11.

Tharu, Susie and K. Satyanarayana (eds). 2013. *The Exercise of Freedom: An Introduction to Dalit Writing*. New Delhi: Navayana Publishing.

Thompson, Scott. 2008. 'Separating the Sheep from the Goats: The United Kingdom's National Registration Programme and Social Sorting in the Pre-electronic Era', in Colin J. Bennett and David Lyon (eds), *Playing the Identity Card: Surveillance, Security and Identification in Global Perspective*, pp. 145–62. London: Routledge.

Thynell, M., D. Mohan, and G. Tiwari. 2010. 'Sustainable Transport and the Modernisation of Urban Transport in Delhi and Stockholm', *Cities*, 27(6), 421–9.

Torpey, John. 1997. Revolutions and Freedom of Movement: An Analysis of Passport Controls in the French, Russian and Chinese Revolutions, Theory and Society, 26 (6): 837–868.

———. 2000. *Invention of the Passport: Surveillance, Citizenship and the State*. Cambridge: Cambridge University Press.

Turner, Bryan. 1990. 'Outline of a Theory of Citizenship', *Sociology*, 24(2): 189–217.

Vaidyanathan, A. 1983. 'The Indian Economy since Independence', in Dharma Kumar and Meghnad Desai (eds), *The Cambridge Economic History of India, c.1757–c.1790*, pp. 947–94, Vol. 2. Cambridge: Cambridge University Press.

Varley, Ann. 2002. 'Private or Public: Debating the Meaning of Tenure Legalization', *International Journal of Urban and Regional Research*, 26(3): 449–61.

Visvanathan, Shiv. 1998. 'The Early Years', *Foul Play: Chronicles of Corruption*, pp. 12–24, New Delhi: Banyan.

Visvanathan, Shiv and Harsh Sethi (eds). 1998. 'By Way of a Beginning', in *Foul Play: Chronicles of Corruption*, pp. 1–12. New Delhi: Banyan.

Weber, Max. 2006. 'Bureaucracy', in Aradhana Sharma and Akhil Gupta (eds), *The Anthropology of the State: A Reader*, pp. 49–70. Malden, Oxford and Victoria: Blackwell Publishing.

Winther, Jennifer A. 2008. 'Household Enumeration in National Discourse: Three Moments in Modern Japanese History', *Social Science History*, 32(1): 19–46.

Zamindar, Vazira Fazila-Yacoobali. 2007. *The Long Partition and the Making of Modern South Asia: Refugees, Boundaries, Histories*. New York: Columbia University Press.

Zureik, Elia. 2001. 'Constructing Palestine through Surveillance Practices', *British Journal of Middle Eastern Studies*, 28(2): 205–27.

Websites

ameshistory.org
blogs.worldbank.org
cgdev.org
dnaindia.com
indiankanoon.org
journal.media-culture.org
moneylife.in
ndtv.com
nhb.org
nvrltd.com
qualitative-research.net
Scroll.in
uidai.gov.in
youtube.com

INDEX

ABOUT THE AUTHOR

Tarangini Sriraman teaches politics and history at the School of Liberal Studies, Azim Premji University, Bengaluru, India. She has previously been a postdoctoral visiting fellow at Centre de Sciences Humaines, New Delhi, India and visiting associate fellow, Centre for the Study of Developing Societies, Delhi, India. She has received the Charles Wallace Research Grant, London, and the South Asian Studies Fellowship at Cornell University. Her work has been published in journals such as *Economic and Political Weekly*, *Contributions to Indian Sociology*, *Indian Economic and Social History Review*, and *South Asia Multidisciplinary Academic Journal*.